THE S. MARK TAPER FOUNDATION

IMPRINT IN JEWISH STUDIES

BY THIS ENDOWMENT

THE S. MARK TAPER FOUNDATION SUPPORTS

THE APPRECIATION AND UNDERSTANDING

OF THE RICHNESS AND DIVERSITY OF

JEWISH LIFE AND CULTURE

Demons in the Details

The publisher and the University of California Press Foundation gratefully acknowledge the generous support of the S. Mark Taper Foundation Imprint in Jewish Studies.

Demons in the Details

DEMONIC DISCOURSE AND RABBINIC CULTURE IN LATE ANTIQUE BABYLONIA

Sara Ronis

UNIVERSITY OF CALIFORNIA PRESS

University of California Press
Oakland, California

 First Paperback Printing 2025
Library of Congress Cataloging-in-Publication Data
Names: Ronis, Sara, 1984– author.
Title: Demons in the details : demonic discourse and Rabbinic culture in late antique Babylonia / Sara Ronis.
Identifiers: LCCN 2021060237 (print) | LCCN 2021060238 (ebook) | ISBN 9780520386174 (cloth) | ISBN 9780520386181 (epub) | ISBN 9780520418363 (pbk: alk. paper)
Subjects: LCSH: Demonology—Iraq—Babylonia. | Rabbis—Iraq—Babylonia. | Incantations, Assyro-Babylonian. | Jewish demonology. | BISAC: HISTORY / Ancient / General | SOCIAL SCIENCE / Jewish Studies
Classification: LCC BF1548 .R66 2022 (print) | LCC BF1548 (ebook) | DDC 133.4/2095675—dc23/eng/20220125
LC record available at https://lccn.loc.gov/2021060237
LC ebook record available at https://lccn.loc.gov/2021060238

30 29 28 27 26 25
10 9 8 7 6 5 4 3 2 1

GPSR Authorized Representative: Easy Access System Europe, Mustamäe tee 50, 10621 Tallinn, Estonia, gpsr.requests@easproject.com

For my grandparents

Elinore (Ellie) Appelbaum Feinberg (z"l)
Dr. Richard (Dick) Feinberg (z"l)

Beatrice (Beaty) Segal Ronis Etinson
Theodore (Teddy) Ronis (z"l)
David (Dave) Etinson (z"l)
Jack Lehman (z"l)

Contents

Acknowledgments xi

Introduction 1

1. Origin Stories 29
2. Classification Matters 56
3. How to Avoid Demonic Dangers 92
4. Legal Demons 128
5. Serving the Rabbinic Project 166
6. Exorcising Demons 195

Conclusion 223

Bibliography 231

Subject Index 255

Index of Jewish Sources 267

Acknowledgments

The rabbis of the Talmud believed that they were surrounded by invisible beings who shaped their lives and learning in innumerable ways. In their discourse about demons, they worked to make the invisible visible and to be in productive relationship with the world around them. This book, too, has been shaped by innumerable people and institutions I would like to make visible here.

This book emerged out of a doctoral dissertation at Yale University. I feel lucky to have been part of such a robust intellectual community there. Christine Hayes, my dissertation adviser, was a supportive interlocutor even before I joined the religious studies program at Yale. She paid attention to everything from the smallest details of my translations to how I was doing as a human being, and she pushed me to become the scholar she knew I could be. She continues to be a source of inspiration and a model of what an incisive and generous mentor can be. Aviva Arad first suggested I "take a look at the weird demon stuff in the tenth chapter of Pesaḥim" when I was debating what to work on and continued to be a friend and colleague throughout the dissertation process and beyond. Renee Reed offered support throughout my time at Yale. Among the faculty of the Religious Studies Department, Kathryn Lofton has been a fierce advocate for me on all fronts. Both Steven Fraade and Stephen Davis gave me essential feedback on this project, pushing me to step back from the details and to look at the bigger picture. Gideon Bohak was an insightful external reader for the project. My other Jewish studies colleagues at Yale—Pratima Gopalakrishnan, Simcha Gross, Rebecca Kamholz, Yishai Kiel, Yoni Pomeranz, Rachel Scheinerman, Annie Schiff, and Shlomo Zuckier—were wonderful conversation partners about specific texts and offered fellowship and support both in and out of the program. Sonja Anderson, Laura Carlson, Elizabeth Davidson, Mary Farag, Christina Harker, Daniel Schriever, Tyler Smith, and Olivia Stewart all read sections of the dissertation and gave me feedback both critical and transformative. Much of the dissertation was written in coffee shops across New Haven, Connecticut, sitting across from T. J. Dumansky, Alex Kaloyanides, Sam Kimport, Sarah Koenig, Emily Johnson, and Shari Rabin, who turned what could have been an isolating project into a joyful community.

I continue to be thankful to Bernadette Brooten at Brandeis University, who first taught me how to set my own research agenda and modeled the importance of being a caring and ethical colleague. The faculty of Midreshet Lindenbaum gave me the time and space to develop my skills reading the Talmud. I would also like to thank Richard Kalmin and David Kraemer at the Jewish Theological Seminary (JTS) for introducing me to the academic approach to Talmud. Finally, I am indebted to Elizabeth Castelli and the late Alan Segal at Barnard College for their help introducing me to graduate work and the types of cross-disciplinary conversations that such work both allows and requires.

I began the project of turning my dissertation into a book as a Starr Fellow at Harvard University's Center for Jewish Studies in 2015. My thanks to Shaye Cohen, David Stern, Rachel Rockenmacher, and Sandy Cantave Vil, who offered their friendship and support during this period and in the following summers. The conversations I had with colleagues Sasha Senderovich, Nadav Sharon, Rachel Wamsley, and Elisha Russ-Fishbane were affirming and challenging in the best possible ways. Yonatan Miller was a wonderful office mate and interlocutor throughout the year and beyond. At the same time, I participated in the Paula Hyman mentorship program of the Association for Jewish Studies; my thanks to the organizers and my mentor Beth Berkowitz for her support and insights throughout the process of figuring out how to write a book.

I presented some of this work at the annual conferences of the Association for Jewish Studies, the American Academy of Religion, and the Society for Biblical Literature. My thanks to the attendees for their tough questions and enthusiasm for this project. A special thank-you to Natalie Polzer, whose comment to me after one panel inspired me to delve far more deeply into how the rabbis use space to think about demons.

The challenge of interdisciplinary work is that it is impossible to be an expert in all things. My deepest thanks to Elitzur Bar-Asher Siegel, Noah Bickart, David Brakke, David Brodsky, Robert Brody, Aaron Butts, Yaakov Elman (z"l), Amit Gvaryahu, Richard Kalmin, Reuven Kiperwasser, Lennart Lehmhaus, Mahnaz Moazami, Shuli Shinnar, Oktor Skjærvø, Shana Strauch Schick, and Shana Zaia for sharing their respective areas of expertise with me and letting me know when I was in danger of being dramatically wrong. I am sure that I am forgetting someone—if that's you, please know that I appreciate you too. All mistakes that remain are my own.

Portions of the introduction were first published as "Intermediary Beings in Late Antique Judaism," *Currents in Biblical Research* 14, no. 1 (2016): 94–120, reproduced with permission. Sections of chapters 4 and 6 were first published as "Space, Place, and the Race for Power: Rabbis, Demons, and the Construction of Babylonia," *Harvard Theological Review* 110, no. 4 (2017): 588–603, reproduced with permission; and "A Seven-Headed Demon in the House of Study: Understanding a Rabbinic Demon in Light of Zoroastrian, Christian, and Babylonian Textual Traditions," *AJS Review* (Spring 2019): 125–42, reproduced with permission. Part of Chapter 5 was first published as "A Demonic Servant in Rav Papa's Household: Demons as Subjects in the Mesopotamian Talmud," *The Aggada of the Babylonian Talmud and Its Cultural World*, edited by Geoffrey Herman and Jeffrey Rubenstein (Providence, RI: Brown Judaic Studies, 2018), 3–21, reproduced with permission. I would like to thank the anonymous peer reviewers of each of these pieces for their incisive feedback and affirmation at the beginning of this project.

I finished this project at St. Mary's University in San Antonio, Texas. I am so very lucky that St. Mary's offers an intellectual community that is kind, collaborative, and deeply committed to the project of accessible higher education. My colleagues in the theology department Jim Ball, Bill Buhrman, Todd Hanneken, and Allison Gray, and my cohort of junior faculty—Amanda Hill, Sue Nash, Betsy Smith, and Lindsey Wieck—have been incredible sources of support and inspiration. My students at St. Mary's continually challenge me to be clearer and more concise in my writing and speaking; if this book is at all readable, it is thanks to them. My research at St. Mary's has been supported by several Speed Faculty Development Grants; my thanks to the Speed family and St. Mary's Center for Catholic Studies for believing in this project.

The rabbis believed that there was safety in numbers. I am so grateful that I am surrounded by a rich community of care with which to walk through the world. Lara Chausow and Rebecca Hirsch have been the most wonderful friends a person could ask for. Rebecca deserves an extra shoutout, since without her willingness to use her awesome archivist powers for good, this book would have taken literally twice as long to write. Rabbi Megan Doherty has been an amazing chavruta and friend for over ten years now. Jenny Caplan is the best writing-accountability buddy and conference copilot. I am also grateful for the friendship of Aliza Libman Baronofsky, Daniel Goldhill, Elie Friedman, and Melissa Weininger. Mathew Schutzer has been my people for too many years to count and read my entire dissertation even when he didn't have to. In San Antonio, my life has been made immeasurably richer by the friendships of Angela Tarango, Jakob Rinderknecht, and Greg Clines.

Finally, I would like to thank my parents, David and Margaret Ronis, for modeling the power of doing what you love. They, my grandmother Beatrice Etinson, and my sisters and brothers-in-law—Tova Ronis and Alex Ziskind, and Aliza Ronis and Michael Hadid—have been important sources of encouragement and support. My nephews, Jack, Sam, and Bo, and nephdogs, Leo, Axl, and Bob, have been important sources of snuggles and WhatsApp cuteness. I thank all of them for this and for so much more. In the last year of this project, I also failed at fostering the greatest dog in the world, Lily. She can't read but has my deepest gratitude for the love, walks, and reminders that sometimes you need to turn off your computer and go outside and smell the white brush.

Sara Ronis
July 2021, San Antonio, Texas

Introduction

RABBIS AND DEMONS

Though of their names in heavenly records now
Be no memorial blotted out and rased
By their rebellion, from the Books of Life.
Nor had they yet among the sons of Eve
Got them new names, till wandering o'er the Earth,
Through God's high sufferance for the trial of man,
By falsities and lies the greatest part
Of mankind they corrupted to forsake
God their Creator, and the invisible
Glory of him that made them, to transform
Oft to the image of a brute, adorned
With gay religions full of pomp and gold,
And devils to adore for deities.

John Milton, *Paradise Lost*

Politicians and scholars will be studying the twists and turns of the 2016 presidential campaign for decades. Reading the reporting on the election cycle, I was struck by the appearance and reappearance of demonic discourse in the national conversation. Voters across the political spectrum accused politicians from the opposing party of being possessed by demons. Gordon Klingenschmitt, a former navy chaplain and one of Republican candidate Ted Cruz's most celebrated supporters, claimed

Epigraph: John Milton, *Paradise Lost*, bk. 1, lines 361–73, in *The Complete Poetical Works of John Milton* (Boston: Houghton, Mifflin, 1899), 107.

that President Barack Obama was demonically possessed.[1] Radio host Alex Jones described Hillary Clinton as "an abject psychopathic demon from hell."[2] While two figures may be dismissed as a statistically insignificant minority, a Public Policy Polling poll of Republican voters in Florida in October 2016 found that "40 per cent of Donald Trump's supporters believe his White House rival Hillary Clinton is an 'actual demon.'"[3] This rhetoric was not restricted to the Republican Party: Alec Ross, a former Clinton adviser, called Trump a "vulgar, demented, pig demon," and one Bernie Sanders supporter explained her resistance to Hillary Clinton by claiming, "She's the devil."[4]

The appearance of demonic discourse in politics is matched by huge popular interest in demons. In 2015 alone, more than twenty horror movies were released in the United States that featured a malevolent demonic being.[5] Since 2010, hundreds, if not thousands, of English-language novels with a demonic hero or antihero have been published.[6] While demons have become "naturalized" in our popular cultural discourse, demons are associated with fringe elements in the political sphere and dismissed. For some mainstream Americans, demons may have lost the very real sense

1. His book *The Demons of Barack H. Obama: How the Gift of Discerning of Spirits Reveals Unseen Forces Influencing American Politics* (CreateSpace, 2012) is self-published on Amazon. See also Trudy Ring, "Ted Cruz's Newest Anti-LGBT Pal: 'Exorcist' Gordon Klingenschmitt," *Advocate,* 11 April 2016, www.advocate.com/election/2016/4/11/ted-cruzs-newest-anti-lgbt-pal-exorcist-gordon-klingenschmitt.

2. Liam Stack, "He Calls Hillary Clinton a 'Demon.' Who Is Alex Jones?," *New York Times,* 13 October 2016.

3. Lucy Pasha-Robinson, "Four in 10 Donald Trump Supporters Think Hillary Clinton 'Is an Actual Demon,'" *Independent,* 31 October 2016, www.independent.co.uk/news/world/americas/us-elections/hillary-clinton-donald-trump-demon-poll-republican-voters-beliefs-a7388546.html. See also Public Policy Polling, "Clinton's Florida Lead Continues to Grow," press release, 14 October 2016, www.publicpolicypolling.com/wp-content/uploads/2017/09/PPP_Release_FL_104161.pdf.

4. Sarah Knapton, "Donald Trump Is a 'Vulgar, Demented, Pig Demon' Says Hillary Clinton's Ex Adviser," *Telegraph,* 30 May 2016, www.telegraph.co.uk/news/2016/05/30/donald-trump-is-a-vulgar-demented-pig-demon-says-hillary-clinton/; Tré Goins-Phillips, "'She's the Devil': Sanders Supporters Open up about What They Really Think of Clinton," *Blaze,* 19 April 2016, www.theblaze.com/news/2016/04/19/shes-the-devil-sanders-supporters-open-up-about-what-they-really-think-of-clinton.

5. "Horror Movies 2015," IMDb, created 5 January 2015, updated 25 March 2019, www.imdb.com/list/ls073680122/.

6. As can be seen by browsing Goodreads.com for the tag *demon* or *demons.*

of presence that they had in earlier periods of human history. Yet they remain a fascinating fiction.

Our fascination with demons represents neither a radical change in outlook nor a devolution to primitive beliefs. Rather, it reflects a range of demonic discourses that have continually existed in some form or another with varying degrees of prominence in different periods and places, in response to varied cultural stimuli.[7] Current claims that particular leaders or groups are possessed by demons or are working with demons suggest that demons continue to be meaningful as modes of group identity formation and policing.

In fact, demons and demonic discourse remain an important lens through which to understand the beliefs, values, and modes of identity formation of cultures modern and ancient. Belief in demons was woven into the social and religious fabric of the late antique Mediterranean world. Although belief in how and when demons manifested varied across ancient religious and ethnic groups, most people shared a belief that visible and invisible intermediary beings existed and could affect the human world. Belief in demons was neither fringe nor associated exclusively with one economic or social class. Demons were a shared yet deeply contested element of the religiously and ethnically diverse world of late antiquity.[8]

This book explores how belief in demons manifested within one religious group in one particular place at one particular time. The Jewish rabbis of late antique Sasanian Babylonia, like other religious groups in late antiquity, believed that the world was full of seen and unseen demons who had a very real presence in people's lives. In rabbinic texts, demons act upon and interact with late antique Jews, rabbinic and non-rabbinic alike. The Babylonian Talmud is filled with stories about rabbinic encounters with demons as well as with laws that regulate and integrate demons into the rabbinic intellectual system. Demons are alternately depicted as dangerous and capricious beings, passive neutral figures, legal actors subject to rabbinic law, and positively marked students and teachers of

7. I adopt the idea of "live" discursive trends from Michael L. Satlow, *Jewish Marriage in Antiquity* (Princeton, NJ: Princeton University Press, 2001), 42.

8. See Rachel Neis, *The Sense of Sight in Rabbinic Culture: Jewish Ways of Seeing in Late Antiquity* (Cambridge: Cambridge University Press, 2013), 106 n. 95.

rabbinic traditions. They challenge rabbinic authority at the same time as they uphold it.

RABBIS IN SASANIAN BABYLONIA

The rabbis were a Jewish scholastic elite that emerged in the long aftermath of the destruction of the Temple in Jerusalem in 70 C.E.[9] By the third century, the rabbinic world was split between two locations: Roman Palestine and Sasanian Babylonia. These two communities shared inherited texts, values, culture, and language, but their literatures also reflect their different geographic and cultural milieus.

Between the second and seventh centuries, the rabbis produced the major works of classical rabbinic literature: in Roman Palestine, the Mishnah and Tosefta (second-to-third-century C.E. legal anthologies), the homiletical and exegetical midrashim (sing. midrash), and the Palestinian Talmud (Yerushalmi); and in Sasanian Babylonia, the Babylonian Talmud (Bavli). Originally composed and transmitted orally, rabbinic literature is characterized by its multivocal, anthological nature.[10] Classical rabbinic literature reflects the richness and dynamism of rabbinic life in the more than four hundred years of its compositional history.

Unlike their Palestinian colleagues, the rabbis of Babylonia primarily produced a single great work of literature that survives to this day, the Babylonian Talmud. Yet this work contains narrative, exegetical, homiletical, legal, and jurisprudential elements. Scholars debate a *terminus ante quem* for the Babylonian Talmud. It seems likely that it was largely collected and organized before the seventh century C.E., though editorial activities may

9. On scholasticism and my use of the term to describe the rabbis of Babylonia, see the discussion in chap. 2.

10. Yaakov Elman, "Order, Sequence, and Selection: The Mishnah's Anthological Choices," in *The Anthology in Jewish Literature*, ed. David Stern (New York: Oxford University Press, 2004), 75; Steven D. Fraade, "Rabbinic Polysemy and Pluralism Revisited: Between Praxis and Thematization," *AJS Review* 31, no. 1 (2007): 1–40. I use the term *anthology* here not to de-emphasize the compositional and redactional work of the editors of these texts, but to emphasize the editors' work of creative juxtoposition of earlier texts to create a dialectical whole.

have continued for another hundred years.[11] This text is a vital piece of historical evidence, both for late antique Judaism and for the complex religious world of late antique Babylonia.

Late antique Babylonia was part of the Sasanian province of Āsōristān. The Sasanian dynasty came to power in 224 C.E. and ruled until 650 C.E. At its height, the Sasanian Empire stretched from modern-day Armenia to Tajikistan and from Kazakhstan to Yemen.[12] Though the Sasanian Empire spanned diverse regions and religious groups, the ruling elite was Zoroastrian, members of a religious system first developed on the steppes of ancient Iran in the first millennium B.C.E.[13] Zoroastrianism's reputed

11. For specific arguments about dating the composition and redaction of the Babylonian Talmud, see Yaakov Elman, "The World of the 'Sabboraim': Cultural Aspects of Post-Redactional Additions to the Bavli," in *Creation and Composition: The Contribution of the Bavli Redactors (Stammaim) to the Aggada*, ed. Jeffrey L. Rubenstein (Tübingen: Mohr Siebeck, 2005), 384; David Weiss Halivni, *The Formation of the Babylonian Talmud*, trans. Jeffrey L. Rubenstein (Oxford: Oxford University Press, 2013); Shamma Friedman, "'Wonder Not at a Gloss in Which the Name of an *Amora* Is Mentioned': The Amoraic Statments and the Anonymous Material in the Sugyot of the Bavli Revisited," in *Melekhet Mahshevet: Studies in the Redaction and Development of Talmudic Literature*, ed. Aharon Amit and Aharon Shemesh (Ramat-Gan, Israel: Bar-Ilan University Press, 2011), 101–44; "Pereq Ha-isha Rabba Ba-Bavli: Be-Ẓiruf Mavo Klali al Derekh Ḥeker Ha-Sugya," in *Texts and Studies: Analecta Judaica*, ed. H. Z. Dimitrovsky (New York: Jewish Theological Seminary of America, 1977), 277–321. For an alternative theory of identifying and dating the anonymous materials of the Talmud, see Robert Brody, "Stam Ha-Talmud ve-Divrei Ha-Amoraim," in *Iggud: Selected Essays in Jewish Studies*, ed. Baruch J. Schwartz, Abraham Melamed, and Aharon Shemesh (Jerusalem: World Union of Jewish Studies, 2008), 1:213–32. Richard Kalmin, "The Formation and Character of the Babylonian Talmud," in *The Cambridge History of Judaism*, ed. Steven T. Katz (Cambridge: Cambridge University Press, 2006), 4:840–76. In this book, I follow Elman in dating the bulk of the composition of the Babylonian Talmud to before the mid-sixth century, but I recognize that redactional and glossing activities continued for several hundred years afterward.

12. For a history of the Sasanian Empire, see A. Shapur Shahbazi, "Sasanian Dynasty," in *Encyclopædia Iranica Online* (2005), www.iranicaonline.org/articles/sasanian-dynasty; Touraj Daryaee, *Sasanian Persia: The Rise and Fall of an Empire* (London: I. B. Tauris, 2009); Josef Wiesehofer, *Ancient Persia: From 550 B.C. to 650 A.D.* (London: I. B. Tauris, 1996); Parvaneh Pourshariati, *Decline and Fall of the Sasanian Empire: The Sasanian-Parthian Confederacy and the Arab Conquest of Iran* (London: I. B. Tauris in association with the Iran Heritage Foundation, 2008).

13. Mary Boyce, *A History of Zoroastrianism*, vol. 1, *The Early Period* (1975; Leiden: Brill, 1989); William W. Malandra, "Zoroastrianism. I. Historical Review up to the Arab Conquest," in *Encyclopædia Iranica* Online (2005), www.iranicaonline.org/articles/zoroastrianism-i-historical-review; Prods Oktor Skjærvø, "Zoroastrian Dualism," in *Light against Darkness: Dualism in Ancient Mediterranean Religion and the Contemporary World*, ed. Armin Lange et al. (Göttingen, Germany: Vandenhoeck & Ruprecht, 2011), 55–91.

founder, named Zarathustra in Avestan and Zoroaster in Greek, taught a fundamental opposition between a good god, Ahura Mazdā (Ohrmazd in Middle Persian), and an evil god, Aŋra Mainyu (Ahriman in Middle Persian). As we will see, as part of this dualistic lens, Zoroastrianism had its own elaborate demonology enacted through myth, ritual, and law.

The Sasanian Empire was also home to rabbinic and non-rabbinic Jews, Christians of different theological bents, Manichaeans, Mandaeans, and followers of other indigenous ancient Near Eastern religious traditions. The Sasanian province of Āsōristān had a significant population that continued to observe in some form the rituals and beliefs of ancient Mesopotamia.[14] The Sasanian Empire's general stance was one of religious toleration, and religious minorities developed in conversation and competition with one another.[15] They produced their own religious laws

14. See discussion in chap. 5.

15. Regarding the Sasanian Empire's stance of toleration, some scholars have argued that an outlier here may be the tenure of the Zoroastrian religious leader Kertir, whose inscription boasts that he suppressed non-Zoroastrian religious minorities in the empire. For more on this inscription within its historical context, see Oktor Skjærvø, "Counter-Manichean Elements in Kerdir's Inscriptions. Irano-Manichaica II," in *Atti Del Terzo Congresso Internazionale Di Studi "Manicheismo E Oriente Cristiano Antico," Arcavacata Di Rende-Amantea 31 Agosto–5 Settembre 1993*, ed. L Cirillo and A. V. Tongerloo (Leuven, Belgium: Brepols, 1997), 314–42; Prods Oktor Skjærvø, "Kartir," *Encyclopædia Iranica Online* (2011, 2012 updated online), www.iranicaonline.org/articles/kartir. For scholarship complicating this assessment, and arguing that any such persecutions were either minimal or entirely fictitious, see Richard E. Payne, *A State of Mixture: Christians, Zoroastrians, and Iranian Political Culture in Late Antiquity* (Oakland: University of California Press, 2015), 26; Richard Kalmin, *Jewish Babylonia between Persia and Roman Palestine* (Oxford: Oxford University Press, 2006), 122–38. Payne argues instead that Sasanian society should be understood through "a model of the differentiated, hierarchical inclusion of religious others rooted in Zoroastrian cosmological thought" (26). For discussions of specific religious communities in Sasanian Iran, see J. P. Asmussen, "Christians in Iran," in *The Cambridge History of Iran*, ed. E. Yarshater (Cambridge: Cambridge University Press, 1983), 3(2):924–48; Adam Howard Becker, "Martyrdom, Religious Difference, and 'Fear' as a Category of Piety in the Sasanian Empire: The Case of the Martyrdom of Gregory and the Martyrdom of Yazdpaneh," *Journal of Late Antiquity* 2, no. 2 (2009): 300–336; Robert Brody, "Judaism in the Sasanian Empire: A Case Study in Religious Coexistence," in *Irano-Judaica II: Studies Relating to Jewish Contacts with Persian Culture Throughout the Ages*, ed. Shaul Shaked and Amnon Netzer (Jerusalem: Yad Izak Ben-Zvi and the Hebrew University of Jerusalem, 1990), 52–62; Richard N. Frye, "Minorities in the History of the Near East," in *A Green Leaf: Papers in Honour of Professor Jes P. Asmussen*, ed. W. Sundermann et al. (Leiden: Brill, 1988), 461–71; Manfred Hutter, "Manichaeism in the Early Sasanian Empire," *Numen* 40, no. 1 (1993): 2–15; G. Widengren, "Manichaeaism and Its Iranian Background," in *The Cambridge History of Iran*, ed. E. Yarshater (Cambridge: Cambridge University Press, 1983), 3(2):965–90; Erica

and narratives, had politically powerful religious leaders, and created communities which were adaptive while also being invested in policing their own religious boundaries. The rabbis thrived in this world, developing scholastic frameworks to shape and transmit their communal identity, and creating a rich corpus of rabbinic culture and thought.

RECEIVING RABBINIC DEMONS

This book examines late antique rabbinic identity formation and cultural interactions through the lens of the rabbis' thinking about demons. It analyzes and contextualizes those Talmudic texts that are directly or indirectly about demons. Given the pervasiveness of demonic discourse in a range of areas of rabbinic thought, this project might seem obvious. Until recently however, many readers of the Talmud have largely ignored or dismissed rabbinic discourse about demons. This dismissal has been part of larger Jewish conversations about normativity, rationalism, authenticity, and antisemitism that have emerged at particular historical moments.

No reader comes to any text a blank slate. Our experiences of reading are always informed by our own life experiences, our families and communities, and the history of textual interpretation. Readers of the Babylonian Talmud have had their experiences conditioned in part by centuries of religious commentary and codification, which both passively and actively downplayed the Talmud's demonic discourse.[16]

The most famous medieval opponent of demonic discourse was Maimonides (c. 1135–1204 C.E.). Maimonides, however, followed the approach first set out by his intellectual forefather, the North African commentator R. Isaac Alfasi (acronym Rif), who lived c. 1013–1103 C.E. Rif compiled an early code of Talmudic law, *Sefer Ha-Halakhot*. To create his compilation,

C. D. Hunter, "Aramaic-Speaking Communities of Sasanid Mesopotamia," *ARAM* 7 (1995): 319–35; Simcha Gross, "Empire and Neighbors: Babylonian Jewish Identity in Its Local and Imperial Context" (PhD diss., Yale University, 2017).

16. Much of this historiographical discussion can be found in Sara Ronis, "Intermediary Beings in Late Antique Judaism: A History of Scholarship," *Currents in Biblical Research* 14, no. 1 (2015): 96. For a succinct survey of medieval and early modern Talmudic interpreters' approaches to the Talmud's demons, see Natan Slifkin, *Wrestling with Demons: A History of Rabbinic Attitudes to Demons* (self-published online, 2011).

Rif made a series of judgments about Talmudic passages and included only those that he determined were legal in nature and normative.[17] In his construction of normative law, Rif left out rabbinic stories, biblical interpretation, and even legal passages on topics he felt were nonnormative, including demons.[18] Barry Wimpfheimer argues that this (medieval) move imposed a classificatory system external to the Talmudic text itself, an imposition which calls "attention to the ways authoritative texts are sometimes marginalized through interpretation."[19]

Maimonides expanded this outlook on demonic nonnormativity into a broader moral stance, railing against superstitious people who "are seduced by [talismanery] with great folly, and with similar things, and think that they are real—which is not so... and these are things that have received great publicity amongst the pagans, especially amongst the nation which is called the Sabians... and they wrote works dealings with the stars, and witchcraft and incantations and calling upon spirits, and horoscopes and demons, and soothsaying in all their forms."[20] In his desire to cast rabbinic literature in a rationalist light, Maimonides explained that demons were really just people who were missing a rational soul; a so-called demon was actually just "an animal in the form and likeness of a person, but with the power to cause all kinds of harm and innovate new evils, which other creations do not have."[21] For Maimonides, the only real demons were irrational humans.

17. Barry S. Wimpfheimer, *The Talmud: A Biography* (Princeton, NJ: Princeton University Press, 2018), 113.

18. See for example, *Sefer Ha-Halakhot* on b. *Pesachim* 109b–112a, which Rif condenses into two paragraphs with only a single brief mention of the demonic ideas that underlie the Talmud's concerns about demons.

19. Barry S. Wimpfheimer, *Narrating the Law: A Poetics of Talmudic Legal Stories* (Philadelphia: University of Pennsylvania Press, 2011), 4–5.

20. Moses Maimonides, *Commentary to the Mishnah, Avodah Zarah* 4:7. Translation from Slifkin, *Wrestling with Demons*, 7. See Avishur Ravitzky, "Maimonides and His Disciples on Linguistic Magic and 'the Madness of the Writers of Amulets,'" in *Jewish Culture in the Eye of the Storm: A Jubilee Book in Honor of Yosef Ahituv*, ed. Aviezer Sagi and Nahem Ilan (Tel Aviv: Ha-Kibbutz Ha-Meukhad, 2002), 431–58; Gad Freudenthal, "Maimonides' Philosophy of Science," in *The Cambridge Companion to Maimonides*, ed. Kenneth Seeskin (Cambridge: Cambridge University Press, 2005), 134–66; Yuval Harari, "Leadership, Authority, and the 'Other' in the Debate over Magic from the Karaites to Maimonides," *Journal for the Study of Sephardic and Mizrahi Jewry* 1 (2007): 79–101.

21. Maimonides, *The Guide to the Perplexed* 1.7.

Rif, Maimonides, and their successors were largely successful in decoupling Talmudic demonology from normative Jewish law and thought. Although groups such as the medieval Ḥasidei Ashkenaz, fifteenth-century Spanish Kabbalists, and the sixteenth-century female pietists of Safed created elaborate demonologies of their own, these demonologies were only superficially related to the earlier rabbinic construction of demons found in the Babylonian Talmud.[22]

The modern reader of the Talmud is also shaped by nineteenth- and twentieth-century academic discourses on the Talmud's nature, historicity, and social location. Judaism first became a subject of academic study in the nineteenth century. The German Jewish scholars who were part of the *Wissenschaft des Judentums* (the scientific study of Judaism) School insisted—to the Jewish community and to the broader public—that Judaism deserved to be studied in German universities. Their work was political, intellectual, and deeply theological—they made their case in part by presenting a Judaism that was just as "rational" and "spiritual" as Protestant Christianity.[23] These scholars downplayed elements of Jewish tradition—legal, ritual, and "irrational"—that did not fit this nineteenth-century German model of religion. [24] Angels, demons, miracles, and popular religious practices were dismissed as "primitive," or as foreign and inauthentic to true Judaism. In 1866, the Hungarian rabbi and scholar Alexander Kohut described rabbinic demonology as "an alien product,

22. See Joseph Dan, *The Esoteric Theology of Ashkenazi Hasidism* (Jerusalem: Bialik Institute, 1968); Rachel Elior, *Dybbuks and Jewish Women in Social History, Mysticism and Folklore* (Jerusalem: Urim Publications, 2008); Jonathan Garb, "Mysticism and Magic: Objections, Doubts, Accommodation," *Mahanayim* 14 (2002): 97–109; Moshe Idel, "Jewish Magic from the Renaissance Period to Early Hasidism," in *Religion, Science, and Magic in Concert and in Conflict*, ed. Jacob Neusner et al. (New York: Oxford University Press, 1989), 82–117; J. H. Chajes, *Between Worlds: Dybbuks, Exorcists, and Early Modern Judaism* (Philadelphia: University of Pennsylvania Press, 2003), 117.

23. On the work of the scholars of the *Wissenschaft des Judentums*, see Michael A. Meyer, "Two Persistent Tensions within Wissenschaft Des Judentums," *Modern Judaism* 24 no. 2 (2004): 105–19. On their relationship to the modern academic study of Judaism, and a critique of Meyer's scholarly reconstruction, see George Y. Kohler, "Judaism Buried or Revitalized? *Wissenschaft des Judentums* in Nineteenth-Century Germany–Impact, Actuality, and Applicability Today," in *Jewish Thought and Jewish Belief*, ed. Daniel J. Lasker (Beer Sheva, Israel: Ben-Gurion University of the Negev Press, 2012), 27–63.

24. These scare quotes are my own; each of these terms has a long historiography and their usage requires caution and care.

obtained through contact with the Persians and the Medes in the exilic period."[25] German historian Heinrich Graetz echoed this approach in 1893. Graetz faulted the Talmud for containing "the various superstitious practices and views of [the Talmud's] Persian birthplace, which presume the efficacy of demoniacal medicines, of magic, incantations, miraculous cures, and interpretations of dreams, and are thus in opposition to the spirit of Judaism."[26] Such scholars dealt with what they saw as an irrational and primitive rabbinic demonology by dismissing it as a foreign corruption; they assumed that the rabbis must have included it in their sacred corpus either because they had themselves been corrupted, or in order to placate the credulous common folk.[27]

The only reason that the author of this book could have been academically trained in ancient Judaism is that, over a hundred and fifty years ago, the scholars of the *Wissenchaft des Judentums* were successful in making the case that Judaism was worthy of study in the secular academy. But their early rejection of rabbinic demonology set a course for modern scholarship that ignored the parts of Jewish tradition that may have seemed primitive or awkward to nineteenth- and twentieth-century readers.[28]

Finally, we cannot overlook the role of antisemitism in framing the way that twenty-first century readers have encountered Jewish texts. In the face of rising antisemitism in the 1930s and 1940s, American Jewish scholars such as Joshua Trachtenberg worked explicitly to decouple demons from normative Judaism. This move was an important part of a critique and undoing of historical antisemitic tropes that associated Jews with demons, devil-worship, and Satanism. As Trachtenberg wrote in 1944, "not a human being but a demonic, diabolic beast fighting the forces of truth and salvation with Satan's weapons, was the Jew as medieval

25. Alexander Kohut, *Ueber die jüdische Angelologie und Daemonologie in ihrer Abhängigkeit vom Parsismus* (Leipzig: Brockhaus, 1866), 7. Translation my own.

26. Heinrich Graetz, *History of the Jews*, 5 vols., vol. 2, *From the Reign of Hyrcanus (135 BCE) to the Completion of the Babylonian Talmud* (1893; Philadelphia: Jewish Publication Society of America, 1967), 633.

27. See also Ludwig Blau, *Das altjüdische Zauberwesen* (Strasbourg: K. Trübner, 1898).

28. See more extensive discussion of this period of study and its impact on understandings of the Talmud, in Ronis, "Intermediary Beings," 98–99.

Europe saw him."[29] In response to the power of these antisemitic beliefs, Trachtenberg reaffirmed that demonology and magic across historical periods were foreign to normative Judaism and were instead primitive and universal "folk" beliefs.[30]

Demons were largely written out of both normative Judaism and Jewish studies as part of specific cultural conversations in particular times and places: the medieval Maghreb, nineteenth-century Germany, and the West in the 1930s and 1940s. These acts of interpretation were meant to affirm Judaism to its supporters and to defend it from its detractors, with varying results. But these rejections of rabbinic demonology as non-normative, foreign superstition continue to lead many readers today to overlook the important roles that demons play in the Babylonian rabbinic imagination.

Overlooking rabbinic demonology has real consequences for understanding rabbinic literature and the rabbis as a movement. Examining the skittishness of many academics to engage in critical scholarship about demons, the religious studies scholar Bruce Lincoln notes that, "as the result of such skittishness, our understanding of many cultures and historic eras remains impoverished, for some of the best minds of numerous peoples were devoted to demonology."[31] In the Babylonian Talmud, the very same "best minds" who created rabbinic literature's legal, ethical, and

29. Joshua Trachtenberg, *The Devil and the Jews* (New Haven, CT: Yale University Press, 1944), 18. Indeed, this is not only a bygone concern. A cursory google search for the words *demons* and *Talmud* when I first began exploring this topic in 2012 yielded a substantial number of links on the first three pages of results to antisemitic websites of various kinds. With renewed academic interest in demonology over the last ten years, the results are now much more scholarly in nature.

30. *Jewish Magic and Superstition: A Study in Folk Religion* (New York: Behrman House, 1939), 1–10; *The Devil and the Jews*, 11–31. For context for Trachtenberg's life, see Sefton D. Temkin, "Trachtenberg, Joshua," *Encyclopaedia Judaica*, 2nd ed., ed. Michael Berenbaum and Fred Skolnik (Detroit: Macmillan Reference USA, 2007), 20:79. For more on Trachtenberg's positionality, see Melissa Margaret Aubin, "Gendering Magic in Late Antique Judaism" (PhD diss., Duke University, 1998), 18–42. Aubin, on p. 36, has noted that Trachtenberg's "emphasis on folklore was [also] meant to counter Christian claims about Judaism's supposed legalistic sterility." This tendency backfired, as Trachtenberg's work has been adopted and deployed in the furtherance of antisemitic tropes in the late twentieth and early twenty-first centuries. See, e.g., Henry Makow, "Covid, The Devil & the Jews," 14 September 2021, http://henrymakow.com/the-devil-and-the-jews.html.

31. Bruce Lincoln, *Gods and Demons, Priests and Scholars: Critical Explorations in the History of Religions* (Chicago: University of Chicago Press, 2012), 33.

theological complexities devoted much time to imagining and regulating the demonic.[32] In the last thirty years, spurred on in part by Gershom Scholem's work in valorizing and valuing Jewish magical and mystical traditions, scholars have finally begun the process of reinscribing demonology into late antique Jewish religion and thought.[33]

In this book, I ask what rabbinic literature, ancient Judaism, and late antique religions look like when demons are reinscribed into them: How did the Babylonian rabbis think about demons? How did demons function in late antique rabbinic theology? How were demons deployed in the construction of the rabbis as a powerful religious elite in late antique Sasanian Babylonia? What broader cultural conversations can be recovered by examining rabbinic discourse about demons? How might demons be a powerful force or framework to "think with" in the late antique world?

I argue that the rabbis' understanding of demons was important to their construction of themselves as a religious and scholastic elite in a complex world. Demons were a particularly rich locus for rabbinic interaction with the diverse cultures and traditions in Sasanian Babylonia; using demons as our test case, we can see the wide range of ways the rabbis used demons to think through contested issues of law, behavior, identity, and belief. Ultimately, the rabbis used all the tools in their respective legal and narrative toolboxes to construct their own belief in demons while their belief in demons helped construct the rabbinic movement.

THEORIZING DEMONS

This study of demonic discourse in the Babylonian Talmud stands at the intersection of three distinct fields of modern scholarship: the study of religion and magic, the social-scientific fields of anthropology and ethnopsychiatry, and the study of the Babylonian Talmud in its cultural context. I use these three intersecting fields to understand how rabbinic demonol-

32. Ronis, "Intermediary Beings," 95.

33. Gershom Scholem, *Major Trends in Jewish Mysticism* (New York: Schocken Books, 1941); David Biale, *Gershom Scholem: Kabbalah and Counter-History* (Cambridge, MA: Harvard University Press, 1979). My thanks to Jordan Rosenblum for suggesting I take into account Scholem's importance to the scholarly trajectory.

ogy functioned within its larger religious intellectual system and within the lives of those rabbis who participated in it.

Magic and/or Religion

Within religious studies, demons have been studied largely within the context of magic. Melissa Aubin, Kimberly Stratton, and Randall Styers have all done thorough work in laying out a scholarly historiography of the study of magic; I offer only a small window into the subject here.[34]

In the nineteenth century, scholars in the nascent fields of religious studies and anthropology began to examine magical practices and beliefs.[35] These scholars proposed a range of ways to distinguish magic—in its essence and in its performance—from religion, whether in terms of the goals of practitioners, the details of rituals, or the social and communal contexts in which it was performed.[36] As in the *Wissenschaft des Judentums,* which was part of this broader trend, demons were classed as magical and understood as primitive "superstition," distinct from a more civilized "religion" that looked very much like Protestant Christianity.[37]

In 1937, British anthropologist E. E. Evans-Pritchard published his groundbreaking study of the Azande people of north-central Africa, *Witchcraft, Oracles and Magic among the Azande.* In it, he criticized existing scholarship for understanding magic through a lens which held up nineteenth-century Western religiosity as the pinnacle of religious practice against which all other religious practice must be judged and found want-

34. Readers who are interested in learning more are encouraged to read Aubin, "Gendering Magic in Late Antique Judaism"; Kimberly B. Stratton, *Naming the Witch: Magic, Ideology, and Stereotype in the Ancient World* (New York: Columbia University Press, 2007), 109–143; and Randall Styers, *Making Magic: Religion, Magic, and Science in the Modern World* (Oxford: Oxford University Press, 2004).

35. Of course, religious leaders had distinguished between these two terms in conversations within a specific religious community for centuries. For discussion of the Christian distinctions between religion and magic, see Stratton, *Naming the Witch,* 109–143; Karen Jolly, "Medieval Magic: Definitions, Beliefs, Practices," in *Witchcraft and Magic in Europe: The Middle Ages,* ed. Bengt Ankarloo and Stuart Clark (Philadelphia: University of Pennsylvania Press, 2002), 1–72.

36. See extensive discussion of these scholars in Aubin, "Gendering Magic in Late Antique Judaism," 26–61; Stratton, *Naming the Witch,* 1–38; Styers, *Making Magic.*

37. Particularly ironic given the importance of demons to early Christian writings in the New Testament and monastic literature.

ing. He argued that magic needed a new definition informed by sensitivity to the self-understandings of its practitioners.[38] With this publication Evans-Pritchard initiated a scholarly approach that sees magic as socially and culturally constructed, rather than static and easily identifiable.[39] As a result, some scholars have recognized that calling something *magic* is itself an ideological act.[40] What "we" (white, male, and rational Christians) do is religion, what "they" (men and women of color, white women, the "primitive," non-Christians) do is magic.[41] As religious studies scholars have begun to recognize the ideological nature of the label *magic*, they have also called into question both the utility of distinguishing between religion and magic and the act of dismissing rites labeled magical.

Jewish studies scholars have followed this trend, moving from early phenomenological accounts of magic in Judaism to more rhetorically nuanced studies of magic that reckon with the ideological and discursive functions of informant claims that certain behaviors or individuals are magical—or demonic—in nature.[42] Most scholarship on late antique Jew-

38. E. E. Evans-Pritchard, *Witchcraft, Oracles and Magic among the Azande* (Oxford: Clarendon Press, 1939), 1–17.

39. For more on Evans-Pritchard's impact on the study of magic, see Aubin, "Gendering Magic," 86–89. Of course, there are still scholars conducting phenomenological studies of magic. See, e.g., H. S. Versnel, "Some Reflections on the Relationship Magic-Religion," *Numen* 38, no. 2 (1991): 177–97, whose approach is partly followed by Yuval Harari, "What Is a Magical Text? Methodological Reflections Aimed at Redefining Early Jewish Magic," in *Officina Magica: Essays on the Practice of Magic in Antiquity*, ed. Shaul Shaked (Leiden: Brill, 2005), 91–124.

40. Stratton, *Naming the Witch*, chap. 1, n. 41.

41. Although almost a truism today, the phrase "what we do is religion, what they do is magic," is often associated with John Gager. See, e.g., John Gager, "The Social Place of Magic in the Graeco-Roman World," paper presented at the Philadelphia Seminar on Christian Origins, Williams Hall, University of Pennsylvania, 5 October 1976 (with minutes available at http://ccat.sas.upenn.edu/psco/archives/psco14-min.htm#b1). I have been unable to identify its earliest use.

42. In his recent work, Yuval Harari has argued that the sociological, cultural studies, gender studies, and comparative religion approaches have

> replaced the traditional scholarship that sought to subordinate the discourse as a whole to one factor within it: the halakha, and to examine it in light of the halakha, alone. The nullification of the essential dichotomy between religion and magic in Jewish studies, part of a more general trend in the study of religion in recent decades, and replacing it with an approach that sees them as parallel and complementary ritual power systems has brought about an important change. It has diverted the focus of discussion about the rabbis' attitude toward magic and magicians (and especially sorceresses) from the ideological to the social. Here, the main concern is

ish magic and ritual power to date has focused on the Jewish communities of the Roman West.[43] Not enough work has been done on the specific character and function of demons in the rabbinic community of the Sasanian East.[44]

Informed by my awareness of the socially constructed and culturally

---

the rabbis' aspiration to acquire a monopoly over knowledge and power and the removal of competition—ideological, ritual, and societal, by labeling such competitors as illegitimate ("The Sages and the Occult," in *The Literature of the Sage*, ed. Shmuel Safrai et al. [Assen, Netherlands: Royal van Gorcum, 2006], 521).

In my own work on demons, I argue that demons are not part of a system parallel and complementary to religion and halakhah; instead, they are very much a part of the halakhic system itself and thus part of normative religion for the rabbis.

43. Scholars of ancient Judaism have examined manifestations of demonology in the Dead Sea Scrolls, *Heikhalot* literature, and the late antique Roman Empire as a whole. On Second Temple demonology, see Philip S. Alexander, "The Demonology of the Dead Sea Scrolls," in *The Dead Sea Scrolls after Fifty Years: A Comprehensive Assessment*, ed. Peter W. Flint and James C. Vanderkam (Leiden: Brill, 1999), 331–53; Esther Eshel, "Demonology in Palestine during the Second Temple Period" (PhD diss., Hebrew University of Jerusalem, 1999). For demons and magic in *Heikhalot* literature, see Michael D. Swartz, *Scholastic Magic: Ritual and Revelation in Early Jewish Mysticism* (Princeton, NJ: Princeton University Press, 1996). For demons and magic in the late antique Roman Empire, see Gideon Bohak, "Jewish Myth in Pagan Magic in Antiquity," in *Myths in Judaism: History, Thought, Literature*, ed. I. Gruenwald and Moshe Idel (Jerusalem: Zalman Shazar Center, 2004), 97–122, 143–226; and his *Ancient Jewish Magic: A History* (Cambridge: Cambridge University Press, 2008).

An important parallel project is that of Mika Ahuvia, whose PhD dissertation, "Israel among the Angels—A Study of Angels in Jewish Texts from the Fourth to Eighth Century C.E." (PhD diss., Princeton University, 2014) and subsequent book explore the essential roles of angels in Jewish exegetical, homiletical, and liturgical texts, as well as in Jewish material culture.

44. One factor contributing to this oversight may be the problem of access, as many scholars of ancient Judaism are trained in Greek, Latin, and Roman history, and thus may more easily study the Palestinian materials in their broader cultural context. Another factor may be the scholarly distance between understandings of magic and understandings of the Babylonian Talmud. On the one hand, many scholars of magic and its relationship to organized religion are hesitant to use the Babylonian Talmud as evidence, both because of linguistic difficulties and because of broader methodological concerns. On the other hand, for the reasons outlined above, scholars who are rigorously trained in Talmudic methodology often dismiss magic as nonnormative and thus irrelevant in the modern context.

Two recent excellent exceptions to this claim are Avigail Manekin Bamberger, "An Akkadian Demon in the Talmud: Between Šulak and Bar-Širiqa," *Journal for the Study of Judaism* 44 (2013): 282–87, and Richard Kalmin, *Migrating Tales: The Talmud's Narratives and Their Historical Context* (Berkeley: University of California Press, 2014), which examine a single incantation and longer Bavli narratives, respectively. Ishay Rosen-Zvi, *Demonic Desires: Yetzer Hara and the Problem of Evil in Late Antiquity* (Philadelphia: University of Pennsylvania Press, 2011), also touches on the demonic as part of a larger discussion of the nature of sin and the evil inclination in rabbinic thought, though his concept of the demonic

contingent nature of definitions of magic, I rely on the rabbis' own definitions of magic *(kishuf)*—the licit, and the forbidden—to understand how and where they do—and do not—situate the demonic within their religious world. The rabbis resist classifying demons together with magic, with consequences for the way modern scholars think about these distinctions in late antique contexts. Building on this awareness, I interrogate *how* and *why* particular attitudes about demons and magic functioned in the social and cultural worlds of the rabbis in late antique Babylonia.

Social Scientists Take Up the Charge

Outside of the discipline of religious studies, the social sciences have had particular interest in demons. Observing Sinhalese demon possessions and exorcisms in 1970s Sri Lanka, anthropologist Bruce Kapferer argued that "demon exorcisms refract the mythical, legendary, historical, and current realities of their participants and, most importantly, bring these realities into conjunction or into relation within the experience of participants"[45]:

> Meaning arises from a process whereby actors project their own action in relation to themselves and others in such a way as to intend further acts, and it is framed in accordance with typifications or ideal conceptions shared by cultural members as to how typical actors within a culture think or act in typical situations.[46]

Demon possession and exorcism are public acts, performed in full view of the community and within the context of community beliefs and practices.

While social anthropologists have traditionally observed demon possession "abroad," ethnopsychiatrists study and treat demon possession "at home." The social-scientific field of ethnopsychiatry rose to prominence in France in the 1960s and 1970s, spearheaded by the work of psychologist and ethnologist George Devereux. These decades saw an influx of

---

is informed by the Christian construction of demons as distinct malevolent forces who enter and possess the body, rather than by Babylonian demonology.

45. Bruce Kapferer, *A Celebration of Demons: Exorcism and the Aesthetics of Healing in Sri Lanka* (Bloomington: Indiana University Press, 1983), 12.

46. Ibid., 5–6.

immigrants to France after the Second World War and a resulting rise in patients describing their mental and physical conditions in the languages of immigrant communities. Western psychiatrists encountered patients who presented as demon-possessed and for whom standard Western drug therapy was ineffective, only partially effective, or refused either by patients themselves or by their communities. Ethnopsychiatry as a field reacted against the impulse to translate immigrant disorders into the language of western European psychology and treat them exclusively with western European therapies and pharmaceuticals.[47] Ethnopsychiatrist Tobie Nathan notes that these acts of translation extended European colonization and set the Western psychologist up as an expert who must get to the obscured truth of the patient's problem. But for Nathan,

> treating language as a thing—more precisely as a system of things—suddenly opens the psychotherapeutic space to real debate in that it henceforth contains a means for the speakers to reach an agreement, instead of finding themselves confined yet again within the closed field of dual conflict where the question is always to determine which of the two better understands the meaning of what is said.[48]

In meeting as equals and recognizing other communities' truth claims, patients and scholars can productively work together to achieve healing.[49]

Following these social scientists, I recognize the rabbis' truth claims about demons, and seek to understand the various ways that demons functioned in rabbinic discourse and rabbinic lives. I am not interested in eliding the rabbis' own talk about demons by asking what demons *really* meant, or what modern psychological or germ-theory equivalent they might have symbolized for the late antique rabbis. Instead, to understand how demons construct and are constructed by rabbinic discourse, I enter

47. It is perhaps no coincidence that both Devereux and Nathan were themselves Jewish immigrants to France, Devereux from Hungary and Nathan from Egypt.

48. Tobie Nathan, "Georges Devereux and Clinical Ethnopsychiatry," trans. Catherine Grandsard, Centre Georges Devereux, 1999–2010, www.ethnopsychiatrie.net/GDengl.htm.

49. See, e.g., Georges Devereux, *Ethnopsychoanalysis: Psychoanalysis and Anthropology as Complementary Frames of Reference* (Berkeley: University of California Press, 1978), 1–19, 265–96; *Essais D'Ethnopsychiatrie Générale* (Paris: Gallimard, 1970); Tobie Nathan, *Nous Ne Sommes Pas Seuls Au Monde: Les Enjeux De L'Ethnopsychiatrie* (France: Points, 2007), 47–68, 187–222; *Du Commerce Avec Les Diables* (Paris: Les Empêcheurs de penser en rond, 2004), 57–86.

into the world of demon-belief inhabited by the rabbis. This is not to say that I believe in demons or practice the rabbinic apotropaic rites laid out in the Babylonian Talmud, but rather that I recognize that the rabbis themselves believed in demons and in the efficacy of their apotropaic and healing practices. By entering into this world, I explore the logic of their system without rationalizing the system to conform to modern expectations or beliefs. I interrogate how demons function in this particular system, in a particular time (late antiquity) and place (Sasanian Babylonia), in conversation with a wide range of contemporaneous social and religious groups. Demons do a wide range of cultural work; though they can be understood symbolically, they cannot be reduced to mere symbols.

The Babylonian Talmud as Babylonian

Late antique Babylonia was a nexus of religious traditions old and new, and rabbinic literature is evidence of the way that one religious group negotiated this complex world. In the last several decades, scholars of the Babylonian Talmud have begun to explore the relationship between the Bavli and discrete cultural communities in and outside the Sasanian Empire. Yaakov Elman and Isaiah Gafni led the charge for rabbinists to study Middle Persian Zoroastrian literature and, together with their students, have begun to examine the fascinating interrelationships between the rabbis and the Zoroastrian elite of Babylonia.[50] Richard Kalmin has

50. Yaakov Elman, "The Other in the Mirror: Iranians and Jews View One Another: Questions of Identity, Conversion, and Exogamy in the Fifth-Century Iranian Empire. Part One," *Bulletin of the Asia Institute*, n.s. 19 (2005): 15–25; "Middle Persian Culture and Babylonian Sages: Accommodation and Resistance in the Shaping of Rabbinic Legal Tradition," in *The Cambridge Companion to the Talmud and Rabbinic Literature*, ed. Elisheva Charlotte Fonrobert and Martin S. Jaffee (New York: Cambridge University Press, 2007), 165–97; Isaiah Gafni, "The Political, Social, and Economic History of Babylonian Jewry, 224–638 CE," in *The Cambridge History of Judaism*, ed. Steven T. Katz (Cambridge: Cambridge University Press, 2008), 4:792–820. Gafni's work was published much before these other works, but it is only more recently that others have answered his call for more study. Elman and Gafni have now been followed by their students and others, including Geoffrey Herman, "'One Day David Went Out for the Hunt of the Falconers': Persian Themes in the Babylonian Talmud," in *Shoshannat Yaakov: Jewish and Iranian Studies in Honor of Yaakov Elman*, ed. Shai Secunda and Steven Fine (Leiden: Brill, 2012), 111–36; Yishai Kiel, "Redesigning *Tzitzit* in the Babylonian Talmud in Light of Literary Depictions of the Zoroastrian *Kustīg*," ibid., 185–202; Shai Secunda, "Reading the Bavli in Iran," *Jewish Quarterly Review* 100, no. 2

done important work exploring broader cultural parallels between Babylonian rabbinic literature and contemporaneous texts from Christian Mesopotamia, the eastern Roman provinces, and Christian Armenia, identifying the fourth century as a pivotal period for the transmission of traditions from the Roman West to the Sasanian East.[51] Mark Geller has examined Talmudic medicine in conversation with much older ancient Mesopotamian medical practices.[52] Building on the insights of these scholars working on rabbinic relationships with diverse religious communities, I argue that the rabbis participated in multiple overlapping and at-times contradictory conversations about demons and demonology in Sasanian Babylonia. I draw upon multiple academic disciplines to compile a data set of Sumerian, Akkadian, Ugaritic, Syriac Christian, and Zoroastrian traditions together with biblical, Second Temple Jewish, and Palestinian rabbinic traditions. Contextualizing rabbinic literature in this broader cultural network sheds light on the ways that the rabbis of late antique Babylonia shared assumptions, narratives, and modes of discourse with those around them, and on the ways that they insisted on charting their own path. It can also begin to help us understand the mechanisms of selection which led the rabbis to any one response in a given situation.

Scholars have theorized cross-cultural interactions in a variety of ways. Different terms—syncretism, bricolage, hybridity—describe different relationships in different academic and cultural contexts.[53] As we will see, there is no one model of interaction which fully explains the variety of ways that the rabbis think about demons in conversation with other religious traditions in late antiquity. Some interactions might have been the result of individualized interaction; others would have been collective

(2010): 310–42; Jason Sion Mokhtarian, *Rabbis, Sorcerers, Kings, and Priests: The Culture of the Talmud in Ancient Iran* (Oakland: University of California Press, 2015); Shana Strauch Schick, "Intention in the Babylonian Talmud: An Intellectual History" (PhD diss., Yeshiva University, 2011).

51. Kalmin, *Jewish Babylonia between Persia and Roman Palestine*, 9–10, 174–75; *Migrating Tales*, 7–9.

52. Mark J. Geller, "An Akkadium Vademecum in the Babylonian Talmud," in *From Athens to Jerusalem: Medicine in Hellenized Jewish Lore and in Early Christian Literature*, ed. Samuel Kottek and Manfred Horstmanshoff (Rotterdam: Erasmus, 2000), 13–32.

53. For an excellent review of scholarship on these terms, see Emily Sigalow, "Towards a Sociological Framework of Religious Syncretism in the United States," *Journal of the American Academy of Religion* 84, no. 4 (2016): 1029–55.

actions patterned on structural similarities between groups and ideas.[54] These interactions cannot be dismissed as foreign corruptions but instead mark particular moments of translation, negotiation, fluidity, and heterogeneity[55] conditioned by the specific realities of rabbinic Judaism in a Sasanian Babylonian world.

PLAN OF THE BOOK

As we have already seen, the study of demons is inherently interdisciplinary. It is a subject of interest from a variety of academic and religious communities. This book is designed to introduce each of these reading communities to some of the engaging and exciting work about demons going on in related fields, and to demonstrate how rabbinic demonology is an important model for thinking about demons, community, and the self in a complicated and contested world.

Throughout the book, we see a diversity of rabbinic approaches to the demonic; the rabbis themselves were not united in their construction of the demonic. While some rabbis and Talmudic texts depict demons as capricious and dangerous, others depict demons as neutral and passive, and many others depict demons as positive members of the rabbinic community. Rabbinic discourse about demons is interconnected but multivocal. Each of the seven chapters of this book traces the threads of a different aspect of this complex rabbinic demonology, while also functioning as a case study that interrogates rabbinic interaction with one or more late antique cultural and religious systems.

Chapter 1 explores stories of demonic origins. Two distinct narratives of demonic origins were told and retold during the Second Temple and early rabbinic periods. One narrative, found first in the Dead Sea Scrolls and later in Pseudo-Philo and the Mishnah, portrayed demons as part of the original divine plan of creation. The other narrative, presented most extensively in the book of Enoch and found later in *Genesis Rab-*

54. Sigalow, "Towards a Sociological Framework of Religious Syncretism in the United States," 1029–55.
55. Ibid., 1032.

bah, described demons as a product of sin and not part of the divine blueprint at all. These two positions point to two distinct conceptions of the demonic essence, one of which insists that demons are intentional elements of God's world, and the other of which associates them with shame, sin, and human failure. This chapter argues that the rabbis of the Babylonian Talmud inherited both of these positions yet privileged the former as a foundation for their own construction of the demonic.

Chapters 2 asks about the ways that the rabbis classified demons. The rabbis were one scholastic elite among many in late antiquity, and they engaged in the kinds of taxonomic projects found across religious and cultural lines. The rabbis of the Babylonian world constructed a differentiated intermediary world. While contemporaneous Christian texts present demons as opposite to angels in both character and essence, this chapter argues that for the Babylonian Talmud demons are not the opposite of angels but part of a monotheism that included a range of distinct and distinctive intermediary beings. For the rabbis, demons are born, reproduce, and die, with lives that are characterized by unlimited and continuous motion. These features construct demons not only as metaphors or symbols but also as real and embodied beings with the ability to materially influence human life. Rabbinic classification of demons also constructs rabbis as the classifiers par excellence, modeling the rabbis as a particular kind of intellectual and scholastic elite competitive with others across the region.

Demons were intermediary beings with a place in the divinely created cosmos; the rabbis believed that demons were also extremely dangerous. Chapter 3 shifts the focus from the rabbis' imaginings of demons to the rabbis' imaginings of their own fraught interactions with demonic forces. The rabbis represent bathrooms and ruins as spaces of demonic danger, palm trees as demonic refuges, and various illnesses as being caused by transgressing specific demonic norms. The cause of different types of danger, rabbinic demons are thus a rich source for understanding ancient ways of spatially and temporally organizing the world, and an important lens through which to understand how the rabbis conditioned particular kinds of bodies to move through their world in distinctly rabbinic ways. This chapter also begins to make the case that the rabbis constructed demonic dangers in such a way as to depict demons as neutral or even positive, and largely passive though capricious figures in the rabbinic imagination, a theme taken up in greater depth in the next chapter.

Where earlier chapters explained how the rabbis understood various aspects of demons, chapters 4 and 5 think through the ways that the rabbis used demons to understand themselves as coreligionists, teachers, and masters of the demonic. Demons are found not only in narrative stories in the Babylonian Talmud; they are interwoven into rabbinic law in ways both explicit and implicit. Chapter 4 outlines the ways that the Babylonian rabbis participated in broader legal conversations about demons while serving their own rabbinic identity formation as an elite. This trend toward "legalizing" demons is not found in earlier Jewish approaches to the demonic, but it is paralleled in contemporaneous Zoroastrian legal texts such as the *Pahlavi Vīdēvdād*. The rabbinic and the Zoroastrian scholastic elites shared an interest in legal discourse. In both these Sasanian religious movements, demons were used as a mechanism to uphold and enforce observance of the law.

However, unlike demons in the Zoroastrian legal discourse, rabbinic demons also appear as subjects, agents, and teachers within Babylonian rabbinic legal discourse. Chapter 5 focuses on these depictions of demons as servants of the rabbis and of the rabbinic project. Whereas the previous chapter explored contemporaneous legalizing trends, this chapter presents a diachronic overview that locates the rabbinic construction of demons as subordinate and servile within much older Sumerian and Akkadian understandings of demons as capricious servants to deities in the Mesopotamian pantheon. Ancient Mesopotamian narratives and inscriptions depict demons as neutral figures whose character as good or bad depends on the nature of their specific missions and on the different perspectives of those with whom they interact. The rabbis built on these still-circulating stories, such that demons became both servants to and students of the Babylonian rabbis. This chapter concludes by tracing the survival of this portrayal of demons into later Syriac Christian and Muslim Arabic narratives.

In light of the complex rabbinic construction of demons, chapter 6 examines rabbinic strategies of imagining, preventing, and treating demonic attacks. Jews and Christians in the Roman West traditionally imagined demons entering a human body and possessing it. The proper response was the performance of an exorcism conducted by a ritual expert. Exorcisms are described in depth in the writings of Josephus and in the apocryphal book of Tobit and are an important part of the successful spread of the early Jesus movement. For the Babylonian rabbis living in a Sasanian world that had inherited earlier Mesopotamian medical models, however, demons were imagined attacking the body from without. The best way to treat a demonic attack was to prevent its occurrence in the first place. Stories of exorcisms are thus largely absent from the Babylonian Talmud, even though the rabbis were also among the heirs of Second Temple Jewish culture. This chapter explores the only two Talmudic stories which feature rabbinic acts of exorcism: a narrative in which a rabbi exorcises a malevolent demon from Abaye's study house in b. *Qiddushin* 29b, and a Talmudic story in which a rabbi performs a traditional "western" exorcism of a person found on b. *Me'ilah* 17a–b. In this story, the rabbis actually collude with a demonic ally to stage a possession and exorcism in Rome. The Babylonian rabbis quite literally *perform* an exorcism to gain credibility and political concessions in the Roman Empire. As we will see, the rabbis deploy and even amplify the differences between Roman and Sasanian demonologies to construct themselves as the religious elite most capable of dealing with demons across imperial borders.

Finally, the book concludes with an examination of the ways that the reinscription of demons into rabbinic text and culture must inform our understanding of Babylonian rabbinic culture and ancient Jewish monotheisms. Rabbinic demonology properly recognized contributes to the scholarly move to complicate and even break down traditional academic distinctions between religion and magic, the normative and nonnormative, and the ancient and late antique. The boundaries between these categories are porous and ever shifting, moving at times to exclude and at times to selectively include a wide range of beliefs, attitudes, and peoples.

NOTE ON LANGUAGE

This book examines demonic discourse in the Babylonian Talmud. On the most basic level, I use *discourse* to refer to the words that are used to talk about demons in the written record. When studying ancient Babylonia, words—composed orally or inscribed on ancient incantation bowls, copied into later manuscripts, and published in premodern and modern books—are some of only a few ways modern scholars can access this world.

Discourse is inherently communicative: it is meant to express ideas and beliefs to a group, an individual, and one's self. My use of discourse as an interpretive lens is informed by the work of French theorist Michel Foucault, who posited an understanding of discourse that moves beyond words to include the unspoken, historically and geographically located conditions which constrain and encourage particular ways of speaking and thinking about the world.[56] The vocabulary, style, and even syntax used by the rabbis were shaped by the rabbis' beliefs and worldview; in turn, the language used shaped the rabbis' beliefs and worldviews. These discourses developed, aggregated, and changed over the hundreds of years that the rabbis were active in Sasanian Babylonia, adding a diachronic element to our understanding of rabbinic discourse about demons.

There is an inherent violence to translating words from one language to another—nuance is lost, difference elided. However, without an act of translation, access is denied to nonnative speakers and readers, and important cross-cultural parallels can be overlooked. The difficulty in translation is no more in evidence than in using the word *demon* to refer to some rabbinic constructions of intermediary beings.

I struggled with this act of translation on two levels: first, in how to translate a variety of Hebrew and Aramaic words that the rabbis appear to be using synonymously; and second, in how to bound a data set of comparanda from contemporaneous cultures that do not all share Proto-Semitic linguistic roots. Indeed, even within a single language family, language is dynamic, and language usage is shaped by time, space, community, and culture.

The modern English word *demon* is most often used to mean "an evil

56. Michel Foucault, "Truth and Power," in *Power/Knowledge: Selected Interviews and Other Writings, 1972–1977*, ed. Colin Gordon (New York: Pantheon, 1980), 109–33, 131; *Discipline and Punish: The Birth of the Prison*, trans. Alan Sheridan (1977; New York: Random House, 1995), 26–31, 67; *The Archaeology of Knowledge*, trans. Alan Sheridan (New York: Pantheon, 1972), 23–43, 46–51, 143.

spirit."[57] It is derived from the Greek δαίμων, which means "god, goddess, divine power, deity, destiny, fate, good or evil genius of a family or person," or evil spirit; in classical Latin, the term was used to describe the "indwelling spirit or genius."[58] It is only with postclassical Latin and the early Christian Fathers that the term *daemōn* came to refer exclusively to an evil spirit, false god, or idol.[59] This shift marked the rejection and demonization of non-Christian gods as part of wider religious changes.[60] The linguistic shift from δαίμων to *daemōn* to *demon* highlights the ways that defining and naming intermediary beings in late antiquity were deeply tied to ideological claims about right religious belief.

Though these nouns were imported into many romance languages, they do not appear in the literature of the rabbis of the Babylonian Talmud and the Sasanian world within which they lived.[61] The rabbis use a combination of three terms: *ruḥot* (sing. *ruaḥ*, lit: spirits); *mazziqin* (sing. *mazziq*, lit: harmers); and *šedim* (sing. *šeid*), from the Akkadian *šēdu*.[62] The Hebrew and Aramaic term *šeid(a)* is usually translated into English as "demon," but in Akkadian the term refers to a beneficent protective male deity.[63] The other speakers of eastern Aramaic dialects—Syriac Christians and Mandaeans—also used these terms. Pahlavi, the language of Zoroastrian religious literature, retained the spelling ŠDYA while pronouncing the word divergently as *dēw*.[64] The Pahlavi *dēw*, from which the English word *devil* is derived, also migrated into Jewish Babylonian Aramaic, as

57. "Demon, N. (and Adj.)," in *Oxford English Dictionary* (2014).

58. Ibid.

59. See discussion in chap. 2.

60. Ian Kidd, "Some Philosophical Demons," *Bulletin of the Institute of Classical Studies* 40 (1995): 217–24.

61. "Demon, N. (and Adj.)," in *Oxford English Dictionary Online* (2014).

62. Michael Sokoloff, *A Dictionary of Jewish Babylonian Aramaic of the Talmudic and Geonic Periods* (Ramat-Gan, Israel: Bar-Ilan University Press, 2003), 1132, s.v. שידא.

63. Jeremy Black and Anthony Green, *Gods, Demons and Symbols of Ancient Mesopotamia: An Illustrated Dictionary* (London: British Museum Press, 1992), 115; A. Löhnert and A. Zgoll, "Schutzgott. A. In Mesopotamien," in *Reallexicon der Assyriologie und Vorderasiatischen Archäologie*, ed. Michael P. Streck (Berlin: De Gruyter, 2009–11).

64. On the phenomenon of arameograms, see Prods Oktor Skjærvø, "Iran. VI. Iranian Languages and Scripts. (3) Writing Systems," in *Encyclopædia Iranica Online* (2006, 2012 updated online), www.iranicaonline.org/articles/iran-vi3-writing-systems.

can be seen from the listing of *devi* along with *šedim, ruḥot, and mazziqin* on many of the Aramaic bowl incantations.[65] For Syriac Christians, Mandaeans, and Zoroastrians, the intermediary beings marked with the term *šed* were unequivocally evil; in translations of the texts of these religious traditions, these terms are often uncomplicatedly translated into English as "demon."

If I restricted this study to an examination of the words *ruḥot, mazziqin,* and *šedim* and their cognates, it would be impossible to properly contextualize the rabbis in their multilingual world. Ideas that first emerge in one language can cross over to the speakers of a different language, even if many or even most of those speakers are not themselves bilingual.[66] It is also possible for individuals and communities to interact with more languages than those in which they construct "tradition," particularly when they are engaged in tradition-construction as a religious or scholastic act. To define a relevant data set within which to understand the rabbis in their own multilingual world, therefore, this work expands its focus beyond cognates of the three terms in Semitic-language texts to include Greek and Latin words. Further, given that language changes as part of broader cultural shifts, this work tracks the development of terms that either start out or end up referring to what we might today think of as demons in late antiquity. Essentially, then, I use as my data set those terms which describe some kind of intermediary being with the potential (realized, or otherwise) to cause serious harm to human beings within a particular worldview. While the Babylonian rabbis do not suggest that these beings as a whole are evil, they clearly think that these beings' very nature *as* intermediary beings with superhuman powers can be dangerous to humankind. Across the wider data set, these beings are all understood to be profoundly dangerous, at least to some, and it is that danger—and the challenges that it poses—which makes such beings useful points of comparison. To not obscure the different linguistic terms as they appear, I

65. Oktor Skjærvø, "Pahlavi Primer," (12 June 2016), 8. The word *δαίμων* does appear in Jewish and Christian writings in the Roman West. The Septuagint uses *δαιμόνιον* to translate the biblical קֶטֶב in Ps. 91:6. The evil spirits who are exorcised by Jesus in the New Testament are referred to as *δαιμόνιον*, a term which also appears in Tobit and other apocryphal works.

66. As an admittedly minor modern example, think of the popularity of the Danish concept of hygge in English-language lifestyle publications.

identify the specific linguistic terms and their particular histories of development and use as they relate to rabbinic demonology in my discussions of the relevant parallels.

But what to call these beings? One of the primary arguments of this book is that the rabbinic subjugation of the demonic to halakhah (rabbinic law) allowed for a discursive construction of demons as mostly neutral forces and followers of the rabbis. The word *demon* with its resonance of evil is thus not the most apt word to describe the actual beings constructed and subjugated by the Babylonian rabbis. Perhaps a more apt descriptor of these beings as they function in the rabbinic system is as follows: neutral intermediary beings who are capricious, powerful, dangerous, and quick to become defensive if they perceive a slight.[67] However, this language is unwieldy and obscures the powerful act of interpretation that the rabbis perform. The rabbis at least partially neutralize the danger of the demonic; this act of neutralization admits the very danger of the original threat. There is a meme from the webcomic *Gunshow,* which circulates widely on various social media platforms. In the first panel, a cartoon dog sits at a table in a room filled with flames and smoke. In the second panel, the artist has focused in on the dog, who is shown saying, "This is fine."[68] The joke is that everything is clearly *not* fine; the dog is trying to convince himself of something that is clearly counter to the reality of his current lived experience. Although it is often impossible to determine tone from the written Talmudic text, I cannot help but think of this meme as I read rabbinic discourse about demons. The rabbis lived in a world where everyone around them believed that demons were ever-present, evil, and maliciously oriented toward humankind. In some rabbis' insistence that the majority worldview is false, are they trying to convince us or themselves? Doth the rabbis protest too much?

For the rabbis, demons could be positive, benevolent members of the rabbinic community; they could also be dangerous and capricious. These might be positions held by different rabbinic individuals, but they may

67. This definition also emphasizes that demons are not the inverse of angels. Chap. 2 addresses in part the rabbis' different construction of angels.

68. "This is Fine," Know Your Meme, https://knowyourmeme.com/memes/this-is-fine. Accessed 3 March 2022.

also be reflective of the complex attitudes held by a single rabbinic thinker. Like the rabbis themselves, demons were understood to be multifaceted and complex. The term *demon* encompasses this complexity, while leaving space for differences in how these beings are understood within different cultural contexts. Thus, throughout this book, I translate all three terms—*šedim, ruḥot,* and *mazziqin*—anachronistically as "demon," while specifying in parentheses which exact term is used.[69] The term *demon* emphasizes the creative act of translation in which the rabbis themselves are engaged, and it serves as an invitation to a broader conversation about intermediary beings, malevolent and otherwise, in the world of late antiquity.[70]

Throughout the book, I present the rabbinic texts as found in the printed edition, except where noted in the footnotes. Information on relevant manuscript variants can also be found in the footnotes. All translations of rabbinic texts are my own, except where otherwise marked. In my translations of rabbinic materials, I have demarcated Hebrew text with italics and left the Aramaic text unitalicized. This demarcation is meant to give a sense of the linguistically disparate sources and complex layers of traditions embedded in these texts. Words in parentheses gloss the text; words in square brackets are meant to make the English translations smoother. The names of rabbis and biblical figures are translated using conventional translations where they exist. Otherwise, they follow simplified transcription: the letter ח is represented by a ḥ, the letter כ by a kh, the letter צ by a ẓ, and the letter ש by a š.

69. Some have attempted to distinguish between *ruḥot* and *šedim,* on the one hand, and *mazziqin,* on the other, suggesting that while *ruḥot* and *šedim* could be neutral or positive, the rabbinic term *mazziqin* is used exclusively to refer to malevolent demons. The impulse to assume that these three terms refer to different types of intermediary beings is a legitimate one and one that this author wishes she could have authentically mapped onto the Talmudic text. However, it simply does not work, as we will see in chap. 5 and its discussion of b. *Ḥullin* 105b, where a *mazziq* is depicted as neutral, passive, and a strict observer of rabbinic dictates.

70. For a discussion of the strengths and weaknesses of this translation choice, see Peregrine Horden, "Afterword: Pandaemonium," in *Demons and Illness from Antiquity to the Early-Modern Period,* ed. Siam Bhayro and Catherine Rider (Leiden: Brill, 2017), 412–18.

1 Origin Stories

In the beginning, God created the Heavens and the Earth.

Genesis 1:1

Every superhero has an origin story. Origin stories add drama and depth, and provide rationales for otherwise irrational behaviors. In the modern media landscape, origin stories are often told through flashbacks, prequels, or companion media. We need to know how an ordinary person becomes a hero, and how a hero becomes a superhero. In late antiquity, demons, too, had origin stories. And, as with modern superhero stories, demonic origin stories gave their audience the context and backstory that allowed readers to categorize and understand demonic powers.

We begin this book at the beginning of demonic life. In this chapter, we shed light on how Jews of different periods and places in the ancient world answered the question, Where do demons come from? Jewish stories of demonic origins are as old as Jewish beliefs in demons themselves. Tracing these origin stories is one way to understand the history of Jewish belief in demons. The rabbis of the Babylonian Talmud did not invent demons out of whole cloth; there was a long Jewish tradition of believing in demons. To understand the demonology of the Babylonian Talmud, then, we must also understand the rich biblical and Second Temple demonological traditions that the rabbis of Sasanian Babylonian inherited.

BIBLICAL BEGINNINGS

A good way to start when studying the Talmud is to explore the biblical background for whatever subject is under discussion. But a student of Talmudic demonology searching for the biblical origins of demons will find herself disappointed. Although most ancient Near Eastern literature is rich in demonological descriptions and stories, demons play little to no role in the biblical narratives about the creation of the world, the wanderings of the Israelites, and the Israelite monarchy.[1] The Hebrew Bible mentions demons only rarely and in passing.

Reading synchronically across the diverse literatures included in the Hebrew Bible, it is possible to cobble together a divine court of beings such as demons, destroying angels, and an accuser known as the *Satan*.[2] Because of his prominent role in later Jewish and Christian theologies, much scholarly ink has been spilled in understanding the figure of Satan. But in his biblical form in the Hebrew Bible, the *Satan* is never associated with a broader class of demonic beings.[3] Indeed all these beings are often ambiguous in nature and in their relationships to one another and to the divine. They appear in different literary and historical contexts and defy neat systematization. And they appear only rarely and always without an origin story.

Some of these intermediary beings function as extensions of God's will; others—and in particular those called *šedim*—seem to function as God's competition. Deuteronomy 32:17 criticizes Israel for sacrificing to "demons *(šedim)*, no-gods, gods they had never known, new ones who came but lately" (NJPS), language echoed in Psalm 106:37, which accuses Israel of sacrificing their own sons and daughters to demons *(šedim)*.

1. Notably, in two episodes, demons deceive and attack divinely disfavored kings (1 Kings 22:22–23; 1 Sam. 16:15, 23). See discussion in chap. 5.

2. See, e.g., Ps. 78, 82; Job 1–2.

3. Loren T. Stuckenbruck, "Satan and Demons," in *Jesus among Friends and Enemies: A Historical and Literary Introduction to Jesus in the Gospels*, ed. Chris Keith and Larry W. Hurtado (Grand Rapids, MI: Baker Academic, 2011), 173–97. On Satan as generic figure and particular being, see Andrei A. Orlov, *Dark Mirrors: Azazel and Satanael in Early Jewish Demonology* (Albany: State University of New York Press, 2011); Henry Ansgar Kelly, *Satan: A Biography* (Cambridge: Cambridge University Press, 2006); C. Breytenbach and P. L. Day, "Satan," in *Dictionary of Deities and Demons in the Bible*, ed. Karel van der Toorn et al. (Leiden: Brill, 1999).

Some scholars have suggested that the worship of *šedim* in the land of Israel is connected to the Mesopotamian worship of divine beings known as *šedu* and *lamassu*.[4] Demons are associated with the worship of foreign deities, and demon-worship thus contravenes Israel's required monolatry.

It can be hard to identify biblical demons. While the demon Lilith and *śĕʿîrîm* (satyrs) appear together in the postapocalyptic wasteland described in Isaiah 34:14, other obscure terms are less clear.[5] Different classes of demons—*îyîm* ("desertlings"), *ṣîyîm* ("howlers") and *ʿōḥîm* (also "howlers")—may appear in Isaiah and Jeremiah's descriptions of a world in ruins, though some scholars prefer to translate these obscure nouns as "jackals," "wildcats," and "owls," respectively.[6] So too, the words *qeteb* and *rešeph* (Deut. 32:24; Ps. 91:5) may be nouns referring to destruction and plague, respectively, but they may also be references to the west Semitic gods Qẓb and Rešeph, integrated into the Hebrew Bible's cosmology as demonic beings whom God sends to punish the Israelites.[7] *Dever* (lit: pestilence) appears to be a demonic force in Psalm 78:48–50, where it is paralleled with both Rešeph and the angels of evil. These verses highlight the difficulty in identifying biblical demons when biblical authors use nouns whose meaning is uncertain or unstable. As we will see, the rabbis seize on to these unstable words and insist on reading them demonically.

The Hebrew Bible's few but evocative mentions of intermediary beings leave space for later interpretation and commentary. The rabbis of the Babylonian Talmud gravitated toward that space and developed an elaborate demonology that renders the rabbis as the true masters of demons

4. Rüdiger Schmitt, "Demons, Demonology. II. Hebrew Bible/Old Testament," in *Encyclopedia of the Bible and Its Reception*, ed. Hans-Josef Klauck et al. (Berlin: De Gruyter, 2012), 6:537.

5. Schmitt, "Demons, Demonology. II," 537. *Śĕʿîrîm* also appear in 2 Chron. 11:15, though Schmitt dismisses this passage as "mere polemic, since there is no evidence for cult veneration of demons in ancient Israel" (ibid.).

6. These animals are themselves predators who dwell in the wilderness and prey on the weak; they are not that far off from one way of imagining demonic beings. For a reading of these groupings as demonic, see ibid. and B. Janowski, "Jackals," in *Dictionary of Deities and Demons in the Bible*, ed. Karel van der Toorn et al. (Leiden: Brill, 1999); on these beings rendered as classes of animals typically found in wastelands, see the 1999 translation of the Jewish Publication Society Tanakh.

7. N. Wyatt, "Qeteb,"in *Dictionary of Deities and Demons in the Bible*, ed. Karel van der Toorn et al. (Leiden: Brill, 1999), 673–74.

biblical and otherwise. Yet, as we will see, the rabbis also recorded and elaborated upon traditions with no prehistory in the constructed biblical canon but which form an essential part of Second Temple demonology.

SECOND TEMPLE ORIGINS

Demons take on a much more prominent role in the Jewish literature produced during the Persian and Second Temple periods (538 B.C.E.–70 C.E.) that did not make it into the biblical canon. Demons begin to appear in biblical retellings, sectarian creeds, and exorcistic ritual texts. Their increased prominence is paired with a new desire to understand how demons came to be at all.

Esther Eshel has argued that Jewish texts had two opposite yet at times overlapping understandings of demonic origins in the pre-rabbinic ancient world. Eshel distinguishes between one narrative trend, found first in the Dead Sea Scrolls and later in Pseudo-Philo, that portrays demons as part of God's original creation, and another narrative trend, found in the books of Enoch and Jubilees, that describes demons as the unintended product of sexual sin and not as part of the divine blueprint at all.[8] Using Eshel's work as a springboard, we will see that traces of both traditions appear in rabbinic literature. These traces allow us to understand how the rabbis read and transmitted older texts, as well as the kinds of interpretive work that the rabbis performed with these stories.

Created Demons

According to Genesis 1, God created the world and everything in it during the seven days of creation. The creation stories of Genesis do not mention demons, but locating demonic origins in the period of creation was a logical move for a people who understood the entire universe to have been created during these seven days. And as we will see, locating demonic origins in the divine creation of the world raises important theological questions about the nature of demons and of God's creation more broadly.

8. Eshel, "Demonology in Palestine during the Second Temple Period," i–ii, 10–78.

The Dead Sea Scrolls are an important primary source for Jewish beliefs in the Second Temple period. Among the scrolls, the Community Rule (1QS) is one of the oldest surviving Jewish texts to describe demons as created ab initio by God. Scholars debate the date of the Community Rule's composition and redaction, but it appears to have been completed and in its current form by the late first century B.C.E. [9] According to the Community Rule's *Treatise on the Two Spirits*,

> 15 Before they [all the sons of man] existed He established their entire design.
>
> 16 And when they have come into being, at their appointed time, they will execute all their works according to his glorious design, without altering anything. In his hand are
>
> 17 the laws of all things and He supports them in all their affairs. He created man to rule
>
> 18 the world and placed within him two spirits (ruḥot) so that he would walk with them until the moment of his visitation: they are the spirits
>
> 19 of truth and of deceit. From the spring of light stem the generations of truth, and from the source of darkness the generations of deceit.
>
> 20 and in the hand of the Prince of Lights is dominion over all the sons of justice; they walk on paths of light. And in the hand of the Angel of
>
> 21 Darkness is total dominion over the sons of deceit; they walk on paths of darkness. From the Angel of Darkness stems the corruption of
>
> 22 all the sons of justice, and all their sins, their iniquities, their guilts and their offensive deeds are under his dominion
>
> 23 in compliance with the mysteries of God, until his moment; and all their afflictions and their periods of grief are caused by the dominion of his enmity;
>
> 24 and all the spirits of his lot *(ruḥe goralo)* cause the sons of light to fall. However, the God of Israel and the angel of his truth assist all

9. Sarianna Metso, *The Textual Development of the Qumran Community Rule* (Leiden: Brill, 1997), 137, 147–48. According to C. Coulot, "L'Instruction Sur Les Deux Esprits (1QS III, 13–IV, 26)," *Religious Studies Review* 82 (2008): 147–60, following Jacob Licht, "An Analysis of the Treatise on the Two-Spirits in DSD," in *Aspects of the Dead Sea Scrolls*, ed. Chaim Rabin and Yigael Yadin (Jerusalem: Magnes Press, 1958), 88–100, the Community Rule is a composite work that attests to different ancient Jewish attitudes toward the "spirits of darkness."

25 the sons of light. He created the spirits of light and of darkness and on them established every deed,

26 [o]n their [path]s every labor . . .[10]

This rich passage introduces us to the spirits of darkness, who are under the command of the Angel of Darkness "in compliance with the mysteries of God."[11] These sons of darkness are intermediary beings who serve a powerful angel. Modern readers might recognize these independent entities as demons, even though the word is not used. The struggle takes place both inside the self and outside it in the broader world. Demons are internal motivators of human beings and external forces upon them. In fact, their actions cause all sins, iniquities, guilts, and "offensive deeds."[12]

According to the theology of the Community Rule, God's original blueprint for creation called for a division between light and darkness, even before God undertook God's primordial act of creation. Within creation, the two parties—light (justice) and darkness (deceit)—are given equal weight and force; they are mirror images of each other in their natures and intentions as much as in their origins. Demonic actions are part of a larger divine system. And yet, in spite of the fact that demons are created by God as part of God's divine plan, or perhaps because of it, their actions in this world are evil and harmful to humans and the good. What does this mean for an understanding of God as both monotheistic and good? The authors do not purport to understand "the mysteries of God."

Pseudo-Philo's *Book of Biblical Antiquities* offers an even more explicit statement that demons and other spirits were intentionally created by God as part of the creation of the world and yet are still troublesome to

10. Text and translation from Florentino Garcia Martinez and Eibert J. C. Tigchelaar, *The Dead Sea Scrolls Study Edition,* 2 vols. (Leiden: Brill, 1997), 1:75–77. I have added the glosses for clarification.

11. For a history of scholarship on 1QS as a whole and the *Treatise on the Two Spirits* specifically, and an analysis of its structural integrity, see Charlotte Hempel, "The *Treatise on the Two Spirits* and the Literary History of the Rule of the Community," in *Dualism in Qumran,* ed. Geza G. Xeravits (London: T&T Clark, 2010), 102–20, 105–13.

12. For a discussion of this concept, see Miryam T. Brand, *Evil Within and Without: The Source of Sin and Its Nature as Portrayed in Second Temple Literature,* ed. Armin Lange et al. (Göttingen, Germany: Vandenhoeck & Ruprecht, 2013), 259–61. See also Eshel, "Demonology in Palestine," 77–78.

humankind.[13] Preserved in Latin, the text was likely written in Hebrew in first- or second-century C.E. Roman Palestine.[14] According to the *Book of Biblical Antiquities'* retelling of 1 Samuel 16:14–23, when the biblical King Saul was rejected as king, the "spirit of God" left him, and he was attacked by an "evil spirit." The boy who would become King David then enjoined the spirit to "not be troublesome, for you are a secondary creation," and the spirit spared Saul.[15] In this text, the creation of intermediary beings, described in the Latin as *tribus spirituum vestrorum*, "the tribe of your spirits," is dated to some point between the second and third days of creation. As part of God's intended creation, demons serve his larger purposes. The spirit of God functions here as a deterrent to attack; its removal leaves the king vulnerable. The "evil spirit" is an attacker, choking King Saul, but self-knowledge of its inferior position persuades it to spare the afflicted king.[16] This text locates the origin of demons with the origins of all other beings in the primeval creation of the world, but their origin as a secondary creation allows exceptional humans to command them in particular ways.

And yet there is an even more prominent tradition of demonic origins found across the Jewish world during this very same time period.

Sinful Demons

As Eshel has compellingly argued, a second tradition of demonic origins in Second Temple literature identifies demons with the offspring of forbidden sexual encounters between angels and humans. Genesis 6:1–4 tells the story of "sons of God" who have sex with daughters of man and reproduce. Second Temple literature expands on this brief and lacunae-filled text.

13. See Howard Jacobson, *A Commentary on Pseudo-Philo's "Liber Antiquitatum Biblicarum": With Latin Text and English Translation* (Leiden: Brill, 1996), 195–224; Frederick James Murphy, *Pseudo-Philo: Rewriting the Bible* (Oxford: Oxford University Press, 1993), 3–7; Eshel, "Demonology in Palestine," iv–v.

14. Daniel J. Harrington, "The Original Language of Pseudo-Philo's *Liber Antiquitatum Biblicarum*," *Harvard Theological Review* 63 (1970): 503–14; Jacobson, *A Commentary on Pseudo-Philo's "Liber Antiquitatum Biblicarum,"* 210–11.

15. LAB LX: 3, in *A Commentary on Pseudo-Philo's "Liber Antiquitatum Biblicarum,"* 188.

16. See Eshel, "Demonology in Palestine," 81–85.

The story is told most expansively within the corpus of literature pseudepigraphically attributed to the biblical figure of Enoch.[17] Among them is the third-century B.C.E. text known as the Book of the Watchers (1 Enoch 1–36). The Book of the Watchers actually contains several slightly different accounts of demonic origins. The Book of the Watchers recounts how the Watchers (a term for angelic beings) descend to earth and share both their secret knowledge and their bodies with human women.[18] According to 1 Enoch 7:2–6, the offspring produced by the unions of human women and fallen angels were enormous giants with monstrously large appetites for animal and human flesh.[19] Their sinful origins were reflected in their sinful character. God tells the angel Michael to destroy "the children of the Watchers, for they have done injustice to man."[20]

With a slight variation, 1 Enoch 15–16 recounts that

> now the giants who are born from the (union of) the spirits and the flesh shall be called evil spirits upon the earth, because their dwelling shall be upon the earth and inside the earth. Evil spirits have come out of their bodies... The spirits of the giants oppress each other; they will corrupt, fall, be excited, and fall upon the earth, and cause sorrow. They eat no food nor become thirsty, nor find obstacles. And these spirits shall rise up against the children of the people and against the women, because they have proceeded forth (from them).[21]

17. For broader discussions of this corpus, see, e.g., Andrei A. Orlov, *The Enoch-Metatron Tradition* (Tübingen: Mohr Siebeck, 2005); Annette Yoshiko Reed, *Fallen Angels and the History of Judaism and Christianity: The Reception of Enochic Literature* (Cambridge: Cambridge University Press, 2005); James C. Vanderkam, *Enoch and the Growth of an Apocalyptic Tradition* (Washington, DC: Catholic Biblical Association of America, 1984); and *Enoch: A Man for All Generations* (Columbia: University of South Carolina Press, 2008).

18. This account functions both as a Prometheus story, where technical and magical knowledge are brought to earth, and as an etiology for demonic presence. A survey of scholarship on this text can be found throughout Eshel, "Demonology in Palestine during the Second Temple Period," 15–76; Reed, *Fallen Angels*; Brand, *Evil Within and Without*, 147–68.

19. The "Fallen Angel" motif likely also draws from interpretations of Isa. 14:12, "How you are fallen from heaven, O Day Star, son of Dawn!"

20. 1 Enoch 10:15–16. English quotations from E. Isaac, "1 (Ethiopic Apocalypse of) Enoch," in *The Old Testament Pseudepigrapha*, ed. James H. Charlesworth (Garden City, NY: Doubleday, 1983), 18. For a discussion of the ways to interpret the linguistic evidence of 1 Enoch, see Eshel, "Demonology in Palestine," 29–36; Dale B. Martin, "When Did Angels Become Demons?," *Journal of Biblical Literature* 129, no. 4 (2010): 667–69.

21. 1 Enoch 15:8–12, from Isaac, "1 (Ethiopic Apocalypse of) Enoch," 21–22. See discussion of linguistic evidence in Eshel, "Demonology in Palestine," 37–42.

The giants are a forbidden mixture of spirit and flesh; these two elements have an uneasy relationship within the gigantic body. Annette Yoshiko Reed notes that "this transgression of categories brings terrible results: after their physical death, the giants' demonic spirits 'come forth from their bodies' to plague humankind."[22] According to 1 Enoch 15–16, demons attack the very part of themselves that they leave behind in death.

Demons' origins in sexual sin can help explain the explicit demonic antipathy toward humans within the Enochic corpus. Loren Stuckenbruck explains that

> as a mixture of heavenly and earthly beings, the giants were composed of flesh and spirit. When they came under divine judgment, the fleshly part of their nature was destroyed, whether through fratricidal conflict (7:5; 10:12) or through the Flood. Spirits or souls emerged from their dead bodies, and it is in this form that the giants are allowed an existence until the final judgment (16:1)... This reconstructed aetiology explains how it is that giants could come to be openly identified as demons at a later stage and, in turn, why it is that demons were thought to be especially desirous of entering the bodies of human beings.[23]

In these texts, demons seek to find new bodies to inhabit when their own stop working. The many possession narratives found in the synoptic Gospels attest to the power and popularity of the belief in demonic possession in first-century Judea. In Stuckenbruck's reading of *1 Enoch*, demonic origins and the demonic drive to possess a human body are logically connected.

The Book of the Watchers slips between two ideas: that demons are the flesh and spirit offspring of the angels and human women, and that they emerge as pure spirits from the fleshly corpses of these offspring. Early sources have been combined and recombined in this text, leading to diverging etiologies. In both accounts, the sinful origins of these children correlate with their acts of injustice.

Second Temple texts elaborate upon this story across a range of texts

22. Reed, *Fallen Angels*, 46.

23. Loren T. Stuckenbruck, "The 'Angels' and 'Giants' of Genesis 6:1–4 in Second and Third Century BCE Jewish Interpretation: Reflections on the Posture of Early Apocalyptic Traditions," *Dead Sea Discoveries* 7, no. 3 (2000): 365.

from this period. This narrative appears to underlie the epithet *mamzerim,* which literally means the offspring of forbidden sexual relationships and is often translated as "bastards" for demons at Qumran. [24] One exorcistic ritual text, 4Q510, promises to "[frighten and terrify] all the spirits of the ravaging angels and the bastard spirits *(ruḥot mamzerim),* demons *(šedim),* Lilith, owls (*'ōḥîm*),"[25] naming spirits of ravaging angels, bastard offspring of forbidden relationships, and perhaps, with *šedim,* demons who were created as part of the original divine plan.

The trope of demons as descending in some way from the angelic Watchers is also picked up in the book of Jubilees, written between 161–140 B.C.E.[26] Jubilees appears to have been important to the Qumran community, and fragments of about fifteen copies of the text have been identified among the Dead Sea Scrolls.[27] According to Jubilees, the angelic Watchers are "the fathers of these spirits," who "cause corruption among the sons of your servant . . . because they are cruel and were created to destroy" (Jub. 10:5).[28] These demons tempt, guide, and destroy the children and grandchildren of Noah.[29] These demons, unlike those in 1 Enoch appear to have been born only as spirit; they had no bodies to lose. But still, their sinful sexual genesis and their harmful actions are intertwined.

While this first mention of demons suggests that Jubilees belongs firmly in the narrative camp attributing demonic origins to sexual sin, Jubilees in fact shows nascent signs of a tendency toward harmonization,

24. Eshel, "Demonology in Palestine," III.

25. 4Q510 1.4–5, in Martinez and Tigchelaar, *The Dead Sea Scrolls Study Edition,* 1029. See discussion in Eshel, "Demonology in Palestine," 309–12.

26. O.S. Wintersmute, "Jubilees," in *The Old Testament Pseudepigrapha,* ed. James H. Charlesworth (New York: Doubleday, 1985), 44. See discussion in Eshel, "Demonology in Palestine," 48–56.

27. Jubilees is also cited by name by the Damascus Document (CD XVI:2–4). For a list of the relevant fragments, see James C. Vanderkam, "Jubilees, Book of," in *Encyclopedia of the Dead Sea Scrolls,* ed. Lawrence H. Schiffman and James C. Vanderkam (Oxford Biblical Studies Online); "The Jubilees Fragments from Qumran Cave 4," in *The Madrid Qumran Congress,* ed. Julio Trebolle Barrera and Luis Vegas Montaner (Leiden: Brill, 1992), 635–48.

28. English quotation from Wintersmute, "Jubilees," 76. Jub. 7:26–28 also mentions demons and their evil activities, but here their origins are left unexplained. Reed, *Fallen Angels*, 128, 150–174, has shown that 1 Enoch and Jubilees are subsequently used as source material for early Christian writings about demons, such as the *2 Apol.* of Justin Martyr, the pseudo-Clementine *Homily* 8:12–13, and 1 Pet. 3:19–20.

29. Jub. 10:1–2.

combining sinful origins together with God's oversight and intentionality. Jubilees introduces a leader of the demons named Satan/Mastema (lit: persecution). When God appears to consider destroying all the demons, Satan/Mastema begs God to spare them, "because if some of them are not left for me, I will not be able to exercise the authority of my will among the children of men because they are (intended) to corrupt and lead astray before my judgment because the evil of the sons of men is great... Let a tenth of them remain before him, but let nine parts go down into the place of judgment" (Jub. 10:7–9). God indeed spares one tenth of the evil spirits, "so that they may be subject to Satan upon the earth" (Jub. 10:11).[30] Analyzing this text, Miryam Brand notes that "Mastema's ability to work his will among humans is part of the divine order, demonstrated by Mastema's right to the assistance of demons in this endeavor."[31] Although not part of God's original blueprint for creation, demons still play an important though limited role in God's divine system. In Jubilees, demons punish evildoers; they do not challenge God's power or control.[32] The author of Jubilees attempts to harmonize the idea that demons are the sinful product of sexual transgression with the belief that everything in God's world is subordinate to God and part of God's divine plan; this attempt is not entirely successful.

In the Enochic accounts, demons are the product of a sin—a forbidden mixing—and not part of God's initial design. They lead people morally and ritually astray, and they bring suffering and sickness upon the righteous. Only the chosen few have the power to protect themselves and their communities from demonic harm. In Jubilees, this protective power is connected to righteous behavior; by design, demons punish the wicked and underline the importance and protective power of doing good.

One final origin story must be mentioned which presents another way that demonic beginnings could be characterized as sinful. The first-century C.E. Jewish historian Josephus writes that demons are "the spirits of wicked men which enter living bodies and kill them if no help can be

30. Wintersmute, "Jubilees," 76; Eshel, "Demonology in Palestine," 53–54.
31. Brand, *Evil Within and Without*, 180.
32. Brand, *Evil Within and Without*, 180–82.

found" (*War* 7.185).[33] As in one of the traditions in *1 Enoch*, demons are the spirits that remain when beings die. However, for Josephus, these beings are not the misbegotten offspring of heavenly beings but ordinary people who were wicked and sinful during their lifetimes. Their wicked origins correlate to their wicked intentions; the only acts attributed to them are demonic possession—the ultimate act of theft—and murder.

We can now see, as Eshel first noted, that Second Temple Jewish origin stories can be divided into two broad tendencies: the first identifies the demonic as part of God's original blueprint for creation; and the second, as the unintentional byproduct of sin.[34] In all accounts, demons intentionally perpetrate evil on humankind.

Fascinatingly, Brand has recently contextualized these two tendencies in an ancient Mesopotamian context, pointing to two distinct narrative trends about the creation of the demon Pashittu, the demon responsible for miscarriage and infant mortality. According to one trend, her creation was intentional; according to the other, it was an accident. Brand argues that the "accidental" creation story is the original, an original that poses theological challenges that the other narrative then came to solve. Yet, as she points out, "while a non-anarchic, god-approved demon may be more palatable from a theological perspective, for a worshiper who actually experiences a malevolent threat this option is less attractive. Calling on the divine for protection, after all, presupposes that the gods are not on the side of the aggressor."[35] Most worshippers were less interested in complex theological abstractions than in actually dealing with the demonic threats to their lives. As Brand demonstrates, the debate about demonic origins was one found across cultures and communities.

Within the ancient Jewish context, the depiction of demons as originating in an angelic sin also appears to have been the more popular, given its

33. Josephus, *The Jewish War*, trans. Martin Hammond (Oxford: Oxford University Press, 2017), 355. See discussion in Gideon Bohak, "Demons, Demonology. V. Judaism. A. Second Temple and Hellenistic Judaism," in *Encyclopedia of the Bible and Its Reception*, ed. Hans-Josef Klauck et al. (Berlin: De Gruyter, 2012), 6:547.

34. See Eshel, "Demonology in Palestine during the Second Temple Period," i–ii, 10–78.

35. Miryam T. Brand, "Demons and Dominion: Forcing Demons into the Divine Order in Jubilees and the Dead Sea Scrolls," in *From Scrolls to Traditions: A Festschrift Honoring Lawrence H. Schiffman*, ed. Stuart S. Miller et al. (Leiden: Brill, 2020), 18–37. Brand discusses the work of Karel van der Toorn on ancient Mesopotamian demons.

frequent appearances in the texts that survive from the Second Temple period. These two accounts of demonic origins are not linked to different time periods; both tendencies are represented for much of ancient Jewish history, in different texts and corpora, and, in at least one instance as we have seen from *Jubilees*, in the very same text. Yet these accounts all produce and reproduce the idea that, regardless of their origins, demons are malevolent attackers and destroyers.

DEMONIC ETIOLOGIES IN RABBINIC PALESTINE

The rabbis of Roman Palestine and Sasanian Babylonia inherited many of the traditions preserved in Second Temple literature. In their transmission of these traditions, the Palestinian and Babylonian rabbis undo both the rough distinction between the two narratives of demonic origin and their shared characterization of the demonic. The rabbis adapt and change each narrative trend in light of the other.

First, a note of caution about rabbinic sources. Rabbinic texts are multivocal and present real and imagined rabbinic opinions and debates on an astonishing range of topics. For much of scholarly history, academics have assumed that the attributions of particular sayings to particular sages were necessarily evidence of their historicity.[36] This assumption was turned on its head by Jacob Neusner, who crucially underscored the literary and theological work of the redactors in attributing traditions to different scholars.[37] It is true that the anthological and composite nature of rabbinic texts means that they preserve traditions that circulated before their collection and redaction. Yet the Talmud's redactors were themselves also literary creators; many other traditions must be characterized as pseudepigraphical. The later literary redactions of all these traditions fur-

36. See, e.g., the works of David Hoffman, *The First Mishnah and the Controversies of the Tannaim* (1881; New York: Maurosho Publications of Cong. Kehillath Yaakov, 1977); and Abraham Weiss, *Le-Heker Ha-Talmud* (New York, 1954).

37. See the shift between his earlier work, Jacob Neusner, *A Life of Rabbi Yohanan Ben Zakkai* (Leiden: Brill, 1962) and his later reworking, *Development of a Legend: Studies on the Traditions Concerning Yoḥanan Ben Zakkai* (Leiden: Brill, 1970). See also Neusner, *In Search of Talmudic Biography: The Problem of the Attributed Saying* (Chico, CA: Scholars Press for Brown Judaic Studies, 1984).

ther complicate our ability to easily identify authentic traditions as they circulated before their collection and redaction.[38] In what follows, I am cautious about assuming the authenticity of purportedly older sources without corroborating evidence of their authenticity.

The rabbis' earliest extant demonic origin story follows the tradition which locates demons' origins in God's original plan for creation. According to Mishnah *Avot* 5:6, redacted in second-century Roman Palestine,

> *Ten things were created [on the eve of the Sabbath] at twilight: The mouth of the earth [that swallowed up Koraḥ and his rebels], the mouth of the well [which sustained the Israelites in the desert], the mouth of [Balaam's] donkey, the rainbow [after the Great Flood], the manna, the rod [of Moses], the Shamir,*[39] *the text, the writing, and the tablets [of the Ten Commandments]. And some say: Also demons (mazziqin) and the grave of Moses and the ram of Abraham our father [which he substituted for his son during the Binding of Isaac]. And some say: Also tongs made of tongs.*[40]

The mishnah lists miraculous events and objects that fundamentally change the course of human—and Jewish—history. The first ten things appear in the Bible at miraculous moments. Of the four proposed additions to the list, only demons and tongs are nonbiblical. For what may be the first time in ancient Jewish literature, here demons are not evil or malevolent at all; though the term used, *mazziqin,* literally means "harmers," their context suggests instead that—like everything else on the list—

38. For scholarly work that identifies at least some traditions as authentic, see Louis Jacobs, "Are There Fictitious Baraitot in the Babylonian Talmud?," *Hebrew Union College Annual* 42 (1971): 185–96; David Kraemer, "On the Reliability of Attributions in the Babylonian Talmud," *Hebrew Union College Annual* 60 (1989): 175–90; Richard Kalmin, "Talmudic Portrayals of Relationships between Rabbis: Amoraic or Pseudepigraphic?," *AJS Review* 18, no. (1993): 165–97; Kalmin, *Sages, Stories, Authors and Editors in Rabbinic Babylonia* (Atlanta: Scholars Press, 1994); and David Brodsky, *A Bride without a Blessing: A Study in the Redaction and Content of Masskhet Kallah and Its Gemara* (Tübingen: Mohr Siebeck, 2006). Although these studies focus on the Babylonian Talmud, similar conclusions can be reached about the rest of the rabbinic corpus. For a history of scholarship, and an analysis of the concept of authorship as it applies to these texts, see Steven Daniel Sacks, *Midrash and Multiplicity: Pirke De-Rabbi Eliezer and the Renewal of Rabbinic Interpretive Culture* (Berlin: De Gruyter, 2009), 44–50.

39. According to the rabbis, a miraculous creation instrumental in the construction of King Solomon's Temple. See discussion in chap. 4.

40. MS Kaufmann. The order of the items differs slightly in the version of the Mishnah attested in manuscripts of the Bavli.

they are positively marked divine creations. Perhaps demons are like the mouth of the earth that swallowed up Koraḥ, intended, from the beginning of creation, to function as a tool that God uses to punish evil. Or perhaps they are like the mouth of Balaam's donkey, intended to call attention to issues beyond human perception. Here we see how a Jewish tradition of intentional creation that appeared in the caves of Qumran in the second century B.C.E., survived and was creatively adapted first by Pseudo-Philo and then by the second- and third-century rabbis of Roman Palestine.[41]

In conversation with this mishnah, the fifth-century Palestinian exegetical midrash known as *Genesis Rabbah* performs a complex act of biblical interpretation in imagining demonic origins.

> *"And God said, Let the earth bring forth [every kind of living creature, cattle, creeping things, and wild beasts of every kind]" (Gen. 1:24). R. Eleazar said: 'Living creature' means the soul of the primordial man—Adam. "And God made wild beasts of every kind" (Gen. 1:25), R. Hoshaya the Elder said: This refers to the snake. R. Ḥama b. Hoshaya said: When speaking of souls [in Gen. 1:24] it lists four, but when discussing their creation [in the next verse], it says "The wild beasts of every kind and cattle of every kind, and all kinds of creeping things of the earth" (ibid.) [listing only three acts of creation, without an act of creation corresponding to the phrase "every kind of living creature" in the command of Gen. 1:24]! Rabbi [Judah the Patriarch] says: These [created souls which had no corresponding bodies] were the demons (šedim), for God created their souls, but when He came to create their bodies, the Sabbath had already been sanctified [begun] and so He did not create them, in order to teach you the proper way to behave from the demons, for if a man is holding in his hand a precious object or a pearl on Friday afternoon when the sun sets, they say to him: Throw it away from you, for the One who spoke and created the world was in the midst in His act of the creation of the world, and had created [demons'] souls and was about to create their bodies but the Sabbath began and He did not create them.*[42]

According to R. Judah the Patriarch's close reading of Genesis 1, God had originally intended to create demons with both spiritual and corpo-

41. I am not suggesting, however, that the rabbis adapt this tradition directly from Pseudo-Philo. Rather, both the rabbis and Pseudo-Philo represent attempts to interpret a widespread earlier tradition.

42. *Genesis Rabbah* 7:5.

real bodies. But, unfortunately, on Friday afternoon God ran out of time and could create only their souls, not their bodies, before the Sabbath. R. Judah the Patriarch's timeline of demonic origins aligns with that of the earlier rabbinic Mishnah *Avot,* in that demons are created on Friday afternoon before the advent of the Sabbath. However, it also integrates the idea of their creation as unintended. And yet even though demonic origins are the same as in 1QS and Pseudo-Philo, the circumstances of their creation and what they mean for demonkind are quite different. Although demons' current noncorporeal forms appear to be unplanned, here demons are not explicitly marked as negative. In fact, they have a positive heuristic function in that their creation is used to demonstrate the importance of stringent Sabbath observance for human beings.

Rabbinic texts also tell a story in which demons are the product of a sinful, forbidden mixing, reminiscent of Enoch and Jubilees. However, Palestinian rabbinic texts point to a different biblical instance in which this mixing occurred. According to another passage in *Genesis Rabbah,* some demons (here ruḥot) are the offspring of Adam and Eve, conceived through sexual sin. In this midrash, Adam and Eve separated from each other for one hundred and thirty years after their expulsion from Eden as penance for their sin in the Garden. During this period of separation, each conceived children with demons and spirits—presumably through sexual intercourse with these demonic beings—and those children, too, were demons and spirits. According to the logic of this account, there must have already been a small number of demons in existence for Adam and Eve to engage with initially. But perhaps the sheer number of demons was not part of the original blueprint for creation. Like their counterparts in the Second Temple period texts, these demons are the product of a primordial sin, but not the sin of a forbidden relationship between humans and angels.

Genesis Rabbah continues the tradition of harmonization first laid out in *Jubilees* and expands it further. And yet, even so, demons function to uphold God's righteousness, punishing the sinners and sparing the righteous.[43] The redactors tie this midrashic narrative to a belief that demons

43. Yishai Kiel has shown that the trope of a primordial couple giving birth to demonic offspring as well as the first human offspring is one that has echoes in Middle Persian Zoro-

are meant to punish the wicked: the midrash continues, "*Therefore it is written, 'If he commit sin, I will chastise him with the rod of men and with the afflictions of the children of man' (2 Sam 7:14)*, which means the children of the first man—Adam." The passage concludes with an anonymous tradition: "One says that house spirits [ruḥot de-beita] are good because they dwell with man, while the other says that they are bad because they understand [man's] inclination. Field spirits [ruḥin de-ḥaqla]—one says that they are good because they do not understand man's inclination, while the other says that they are evil because they do not dwell with man."[44] Even when attributing demonic origins to sexual sin, the rabbis demonstrate an attitude toward demons which suggests that they are not entirely sinful or evil in nature. The Palestinian rabbis insist that some demons have the capacity to recognize man's innate nature, while others—though the rabbis are not sure which ones—are endemically good.

DEMONIC ORIGINS IN RABBINIC BABYLONIA

Like their Palestinian colleagues, the Babylonian rabbis attempted to synthesize their early inherited traditions. And like their Palestinian colleagues, the Babylonian rabbis did so by locating demonic origins in the period after Adam and Eve were expelled from the Garden of Eden. But the Babylonian rabbis go further than their Palestinian colleagues by insisting that the creation of demons was the *accidental* product of an *accidental* sin, rather than the product of intentional acts of inappropriate sexual intercourse. According to b. *Eruvin* 18b,

> *R. Jeremiah b. Eleazar said: All the years during which Adam was in a state of banishment, he gave birth to demons (šedim), spirits (ruḥin), and liliths (lilin, a type of female demon), as it says, "And Adam lived one hundred and thirty years and gave birth to a son in his own image and form" (Gen. 5:3), which suggests that until now, he gave birth to offspring who were not in his*

astrian texts. See Yishai Kiel, "Creation by Emission: Recreating Adam and Eve in the Babylonian Talmud in Light of Zoroastrian and Manichaean Literature," *Journal of Jewish Studies* 66, no. 2 (2015): 295–316. See discussion below.

44. *Genesis Rabbah* 20:11.

> *form. An objection was raised. R. Meir used to say: Adam was a pious man; when death was imposed [on humankind] because of him, he fasted for one hundred and thirty years, and separated from the woman for one hundred and thirty years, and wore clothing made of fig leaves for one hundred and thirty years! This statement was made about the semen that he ejaculated unintentionally.*[45]

While R. Jeremiah seems to agree, intentionally or otherwise, with the Palestinian tradition of Adam's intercourse with demons and spirits during the period that he was separated from Eve, the Babylonian Talmud minimizes the sexual transgression in several ways. First, in b. *Eruvin,* only Adam is responsible for the creation of these demons; Eve is notably absent. Second, whereas in *Genesis Rabbah* Adam inflames female demons and impregnates them, in the Babylonian Talmud the demons are created from Adam's semen with no female involvement. Finally, whereas in *Genesis Rabbah* Adam and Eve have actual sexual intercourse with demonic beings, the Talmud's anonymous Aramaic voice insists that Adam does not actually engage sexually with demons. Demons are created accidentally, without any direct contact between Adam and the demonic world.[46]

The accidental creation of demons is a trope evident from Second Temple texts. However, despite the Second Temple undertones, and the fact that the two rabbis named in this Talmudic passage are themselves Palestinian, the ideas attributed to them are remarkably Babylonian in nature. Yishai Kiel demonstrates that the motif of "creation by emission" is found in Zoroastrian stories of the first man, who in Pahlavi tradition is named Gayōmard.[47] In Zoroastrian creation narratives, Gayōmard's seminal emission at the moment of his death leads to the creation of the first human couple, "from whose incestuous coupling the world of the living was filled up, the demons cut off, and the Foul Spirit undone."[48] The belief that semen spilled on the ground can produce offspring outside a womb and without any assistance is a uniquely Persian concept, found

45. Translation of MS Munich 95.
46. See further discussion of b. *Eruvin* in Kiel, "Creation by Emission," 304–09.
47. Kiel, "Creation by Emission," 311, quoting *Bundahišn* 6f.7–9, 14.5–6; *Dēnkard* 3.80.7.
48. *Bundahišn* 6f.9, in Prods Oktor Skjærvø, *The Spirit of Zoroastrianism* (New Haven, CT: Yale University Press, 2011), 100.

in contemporaneous Middle Persian Zoroastrian texts.[49] The Zoroastrian creation texts share with b. *Eruvin* the association of creation through seminal emission with the demonic. The exact nature of that association, however, is inverted. In Zoroastrian tradition, demons are servants of the evil god and work to propagate evil in our world. Gayōmard's seminal emission in this tradition leads to the demons' eventual destruction. In the Talmudic tradition, Adam is the father of all demonic forces. And, rather than being the source of all evil, all we know about demons from the passage in the Babylonian Talmud is that, while they appear to be in Adam's likeness, they "are not in his form."

Thus, though b. *Eruvin* 18b belongs firmly in the category of accounts that attribute demonic origins to events after God's creation of the world, and though it has a parallel in *Genesis Rabbah* 20:11, it contains elements which firmly locate its creation in the Sasanian Empire. It represents one culturally specific way that the rabbis of Sasanian Babylonia harmonized the tradition in which demons were intended creations of God with the tradition in which demons are the malevolent product of sin.

However, like the Palestinian rabbis and Second Temple Jewish writers before them, the Babylonian rabbis were multivalent, and the text they produced—the Babylonian Talmud—contains multiple and sometimes contradictory accounts of demonic origins. Another tradition also attributed to R. Jeremiah b. Eleazar states that God transformed some human beings into demons as punishment for their part in the attempt to build the Tower of Babel. The consequence of their rebellion against God was to be "*turned into apes, spirits (ruḥin), demons (šedim), and lilin*" (b. *Sanhedrin* 109a).

Though R. Jeremiah b. Eleazar was a Palestinian rabbi, this tradition demonstrates the complex cultural context of the Bavli's recorded traditions about demons. The triptych of spirits, demons, and *lilin* is exclusively found in these Babylonian rabbinic texts. The association of apes and demons in b. *Sanhedrin* 109a, however, is reminiscent of a tradition

49. See Kiel, "Creation by Emission." This idea is different from Greco-Roman understandings of the creation of the world, in which the earth goddess Gaia functions as the womb for the spilled semen of the sky god Uranus. In the Babylonian rabbinic account, the location of the spilled semen is unstated and the female role entirely downplayed.

in *Genesis Rabbah* which teaches that, during the days of Enosh son of Seth, "*men's faces became ape-like, and they became vulnerable to demons (mazziqin). R. Isaac said: They themselves caused themselves to become vulnerable to demons* [because they said:] What is the difference between prostrating oneself to an icon and prostrating oneself to a human being?"[50] In this Palestinian midrash, humanity's transformation in both form and vulnerability is punishment for the moral decay associated with the generation of the biblical Enosh.[51] Demons are not the product of this decay, but the fraught relationship between demons and human beings is. By comparison, in b. *Sanhedrin*, these demons are the direct product of humanity's sin of building the Tower of Babel. Humans become demons, demons who might then afflict other humans.[52]

The identification of both of these Talmudic accounts of demonic origins with R. Jeremiah b. Eleazar, consistent across almost all textual witnesses, raises the possibility for either R. Jeremiah, if we take the attribution seriously or, at the very least for the redactors of the Bavli, that demons were created on numerous occasions in biblical history when human beings failed to live up to the divine standard.[53]

EVOLVING ACCOUNTS OF DEMONIC ORIGINS

These rabbinic texts transmit the tradition that demons are the product of sin while also reflecting the belief that they are created by the divine plan. Yet, one strange rabbinic text focuses entirely on demons as an intentional part of the divine cosmos. The text is attached to a mishnah in *Baba Qamma*, which discusses which animals are categorized as "always

50. *Genesis Rabbah* 23:6.

51. For analysis of the figure of Enosh in the early rabbinic period, see Steven Fraade, *Enosh and His Generation: Pre-Israelite Hero and History in Post-Biblical Interpretation* (Chico, CA: Scholars Press, 1984). See also Archie T. Wright, *The Origin of Evil Spirits: The Reception of Genesis 6:1–4 in Early Jewish Literature*, 2nd ed. (Tübingen: Mohr Siebeck, 2013), 56–58.

52. Note the similarities of this idea to that of Josephus, discussed above.

53. With the exception, in the case of b. *Sanhedrin* 109a, of MS Florence II-I-9. It is also possible that a later redactor associated teachings about demonic origins with R. Jeremiah b. Eleazar and extrapolated from one teaching to the other.

dangerous" and thus require special caution in their handling. One of the animals listed is the female hyena, and so the Talmudic redactor attaches a relevant teaching:

> *As was taught in a baraita [earlier tradition]: after seven years the male hyena becomes a female [hyena], and after another seven years becomes a bat. After seven years the bat becomes a vampire bat. After ten years the vampire bat becomes a nettle. After seven years the nettle becomes a thorn. The thorn after seven years becomes a demon (šeid).*[54]

In a metamorphical account, the male hyena transforms into a demon over a forty-five year span. Each transformation turns it into something that takes up less physical space and is perhaps less aggressive than it was before.[55] Whereas wild hyenas will attack when hungry both at night and during the day, bats and vampire bats only hunt at night. While all the animals named seek out prey, a thorn or nettle causes harm only when one is extremely close to it; these plants do not seek out victims to harm. According to the general organizational logic of the text, the author of this baraita sees demons as less aggressive than predatory wild animals and plant morphology.[56]

This last account of demonic origins is unique in rabbinic literature and has no Second Temple parallels. It bears a resemblance to the class of accounts which ascribe demonic origins to a divine plan rather than an accident, even though the plan is neither explicitly divine, nor located in the original six days of creation. According to the baraita, demons are harmful in the same way as predatory animals whose instincts are to attack and kill human beings. Like the other things listed here, then, demons are not necessarily malicious or evil; they simply live out their natures in ways that may cause harm to those who get too close. Their harm is contained

54. B. *Baba Qamma* 16a. Although attributed to an earlier Tannaitic source, the text has no parallels in Tannaitic writings. It may be an invention of the Babylonian rabbis or an authentic earlier tradition only preserved by the Babylonians; either identity highlights its importance to the Babylonian redactors of the Babylonian Talmud as opposed to the Palestinian compilers of their own rabbinic texts.

55. This distinction does not hold for the male and female hyenas, however, as female hyenas are substantially more aggressive than the males. See Kay E. Holekamp, "Male or Female? Good Question!," *New York Times*, 29 June 2011.

56. My thanks to Christine Hayes for suggesting this reading.

by proximity or passivity. This unique account thus harmonizes aspects of earlier traditions, again, to limit or soften them.

The rabbinic texts of late antique Roman Palestine and Sasanian Babylonia reveal traces of earlier Jewish demonological origin stories. These texts are composite and multivocal. But as we can see, the redactional instinct appears to harmonize the different traditions while privileging the idea that demons are part of the divine plan, whether or not they were part of that plan originally. Yet in all these texts, this harmonization rejects the idea that demons are unequivocally evil.

SEEKING THE ANGELS

But as much as the rabbis harmonized earlier Jewish demonological origin stories, they did not integrate all the Second Temple traditions about demons into their work. One of the fundamental curiosities of ancient Jewish angelology and demonology is the absence of the story of the angelic Watchers from the rabbinic imagination. The story of the Sons of God having sex with human women and producing monstrous offspring was extremely popular during the Second Temple period. But, while the rabbis continued to attribute demonic origins to a sexual sin in the primeval history, they pointed to a *different* instance of sexual sin. Shifting the locus of demonic origins from the actions of fallen angels right before the Flood to the actions of Adam and Eve after they had been expelled from the Garden of Eden was part of a larger move to shift the origins of sin and danger away from the Watchers.[57] Why did the rabbis make this interpretive move? How did the story of the Watchers disappear from the late antique Jewish literary tradition?[58]

57. Reed has noted that the first seeds of this move are embedded in 1 Enoch 69.6, which purports to tell the story of the fallen angels but inserts Eve into the account: "The third [angel] was named Gader'el; this one is he who showed the children of the people all the blows of death, who misled Eve, who showed the children of the people [how to make] the instruments of death" (Isaac, "1 [Ethiopic Apocalypse of] Enoch," 47). See Reed, *Fallen Angels*, 114. Reed also notes a similar shift in the New Testament book of Revelation 12.9, where the fallen angels are hurled to earth at the beginning of time, and not in connection to the flood story (116).

58. This disappearance can also be found beyond rabbinic literature, in the paraphrastic interpretive work of the Targumim. This disappearance is in contrast to some manuscripts

Several pieces of evidence suggest that it was in fact intentionally suppressed. Philip Alexander argues that this suppression is part of a larger trend in which "rabbis in Palestine from the second century onwards engaged in a polemic against angelology."[59] A primary piece of evidence for Alexander is *Genesis Rabbah*. In its commentary on Genesis 6:1–4, *Genesis Rabbah* 26:5 states, "'*And the sons of God saw the daughters of men' (Gen. 6:2).* R. Simeon b. Yoḥai called them 'sons of judges.' R. Simeon b. Yoḥai cursed all whose who called them 'sons of God.' . . . [And] Why are they called "sons of God"? Rabbi Ḥanina and Reish Laqish both said: *Because they had long lives (Gen. 6:3) without trouble or suffering.*"[60] *Genesis Rabbah* was compiled in the fifth century C.E., but R. Simeon b. Yoḥai is said to have lived in the second century C.E.; Alexander sees R. Simeon b. Yoḥai's curse as a reflection of actual historical events in the second century.[61]

The second-century Christian writer Justin Martyr's *Dialogue with Trypho* supports Alexander's contention that ancient Jews rejected this story possibly as early as the second century C.E. Justin imagines his Jewish dialogue partner saying that "the words of God are indeed holy, but your interpretations are contrived, as is evident from those which you have given—nay more, they are blasphemous, for you affirm that angels have sinned and rebelled against God" (1, 79, 1).[62] The fictional Jew alleges that the belief that angels descended to earth in rebellion of God is a blasphemous Christian innovation. In contrast, Justin insists that "in ancient times wicked demons appeared and defiled women."[63] Justin's words suggest that Jews had a different interpretation of Genesis 6:1–4,

of the earlier Septuagint, where "sons of God" is rendered "angels of God." See Reed, *Fallen Angels*, 217.

59. Philip S. Alexander, "Targumim and Early Exegesis of 'Sons of God' in Genesis 6," *Journal of Jewish Studies* 23, no. 1 (1972): 60–71, 68.

60. Translation partly adapted from Reed, *Fallen Angels*, 209.

61. Alexander, "Targumim and Early Exegesis of 'Sons of God,'" 61–63, 68–69. As a countervailing view, Reed, ibid., 136, posits that "it is possible that the Rabbinic movement simply ceased to copy Enochic literature without any thought to the loss of books that they held to be insignificant," and notes that "it is important to recall that the transmission of texts in antiquity was both a laborious and an expensive endeavor, and it is to this that we owe the loss of many texts. If no motivation existed to continue producing new copies to replace the old, a text could just fall out of circulation" (136 n. 51). Reed herself is unconvinced by this possibility, as discussed below.

62. Alexander, "Targumim and Early Exegesis of 'Sons of God,'" 62.

63. *First Apology* V, 2, in ibid.

and that this difference became a key marker of distinction between Jews and Christians in second-century Ephesus, where he was writing. But the question remains, Why did a story so popular and widespread disappear from rabbinic Jewish literature during late antiquity?

Reed has pointed to the popularity of the account of the Watchers and Enochic literature more broadly with contemporaneous Christians as a possible element of their suppression in rabbinic literature.[64] She convincingly argues that

> proto-orthodox Christians preserve two different poles in a broader continuum. In light of the widespread use of the *Book of the Watchers* in pre-Rabbinic literature and its scriptural status among some groups of Second Temple Jews, it is likely that other Jews also continued to use these books, at least in the early period. In attempting to undermine the biblical basis for the Enochic tradition, early Rabbis may thus be reacting to a number of groups that continued to use these and other apocalypses, including Christ-believing Jews. Yet, it is not their Christianity (or Christology, or even messianism) that is at stake here. Rather, in this critical era of Rabbinic self-definition, Rabbis seem to counter those who retain elements of earlier Jewish tradition, other than those that they themselves adopt and adapt to fit the new needs of the time.[65]

Many Christians and, perhaps, non-rabbinic Jews, were thus continuous with Second Temple narrative traditions about the Sons of God and the daughters of man. The importance of the fallen angels to Justin Martyr's genesis of sin is evident in the primeval history in his *Second Apology*. Reed has noted that according to Justin's narrative of history, the sin of the fallen angels immediately followed the creation of the world; Adam and Eve are surprisingly absent.[66] This approach is the inverse of the rabbinic approach, where the human Adam and Eve take center stage and the fallen angels have all but disappeared. Justin was largely continuous with Second Temple Enochic traditions; by contrast, the rabbis broke with

64. Ibid., 128, has shown that "Enochic traditions can be found in multiple strata of the Pseudo-Clementine literature (*Rec.* 1.29, 4.26–27; *Hom.* 8.12–18)."

65. Ibid., 147.

66. See Justin Martyr, 2 *Apol.* 4–5. This is particularly interesting given that Justin discusses Gen. 2–3 and the primeval couple extensively. See thereon in Reed, *Fallen Angels*, 166–67.

the early Enochic narrative traditions in their details while continuing to attribute demonic origins to an original sexual sin.

Notably, while the rabbis' discontinuity was successful in late antiquity, they were unable to completely eradicate the story of the Watchers from normative Jewish tradition. The story reappears in the eighth-century Palestinian midrashic work *Pirqe de-Rabbi Eliezer*, attributed to the very redactor of the Mishnah, R. Judah the Patriarch.[67]

> *Rabbi said: The angels who had fallen from their holy place in heaven saw the daughters of Cain walking about naked, with their eyes made-up like whores, and they went astray after them, and took wives from among them, as it says, "the Sons of God saw how beautiful the daughters of men were (and took wives from among those that pleased them [Gen. 6:2])."*[68]

The author of *Pirqe de-Rabbi Eliezer* resurfaces and creates anew the story of the Sons of God and the daughters of man, in ignorance, apathy, or defiance of the teachings of *Genesis Rabbah*.[69] As Rachel Adelman notes, "one can only appreciate the audacity on the part of the author of [*Pirqe de-Rabbi Eliezer*] in de-compressing the biblical text."[70] However, the rabbinic disassociation of demonic origins from the story of Genesis 6:1–4 continued to be upheld; in the account in *Pirqe de-Rabbi Eliezer*, the forbidden union produces offspring gigantic but not demonic. The rabbis of late antiquity have both lost and won the battle of ideas at the same time.[71]

In a strange complementarity, later Christian texts also point to Adam and Eve as the origin of sin, as well as of all the dangers and decay that sin brought to the world. This shift of emphasis is paired, in the Christian sphere, with a devaluation of the Enochic corpus and its categorization as

67. For a discussion of the history of scholarship on the dating of this text, see Rachel Adelman, *The Return of the Repressed: Pirqe De-Rabbi Eliezer and the Pseudepigrapha* (Leiden: Brill, 2009), 35–42.

68. *Pirqe de-Rabbi Eliezer* 22:4, translated in ibid., 113.

69. Ibid., 112–18.

70. Ibid., 114.

71. The story, associated with the antediluvian angels, does resurface and gain popularity in later medieval Jewish texts including *Yalqut Shimoni* on Gen. 44 and the *Chronicles of Jerahmeel*. For a discussion of these texts, see Adelman, *Return of the Repressed*, 116 n. 20. It also enters the folktale canon; see Howard Schwartz, *Miriam's Tambourine: Jewish Folktales from around the World* (New York: Seth Press, 1986).

heretical.[72] Texts that were once popular and important to ancient Jewish and Christian theology were later intentionally suppressed by both communities, for reasons of politics, interreligious competition, and internal disputes about canonicity. But this suppression was always incomplete.

In attributing demonic origins in part to an earlier sexual sin on the part of Adam (and to a lesser extent Eve), the late antique rabbis were not ignorant of the earlier Enochic account. They were also not passive transmitters of older traditions. Instead, as inheritors of Second Temple Jewish traditions, they made a conscious interpretive choice within a complex cultural network of boundary drawing, theological debate, and competing biblical exegeses. Demonic origins are one lens on this process of identity formation; they shed light on the relationship between rabbinic Jews and others past and present as much as they do on the nature of unseen forces.

CONCLUSIONS

The rabbis of Roman Palestine and Sasanian Babylonia were the inheritors of a rich Second Temple demonological tradition. These older Jewish traditions—as seen by the pseudepigraphical literature and biblical retellings found among the Dead Sea Scrolls—tell two very different stories of demonic origins. However, with the exception of *Jubilees*, in all these stories, demons are evil. They may be part of God's divine system, but their innate natures are evil and their actions on earth are harmful toward humankind. The rabbis of Roman Palestine and Sasanian Babylonia attempt, at times unsuccessfully, to harmonize these traditions as a foundation for their own construction of the demonic, while leaving open room for a moral system in which demons are more nuanced characters.

Such acts of creative excision and synthesis shed light on rabbinic attitudes toward Second Temple literature and provide insight into rabbinic understanding(s) of the demonic nature. Late antique rabbinic acts of harmonization in part uphold God as the all-powerful creator of

72. This trend is first seen in writings of the fourth-century Athanasius, Epistle 39. See Reed, *Fallen Angels*, 200–04.

everything, including demons, and in part defang demons, suggesting that some demons are neutral and others—as we shall see—are perhaps even good. But if demons—powerful intermediary beings subordinate to God—can be neutral or even good, what distinguishes them from angels? The rabbinic urge to categorize takes on this very question.

2 Classification Matters

Deus Creavit, Linnaeus Disposuit

"God created—Linnaeus arranged"

What does it mean to be more, or less, than human? As we saw in chapter 1, the rabbis were largely committed to the idea that demons were created by God. Demonic origins, like those of humans, were divine. So what makes demons different from humans? What makes them different from other intermediary beings such as angels? How do demons fit into the cosmos? And what do they *look* like? This chapter explores how the rabbis answered these questions.

The previous chapter looked at demonic origins in Jewish literature from the Second Temple period and rabbinic literature; this chapter turns to Greek philosophy and early Christian thought to understand how the rabbis constructed demons within the context of earlier and contemporaneous scholastic elites. While it is certainly true that almost everyone in the ancient world believed in demons, it was the scholastic elites who organized and systematized thinking about demons. By *scholastic elites*, I mean networks of individuals who saw themselves as a com-

Epigraph: Quoted from D. H. Stövers' biography of Linnaeus from 1792, in "The Order in Nature," Linné on line, Uppsala University, 2008, http://www2.linnaeus.uu.se/online/animal/1_0.html.

munity of scholars in a shared discursive intellectual project, a project which included traditions transmitted from their intellectual forebears.[1] These networks were often manifest in loosely or more formally organized schools. Their attempts at systematization of a world that included demons were designed to contrast with more popular understandings of intermediary beings, at the same time as these scholastic elites were indeed engaged with broader cultural conversations.

This chapter situates the rabbis as a scholastic elite within the ancient world and traces the ways that three different but interrelated scholastic elites—Greek philosophers, early Christian writers, and Jewish rabbis—attempted to theorize and systematize how demons fit into a broader cosmos they believed followed certain logical rules. While all these communities thought about demons in varied contexts, this chapter will focus on the ways that they categorized demons as they related to other intermediary beings. Scholarly research on ancient taxonomies of intermediary beings has blossomed over the last fifteen years. Most notably, Heidi Marx-Wolf has traced continuities and distinctions between the demonologies of Greek philosophers and early Christian writers, and Ellen Muehlberger has done excellent related work on early Christian angelologies.[2] But Greek philosophers and early Christian writers often lived in the same cities and towns as Jews, some of whom also participated in related inter-

1. I use this term instead of *literary elite* to resist associating late antique intellectual communities with writing; many of the learned traditions discussed here were composed and circulated orally. For more on late antique scholasticism and the formation of elite identities, see Catherine Hezser, "Rabbis as Intellectuals in the Context of Graeco-Roman and Byzantine Christian Scholasticism," paper presented at the SOAS, University of London, 2017; Adam Howard Becker, *Fear of God and the Beginning of Wisdom: The School of Nisibis and Christian Scholastic Culture in Late Antique Mesopotamia* (Philadelphia: University of Pennsylvania Press, 2006), 1–21; Kendra Eshleman, *The Social World of Intellectuals in the Roman Empire: Sophists, Philosophers, and Christians* (Cambridge: Cambridge University Press, 2012), 1–20; José Ignacio Cabezón, "Introduction," in *Scholasticism: Cross-Cultural and Comparative Perspectives*, ed. José Ignacio Cabezón (Albany: State Uuniversity of New York Press, 1998), 1–8.

2. In the interest of disclosing my own intellectual genealogy on these issues, I must acknowledge two of Dale B. Martin's works: *Inventing Superstition: From the Hippocratics to the Christians* (Cambridge, MA: Harvard University Press, 2004) and "When Did Angels Become Demons?" as foundational to my first encounters with many of the relevant primary sources and my early thinking about these questions. I include references to his work in the footnotes.

pretive activities. This chapter first surveys the work of these scholars of late antique Christianity and then brings the late antique rabbis into the conversation to demonstrate how and when rabbinic taxonomies aligned with those of these other communities, and when they decidedly did not. Taxonomy was an important part of how these scholastic elites addressed the demonic as part of a larger understanding of the world, but, as we shall learn, they took three somewhat different approaches.

ROMANS AND CHRISTIANS IN THE SCHOOLS OF PHILOSOPHY

In this section, I focus on four major thinkers across this time period—Plutarch, Justin Martyr, Origen, and Iamblichus—to explore the ways that overlapping scholastic communities interrogated the demonic in their world. These are not the only ancient writers who thought seriously about demons and the demonic, but they represent particular moments in the systematization of Greek and Christian traditions about demons that are instructive points of comparison with the Babylonian rabbis.[3] These particular moments highlight continuities and discontinuities as well as key linguistic and interpretive choices across scholastic communities in late antiquity.

To fully understand Plutarch and indeed all four figures, we must explore the Greek culture and philosophy that set the scene for this later thinking and discuss how Plutarch sets himself within this tradition. To understand Justin Martyr and the later Christian taxonomers, we must also examine how the New Testament described demons as they relate to other intermediary beings in the world. This attention to context sheds light on the interactions between these four thinkers and the distinctive interpretive choices each makes to achieve their own theological and rhetorical aims.

Marx-Wolf has pointed to the late second and third centuries C.E. as a time when thinkers across religious groups began "to produce systematic

3. They have the additional benefit of being some of the thinkers that both Martin and Marx-Wolf put into conversation with one another, and they thus represent a productive entry point into triangulating the rabbinic approach with these earlier efforts.

discourses that ordered the realm of spirits in increasingly more hierarchical ways" that she calls "spiritual taxonomies."[4] Greek philosophy and Christian theology were elite pursuits undertaken by only a small percentage of the population of ancient Greece and the Roman Empire. But despite their small numbers, Greek philosophers and early Christian writers undertook to interrogate and understand the entire world and, in so doing, shaped the world itself.[5] Marx-Wolf notes that Greek philosophers and early Christian writers were tied to each other by social class, educational experience, and a conception of themselves as potential leaders of a broader populace.[6] That both scholastic elites in the Roman West undertook this systematization at the same time is therefore not surprising. They did so very much in dialogue with each other but part of increasingly distinctive theological understandings of the world.

Plutarch, Justin Martyr, Origen, and Iamblichus all inherited a scholastic worldview shaped by Plato and his students. These early founding fathers of Greek philosophy were themselves responding to even earlier developments in the philosophical understanding of *daimones*, intermediary beings. As noted in the introduction, the English word *demon* comes from the Greek *daimōn* (δαίμων, pl. *daimones*). For much of its early history, the word *daimōn* did not refer to what we would today call *demons*. Yet the word and the changing concepts to which it referred were crucial building blocks in the self-understandings of Greek philosophers and early Christian writers. The rabbis lived in a world shaped in part by these self-understandings.

In its earliest usages, the word *daimōn* referred simply to the gods and goddesses of the Greek pantheon. These gods could bring blessings or plagues to cities and states. Ian Kidd has identified the eighth-century B.C.E. poet Hesiod's *Works and Days* as containing the earliest explicit and influential reference to daimones being separate from the gods. Hesiod describes daimones as "fine spirits upon the earth, guardians of mortal human beings: they watch over judgments and cruel deeds, clad in invis-

4. Heidi Marx-Wolf, *Spiritual Taxonomies and Ritual Authority: Platonists, Priests, and Gnostics in the Third Century C.E.* (Philadephia: University of Pennsylvania Press, 2016), 1.

5. Martin, *Inventing Superstition*, 168–69.

6. Marx-Wolf, *Spiritual Taxonomies and Ritual Authority*, 84–85.

ibility, walking everywhere upon the earth, givers of wealth."[7] Over time, these daimones developed from the guardians of humankind in general to individuated superhuman beings who govern the destiny of specific individuals or families. A tripartite hierarchy of superhuman beings emerged: gods, daimones, and heroes (a superhuman race of men who performed great deeds).[8] Daimones intervened in human lives in ways both kind and cruel. While Greek households often ended their meals with a toast to the *Good Daimōn* associated with wine and the cult of Dionysus, the Greek tragedies are full of stories of daimones who lead men to their doom.[9] It is clear that many Greeks believed that daimones could be evil and required propitiation. But as we will see, Greek philosophers disagreed.

In the face of popular belief, Plato asserted that daimones are both physically superior than human beings and entirely good. In his *Timaeus*, Plato (c. 429–347 B.C.E.) writes that "we ought to think of the most sovereign part of our soul as god's gift to us, given to be our guiding spirit [lit: *daimōn*]. This, of course, is the type of soul that, as we maintain, resides in the top part of our bodies. It raises us up away from the earth and toward whatever is akin to us in heaven, as though we are plants grown not from the earth but from heaven."[10] A man who obeys his daimōn ascends the cosmic hierarchy to the stars; one who ignores his daimōn and falls prey to his own base passions descends the cosmic hierarchy and may be reborn

7. Hesiod, *Works and Days* 123, in Hesiod, *Theogony; Works and Days; Testimonia*, trans. Glenn W. Most (Cambridge, MA: Harvard University Press, 2007), 97, and the discussion in Kidd, "Some Philosophical Demons," 218.

8. Kidd, "Some Philosophical Demons," 218–19. For more on the ancient Greek usage of the term *daimōn*, see Henry George Liddell and Robert Scott, *A Greek-English Lexicon* (Oxford: Clarendon Press, 1996), 365. For analyses of this usage, see Ruth Padel, *In and Out of the Mind: Greek Images of the Tragic Self* (Princeton, NJ: Princeton University Press, 1992), 141, discussed in Rosen-Zvi, *Demonic Desires*, 7, and notes thereon; Kidd, "Some Philosophical Demons," 218; Martin, *Inventing Superstition*.

9. On the tragedies, see, e.g., Sophocles, *Antigone* 376, 824–34 in Sophocles, *Antigone. The Women of Trachis; Philoctetes; Oedipus at Colonus*, ed. and trans. Hugh Lloyd-Jones (Cambridge, MA: Harvard University Press, 1994). On the *Good Daimōn*, see Liddell and Scott, *A Greek-English Lexicon*, 366; Kidd, "Some Philosophical Demons," 218. This daimōn was often depicted visually as a snake and understood as a chthonic bearer of blessings and protection.

10. *Timaeus* 90A, in Plato, *Timaeus*, trans. Donald J. Zeyl (Indianapolis: Hackett, 2000), 85–86; and see Martin, *Inventing Superstition*, 58; Kidd, "Some Philosophical Demons," 221.

as a woman or an animal.[11] For Plato, daimones help worthy men ascend to heaven; the unworthy are dragged down further into the world of base physicality.

In the writings of Plato, daimones are not demons, malevolent and unworthy. This point is not simply stylistic; Plato has no word for entirely malevolent intermediary beings. Indeed, Plato's understandings of the world precluded such an idea entirely. Plato believed daimones were good because he maintained that the taxonomy of power mapped perfectly onto a moral taxonomy: the more powerful a being, the more ethical it was.[12] For the world to make philosophical sense, Plato insisted that those beings who were more powerful than humans—such as gods and daimons—were also ethically better than human beings.[13] And Plato and his students integrated this insistence into comprehensive philosophical systems that shaped all of Greek philosophy and early Christian thought going forward.[14]

The writings of Plutarch (c. 45–120 C.E.) demonstrate how much these earlier philosophers continued to affect philosophical thinking five hundred years after Plato's death. Plutarch, too, criticizes those so-called superstitious fools who misunderstand the nature of daimones and fear them.[15] In *On the Sign of Socrates,* Plutarch suggests that daimones are free from corruption and desire to aid the most worthy of men: "One dae-

11. *Timaeus* 42A-C, in Plato, *Timaeus,* 29–30; and see Martin, *Inventing Superstition,* 56–59.

12. Martin, *Inventing Superstition,* 76.

13. Ibid., 61.

14. Aristotle (c. 384–322 B.C.E.) articulates his heavenly hierarchy more systematically. In *Parts of Animals,* vol. 1, Aristotle divides the works of nature into two groups: those that are born and die, and those that are neither born nor die. At the top of his hierarchy are divinities, who are not born and do not die, and who are characterized by their excellence and worth. At the bottom of the hierarchy are animals, who are born and die and have no stake in divinity. Aristotle places humankind between animals and divinities in his cosmic hierarchy. Human beings are closer to animals than gods but share the divine "nature and essence." Daimones are not explicitly named in this hierarchy. See *Parts of Animals* 644b, 686a, in Aristotle, *Parts of Animals; Movement of Animals; Progression of Animals,* trans. A. L. Peck and E. S. Forster (Cambridge, MA: Harvard University Press, 1937), 96–99, 366–67; and see Martin, *Inventing Superstition,* 67–68.

15. *On Superstition,* 167F–168F, in Plutarch, *Moralia,* vol. 2, *How to Profit by One's Enemies; On Having Many Friends; Chance; Virtue and Vice; Letter of Condolence to Apollonius;. Advice About Keeping Well; Advice to Bride and Groom; The Dinner of the Seven Wise Men; Superstition,* trans. Frank Cole Babbitt (Cambridge, MA: Harvard University Press, 1928), 468–77.

mon is eager to deliver by his exhortations one soul, another another, and the soul on her part, having drawn close, can hear, and thus is saved; but if she pays no heed, she is forsaken by her daemon and comes to no happy end."[16] Since these physically superior beings must be morally superior as well, they cannot be evil; fearing daimones is a sign of a grave and even offensive misunderstanding of the daimonic nature.[17] And yet for all his insistence on this idea, Plutarch opens the door to a belief that daimones may *not*, in fact, be kindly disposed to human beings.[18] In *On Isis and Osiris,* Plutarch appears to give up ground to those who believe that daimones can indeed be evil. Citing Plato, Pythagoras, Xenocrates, and Chrysippus, Plutarch locates daimones between gods and men, "stronger than men and, in their might, greatly surpassing our nature, yet not possessing the divine quality unmixed and uncontaminated, but with a share also in the nature of the soul and in the perceptive faculties of the body."[19] Because of the vagaries of this metaphysical "mixture," Plutarch goes on to suggest that "in *daimones*, as in men, there are divers degrees of virtue and of vice."[20] Like human beings then, daimones have the capacity to be wicked. For some, this wickedness might be inherent, essential to their very nature. Others may be struggling to overcome their evil tendencies and ascend within the cosmic hierarchy themselves.[21] Plutarch's writings thus present an apparent contradiction: on the one hand, he insists that

16. *On the Sign of Socrates,* 594A, in Plutarch, *Moralia,* vol. 7, *On Love of Wealth; On Compliancy; On Envy and Hate; On Praising Oneself Inoffensively; On the Delays of the Divine Vengeance; On Fate; On the Sign of Socrates; On Exile; Consolation to His Wife,* trans. Phillip H. De Lacy and Benedict Einarson (Cambridge, MA: Harvard University Press, 1959), 482–85. See also 590E, in ibid., 470–71. See also Martin, *Inventing Superstition,* 99–103; Frederick E. Brenk, "'A Most Strange Doctrine.' *Daimon* in Plutarch," *Classical Journal* 69, no. 1 (1973): 1–11, 9.

17. Martin, *Inventing Superstition,* 97.

18. This point is noted by Martin, *Inventing Superstition,* 108.

19. *Isis and Osiris* 360E-F, in Plutarch, *Moralia,* vol. 5, *Isis and Osiris; The E at Delphi; The Oracles at Delphi No Longer Given in Verse; The Obsolescence of Oracles,* trans. Frank Cole Babbitt (Cambridge, MA: Havard University Press, 1936), 58–61.

20. *Isis and Osiris* 360E–F, in ibid., 58–61; and see Martin, *Inventing Superstition,* 103. In *The Divine Vengeance* 567B-C, Plutarch depicts daimones as punishing evildoers in the afterlife; however, these should be understood not as independent evil daimones but as an extension of divine punishment for immoral actions. See Brenk, "'A Most Strange Doctrine,'" 8–10.

21. Jeffrey Burton Russell, *Satan: The Early Christian Tradition* (Ithaca, NY: Cornell University Press, 1981), 49–50.

Plato is correct and that daimones are innately and entirely good; on the other hand, he cites Plato among others as suggesting that daimones may not all be morally upstanding.[22] His writings make possible a philosophical construction of daimones as *not* morally superior to human beings while he sees himself following Plato's modes of thinking.

The Christian apologist Justin Martyr emerged out of the scholastic tradition that traced itself to the Greek philosophical schools but used its ideas in conversation with Second Temple Jewish ideas and the emerging texts of the New Testament. Hundreds of years after Plato, the New Testament testifies to the development of Jesus-oriented communities that also thought about angels and demons. Like the Second Temple Jewish communities out of which they emerged, the New Testament authors had no interest in tying intermediary beings' ontological superiority to any sort of moral superiority. Throughout the New Testament, demons are consistently and wickedly opposed to Jesus's mission.

New Testament authors make no real attempt to create or enforce a systematic taxonomy or hierarchy of intermediary beings. Paul's letters reveal a deep anxiety that God, angels, demons, and human beings will be confused for one another, and that this confusion will lead human beings to err, and yet Paul does not attempt to solve this problem by demarcating these beings more clearly.[23] The gospel writers are similarly vague in their discussions of demons and angels. Thus, for example, in Matthew 4, the Devil *(diabolos)* tempts Jesus in the desert and when Jesus resists the Devil's temptations, "then the devil left him, and angels came and attended him," which suggests that angels are in some way opposed to the Devil. Yet in Matthew 25:41, Jesus promises that the Son of Man has prepared the eternal fire for "the devil and *his* angels" (emphasis added).[24] The Son of Man himself is also described as being accompanied by angels (Matt. 25:31). In this period, the term *angeloi* can simply refer to messengers;[25]

22. Martin, *Inventing Superstition*, 105–07.

23. See, e.g., 2 Cor. 11:12–15; and see Ellen Muehlberger, *Angels in Late Ancient Christianity* (Oxford: Oxford University Press, 2013), 29–30. Note that Paul does not, however, use the term *daimōn* in this text.

24. NIV translation. See Elaine Pagels, *The Origin of Satan* (New York: Random House, 1995), 86. See also Martin, "When Did Angels Become Demons?," 673–75.

25. Liddell and Scott, *A Greek-English Lexicon*, 7.

the author of the Gospel of Matthew does not sharply distinguish between angels as servants of God and demons as servants of the Devil. Similarly, in Revelation, angels are the foot soldiers in God's army, but angels also appear to serve the (destructive) will of Satan.[26] Angels and demons both appear in these first- and second-century texts, but these terms have not yet hardened into distinctive and opposing labels. Instead, these texts build on the particular Second Temple demonological trends conflating angels and demons discussed in chapter 1.

Kidd notes that "demons really received a pasting from the gutter press of the Greek Church Fathers."[27] This "pasting" was designed to achieve particular theological and polemical aims. As we will see, Justin Martyr and other early Christian writers took Greek daimones and divided them into two distinct groups—benevolent angels and evil demons—that these early church fathers imagined as opposing armies in a cosmic battle between God and Satan. These church fathers worked to construct human beings at the center of a highly differentiated spectrum which ranged from God to Satan, with angels and demons working to pull human beings in opposite directions in a cosmic game of tug of war.[28] They imagined not simply a spiritual taxonomy but a moral one which posed real dangers to the humans caught in the middle.

The second-century Christian writers Justin Martyr and his student Tatian combined Greek philosophical ideas with Second Temple Jewish demonological traditions in order to clearly distinguish demons from angels. Justin agrees with the Greek philosophers that daimones are superhuman beings. However, Justin insists that all the Graeco-Roman

26. Rev. 16:14; and see T. J. Wray and Gregory Mobley, *The Birth of Satan: Tracing the Devil's Biblical Roots* (New York: Palgrave, 2005), 147–48.

27. Kidd, "Some Philosophical Demons," 224.

28. At times, this association led to Satan being identified with demons even more closely. In *Patrologia Graeca* 37.1400–01, Gregory of Nazianzus proclaims, "Flee from my limbs, flee from my life. / Thief, serpent, fire, Belios, evil, doom, chasm, dragon, beast, / Night, ambush, rage, chaos, bewitcher, manslayer; / You who also hurled those firstborn of our kind into ruin, / Having tasted evil, baneful one, and death./ Christ Lord orders you to flee to the depth of the sea, / Down from the peaks or into the herd of swine,/ Just as the arrogant legion before" (quoted in Dayna S. Kalleres, "Demons and Divine Illumination: A Consideration of Eight Prayers by Gregory of Nazanzus," *Vigiliae Christianae* 61 [2007]: 164). *Satan* here is the demonic horde known as Legion in the synoptic Gospels as much as he is the one who corrupted Adam and Eve.

superhuman beings he had once worshipped—Dionysus, Apollo, and other gods—are not simply daimones but "foul *daimones*."[29] For Justin, the characterization of daimones as demons served to delegitimize the Greek pantheon and other religions' deities, reframing non-Christian belief as morally and ontologically inferior to Christianity. Following Second Temple narratives of demonic origins, Justin identifies these demons/daimones as the offspring of fallen angels who reproduced with human women.[30] Demons thus share some characteristics with angels, but, because of their human mothers, they are fundamentally different from angels, whether fallen or still in heaven. Justin's student Tatian further systematizes this distinction. Tatian explicitly distinguishes between physical and moral superiority. Tatian explains that, ontologically, demonic bodies are made of pneuma (spirit), rather than flesh. Pneuma weighs less than flesh, and so demons, like angels, live higher up than human beings, in the air. Physically, demonic beings are able to make themselves visible or invisible to human beings, but morally, demons deploy this ability as part of their evil mission to impede human attempts to ascend spiritually to heaven.[31] For Tatian, "the substance of demons has no 'room for repentance', for they are reflections of matter and of evil, and matter wished to exercise authority over the soul. Of their own free will they have handed down the laws of death to man."[32] Thus, even though humans are physically inferior to demons, they are spiritually superior and closer to God.[33] Justin and Tatian work to disentangle angels and demons, and at the same time break the association of ontological superiority with moral superiority. Demons have powers that humans do not, but they use these powers to perpetrate wickedness in the world.

29. Justin, *1 Apol.* 25, in Pagels, *The Origin of Satan,* 120.

30. Justin, *2 Apol.* 5:3–4. Angels are appointed over human beings and everything in this world; when some fell in the primordial history, they created a hierarchy of (good) angels, fallen angels, and their hybrid offspring, demons. See Justin, *2 Apol.* 5:2; 7:1–2. See Reed, *Fallen Angels,* 160–70; Eshel, "Demonology in Palestine," iii–iv.

31. Single quotation marks in the original. Tatian, *Oratio ad Graecos,* 12.1–4; 16.1 in Tatian, *Oratio ad Graecos* and *Fragments,* ed. and trans. Molly Whittaker (Oxford: Clarendon Press, 1982), 22–27, 32–33. See Gregory A. Smith, "How Thin Is a Demon?," *Journal of Early Christian Studies* 16, no. 4 (2008): 490–92; my thanks to Annette Yoshiko Reed for suggesting Smith.

32. Tatian, *Oratio ad Graecos* 15, in Tatian, *Oratio ad Graecos and Fragments,* 30–31.

33. Russell, *Satan,* 76–77.

Building on the work of both earlier Christian thinkers and Greek philosophers, the Christian theologian Origen (c. 184–254 C.E.) further heightens the danger of demons and extend the impact of both angels and demons in human life. His work is in turn important for later Christian theologians and Greek philosophers. Scholars have noted that Origen also appears to have had extensive contact with Jewish teachers and thinkers in the Roman Empire.[34] As we will see in the next section, Origen's contacts with Jews do not translate to similar demonic taxonomies, at least in the surviving rabbinic literature.

Like Justin, Origen asserts that the non-Christian gods are really evil demons pretending to be gods.[35] Like Tatian, Origen insists that daimones are always evil, intending to "lead men astray and distract them, and drag them down from God and the world beyond the heavens to earthly things."[36] According to Origen, this demonic goal is also enacted by causing heretical conflicts within the church as well as Roman persecutions of Christians.[37]

But how did demons get to be so evil? Justin had answered this question with reference to Second Temple accounts of the offspring of fallen angels and human women. For Origen, however, demonic wickedness could be traced back even further, to the beginnings of the cosmos. According to

34. See the foundational work in this area of study, N. R. M. de Lange, *Origen and the Jews: Studies in Jewish-Christian Relations in Third-Century Palestine* (Cambridge: Cambridge University Press, 1976). See discussion of this work in its scholarly context in William Horbury, "Origen and the Jews: Jewish-Greek and Jewish-Christian Relations," in *The Jewish-Greek Tradition in Antiquity and the Byzantine Empire*, edited by James K. Aitken and James Carleton Paget (Cambridge: Cambridge University Press, 2014), 79–90. My thanks to Beth Digeser for noting Origen's interactions with contemporaneous Jewish communities.

35. As noted by David Brodsky in private conversation, a similar move is made by the fifth- or sixth-century Syriac text *The Acts of Mār Mārī*, in which the author claims that the statues of the polytheistic gods are actually inhabited by demons who work to prevent the people's recognition of Christianity and ultimate salvation. See also the extensive and thorough discussion of this phenomenon in Sonja Anderson, "Idol Talk: The Discourse of Idolatry in the Early Christian World" (PhD diss., Yale University, 2016); and see discussion below in chap. 5.

36. Origen, *CC* 5.5, in Henry Chadwick, *Origen: Contra Celsum* (1953; Cambridge: Cambridge University Press, 1965), 267; and see Martin, *Inventing Superstition*, 177–78.

37. Origen, *CC* 3.25, 5.46, 6.11, 8.43, in ibid., 143, 301, 25, 483; and see Martin, *Inventing Superstition*, 179–80. According to Origen, any positive acts performed by intermediary beings are really performed by angels (Origen, *CC* 8.57, in Chadwick, *Origen: Contra Celsum*, 495).

Origen, God originally created all intelligent beings equal and with free will. With the notable exceptions of Christ and the Holy Spirit, all created beings then chose to distance themselves from the divine unity, to varying degrees. The more created beings distanced themselves—or emanated—from God, the more debased their status, creating a descending hierarchy of God/Christ/Holy Spirit, "archangels, angels, gods, human beings, demons, and the devil."[38] Humans are in the middle of this hierarchy, nestled between the forces of good and the forces of evil.[39] Demons, as servants of the Devil, work to distance people from God. Only good angels can and do protect right-thinking Christians from the attractions of the demonic.[40] Humanity is the rope in the cosmic game of tug of war played between angels and demons.

For Origen, humans are not only torn between angels and demons in a cosmic sense; they are also torn between good and evil intermediary beings in their everyday lives: "Two angels attend each human being. One is an angel of justice, the other an angel of iniquity. If good thoughts are present in our hearts and justice springs up in our souls, the angel of the Lord is undoubtedly speaking to us. But, if evil thoughts turn over in our hearts, the devil's angel is speaking to us."[41] The image of the angel and the demon sitting on one's shoulders is an old one indeed.

Origen attempts to rank and highly differentiate these beings in form and function. And yet, as Marx-Wolf points out, "across Origen's works we encounter imprecision and context-specific usage of names and terms referring to spirits that aid or obstruct humans in their quest to achieve

38. Muehlberger, *Angels in Late Ancient Christianity*, 34, discussing Origen, *De Principis* I.6.2–3, II.9.6. See Adam Ployd, "Participation and Polemics: Angels from Origen to Augustine," *Harvard Theological Review* 110, no. 3 (2017): 421–39; Marx-Wolf, *Spiritual Taxonomies and Ritual Authority*, 45; Russell, *Satan*, 125–27. Notably, animals are absent from this taxonomy.

39. Angels and demons are two sides of a coin; though Origen has an articulated taxonomy of intermediary beings, notably, he uses the word *daimōn* interchangeably with the expression "the Devil's angels." See, e.g., Origen, *De Principis* I.6.2–3.

40. Origen, *CC* 8.36, in Chadwick, *Origen: Contra Celsum*, 477–78; and see Martin, *Inventing Superstition*, 182.

41. Origen, *Homilies on Luke* 12.4, in Origen, *Homilies on Luke; Fragments on Luke*, trans. Joseph T. Lienhard (Washington, DC: Catholic University of America Press, 1996), 49–50, and the discussion in Russell, *Satan*, 135.

salvation."[42] We see some of the same linguistic slippage between angels and demons evident in the Gospel of Matthew. This phenomenon is reminiscent of the inconsistency of terminology for demons in the Babylonian Talmud, moving seemingly without logic between the terms *šedim, ruḥot,* and *mazziqin.* But in contrast with the rabbis, Origen seems explicitly aware of the slipperiness of his terminology, noting that both the Devil and Jesus are accompanied by beings referred to, imprecisely, as angels.[43] Origen's attempts to systematize are undermined by his commitment to the slippery earlier texts that he saw as both foundational and sacred.

Although not himself committed to New Testament texts, Iamblichus (c. 245–c. 325 C.E.) was a Syrian polytheist in conversation with both Origen and earlier Greek philosophers in his thinking about demons.[44] Like Origen, Iamblichus adopts an "emanational framework" in which distance from the Highest God determines your species;[45] Iamblichus defines demons as "the generative and creative powers of the gods in the furthest extremity of their emanations and in its last stages of division" from the Highest God.[46] Unlike the Christian Origen, Iamblichus has no concept of the devil, and so demons are those beings most distant from the Highest God. In further contrast to Origen, Iamblichus does not necessarily correlate this distance with moral status. Indeed, Iamblichus believes that one can actually change one's species and ascend toward the supreme being through the practice of particular rituals meant to refine the soul, known as theurgy.[47]

A belief that one can ascend the ranks of species requires an ordered hierarchy of species. In *De Mysteriis,* Iamblichus purports to describe each species in the cosmos and to compare a variety of their features,

42. Marx-Wolf, *Spiritual Taxonomies and Ritual Authority,* 42; and see also Martin, "When Did Angels Become Demons?"

43. Origen, *De Principis* I.5.2.

44. Martin, *Inventing Superstition,* 196. Iamblichus explicitly engages with Porphyry, but it is his dependence on Origen that is of interest here.

45. Marx-Wolf, *Spiritual Taxonomies and Ritual Authority,* 55.

46. Iamblichus, *De Mysteriis* 2.1, in Iamblichus, *De Mysteriis,* trans. Emma C. Clarke et al. (Atlanta: Society for Biblical Literature, 2003), 83, cited in Marx-Wolf, *Spiritual Taxonomies and Ritual Authority,* 57.

47. Marx-Wolf, *Spiritual Taxonomies and Ritual Authority,* 55.

including appearance, ability, swiftness, celestial light, and matter.[48] So, for example, he writes that

> the appearances of the gods are uniform; those of *daimones* are varied; those of angels are simpler than those of *daimones*, but inferior to those of the gods. Those of archangels are closer to divine principles, but those of archons, if you take these to be rulers of the cosmos, who administer the sublunary elements, are varied, but structured in an orderly manner; and, if they preside over matter, they are more varied and more imperfect than archangels; and the appearances of souls come in all sorts of forms.[49]

Daimones have a range of appearances; further on in the text Iamblichus describes daimons as characterized with "tumult and disorder,"[50] able to change their size at will,[51] able to appear to move more swiftly than they actually can, and visibly glowing with "smouldering fire."[52]

Like Plato and Plutarch before him, Iamblichus believes that daimones can be good. Like Origen and the early church fathers, however, he explicitly states that at least some daimones are inherently evil. Thus, when Iamblichus describes how different celestial beings manifest to human sight, he writes that the viewer sees "good *daimones* presenting for contemplation their own productions, and the goods which they bestow; punitive *daimones* displaying their forms of punishment; the other *daimones* who are wicked in whatsoever way surrounded by harmful beasts, greedy for blood and savage."[53] Daimones are here divided into three categories, two of which (good daimones and punitive daimones) appear to be on the side of good, and one of which (the wicked daimones) are entirely evil. A wicked daimon is "by nature wicked," and though he may pretend "to resemble the divine race," he is inherently other.[54]

Iamblichus explicitly ranks each being relative to the others in a range

48. *De Mysteriis* 2.3–9, in Iamblichus, *De Mysteriis*, trans. Emma C. Clarke et al., 87–107; and see Marx-Wolf, *Spiritual Taxonomies and Ritual Authority*, 56–57.

49. Adapted from *De Mysteriis* 2.3, in Iamblichus, *De Mysteriis*, 87.

50. *De Mysteriis* 2.3, in ibid., 89.

51. *De Mysteriis* 2.3, in ibid., 89.

52. *De Mysteriis* 2.4, in ibid., 95; and see also the rest of *De Mysteriis* 2.3 and 2.4.

53. Adapted from *De Mysteriis* 2.7, in ibid., 101.

54. *De Mysteriis* 4.7, in ibid., 215; and see discussion of Iamblichus's daimonic divisions in Martin, *Inventing Superstition*, 198–99.

of areas.[55] This ranking is especially notable in his discussion of "the fineness of the light" that each being "radiates."[56] Using the human being and the human power of sight as his center point, Iamblichus describes the relative abilities of humans to view the light that radiates from gods, archangels, and angels. Humans cannot view the light that radiates from the gods because it is too fine, whereas the light radiating from archangels and angels is less fine and thus partly visible to the human eye. Humans are unable to see the light of daimones, heroes, archons, and souls, but here it is not because their light is too fine but, rather, it is because these lesser beings do not radiate this special kind of light at all.[57] This discursive move to rank cosmic beings according to their ability to be seen is particularly striking in light of *Pesiqta Rabbati's* interest in ranking beings according to ability to see, discussed below.

Iamblichus represents one attempt to synthesize Greek philosophical taxonomic traditions with Christian ideas. In his extensive taxonomic project as represented by *De Mysteriis*, daimones appear consistently somewhere between the Supreme God and human beings; but they are morally complex, and different classes of daimones are categorized differently.

TESTAMENTS OF HIERARCHIES

In the western Mediterranean, the late antique impulse to categorize intermediary beings reached its apex in two very different Christian texts: Pseudo-Dionysius's *Celestial Hierarchy* and the *Testament of Solomon*. Texts by early Christian writers Justin Martyr, Tatian, and Origen discuss demons in a range of theological contexts without articulating a completely unified cosmic order as Plato and Iamblichus did. Yet these two later texts organize, systematize, and, in the case of Pseudo-Dionysius, also rank those unseen intermediary beings who share the world with humankind.

55. *De Mysteriis* 2.3–9 in ibid., 87–107; and see Marx-Wolf, *Spiritual Taxonomies and Ritual Authority*, 56–57.

56. *De Mysteriis* 2.8, in ibid., 103; and see Marx-Wolf, *Spiritual Taxonomies and Ritual Authority*, 56–57.

57. *De Mysteriis* 2.8, in ibid., 103–05.

An unnamed Christian theologian and philosopher, the author of the *Celestial Hierarchy* lived in the late-fifth or early-sixth century C.E. and would come to be known as Pseudo-Dionysius the Areopagite.[58] Pseudo-Dionysius delineates an angelology with nine ranks of angels who attend God and the cosmos. Muehlberger argues compellingly that the *Celestial Hierarchy* "represented a break from other late ancient thought, in that it treated angels as a discrete subject, a 'hierarchy' that stood between God and Christians."[59] Pseudo-Dionysius writes that "the goal of a hierarchy... is to enable beings to be as like as possible to God and to be at one with him."[60] While he admits that angels at times enact God's judgment on human beings, entirely evil demonic beings have no place in his idealized world.[61]

By contrast, the *Testament of Solomon* presents a fascinating taxonomy of demons, offering what Philip Alexander has called an "encyclopaedia of demonology."[62] A highly syncretistic work written in Greek which includes elements of ancient Jewish, Egyptian, and Hellenistic thought, the *Testament of Solomon* tells the story of how King Solomon built the Temple using demonic forced labor.[63] Although a composite work, the text appears to have been ultimately redacted by an early medieval Christian writer.[64] The text identifies over fifty named and highly individuated

58. For a discussion of Pseudo-Dionysius and his philosophical influences, see John Dillon and Sarah Klitenic Wear, *Dionysius the Areopagite and the Neoplatonist Tradition: Despoiling the Hellenes* (Farnham, UK: Ashgate, 2007).

59. Muehlberger, *Angels in Late Ancient Christianity*, 21–22.

60. Pseudo-Dionysius, *The Celestial Hierarchy* 165A, in Colm Luibhéid and Paul Rorem, eds., *Pseudo-Dionysius: The Complete Works*, rev. ed. (New York: Paulist Press, 1987), 154. For Pseudo-Dionysius, "a hierarchy is a sacred order, a state of understand and an activity approximating as closely as possible to the divine. And it is uplifted to the imitation of God in proportion to the enlightenments divinely given to it" (164A, in ibid., 153).

61. Pseudo-Dionysius, *The Celestial Hierarchy* 333C, in ibid., 187.

62. P. S. Alexander, "Incantations and Books of Magic," in Emil Schürer, *A History of the Jewish People in the Age of Jesus Christ (175 B.C.--A.D. 135), a New English Version*, vol. 3, pt. 1 (Edinburgh: T&T Clark, 1986), 373, cited in Pablo Torijano, *Solomon the Esoteric King: From King to Magus, Development of a Tradition* (Leiden: Brill, 2002), 54.

63. Torijano, *Solomon the Esoteric King*, 144.

64. Sarah Schwartz has argued that "while we only find evidence in the late medieval manuscripts of fuller forms of the *TSol* collection, variously combining testament framework, demonological narratives, and spells, there is no doubt that some (perhaps many) elements go back much further... It seems nearly impossible to say more (without the discovery of more information) than that some elements which would ultimately come together in the late collection were circulating as early as the first century C.E., and by the fourth and fifth centuries C.E. we find flourishing evidence of the popularity of multiple elements of

demons. Some of these demons are described as fallen angels, others are the offspring of angels and human women, and still others are generic spirits.[65] Many of the demons described in the *Testament of Solomon* "reside in" a particular star or constellation, and human beings who are born under that star are particularly vulnerable to that demon's attack.[66] As a demon named Ornias explains, because of their lighter bodies and their wings, "we demons go up to the firmament of heaven, fly around among the stars, and hear the decisions which issue from God concerning the lives of men. The rest of the time we come and, being transformed, cause destruction, whether by domination, or by fire, or by sword, or by chance."[67] The *Testament of Solomon's* primary contribution to late antique demonology comes in its articulation of the means of repelling these demonic attacks; each of the demons reveals the name of his or her thwarting angel, a specific heavenly being who opposes and controls that demon when invoked by human beings.[68] Though they may have shared origins, demons and angels are fundamentally opposed to each other in this text. Human beings exist between these two cosmic poles, attacked by the one but invoking the other for protection.

The *Celestial Hierarchy* and *Testament of Solomon* represent the ultimate attempts on the part of late antique Christian thinkers to categorize intermediary beings. Each text appears to be interested in only one type of intermediary beings, but each also reveals a great deal about other intermediary beings in their discussions. Taken together, these texts model the ways that some Christian scholastic elites divided benevolent Greek daim-

what would eventually be included in the *TSol* collection." See Sarah L. Schwartz, "Building a Book of Spells: The So-Called *Testament of Solomon* Reconsidered" (PhD diss., Philadelphia, University of Pennsylvania, 2005), 135. See also Schwartz, "Reconsidering the *Testament of Solomon*," *Journal for the Study of Pseudepigrapha* 16, no. 3 (2007): 203–37; Kalmin, *Migrating Tales*, 95–96. For alternative views of the dating of this text, see D. C. Duling, "The Testament of Solomon," in *The Old Testament Pseudepigrapha*, ed. James H. Charlesworth (Garden City, NY: Doubleday, 1983), 940–44; Philip S. Alexander, "Contextualizing the Demonology of the Testament of Solomon," in *Die Dämonen—Demons: Die Dämonologie der Israelitisch-Jüdischen und Frühchristlichen Literatur im Kontext ihrer Umwelt*, ed. A. Lange et al. (Tübingen: Mohr Siebeck 2004), 613–35.

65. *TSol* 5:3; 6:2; 25:1, in Duling, "The Testament of Solomon," 966–68, 85.

66. *TSol* 2:2, in ibid., 963.

67. *TSol* 20:12–13, in ibid., 983.

68. Demons in the *Testament of Solomon* can be either male or female and can also change their gender at will. See *TSol* 15:1–6, in ibid., 975.

ones into two distinct groups: benevolent angels and malevolent demons. For the authors, that demons are and must be malevolent emphasizes the protections that Christianity affords its followers. Only the Christian readers of these texts and their disciples have the knowledge to access the angelic cohorts and repel demonic attacks.

Although the late antique Christian theologians discussed here differ in the details, they all agree that both angels and demons are physically superior to human beings. Yet only angels are morally superior and thus worthy of being emulated. Humans stand between angels and demons, pulled in both directions. But angels, in their moral superiority, stand in opposition to demons and so protect faithful Christians from demonic influence. [69] In the late antique world, taxonomy is both a form of anthropology and a form of theology.

To take a step back then, early Christian writers reinterpreted neutral or even beneficent Greek daimones as malevolent demons who serve the cause of evil. This act of interpretation synthesized Greco-Roman philosophical ideas with emerging Christian understandings of the world in a profoundly ideological way, equating other religions' divinities with false gods and demonic actors. In making this claim, these writers appropriate the Greek term *daimones* and subvert its meaning. With Christianity's eventual victory over the Roman world, the world *demon* has taken on this resonance entirely. But early Christian polemicists and their counterparts in the world of Greek philosophy were not the only late antique scholastic elites to offer a taxonomic understanding of possibly dangerous intermediary beings.

RABBINIC TAXONOMIES

We have read Greek philosophers and early Church fathers as individuals before attempting to make larger comments about the trends and tensions in philosophical and Christian taxonomies. Yet the character of rabbinic literature—the nature of the Talmud as a communal and dialectical project, its cross-generational aspects, and the prominent role of redaction in

69. See also Martin, *Inventing Superstition*, 181–83.

compiling it—requires us to read it from the start with attention to a range of discursive attitudes and approaches.

By reading across the Babylonian Talmud, we learn a surprising amount about rabbinic demons in the Babylonian world over the course of several centuries. For the rabbis, demons can be named. Some have biblical names such as Joseph and Jonathan,[70] while others have Aramaicized names such as Lilith, Agrat bat Maḥlat, Ben Talamion, and the demon king Ashmedai.[71] Some demons appear nameless in groups of šedim, ruḥot, and mazziqin. Demons can be male or female, though, consistent with its general approach to gender, the Talmud discusses male demons more than it does female demons. Demons can move rapidly from place to place.[72] These details are scattered across the Babylonian Talmud, crucial to our understanding of rabbinic demonology but presented as largely incidental to larger halakhic and aggadic concerns. But these were not sustained attempts at taxonomy.

The rabbis of late antiquity did not necessarily see themselves as philosophers or even as systematizers. In much of their writings, they are

70. For Joseph the demon, see b. *Pesaḥim* 110a, cited by R. Joseph and R. Papa, and the anonymous teaching in b. *Eruvin* 43a. B. *Yevamot* 122a may introduce us to another demonic teacher, Jonathan or Yoḥanan. The manuscript tradition is extremely corrupted, and the identity of this demon remains uncertain. According to the Pesaro print edition, R. Ḥanina cites a tradition in the name of Yoḥanan the demon. According to the Vilna print edition, R. Ḥanina cites a tradition in the name of Jonathan the demon. Yet MSS Oxford Opp. 248 (367), Munich 141, and Munich 95 have R. Ḥanina cite the same tradition in the name of Yoḥanan my son [יוחנן בני]. MS Vatican 122a has the tradition cited by R. Joseph in the name of Jonathan my son [יונתן בני]. MS Moscow-Guenzburg 1017 has the tradition cited by R. Ḥanina in the name of Yoḥanan, with no descriptor of who this Yoḥanan was, and MS Moscow-Guenzburg 594 has the same form of citation but in the name of Jonathan. The print editions may be drawing on a textual tradition that has not come down to us, or, alternatively, this may be a rare case of the scribal amplification of the demonic in the early modern period, in contrast to the dominant tendency to explain away and suppress the demonic which began in the medieval period. Note, however, that none of these names points to sins or failings—unlike early Christian and Zoroastrian demons, rabbinic demons are never named Wrath, Gluttony, or Sloth.

71. Except for the name Lilith, the Aramaicized names appear only in the anonymous stratum of the Babylonian Talmud. For Lilith, see b. *Eruvin* 18b, attributed to R. Jeremiah b. Eleazar; b. *Niddah* 24b, attributed to R. Judah in the name of Shmuel; b. *Shabbat* 151b attributed to R. Hanina, and a possible baraita at b. *Eruvin* 100b. For the anonymously named Agrat bat Maḥlat, see b. *Pesaḥim* 112b–113a and the discussion in chap. 3. For Ben Talamion, see b. *Me'ilah* 17a–b, and the discussion in chap. 6. For Ashmedai, see b. *Gittin* 68a–b, and the discussion in chap. 4.

72. B. *Eruvin* 43a.

frustratingly and excitingly unsystematic. However, the rabbis bring their powers of categorization to bear on intermediary beings in one key tradition that appears in both *Avot de-Rabbi Natan* A and b. *Ḥagigah*. Second Temple Jewish literature and Tannaitic texts do not preserve interest in classifying and ranking intermediary beings relative to other species; the tradition recorded in b. *Ḥagigah* and *Avot de-Rabbi Natan* is thus the earliest extant evidence for this kind of systematization. As we will see, a sustained analysis of this single rabbinic tradition that categorizes intermediary beings as part of the cosmos highlights the ways that the rabbinic authors of this tradition emphasize both demons' mutability and their moral neutrality.

This tradition appears in *Avot de-Rabbi Natan* A as part of a series of lists and taxonomies of God's creations. Dating *Avot de-Rabbi Natan* A is a complicated task, with different scholars positing dates between the third and ninth centuries C.E.[73] The text is paralleled in b. *Ḥagigah* 16a as part of a larger *sugya* that explores *Ma'aseh Merkavah*, Ezekiel's vision of the Heavenly Chariot. In the course of their discussion of the heavens, the Talmud goes on to discuss angels and other heavenly beings. I treat both passages as roughly contemporaneous. The two parallels are presented here in tandem.

Avot de-Rabbi Natan A 37	b. *Ḥagigah 16a* MS Munich 6
Six things were said about human beings: Three like an animal, and three like the ministering angels.	
Three like an animal: They eat and drink like an animal, procreate like an animal, and excrete like an animal.	

73. Judah Goldin, *The Fathers According to Rabbi Nathan [Version A]* (New Haven, CT: Yale University Press, 1955), xxi, dates the text to the third century. However, both M. B. Lerner, "The External Tractates," in *The Literature of the Sages*, ed. Shmuel Safrai (Philadelphia: Fortress Press, 1987), 367–409, and Menahem Kister, "Avot De-Rabbi Nathan: Studies in Text, Redaction and Interpretation," (PhD diss., Jerusalem: Hebrew University of Jerusalem, 1993), 214–219, date both texts to the post-Talmudic period, based on their being grouped with the seventh- to ninth-century minor tractates. I have chosen to treat this text as Amoraic based primarily on its loose treatment of the mishnah, which suggests a date before the Mishnah's canonicity was affirmed, and its use of mishnaic and Amoraic Hebrew. ARN B is very likely the older version of the two.

Three like a ministering angel: They have reason [בינה] like ministering angel, walk upright like a ministering angel, and speak in the Holy Tongue like a ministering angel.[74]

Six things were said of demons (šedim): three like human beings and three like the ministering angels.

Three like human beings: They eat and drink like human beings, they procreate like human beings, and they die like human beings.

Three like the ministering angels: They have wings like the ministering angels, they know what will happen in the future like ministering angels, and they can travel from one end of the world to the other like ministering angels.

Our rabbis taught: Six things were said of demons (šedim): Three like the ministering angels and three like human beings.

Three like the ministering angels: They have wings like the ministering angels, and they fly from one end of the world to the other like the ministering angels, and they know what will happen in the future like the ministering angels.

Do you really think they know? Rather say that they hear what will happen in the future like the ministering angels.[75]

Three like human beings: They eat and drink like human beings, they procreate[76] *like human beings, and they die*[77] *like human beings.*

74. On speech, angels, and the Holy Tongue in this tradition, see Willem F. Smelik, *Rabbis, Language and Translation in Late Antiquity* (Cambridge: Cambridge University Press, 2013), 14, 42. See also b. *Shabbat* 12b, b. *Sotah* 33a, which insist that angels do not understand Aramaic.

75. Emphasis added.

76. Munich 95 has מולידים ומזריעים.

77. Oxford Opp. Add. 23 has רעי ומוציאין.

And some say they can change their faces into any appearance they desire, and they see but cannot be seen.

Six things were said of human beings: Three like the ministering angels and three like animals.

Three like the ministering angels: They have reason [דעה] like the ministering angels, and they walk upright like the ministering angels, and they speak in the Holy Tongue like the ministering angels.

Three like the animals: They eat and drink like animals, they procreate like animals, and they excrete like animals.

The Talmud's text, presented as a baraita, comes immediately after a discussion of God and the heavenly court. It begins with demons and moves on from there to discuss human beings. The passage in *Avot de-Rabbi Natan* has a reverse order of beings, discussing first humans and then demons. But both texts classify humans and demons as they relate to the ministering angels and to animals.

In these texts, we learn a tremendous amount about demons: They have wings and can use them to travel large distances. They know the future (or, as the anonymous interjection in b. *Ḥagigah* insists, they do not themselves know the future, but are able to *hear* the future as it is spoken [?] by God).[78] Their wings put them solidly between heaven and earth, enabling them to travel not just across the world but between worlds. They eat and drink,[79] procreate, and die. That demons procreate may suggest another

78. As in the *Testament of Solomon*, discussed above.

79. By contrast, a belief that demons do *not* eat is found in some of the Aramaic magic bowls, where serving food is one way to distinguish between humans and demons: humans will eat it while demons will leave it untouched; see Joseph Naveh and Shaul Shaked, *Amu-*

story of demonic origins: some demons are the offspring of other demons. Demons have bodies and know how to use them. That demons can die suggests that they can also be killed;[80] in chapter 6, we further discuss the exorcistic impulse.

This text also teaches us about the relationships between demons and other divine creations. Demons are not ontologically identical to angels, that is, fallen angels. They are not the inverse of angels, opposed to angels, or controlled by angels.[81] They are their own species, which has features in common with both angels and humans. They exist in a space between the ministering angels and humankind. Humans are not pulled in two directions by angels and demons; it is demons who exist between humans and angels in this cosmic taxonomy. Curiously, angels are not themselves subject to this taxonomy; they appear only instrumentally to help classify demons and humans.[82] Perhaps angels, who might legitimately be expected to share some similarities with God, were too heavenly to fully classify. To whom might they be compared?

This tradition pulls in two opposite directions. On the one hand, it is morally neutral: animal and human qualities are not marked as bad, and angelic features are not marked as good. This tradition simply recognizes the different bodies and abilities of different species. This neutrality is particularly striking given that the word these traditions use for demons, *šedim,* is used contemporaneously by Zoroastrian texts as the spelling for the Pahlavi word *dēw* to refer to unequivocally evil servants of the evil god Ahriman.[83] On the other hand, the structure of these texts also suggests that the connections between humankind and demons are complicated;

---

lets and Magic Bowls: Aramaic Incantations of Late Antiquity (Jerusalem: Magnes Press, 1985), 75–76.

80. Gideon Bohak, "Conceptualizing Demons in Late Antique Judaism," in *Demons and Illness from Antiquity to the Early-Modern Period*, ed. Siam Bhayro and Catherine Rider (Leiden: Brill, 2017), 114, suggests that "the number of demons alive and active at any different moment clearly fluctuates, adding a measure of instability to an otherwise orderly celestial realm."

81. The Amoraic rabbis' resistance to opposing demons and angels is not found in either earlier or later rabbinic tradition. See *Sifrei Numbers Naso*, §40, and *Midrash Tanhuma* on Exod. 23:20, and the discussion in Ahuvia, "Israel among the Angels," 75.

82. See ibid., 67–83, for a discussion about how the rabbis "think with" angels about intermediary beings.

83. See the introduction.

while demons are compared with humankind, humans are not compared with demons but rather with animals and the ministering angels. There are, in fact, several traditions in late antique rabbinic literature that locate human beings in the midpoint between angels and animals.[84] The tradition found in *Avot de-Rabbi Natan* A 37 and b. *Ḥagigah* 16a is the only late antique rabbinic example in which demons have been inserted into the taxonomy. And in this tradition, they have been inserted only roughly; the various classes of beings are not equally enchained with one another. Instead, while humans have nothing in common with demons, demons have a great deal in common with humans.[85]

While the list of similarities is the same in both texts, *Avot de-Rabbi Natan* concludes its discussion of demons with a fascinating addition: "And some say they can change their faces into any appearance they desire, and they see but cannot be seen." These two features rely on demonic embodiment (with faces, bodies, and eyes) as the starting point for demons' ability to alter their physical forms. The mutability of demons is part of their danger—you never know who you are talking to. The sense of sight is important, but you cannot trust your eyes. This addition is consistent with the "visual turn" that Rachel Rafael Neis describes as "a hitherto overlooked but crucial component of later (that is, Amoraic and later), rabbinic piety."[86] Demons are radically corporeal, not metaphorical or spiritual in nature, and thus they are experienced through the senses.

Elsewhere, the Babylonian Talmud shares *Avot de-Rabbi Natan's* focus on the visual and its fear of identity-confusion when it comes to demons. The Mishnah in *Gittin* 6:6 states that a woman may be given permission

84. See b. *Shabbat* 112b; *Sifrei Numbers Koraḥ* 119.

85. While lists of six are found in several places in the Babylonian Talmud, the particular structure of this text, a list of six followed by a division into two groups of three, is only found in one other location in the Bavli, b. *Beiẓah* 32b, where the late Tanna/early Amora Bar Kappara provides a list of six teachings about the laws relating to a candlewick, which is then divided into three leniencies and three stringencies. Other lists of six can be found at b. *Berakhot* 51a–b, b. *Pesaḥim* 49b and 113b, all of which are presented as baraitot. Interestingly enough, there are no other explicit lists of six found in *Avot de-Rabbi Natan* A, or in Palestinian Amoraic midrashim.

86. Neis, *The Sense of Sight in Rabbinic Culture,* 10. The imbrication of sight and power was also highly gendered. See ibid., 116, 98.

to remarry based on a voice affirming that she is divorced or widowed, even if the person whose voice it is remains unseen.[87] The anonymous voice of the Babylonian Talmud raises the concern that a voice, when not visibly attached to a human body, may belong to a demon—and a demon has no legal agency to enact the dissolution of someone else's marriage:

> But should we not fear that he is a demon (šeid)? R. Judah said: *This is a case where he was seen to have the appearance of a human.* But [demons] can also look like men?! This is a case where they can also see his shadow. But [demons] can also have a shadow?! This is a case where they also saw the shadow of his shadow. And should you say that [demons] also have a shadow of a shadow, didn't R. Ḥanina say: My son[88] Jonathan taught me that they do have a shadow, but they do not have a shadow of a shadow.[89]

The Talmud's anonymous voice undercuts the legal force of the potentially demonic voice and refocuses on visual signals of humanity. Steven Fraade has also shown that the elision of the distinction between hearing and seeing and the simultaneous privileging of the visual over the auditory is an interpretive strategy given greater force in the rabbinic period.[90] This emphasis on the visual further embodies the demonic in the physical world. Demons are not disembodied voices of malevolence. Instead, demons differ from humans only in that their shadows do not have shadows. And the shadow of a shadow is of little substance at all.[91] The rabbinic insistence that demons were embodied but could control and alter their embodiments created new anxieties around the forms that those bodies could take, anxieties that—as we will see in chapters 3 and 4—could be resolved only through the back and forth of halakhic discourse.

87. See also the parallel in m. *Yevamot* 16:6.

88. All the extant manuscripts read בני, yet the print edition of the exact parallel at b. *Yevamot* 122a reads שידא, pointing to either an alternative tradition or a later interest in redemonizing the Talmud. See discussion in note 70.

89. B. *Gittin* 66a, MS Arras 889.

90. Steven D. Fraade, "Hearing and Seeing at Sinai: Interpretive Trajectories," in *The Significance of Sinai: Traditions about Sinai and Divine Revelation in Judaism and Christianity*, ed. George J. Brooke et al. (Leiden: Brill, 2008), 247–68. Fraade there explores a number of Philonic and midrashic texts that discuss the visual aspects of the revelation at Sinai.

91. The character Guildenstern in Shakespeare's *Hamlet* thus states: "Truly, and I hold ambition of so airy and light a quality that it is but a shadow's shadow" (2.2.280–81). In Shakespeare's time, the expression "shadow's shadow" appears to imply that it is nothing at all and thus one need not deal with it.

RABBINIC RANKINGS

The taxonomies of b. *Ḥagigah* 16a and *Avot de-Rabbi Natan* A37 present demons as another species in a broader world, albeit a species with some of the strengths and characteristics of both angels and human beings. Juxtaposing this tradition with two rabbinic parallels, one earlier and one later, further highlights its particular interest in demons and its almost aggressive moral neutrality.

The earlier parallel to this rabbinic taxonomy is found in *Genesis Rabbah* 8:11, as part of a midrashic discussion of Genesis 2:5, "Male and female He created them."

> *R. Joshua b. Neḥemiah in the name of R. Ḥanina b. Isaac and the Rabbis in the name of R. Eleazar say: He created [man] with four creations from above, and four from below. He eats and drinks like an animal, procreates like an animal, excretes like an animal, and dies like an animal. From above—he stands like a ministering angel, speaks like a ministering angel, has reason [דעת] like a ministering angel, and sees like a ministering angel. An animal doesn't see?! Rather, [man] has binocular vision [unlike an animal].*
>
> *R. Tifdai [said] in the name of R. Aḥa: "The upper beings were created in the image and likeness [of God] and do not procreate; and the lower beings procreate and are not created in the image and likeness [of God]. The Holy One blessed be He said: "I will create [man] in the image and likeness [of God], of the upper beings, and able to procreate, of the lower beings." R. Tifdai [said] in the name of R. Aḥa: "The Holy One blessed be He said: If I create [man] of the upper beings, he will live and not die, of the lower beings he will die and not live. Rather, I will create him of the upper beings and of the lower beings. If he sins, he will die, and if he does not sin, he will live.*

According to *Genesis Rabbah*, humankind shares four features with animals and four with the ministering angels. The structure is similar enough to the tradition found in b. *Ḥagigah* and *Avot de-Rabbi Natan* A that there must be some kind of relationship between the texts. And yet there are three immediate differences. First, this description is focused exclusively on human beings and "upper beings"; either demons are not considered in this taxonomy at all, or they, too, are part of an undifferentiated group of "upper beings" created in the image of God. Second, here the ability to see is ascribed to humankind, not demons, and understood literally to refer to binocular vision, which is the ability to have one's field of vision in each eye overlap creating depth perception.[92] And third, the teachings of R. Tifdai introduce another very important figure into this taxonomy, God. Both the discussions of the image of God and the inclusion of God's own speech orient this text not just toward creations, but also toward their Creator.[93]

There are two obvious ways to understand the differences between the earlier *Genesis Rabbah* taxonomy and the later Babylonian rabbinic taxonomy: either an independent tradition circulated and was composed and edited in two different ways by two different rabbinic communities, or the Babylonian redactors consciously adapted and transformed a Palestinian tradition. Regardless of which model of transmission is correct, the authors of b. *Ḥagigah* 16a and *Avot de-Rabbi Natan* A clearly share an interest in the taxonomy of demons that this earlier tradition does not.[94] And where this earlier text is focused on God's thought process as it relates to man's moral nature, the later texts are interested in describing bodies and abilities in morally neutral ways detached from expectations of the image of God, and thereby sidestep the question of whether demons themselves were created *b'tzelem Elohim,* in the image of God.

A later tradition in *Pesiqta Rabbati* further illuminates the late antique rabbis' redactional choices.[95]

> *Come and see the wonders of the Holy One Blessed be He. He creates worlds within worlds. He created the world and created within it human beings. He created His world and created within it human beings and demons*

92. My thanks to my mother, Dr. Margaret Ronis, O.D., for explaining binocular vision to me. In private conversation, David Brodsky has noted the oddness of the midrash's inaccurate assumption that no animal species have binocular vision. Dogs and snakes, e.g., which are species with which the rabbis were familiar, both have binocular vision.

93. And see discussion of this text in Jonathan Wyn Schofer, *Confronting Vulnerability: The Body and the Divine in Rabbinic Ethics* (Chicago: University of Chicago Press, 2010), 170–76.

94. Where *Genesis Rabbah* understands sight as a purely visual phenomenon, *Avot de-Rabbi Natan* A sees sight as an important marker of a supernatural ability shared by angels and demons.

95. The date of *Pesiqta Rabbati* is difficult to determine. Rivka Ulmer, *A Bilingual Edition of Pesiqta Rabbati* (Berlin: De Gruyter, 2017), 28, has identified four "major stages in its textual development: (1) 4th century C.E. amoraic formation of rabbinic interpretations in the Land of Israel; (2) the collection of the core material, probably in the fifth or sixth century Land of Israel when the material was structured into a coherent work; (3) 'congealing' of the text into a fixed form in the 12th/13th century; (4) supplementing and expanding the text in the nineteenth century printed editions."

(mazziqin). Demons see human beings, but human beings do not see them. He created demons (mazziqin) and ministering angels. The ministering angels see demons, but demons do not see ministering angels. He created ministering angels, demons, and human beings. He sees everything, but none of these creations sees Him.[96]

As in *Genesis Rabbah*, the real focus in this text is on God and God's acts of creation. And as in *Avot de-Rabbi Natan* A, vision is a key feature of what it means to be a demon. But where the power inherent in vision is implied in *Avot de-Rabbi Natan* A, *Pesiqta Rabbati* makes it explicit and ties it not only to a taxonomy but also to a hierarchy of beings.[97] Here, for the first time, humans, demons, ministering angels, and God Godself, are explicitly ranked relative to one another. This hierarchy is interested in power and authority; the more a being can see and control who sees it, the more powerful it is. The goal of this text is to uphold God as the supreme power over all other beings in the universe.[98] Visibility and vision are inextricably bound up with divine power.

The rabbis of the Talmud certainly agree that power and visuality are connected. In their discussions about the demonic, the rabbis worry about the power imbalance that demonic mutability and invisibility can cause, a power imbalance all the more striking for the rabbis' insistence that demons are subject to rabbinic authority (see chapters 4 and 5). B. *Berakhot* 6a includes instructions for two rituals that one might perform if one wishes either to know without a doubt that demons exist or to see demons for oneself.[99]

One who wants to become aware of [demons]—let him take sifted ash and place it around his bed, and in the morning, he will see something like [the

96. *Pesiqta Rabbati* 6.

97. For this language, see Kidd, "Some Philosophical Demons," 221. Another rabbinic text to use vision as an arbitrator of status is the Palestinian homiletic midrash *Leviticus Rabbah* 4:8, in which the ability to see but not be seen is a key status marker of God and the human soul relative to the world and the body, respectively. Again, demons are absent from the discussion. Note, however, that demons *do* appear in *Genesis Rabbah* in other contexts, such as the discussion of demonic origins explored in chap. 1.

98. In fact, this tradition is explicitly attached to Ps. 92:6, "How great are your works, Oh Lord!"

99. This passage immediately follows an explicit discussion of the number and location of demons, discussed in more depth in chap. 4.

> prints from] a rooster's feet. One who wants to see them—let him take the placenta of a black female cat [who is] the offspring of a black female cat,[100] the firstborn of a firstborn, let him roast it in the fire and grind it down, and then let him paint his eye with it,[101] and he will see them. Let him also put [the ash] in an iron tube and seal it with an iron seal, lest [the demons] steal it from him. Let him also close his mouth, so that he does not come to harm. R. Bibi b. Abaye did so, saw them, and was harmed. The rabbis asked for mercy for him [i.e., prayed] and he was healed.

The Talmud lays out two rituals that allow the practitioner to know and see the demons who fill out their world. These rituals point to both the omnipresence and the hybridity of demonic bodies; demons apparently have chicken feet, a belief that also appears in b. *Gittin* 68b and is discussed in chapter 5.[102] Through these rituals, the rabbis circumvent the natural order of things and seize control of demonic visibility, both within the context of the ritual and within the context of the text. By writing about demonic bodies and ways to see them, the rabbis make these bodies visible to their followers through the rhetoric of description. Even if one does not perform the rituals described (and given its danger, one is probably advised not to try), by studying and repeating the tradition, one asserts the authority and ability of the rabbis and their followers to truly see demons, even when lived experience suggests otherwise.

While earlier rabbinic texts were interested in taxonomy, the rabbinic tradition found in b. *Ḥagigah* 16a and *Avot de-Rabbi Natan* A is the first to inscribe demons into its taxonomic project. These specific Amoraic texts are interested in describing demonic bodies and abilities as part of broader descriptions of bodies and abilities, in morally neutral ways.

100. On the specifical cultural valences of a black cat, see Beth A. Berkowitz, *Animals and Animality in the Babylonian Talmud* (Cambridge University Press, 2018), 147 n. 109.

101. Following Sokoloff, *A Dictionary of Jewish Babylonian Aramaic*, 678, s.v. מלי 1.

102. The association of demons with chicken feet may be simply a function of understanding their bodies as hybrid and as able to take flight—if they can fly they must have wings, and if they have wings they must have the matching feet. However, it is noteworthy that the ancient Mesopotamian evil goddess/demon Lamaštu is depicted as having "the feet of Anzu," i.e., bird talons. See Black and Green, *Gods, Demons and Symbols of Ancient Mesopotamia*, 116. This association of demons and birds' feet may have continued to be salient in late antique Babylonia. As discussed in chap. 5, rabbinic demonology aligns with ancient Mesopotamian demonology in a range of interesting ways. Perhaps this physical marker of the demonic is one of these ways. Yet we must not obscure the differences between these two demonologies: Lamaštu is one of only a few demons who are depicted as unequivocally evil in Mesopotamian demonology; for the rabbis, however, this morphology is found in neutral demonic beings.

As we have seen, the rabbis are not the only scholastic elite in late antiquity to categorize demons and other cosmic species. They are not the first nor even the second scholastic elite to enter into this project; in some ways, they come surprisingly late to the party. To understand how and why the rabbis begin to include demons in their taxonomic project, let us now put all three scholastic communities in conversation with one another.

TRIANGULATING LATE ANTIQUE DEMONS

This brief and highly selective exploration of late antique scholastic approaches to classifying daimones throws into sharp relief the distinctive discursive choices of the rabbis working to systematize the cosmos. All three scholastic elites see demons as real. They all think demons play a significant world in the cosmos as a whole and in the lives of human beings. They all believe that demons and other intermediary beings are physically superior to humans—that demonic bodies are either made of better stuff, or can be used to interact with the world in better ways than humans can. They also all believe that daimones/demons have more power and control over the universe than the average human being. Like Justin Martyr, Plutarch, Origen, Iamblichus, and others, the rabbis divide intermediary beings into at least two groups of beings. But unlike these thinkers, the rabbis are marked by their insistence on moral neutrality, their refusal to rank various intermediary beings, and the very lateness of their interest in classifying cosmic beings.

In *Avot de-Rabbi Natan* and the Babylonian Talmud, these beings are not ranked by their distance from God or their descent into a fallen state. They are not ranked at all. The rabbis in *Avot de-Rabbi Natan* A and the Babylonian Talmud do not distinguish between these two groups morally: angels are not marked as good, and demons are not marked as bad.[103] In fact, demons are *never* associated with the Devil or Satan in late antique

103. There are, however, Babylonian rabbinic discussions in which different angels are classed as either good or evil. See, e.g., b. *Shabbat* 119b, where two ministering angels accompany a man home from synagogue on Friday nights, one good and one evil. See also b. *Ta'anit* 11a; and see discussion in Tal Ilan, *Massekhet Ta'anit: Text, Translation, and Commentary* (Tübingen: Mohr Siebeck, 2008), 150–51.

rabbinic literature.[104] For the Amoraim and their redactors, demons are not opposed to angels but constitute their own unique part of a created world with a range of distinct and distinctive intermediary beings. They are their own distinct species, with no possibility that one kind of intermediary being could become another (as in Second Temple Jewish texts and Justin Martyr), or that humans could become daimones through theurgical practices (as in Iamblichus).[105] In this choice, the rabbis have more in common with Plato than they do with Justin Martyr or even Plutarch.[106] The rabbis appear to insist that, if demons originate in God's creation and God maintains total control over the cosmos, then demons must be just another part of the universe. And yet, where Plato insisted that all daimones are morally good, the rabbinic taxonomy is almost aggressive in its neutrality. The rabbinic taxonomy insists on moral neutrality even when the careful reader can see rabbinic resistance to the idea that human beings have anything in common with demons.

One remarkable element becomes clear when we triangulate the rabbinic interest in classifying demons with other late antique scholastic elites: namely, the time gap. Plutarch, Justin Martyr, Tatian, and even Origen did their taxonomic work in the first two and a half centuries of the first millennium, when the rabbinic Tannaim were active. The Tannaim, however, show no interest in recording taxonomic traditions about intermediary beings. It is only in a tradition which is likely Amoraic, and possibly quite late, that we begin to see rabbinic taxonomic impulses applied to angels and demons in an organized vision of the cosmos.

What can account for the time gap between when Greek and Christian scholastic elites begin to do this work and when the rabbis engage with it? Geographic factors may play a role here. These Greek philosophers and

104. This is in contrast to angels. B. *Baba Batra* 16a contains a tradition in the name of R. Shimon b. Laqish that "*Satan, the yeẓer hara, and the Angel of Death are all one.*" See also b. *Berakhot* 51a.

105. Note, however, b. *Sanhedrin* 109a, discussed in chap. 1, in which some sinful humans were transformed into demons as part of their punishment for building the Tower of Babel. In its context, this narrative is not part of a larger taxonomic discussion.

106. Shana Strauch Schick, "Reading Aristotle in Mahoza? Actions and Intentions in Rava's Jurisprudence," *Jewish Law Association Studies* 25 (2014): 262–91, has noted particular similarities between the legal thinking of fourth-generation Amora Rava and Aristotle. Schick, too, resists making an argument about causality, but notes striking overlaps and shared conclusions between this rabbi and one of the most famous Greek philosophers.

Christian theologians worked entirely in the Roman Empire, from Rome to Syria, Greece, Roman Palestine, and Egypt. Extant ancient Mesopotamian texts and the earliest Zoroastrian texts do not seem interested in classifying divine and intermediary beings. The impulse to classify creation appears to have crossed imperial borders into the Sasanian Empire only in the fourth or even fifth centuries C.E.[107] Writers began to translate the kinds of specialized knowledge produced by the scholastic communities of the west from Greek into Syriac in the fifth century. Much of this translation work took place in Edessa and Nisibis, on the border between the Roman and Sasanian Empires.[108] These translations of specialized, scholastic knowledge included taxonomies and classifications of the beings both visible and invisible in our world. It is perhaps no coincidence that it is during this period when the rabbis—members of a dynamic scholastic community with its own systems of specialized knowledge—themselves become interested in classifying intermediary beings. While the rabbis are rather late to the ancient-cosmic-classification game, they stake out a new position which overlaps with and diverges from the positions of other scholastic elites in late antiquity.

To be clear, I am not arguing that rabbinic taxonomy explicitly or intentionally rejects early Christian and Greek philosophical approaches. As we saw in the last chapter, rabbinic literature is the product of a complicated culture with a variety of conversation partners, including biblical and Second Temple traditions, Greek and Roman philosophy, early Christian texts, and, as we will see in later chapters, also Mesopotamian and Zoroastrian traditions. The impulse to classify the cosmos is one that was clearly shared by scholastic elites laying claim to elite, authoritative systems of knowledge. But in triangulating these three scholastic elites' taxonomies of intermediary beings, we can see the ways that different scholastic communities both held similar concerns and approaches, and manifested these concerns and approaches in very different time periods, geographies,

107. This is consistent with a broader trend identified by Kalmin, *Jewish Babylonia between Persia and Roman Palestine*. Kalmin identifies "the mid-fourth century as an important period when this shared culture between the empires began to manifest itself in Babylonian rabbinic literature, and . . . in changing rabbinic behavior as well" (174–175). See discussion in the introduction.

108. Hidemi Takahashi, "Syriac as the Intermediary in Scientific Graeco-Arabica: Some Historical and Philological Observations," *Intellectual History of the Islamicate World* 3 (2015): 68–69. My thanks to Shulamit Shinnar for this bibliographic suggestion.

and theological frameworks. A single benevolent class of daimones made sense as part of the benevolent and united cosmos constructed by early Greek philosophers. A highly bifurcated opposition between good and evil beings made sense to early Christian theologians both appropriating and rejecting the force and power of Greco-Roman religion, and presenting themselves as continuous with Second Temple traditions. And for the rabbis, morally neutral or benevolent angels *and* demons functioned to uphold God's omnipotence and benevolence, integrating the older traditions of angels and demons discussed in chapter 1 and setting themselves up as the sole purveyors of sacred truth in the busy marketplace of ideas.

In many ways, the rabbis and the late antique Greek philosophers were like two ships passing in the night. The rabbis had inherited traditions in which demons were evil angels, or at the very least evil, and had begun to neutralize them; the Greek philosophers had inherited traditions from Plato insisting that daimones were benevolent and had begun to allow space for evil demons. And early Christians, inheriting both types of traditions, insisted consistently that demons were, and always had been, entirely evil servants of Satan. These were not the only positions available to these scholastic elites. But they were the paths taken in this crucial period in late antiquity.

CLASSIFICATION MATTERS

Late antique scholastic elites attempted to understand the cosmos by classifying the beings found within it. Some of these classifications are hierarchical, where beings are ranked against one another. Others are simply neutral descriptions of different groups and categories. But why was classification such a powerful tool with which to make sense of the cosmos?

Scholars have noted that taxonomy and systematization are common features of oral culture.[109] Well-organized traditions are easier to remember and recite aloud. While it is certainly true that organization serves

109. On rabbinic literature, see, e.g., W. Sibley Towner, *The Rabbinic "Enumeration of Scriptural Examples": A Study of a Rabbinic Pattern of Discourse with Special Reference to Mekhilta D'R. Ishmael*, ed. J. C. H. Lebram (Leiden: Brill, 1973), 14–18, 23, 53–65.

mnemonic purposes, it also serves two complementary discursive aims: comprehensiveness and abstraction.

In the first century C.E., Pliny the Elder published his encyclopedic *Natural History*, a thirty-seven-volume work that catalogued the natural world as he understood it. Trevor Murphy has argued that the *Natural History*

> collects the phenomena of the universe and reassembles them as a universal Latin text, a book patterned after the vast empire that has made the universe available for knowing . . . the structure and content of the *Natural History* entwined with Roman political imperium in a relationship of mutual benefit, in that one of the functions of an encyclopedia is to embody how much is known and to demarcate it all from the perspective of central authority.[110]

The acts of cataloguing and classifying are never neutral but serve a range of ideological and theological interests. The ability to collect extensive information can be seen as a sign of the authority and knowledge of an author or a community. Although Pliny was a first-century Roman writer, these impulses continued into late antiquity. Andrew Jacobs argues that "one new mode of articulating Christian identity" that became popular in late antiquity involved refashioning "the Christian world in a newly comprehensive manner. This Christian view was comprehensive in two senses of the word: *totalizing*, seeking to gather together all that existed into clear and definable intellectual and cultural categories; and *knowing*, seeking to create a cognitive mastery of all that existed in the Christian world."[111] Jacobs points out that this type of comprehensive worldview

110. Trevor Morgan Murphy, *Pliny the Elder's "Natural History": The Empire in the Encyclopedia* (Oxford: Oxford University Press, 2004), 2. I first encountered Murphy's work in Aude Doody, "Pliny's *Natural History*: *Enkuklios Paideia* and the Ancient Encyclopedia," *Journal of the History of Ideas* 70, no. 1 (2009): 1–21; her excellent critique of the "encyclopedic" nature of the *Natural History* is an important reminder that generic terms have particular meanings and that our standpoints shape our conclusions. For Pliny's relationship to the rabbis in at least one sphere, see Giuseppe Veltri, "The Rabbis and Pliny the Elder: Jewish and Greco-Roman Attitudes toward Magic and Empirical Knowledge," special issue: Hellenism and Hebraism Reconsidered: The Poetics of Cultural Influence and Exchange, pt. 1, *Poetics Today* 19, no. 1 (1998): 63–89. My thanks to the anonymous reviewer who suggested I look at this ancient text.

111. Andrew S. Jacobs, *Remains of the Jews: The Holy Land and Christian Empire in Late Antiquity* (Stanford, CA: Stanford University Press, 2003), 23.

is not exclusive to late antique Christians. The modern colonial project was in many ways undergirded by attempts to classify colonized subjects according to castes, races, and religions.[112] Of colonial attempts to classify human beings in southern Africa, David Chidester writes, "The conceptual organization of human diversity into rigid, static categories was one strategy for simplifying and thereby achieving some cognitive control over the bewildering complexity of a frontier zone."[113] Intermediary beings exist in a different frontier zone, on the borders between humanity and the divine. Classification serves political aims, imposing new ways of knowing and being in contested territory.

Ellen Muehlberger and David Frankfurter have both argued that taxonomies can abstract the subjects to be classified.[114] Abstraction further shapes the knowledge and information to be categorized by creating distance between the categorizers and their subjects. Classification requires simplification, and, as Frankfurter notes, "abstracting immediate experience for the sake of cosmic structures."[115] All the thinkers examined here believed that demons can be both invisible and mutable. Demons have superhuman abilities but are chaotic and outside human control. An ostensibly comprehensive taxonomy was one way that these scholastic elites could restrain and fix that demonic mutability into a recognizable, controllable shape, to impose order and construct a newly understandable world. A wild force of nature is tamed and can now be put in a little box, a box that promises to hold its shape forever. Taxonomy is both totalizing and also limiting, a promise to followers that any new knowledge, if there ever is any, will conform

112. See Nicholas B. Dirks, *Castes of Mind: Colonialism and the Making of Modern India* (Princeton, NJ: Princeton University Press, 2001); David Chidester, *Savage Systems: Colonialism and Comparative Religion in Southern Africa* (Charlottesville: University of Virginia Press, 1996).

113. Chidester, *Savage Systems*, 21–22, quoted in Jacobs, *Remains of the Jews*, 23–24; Neis, *The Sense of Sight in Rabbinic Culture*, 173.

114. David Frankfurter, *Evil Incarnate: Rumors of Demonic Conspiracy and Ritual Abuse in History* (Princeton, NJ: Princeton University Press, 2006), 15–18; Muehlberger, *Angels in Late Ancient Christianity*, 207–12.

115. Frankfurter, *Evil Incarnate*, 27, cited in Muehlberger, *Angels in Late Antique Christianity*, 207.

to existing structures of information.[116] But as history has shown us, this is a promise often broken.[117]

A taxonomy was not only a way to construct intermediary beings along particular lines. It was also a way to construct the taxonomists themselves. In his exploration of the rabbis' efforts to categorize and classify magical practices, Joshua Levinson writes,

> This process of constructing magic as a discourse of knowledge, of creating knowledge about an inferior Other, places the Babylonian sages in a position of authority, structuring magic as an object to be known. As described by Edward Said, "to have such knowledge of a thing is to dominate it, to have authority over it. And authority here means for 'us' to deny autonomy to 'it'... since it exists as we know it."[118]

Insisting that one has the power and knowledge to accurately categorize such beings is one way of asserting control over classes of beings who are not only bewilderingly complex but also largely invisible. The unknown becomes known, the invisible made visible, and chaos is turned into order. Taxonomies are a crucial tool in the formation of a group *as* a scholastic elite with knowledge and authority over everything known and to-be-known. Demons' invisibility and their mutability made demons the perfect tool for the rabbis to use to interrogate the nature of humanity, the structure of the cosmos, and their own position in the world.[119]

The rhetoric of taxonomy shaves the edge off of potential danger by imposing order and obscuring uncertainty. In insisting that there is no danger, however, taxonomies run the risk of "protesting too much." And as the next chapter explores, the rabbis, like all late antique scholastic elites, were actually very aware of the dangers that demons could pose.

116. Muehlberger, *Angels in Late Ancient Christianity*, 207–08. On the rabbinic interest in this promise, see also James Adam Redfield, "Embedding, Sublation, Ambivalence: Ethnographic Techniques in Early Rabbinic Law," article circulated for a seminar at the annual conference of the Association for Jewish Studies, Washington, DC, December 2017.

117. Thomas S. Kuhn, *The Structure of Scientific Revolutions*, fiftieth anniversary edition (4th ed.) (Chicago: University of Chicago Press, 2012), 66–77.

118. Joshua Levinson, "Enchanting Rabbis: Contest Narratives between Rabbis and Magicians in Rabbinic Literature of Late Antiquity," *Tarbiz* 75 (2006): 295–328, 70–71, citing Edward W. Said, *Orientalism* (New York: Vintage Books, 1978), 32.

119. Andrew Jacobs, *Remains of the Jews*, 25, makes a similar argument about the Jew in the post-Constantinian Holy Land, a period in which Jews were also largely absent from the Palestinian landscape.

3 How to Avoid Demonic Dangers

Now I pierce the darkness, new beings appear,
The earth recedes from me into the night,
I saw that it was beautiful, and I see that what is not the earth
is beautiful.

Walt Whitman, "The Sleepers," *Leaves of Grass* (1855)

For all their taxonomic insistence that demons are neutral, the rabbis did not completely reject the belief that demons are also dangerous. Instead, they used demonic dangers to undergird their understandings of time, space, and bodily experiences. This chapter examines the ways that the rabbis named, located, and worked to avoid demonic dangers. When demons posed dangers, the rabbis shaped their lives to avoid such dangers, conditioning a particular and particularly rabbinic way of existing in a world filled with demons. In constructing demonic dangers, then, the rabbis also constructed what it meant to be a rabbinic person in the world.

Talmudic discourse about demonic dangers is found throughout the Babylonian Talmud; this chapter uses one extended passage, or *sugya,* in tractate *Pesaḥim* as its focal point and expands out from there. The tenth chapter of tractate *Pesaḥim* describes the ritual meal to be eaten on the first night of Passover. The Mishnah begins its chapter with the statement that *"one should have no fewer than four cups of wine"* as part of this ritual meal. The rabbinic redactors of the Babylonian Talmud use this mishnah as the springboard to an extended discussion of demonic dangers. This sugya is a loosely unified redaction particularly rich in rabbinic discourse about demonic dangers. In this and the following chapter, I discuss various aspects of the sugya in conversation with a range of other Talmudic texts. Here is that sugya in full. The divisions are my own to facilitate reading.

B. *PESAḤIM* 109B–112A[1]

Mishnah: *One should have no fewer than four cups of wine.*

[A1] How could our Rabbis institute something that would ultimately lead to danger? For surely it was taught in a baraita: *One should not eat in* even numbers, *or drink* in even numbers, *nor wipe himself* in even numbers, *nor fulfill his [sexual] needs* in even numbers.

[A2] *R. Naḥman b. Yitzḥak said: "It is a night that is guarded" (Exod. 12:42). It is a night that is guarded from the demons (mazziqin). Rava said: The cup of blessing [on which Grace after Meals is recited, i.e., the third cup] combines for good things but not for bad things.* Ravina said: Each cup is a separate commandment [and thus they do not combine to create a total number that is either odd or even]

> [A1.2] "*One should not fulfill his [sexual] needs* in even numbers." Has he not *newly decided [to engage in intercourse each time]?* Abaye said: It was taught thusly: *One should not eat* in even numbers *and [then] fulfill his [sexual] needs even once*, lest he become ill and bad things befall him.[2]

[A3] Our rabbis taught: *One who drinks in even numbers, his blood is upon his head [meaning, he takes his life into his own hands]. R. Judah said: When? When he has not gone out into the street [lit. seen the face of the market],[3] but if he has gone out into the street, he is permitted [to drink in even numbers].*

1. As a reminder, the text in Hebrew is marked by italics, and Aramaic language is marked by plain text. To make these linguistic shifts clear to the reader, I have chosen not to italicize transliterated foreign words in my translation of this text, though I continue to do so throughout my own discussion of the text.

My translation is based on MS Vatican 125. On b. *Pesaḥim*, I follow Stephen G. Wald, *B.T. Pesahim III. Critical Edition with Comprehensive Commentary* (New York: Jewish Theological Seminary of America, 2000), 274–82, in seeing MS Vatican 125 as part of a branch of manuscripts originating in Ashkenaz and the eastern Mediterranean that are more conservative than the manuscripts from Spain and Yemen.

2. Although it appears out of order, A1.2 is a dependent gloss on A1. I mark it as such by my numbering system and by my choice of indentation. See also A3.2.1 and A3.2.2 below.

3. Following Sokoloff, *A Dictionary of Babylonian Aramaic*, 445, s.v. חזי.

[A3.1] R. Ashi said: I saw that R. Ḥinena b. Bibi, [after] every cup, would go out into the market.

[A3.2] And this applies only to one who [plans] to set off on a journey [after drinking the even number of cups], but if he [plans] to stay home, it is not [harmful.]

[A3.3] R. Zeira said: And going to sleep is like setting off on a journey.

[A3.4] R. Papa said: And going out to the outhouse is like setting off on a journey.

[A3.2.1] "If he intends to stay home, it is not harmful"? Did Rava not count the beams [of his own home in order to keep track of the number of drinks he was drinking], and Abaye, when he would drink one cup, his mother would hold out to him two [more] cups in her two hands. [Similarly] R. Yitzḥak [b. R. Yehuda], when he would drink one cup, his attendant would hold out to him two cups in his two hands.

[A3.2.2] An important person is different [and more susceptible to harm].

[A4] *Ulla said: Ten cups are not subject to "even numbers."*

[A4.1] Ulla is consistent in his reasoning, for Ulla said, and some say it was taught in a mishnah: *ten cups were instituted by the sages in a house of mourning*. And if you should think *that ten were susceptible to "even numbers,"* would our rabbis have enacted something that would lead to danger? But for eight [cups], we do take care [about even numbers.]

[A4.2] R. Ḥisda and Rabbah b. R. Huna both said: *[The number seven, as represented by the seventh word] "Shalom" [in the priestly blessing of Num. 6:24–26], does not combine for evil [with one to make the number eight, so the number eight is not dangerous]*. But for six [cups], we do take care [about even numbers].

[A4.3] Rabbah and R. Joseph both said: *[The number five, as represented by the fifth word] "Vayehunekha" [in the priestly blessing] does not combine for evil [with one to make the number six, so the number six is not dangerous]*. But for four [cups], we do take care [about even numbers].

[A4.4] Abaye and Rava both said: *[The number three, as represented by the third word] "Vayishmerekha" [in the priestly blessing] does not combine for evil [with one to make the number four, so the number four is also not dangerous]*.

[A.4.4.1] And Rava followed his own approach, for Rava sent away the sages [from his home] after having four cups of wine. And even though Rabbah b. Levai was harmed, [it was] because [Rabbah b. Levai] used to answer back to [Rava] during his public lecture.

[A5] R. Joseph said: Joseph the demon (šeida) told me: Ashmedai the king of the demons (malka d'šeidei) is appointed over even numbers, and a king is not called a mazziq [harmer]. And some say, on the contrary, a king has the authority in his hands [to harm whomever he pleases].

[A6] R. [Papa] said: Joseph the demon (šeida) told me: For two we kill, for four we [only harm]. With two, [we punish] whether it was accidental or intentional [to drink an even number]; with four, if it was accidental, no, but if it was intentional yes. And if he happens to go out [having drunk even numbers], let him hold his straight right arm in his left arm [sleeve] and that of the left in his right arm [sleeve],[4] and let him say: You (pl.) and I are three. And if he hears someone say [You and I are] four, let him say, [You and] I are five. And if he hears someone say [You and I are] six, let him say, [You and I are] seven.

[A6.1] This once happened and when they reached one hundred and one, the demon (šeida) burst.

[A7] Amemar said: The head of the female witches said to me: If one comes upon female witches, let him say thusly: Hot excrement in a perforated basket to your mouths, you sorcerous women! A storm in your cooking pot,[5] may your flying things fly away, may your spices be scattered, may the wind blow away the new saffron that you are holding! As He has shown grace to me and to you, I never encountered you, but now that I have encountered you, you have cooled [toward me] and grace is upon you [and not upon me].

[A8] In the west, they are not particular about even numbers. In Nehardea (a rabbinic center in Babylonia), they are particular about even numbers. R. Dimi from Nehardea was particular even about the marks on a jug. The general rule on the matter is: Anyone who is particular [about even numbers], [the demons] are particular about him. Anyone who is not particular, they are not particular about him.

4. My translation here follows Sokoloff, *A Dictionary of Jewish Babylonian Aramaic*, 537, s.v. ימינא. Soncino, however, translates it as, "Let him take his right-hand thumb in his left hand and his left-hand thumb in his right hand."

5. Meaning of this clause uncertain. Soncino translates it as, "May you become bald."

[A8.1] When R. Dimi came, he said: *Two eggs, two cucumbers, two nuts, and something else are a halakhah from Moses at Sinai.* And the identity of the "something else" was doubtful to the rabbis, and so they decreed [that the law of evens applies] in all things.

[A4.5][6] And that which you said, that ten, eight, six and four are not susceptible to "even numbers," was only said in places where one does not have to be careful of witches, but in a place where one has to be careful of witches, we must be careful even of large numbers [that are even].

[A4.5.1] A certain man divorced his wife. She went and married the tavern-keeper at the [tavern] where [her ex-husband] regularly drank wine. Every day she would work witchcraft on him, but she could not affect him adversely because he was careful of even numbers. One day he drank a lot; up to sixteen cups he was sober and took care [of even numbers], but beyond that, he was not sober enough to take care, and she served him even numbers. When he went out, he met a certain Arab.[7] [The Arab] said to him: You are a dead man walking! He went and grasped a [palm] tree. The palm tree withered and exploded.[8]

[A9.1] *R. Avira said: Dishes, (cups),* [9] *and loaves of bread are not susceptible to even numbers.*

[A9.2] The general rule on the matter is: *We do not take particular care [about even numbers] with anything that was completed by human hands. Anything finished by God, however, we do take particular care [about even numbers].*

[A9.3] *Shops are not susceptible to even numbers.*

[A9.4] *If one changes his mind [and drinks another cup], he is not susceptible to even numbers.*

[A9.5] *A guest is not susceptible to even numbers.*

[A9.6] *A woman is not susceptible to even numbers. However, if she is an important woman, then she is susceptible to even numbers.*

6. Although they appear at this point in the sugya, this statement and the next appear to actually be responding to the discussion in A4.

7. On this figure, see Sara Ronis, "Imagining the Other: The Magical Arab in Rabbinic Literature," *Prooftexts* 39, no. 1 (2021): 1–28.

8. MSS Vatican 109, Munich 95, and Oxford Opp. Add. fol. 23 read "ופקע הוא" (and the man exploded).

9. This word appears only in MS Vatican 125, and in MS Vatican 109 where it has been crossed out. It makes no sense in the context of the sugya as a whole.

[A10.1] *R. Huna b. R. Joshua said: Ispargos [a drink made of fermented asparagus] combines [to make even numbers],* and some say*: It does not combine.* And they do not disagree, for the one is saying "for good" and the other, "for evil."

[A10.1.1] Ravina said in the name of Rava: [Even numbers are treated] leniently. [And some say: even numbers are treated stringently.][10]

[A10.2] R. Joseph said: Two [cups] of date beer and one of wine combine. Two [cups] of wine and one of date beer do not combine.

[A10.2.1] And your sign for this is as [the rabbis] taught: *This is the general rule: Anything which has attached to it something that is treated more severely than it is impure. Anything which has attached to it something that is treated more leniently is pure.*

[A10.3] R. Naḥman said: Two [cups] before the meal, and one during the meal combine. One [cup] before the meal, and two during the meal do not combine.

[A10.3.1] R. Mesharsheya raised an objection: Are we trying to fix the table? No, we are trying to fix the man. And surely the man stands fixed!

[A10.3.2] Yet everyone agrees that two during the meal and one after the meal do not combine, because of the incident of Rabbah b. Naḥmani.[11]

[A10.4] *R. Yehuda said in the name of Shmuel: Anything that is poured combines except for water. R. Yoḥanan said, even water.* R. Papa said: We only said this [in reference to water combined by] [pouring] hot water into cold, or cold water into hot, but hot water into hot, or cold water into cold, do not [combine].

[B] *R. Shimon b. Laqish said: There are four things, for which the one who does them, his blood is upon his head, and he pays with his life: One who turns aside between a palm tree and a wall to relieve oneself; one who passes between two palm trees; one who drinks borrowed waters; and one who passes over spilled waters, even if his daughter spilled them out in front of him.*

10. Vatican 109 and Munich 6 read "זוזי לקולא ואמרי לה זוזי לחומרא" (zuzim [coins] are treated leniently, and some say zuzim are treated stringently), which is a clear error in the context of the sugya. JTS Rab. 1608 (ENA 850), Oxford Opp. Add. fol. 23, Vatican 134, Columbia X893T14a, NY JTS 1623/2, Enelow Manuscript Collection 271, Cambridge T-S F1 (1) 116, and Sassoon 594 read "זוגי לחומרא ואמרי לה זוגי לקולא" (Even numbers are treated leniently. And some say: even numbers are treated stringently).

11. On this incident, see discussion in chap. 4.

[B1] The statements "*One who turns aside between a palm tree and a wall to relieve oneself, and one who passes between two palm trees,*" apply only if there were fewer than four amot between them, but if there were four amot [cubits] between them, then no [it is not harmful].

[B1.1] And even if there were fewer than four amot, this applies only if there was no other path, but if there were another path, then no [it is not harmful].

[B2] "*And one who drinks borrowed waters*" applies only when a minor borrowed it, but if an adult has borrowed it, then no [it is not harmful].

[B2.1] Even if a minor borrowed it, this applies only if [he borrowed it] in a field in which water was not common, but in the city [where water is common], no.

[B2.1.1] And in a field applies only about water, but wine or date-beer, no [these are not harmful.]

[B3] "*And one who passes over spilled water,*" applies only if he had not separated them with spittle or with dust, and if he had not separated them with the sun,[12] and had not separated from them sixty paces, and if he was not riding a donkey, and not wearing his shoes. But if he was riding a donkey and wearing shoes, then it is not harmful.

[B3.1] And these words apply where there is no need to be careful of witchcraft, but where there is a need to be careful of witchcraft, then even if one is riding a donkey and wearing shoes [it is still harmful.]

[B3.2] It once happened [that he was riding a donkey and wearing shoes] and his shoes were destroyed and his feet lashed.

[C1] *Our rabbis taught: There are three whom one should not allow to pass between him and a fellow, and whom one himself should not pass between, and these are the dog, the palm tree, and the woman. And some say: Also the pig. And some say: Also the snake.*

[C1.1] And if you allow them to pass between you, what should you do? *R. Papa said: Let him open with "Al" and let him end with "Al,"*[13] *or let him open with "Lo" and end with "Lo."*

[C1.2] When a menstruant woman passes between two men, if it was

12. MS Vatican 109 reads "לא נפל עלייהו שימשא אבל נפל עלייהו שימשא לית לן בה" (and the sun did not fall upon it, but if the sun fell upon it, then no [it is not harmful]).

13. My thanks to Galit Hasan-Rokem for her suggestion regarding this translation.

the beginning of her niddah period, she will kill one of them, and if it is the end of her niddah period, she will cause conflict between them.

[C1.3] When two women sit at a crossroads directing their glance at each other, they are [obviously] working witchcraft. If there is another road, let him go there. And if there is another man with him, let them grasp each other's hand and let them pass. And if there is no other man with him, let him say thusly: Agrat disappear! Asya Blusya,[14] let them be slain! Receive this in your bosom!

[C1.4] One who meets a woman when she is ascending from her ritual immersion [after her niddah period], if he is the first to have sex, the *demon (ruaḥ) Znunim [immorality]* seizes him. If she is the first to have sex, the *demon (ruaḥ) Znunim* seizes her. What is the solution?[15] Let him say thus: *"He pours contempt on great men and makes them lose their way in trackless deserts"* (Ps. 107:40, NJPS).

[C2] *R. Yitzḥak said: What is meant by the verse, "Though I walk through the valley of the shadow of death, I fear no harm [for You are with me (Ps. 23:4)]?" This refers to one who sleeps in the shade of a single palm tree, or in the moon's shadow.*

[C2.1] *"The shade of a single palm tree"* applies only when the shadow of its fellow did not fall upon it, but if the shadow of its fellow falls upon it, then no [it is not harmful].

[C2.2] *"The moon's shadow"* applies only in the west [Roman Palestine], but in the east [Sasanian Babylonia], it is not harmful.

[C2.3] And these words [regarding the palm tree] apply only about the field, but in the courtyard, even if the shadow of its fellow falls upon it, it is still harmful,

[C2.3.1] as it says in a baraita: *One who sleeps in the shade of a single palm tree and he is in a courtyard, his blood is upon his head.* In a courtyard, yes, but in a field, no. From this we learn that even if the shadow of its fellow falls upon it [in a courtyard], it is still harmful.

14. Based on MSS Vatican 109, JTS Rab. 1608 (ENA 850), Oxford Opp. Add. fol. 23, Vatican 134, Columbia X893T14a, NY JTS 1623/2, Enelow Manuscript Collection 271. This phrase could possibly be translated as "Blusya [meaning unknown] in your nostril, be killed!" But it is also possible that these are names of demons or *vocae magicae* without specific meanings.

15. On the word *tqnt'h,* which I have translated as "solution," see Monika Amsler, "Medical Theory + Grammar = Voces Magicae," paper presented at the Association for Jewish Studies annual meeting, San Diego, December 2019.

[C3.1] One who relieves himself on the stump of a date-palm tree, the demon (ruaḥ) Palga will seize him.

[C3.2] One who rests his head on the stump of a date-palm tree, the demon (ruaḥ) Ẓreida will seize him.

[C3.3] One who steps on a date-palm tree, if he is to be executed, he will be executed, if he is to be uprooted, he will be uprooted.

[C3.4] And what is the solution? Let him rest his feet upon it.

[C4.1] There are five shadows: the shadow of a single date-palm tree, the shadow of a lote tree, the shadow of a fig tree, the shadow of a caper bush, and the shadow of a zardata reed. And some say also the shadow of a ship and the shadow of a willow tree. The general rule of the thing is: any [tree] with many branches has harmful shadows. And any [bush] with many thorns has harmful shadows, except for the sorb tree.[16]

[C4.1.1] For a female demon [šidata] said to her son: Fly away from the sorb tree, for it is he who killed your father, and he will kill you too.

[C4.1.2] R. Ashi said: I saw R. Kahana separate himself from all shadows.

[C4.2] The [demons] of caper shrubs are [called] ruḥe. The [demons] of zardata reeds are [called] šeda. The [demons] of the roof are [called] rišpei.

[C4.2.1] The [demons] of caper shrubs are creatures that have no eyes.

[C4.2.1.1] What is the relevance of this [fact]? [One can] detour around it [the caper shrub without the demon seeing you].

[C4.2.1.2] One time, a Ẓurva de-Rabbanan[17] went to relieve himself among the caper shrubs. He heard it [a ruḥa] coming toward him and detoured around him. [The ruḥa] went and grasped a date-palm tree, attempting to harm it. The date-palm tree shouted and burst.

[C4.2.2] "The [demons] of zardata reeds are called šeda." These zardata reeds that are close to the city have no fewer than sixty demons (šeidei).

[C4.2.2.1] What is the relevance of this [fact]? For the writing of amulets.

[C4.2.2.2] A certain city official went and relieved himself near zar-

16. I have emended this word on the basis of MS Munich 95.
17. See discussion of this class of people below.

data reeds near a city. He became seriously ill. A certain one of the rabbis[18] who didn't know that zardata reeds are infested with sixty demons (šeidei) went and wrote an amulet for one [demon]. He heard that they had suspended a hinga [a musical instrument common in Babylonia] within [the reeds] and sang: That man's soudarion [neck cloth] is like that of our Rabbis, but when they examined him, [they discovered that] he did not [even] know "*Blessed art Thou*" [the traditional opening of many rabbinic blessings]. A certain one of our Rabbis who did know that the zardata reeds are infested by sixty demons (šeidei) wrote an amulet for sixty demons (šeidei). He heard them say: All of you, remove yourselves from here!

[C4.2.3] "The [demons] of the roof are called rišpei."

[C4.2.3.1] What is the relevance of this [fact]? For the writing of amulets.

[C4.3] *Qetev Meriri*: There are two *Qetevs*, one before noon and one after noon. The one before noon *is named Qetev Meriri*, ["deadly pestilence" (Deut. 32:24, NJPS)] and looks like a milk jug in which the stirrer turns around [of its own volition]. The one after noon *is named Qetev Yašud Ẓaharaim* ["the scourge that ravages at noon" (Ps. 91:6, NJPS)] and looks like a goat's horn, and it turns around like a sieve.

[C4.3.1] Abaye was once walking along with R. Papa to his right and R. Huna b. R. Joshua to his left. He saw a certain *Qetev Meriri* coming toward him from the left and switched R. Huna b. R. Joshua to his right side. R. Papa said: And what about me? [Abaye] responded: This is a propitious time for you [and you are protected].

[C4.4] From the cycle of Tammuz [the summer solstice][19] to the sixteenth [of Tammuz], [demons] are certainly common. From the sixteenth on, it is unclear whether or not they are common.

[C4.5] And they are common in morning shadows that are no shorter than a cubit. And [they are common in] evening shadows that are not a cubit long, and primarily, they are found in the shadows of the privy.

[C5.1] R. Joseph said: Three things make the eyes blind[20]: One who combs [his hair] when it is dry, one who drinks drop by drop, and one who puts on his shoes when his feet are still wet.

18. MSS Vatican 134 and Cambridge T-S F1 (1) 116 read Ẓurva me-Rabbanan.

19. Following Marcus Jastrow, *Dictionary of Targumim, Talmud and Midrashic Literature* (London: Luzac, 1903), 1690, s.v. תקופה.

20. Following Sokoloff, *Dictionary of Babylonian Aramaic*, 163, s.v. ארבונא.

[C5.2] [Foods] suspended in the house lead to poverty. And this applies only to bread, but meat and fish are not harmful. Bran in the house leads to poverty, crumbs in the house lead to poverty.

[C5.3] Demons (mazziqin) are let loose on Tuesday nights and Friday nights.[21]

[C5.4] The genius [a type of intermediary being][22] appointed over food is named *Naqid* [lit: clean, clear]. The genius appointed over poverty is named *Navil* [lit: defiled].

[C′5.2] A dish on the mouth of a pitcher leads to poverty. Drinking water from a plate[23] leads to cataracts.

[B′1] One who eats cress and does not wash his hands is afraid for three days. One who lets blood and does not wash his hands is afraid for seven days. One who cuts his hair and does not wash his hands is afraid for three days. One who cuts his nails and does not wash his hands is afraid for one day and does not know why he is so afraid.

[B′2] A hand on the cheek is a path to fear. A hand on the forehead is a path to sleep.

[A′1] *Food and drink under the bed, even if they are covered with an iron utensil, an evil demon [ruaḥ ra'ah] dwells upon them.*

[A′2] *Our rabbis taught: A man should not drink water on Tuesday nights and Friday nights, and if he did drink, his blood is upon his head.*

> [A′2.1] And if he is thirsty, what [should he do]? Let him say seven kolot (Ps. 29) and then drink.
>
> [A′2.2] And if not, let him say thusly: Lul Shafan, Anigron, Anirdefai. I dwell between the stars, [24] I become fat among the thin ones/the superior ones between the chasms.
>
> [A′2.3] And if not, if there is another person lying next to him, let him wake him up and say: Ploni son of Plonita, I am thirsty for water, and then let him drink.

21. Literally "the nights of the fourth and Sabbath [days]." Given that the rabbinic week starts on Sunday, and that rabbinic days start in the evening of the day before, this phrase is best translated as "Tuesday and Friday nights."

22. MSS Munich 6, Munich 95, Vatican 134 and Columbia X893T14a all offer instead some form of "שידא" (šeda).

23. I have emended the text here based on MSS Vatican 109, Munich 95, on JTS Rab. 1608 (ENA 850), Oxford Opp. Add. fol. 23, Vatican 134, Columbia X893T14a, NY JTS 1623/2, Enelow Manuscript Collection 271 and Cambridge T-S F1 (1) 116, which have "בצעא" (plate, flat dish).

24. So Sokoloff, *A Dictionary of Jewish Babylonian Aramaic*, 212, s.v. בי כוכבי-. Another possible translation is: I dwell among the great chasms.

[A′2.4] And if [there is no other person there], let him rattle the cover of the pitcher, and then let him drink.

[A′2.5] And if not, let him spit into [the waters], and then let him drink.

[A′3] *Our rabbis taught: One should not drink water from the rivers or the lakes at night, and if he does, his blood is upon his head, because of the danger.*

[A′3.1] What is this danger? The danger of day and night blindnesses.

[A′3.2] And if he is thirsty, what [should he do]? If he has a friend with him, let him say: [Ploni son of Plonit, I am thirsty for water,[25]]

[A′3.3] and if not, let him say to himself: Ploni son of Plonit, *your mother told you to be careful of shavriri [day and night blindness] vriri riri iri ri* in an unglazed cup.

The unit as a whole is structured as a loose and uneven chiasm.

A. Drinking liquids

B. Four things that put one in danger.

C. Demons and physical space

B′. Four things that make one afraid

A′. Drinking liquids

It begins and ends with an exploration of the demonic dangers inherent in drinking various liquids, and centers on an extended discussion of demons and space; this structure suggests an intentional strategy of organization. In centering this text on demons, the rabbis create a world in which demons constitute an organizing principle, underlying constructions of time, space, and the human body, even when at times they appear to recede from the text. Next I explore each of these themes with reference to their expressions within this core text and related rabbinic texts.

CONSTRUCTIONS OF TIME

While some might argue that time exists entirely independent of human experience, many sociologists, anthropologists, and religious studies

25. Emended on the basis of Munich 95, Oxford Opp. Add. fol. 23, and Vatican 134.

scholars have problematized this assertion. It is humans who organize time, divide it into units, and make it meaningful through stories, calendars, and rituals.[26] As Sarit Kattan Gribetz notes,

> the heavenly bodies—the sun, moon, stars, and planets—and related natural phenomena such as light levels and visibility, the tides, animal migrations, plant cycles, and so on, are used as points of reference and time markers through which calendars, festivals, and rituals are ordered, organized, and kept on schedule, but they are not, on their own, fully significant without the communal meaning and system of values attached to them.[27]

Late antique Sasanian Babylonia had a number of religious communities with their own calendars and ritual practices, as well as an official calendar used for government documentation.[28] These calendars overlapped and competed for meaning and communal adherence. For the rabbis of the Babylonian Talmud, "the communal meaning and system of values" attached to time was one in which demons played a prominent role. The rabbis "thought with" or through the demonic to help shape rabbinic time on a small scale—the hours of the day, the days of the week—and on a larger scale—the calendar year.

According to b. *Pesaḥim* 109b–112a [C4.3], the rabbinic day is divided by the two demons marking the position of the sun: the morning demon—*Qetev Meriri*—and the afternoon demon—*Qetev Yašud Ẓaharaim*. Both demons have bizarre, nonhumanoid appearances and are characterized by whirling motions.[29] The narrative which follows the Talmud's description of these demons further embeds these demons in time. According to the

26. Sarit Kattan Gribetz, "Time, Gender, and Ritual in Rabbinic Sources," in *Religious Studies and Rabbinics: A Conversation*, ed. Elizabeth Shanks Alexander and Beth A. Berkowitz (London: Routledge, 2017), 139–57, 139.

27. Gribetz, "Time, Gender, and Ritual," 141, discussing Durkheim, *The Elementary Forms of Religious Life*, trans. Joseph Ward Swain (London: Hollen Street Press, 1915), 10–17. Gribetz importantly notes the ways that, for the rabbis, gender played a role in different constructions and experiences of time. The texts discussed are written by a male audience for a male audience; even the discussion of Agrat bat Maḥlat imagines a female demon limited and controlled by powerful men. Human women are absent from the discussion.

28. Panaino, Antonio, et al. "Calendars," in *Encyclopædia Iranica Online* (1990), www.iranicaonline.org/articles/calendars.

29. These two demons are grounded in a rabbinic reading of Deut. 32:24 and Ps. 91:6. In Deut., Moses describes God's punishments for idolatry to the Israelites as "מְזֵי רָעָב וּלְחֻמֵי רֶשֶׁף וְקֶטֶב מְרִירִי; וְשֶׁן-בְּהֵמֹת, אֲשַׁלַּח-בָּם עִם-חֲמַת, זֹחֲלֵי עָפָר" (Wasting famine, ravaging plague, deadly pestilence

brief account, Abaye and his students R. Papa and R. Huna b. R. Joshua were out walking when a Qetev Meriri came toward them approaching R. Huna b. R. Joshua. Abaye immediately switched the positions of R. Papa and R. Huna, distancing R. Huna from the demon and bringing R. Papa closer, because he (correctly) noted that "this is a propitious time [lit: hour]" for R. Papa, who was therefore protected. Morning and evening are further differentiated in b. *Pesaḥim* by instituting distinctions between morning shadows and afternoon shadows as demonically dangerous. One must be appropriately aware of the position of the sun, the hours of the day, and one's own time as auspicious or inauspicious to both identify demonic dangers and successfully ward against them. But the dangers of daylight shadows are only a prelude to even more prominent dangers found in the dark of night.

According to the Talmud, nighttime has its own set of pervasive demonic dangers. Associations between demons and the night are common within the Babylonian Talmud and in the ancient world more broadly. According to a tradition cited in b. *Sanhedrin* 44a,

> *Once, when Joshua was near Jericho, he looked up and saw a man before him, drawn sword in hand. [Joshua went up to him and asked him: Are you one of us or of our enemies?] He replied: No, I am captain of the LORD's host. Now I have come!* [Josh. 5:13–14, NJPS]. How could he do this? Didn't R. Yoḥanan[30] say: *One is forbidden from greeting his fellow at night.* We take care, lest [the man greeted] be a demon (šeid). This case is different because he said to him: *I am the captain of the LORD's host.*[31] But maybe he lied? We have a tradition that these [demons] do not take the name of God in vain. [32]

Greeting a demon at night apparently provokes demonic dangers. Perhaps it is seen as an aggressive move requiring a demon to defend himself;

[Qetev Meriri], and fanged beasts will I let loose against them, with venomous creepers in dust [NJPS]). *Lamentations Rabbah* 1:29 offers further descriptions of the Qetev Meriri.

30. Note that in b. *Megillah* 3a, the teaching is attributed to R. Joshua b. Levi, a first-generation Palestinian Amora. The statement's Palestinian character is thus upheld, though the specific Amora is different. See discussion below about the Babylonian and Palestinian rabbinic approaches to the demonic.

31. Of course, Joshua greets the man before the man introduces himself and says that he is the captain of the Lord's host. Thus logically, Joshua would not have had the man's response to be able to know at this point whether the man was in fact human.

32. MS Florence II-I-9. This text is paralleled at b. *Megillah* 3a.

perhaps nighttime is the demons' time to roam free, and human beings' walking outside at night at all is itself an encroachment on this demonic domain. Demons, who (as discussed in chapter 2) can appear humanoid and who apparently need no biblical commandment to prevent them from using God's name in vain, mark the nighttime as particularly dangerous even for those just trying to offer a friendly greeting. Then what is a person to do? In the next passage in tractate *Pesaḥim*, the Tanna R. Judah the Patriarch commands the first-generation Amora Rav to *never* go out alone at night. Far safer to just stay home.

But dangers lurk even at home. According to b. *Berakhot* 5a, the third-century Palestinian Amora R. Isaac states that demons (mazziqin) keep their distance from all who recite the Shema in bed before they go to sleep. The statement assumes that without the Shema, demons will attack unsuspecting sleepers in their homes, in their very beds. R. Isaac's statement casts the recitation of the Shema in bed as a universally successful exorcistic practice, while framing the night and the vulnerability of sleep as particularly dangerous moments in the human experience. Although its demonic connection is today underplayed, this understanding of the Shema in bed continues to resonate in modern Jewish practice; bringing together the discussions in b. *Berakhot* 5a and b. *Pesaḥim* 109, many communities still have the custom of not reciting the Shema in bed on the first night of Passover because, as R. Naḥman b. Yitzḥak states, "*It is a night that is guarded from the demons (mazziqin).*"[33] Particular practices can protect people from nighttime demonic dangers. The twenty-four-hour cycle of the day contains particular demonic dangers marking its hours; rabbinic knowledge and practice serve to protect those in the know.

To safely and rabbinically navigate the world, one must be aware not only of the hour of the day but also of the day of the week. The anonymous voice of the Talmud in b. *Pesaḥim* specifies that demons "are let loose on

33. B. *Pesaḥim* 109b. For the survival of this practice into later Jewish law codices, see *Shulḥan Arukh Oraḥ Ḥayim* 481. For the ways that both the practice is encouraged and the demonic elements underplayed, see, e.g., Eliyahu Kitov, *The Book of Our Heritage: The Jewish Year and Its Days of Significance*, trans. Nachman Bulman and Ruth Royde, rev. Dovid Landesman, adapted and expanded ed. (1968; Feldheim, 1997), 635–36, which quotes the *Shulḥan Arukh* but leaves off its explanation as it relates to demons.

Tuesday nights and Friday nights." A gloss on R. Judah the Patriarch's prohibition on going out at night explains why:

> *"Do not go out alone [at night]"* as it is taught in a baraita: *One should not go out alone at night on Tuesday or Friday nights because Agrat bat Maḥlat goes out, and eighteen thousand myriads of destructive angels (malakhei ḥabalah) go out with her. And each of these [destructive angels] has individual permission to destroy [anything].* They used to be found [outside] every night. One time, she met R. Ḥanina b. Dosa and said to him: If they did not announce concerning you in heaven, "Be careful of R. Ḥanina b. Dosa, my son," I would certainly have put you in danger! He said to her: And if I am important in heaven, I decree upon you that you never pass through settled regions. She said to him: I beg you, leave me room! He left her Tuesday nights and Friday nights. Another time, she met Abaye. She said to him: If they did not announce concerning you in heaven, "Be careful of Naḥmani, my son," I would certainly have put you in danger! He said to her: If I am important in heaven, I decree that you never pass through settled regions.
>
> But we see that they do pass through! Those are the female gezita [demons] whose horses fell out from under them.[34]

According to this anonymous account, Agrat bat Maḥlat and her malevolent hordes used to menace the populace every night, but the rabbis' clever thinking and divine support limited her dangerous minions' roaming to only two nights a week, and even then only in certain regions. And yet the final gloss on the narrative destabilizes the negotiations described, suggesting that, in fact, some demons are at least accidentally in violation of the agreement and poised to harm human beings more broadly.

This tension—between limiting demonic dangers to two nights a week and undercutting those limitations—is seen elsewhere in the Babylonian Talmud. A baraita in b. *Ta'anit* 22b-23a explains when Israel obeys God's commands, they will be given "rain in their season" (Lev. 26:4, NJPS). An anonymous gloss explains that this phrase means that the earth will be fruitful even though it will rain only on Tuesday and Friday nights. These are the nights when demons roam, and good rabbinic Jews stay home—

34. B. *Pesaḥim* 112b–113a, translation of MS Vatican 125. It is possible that this means that these demons are out looking for their horses, or that they are lost in the public arena and cannot find their way home.

the perfect nights for copious amounts of rain! And yet a pseudo-baraita in b. *Pesaḥim* 109b–112a brings the danger indoors, prohibiting drinking water entirely on Tuesday and Friday nights; even at home, the danger still lurks.[35]

While Tuesdays and Fridays were particularly dangerous demonically, there might be a range of demonic dangers on other nights of the week depending on the season. According to the anonymous voice of the *Pesaḥim* passage that is the focus of this chapter, demons are particularly common in the height of summer from the first of Tammuz to the sixteenth of Tammuz, the day before the fast of the seventeenth of Tammuz, though they may persist even past the sixteenth [C4.4]. B. *Gittin* 70a also discusses the dangers of this period. There, R. Joshua b. Levi is recorded saying that if one eats beef with turnips and then sleeps in the moon on the nights from the summer solstice to the sixteenth of Tammuz, he is liable to great danger. Although this scenario is oddly specific, it highlights a persistent belief that this time period is particularly dangerous.[36] Curiously, a fifth-century Palestinian midrash in Lamentations Rabbah describes the period from the fast of the seventeenth of Tammuz to the fast of the ninth of Av as a time in which the *Qetev Meriri* demon roams, particularly in the

35. On the debate over the authenticity of some of the baraitot in the Babylonian Talmud, see Jacobs, "Are There Fictitious Baraitot in the Babylonian Talmud?" According to Friedman, "'Wonder Not at a Gloss in Which the Name of an *Amora* Is Mentioned'," 103, "there are *baraitot* from the Tosefta which are parallel to the language of the Mishnah with some enhancements and treatments, there are *baraitot* which are entirely or in part late Babylonian, and there are *baraitot* which are designed according to the sayings of the Amoraim, and are not Tannaitic *baraitot* at all." This phenomenon was already noted by Jacob Nahum Epstein, *Mavo Le-Nusakh Ha-Mishnah*, 2 vols. (1948; Jerusalem: Y. L. Magnes, 1999), 171–77. Significantly more work has been done on the pseudo-baraita in rabbinic narratives. See, e.g., Jeffrey L. Rubenstein, *Talmudic Stories: Narrative Art, Composition, and Culture* (Baltimore: Johns Hopkins University Press, 1999), 262. I do not assume that all baraitot that have no parallels in Palestinian materials are Tannaitic, or that they are all invented Babylonian fictions. They may well be Tannaitic traditions that are absent from Palestinian Tannaitic compilations, or Tannaitic traditions that have undergone Babylonian editing to bring them in line with Babylonian rabbinic cultural concerns. This point has also been made by Kalmin, *Migrating Tales*, 90–92. In light of supporting linguistic and thematic evidence for a later Babylonian context, however, the designation of these baraitot in b. *Pesaḥim* as "pseudo-baraitot" invented by later Amoraim or by the *Stam* and patterned after authentic baraitot seems reasonable. See also discussion in chap. 1, n. 30.

36. This time period overlapped with a period of cultic mourning across the region for the god Dumuz (Tammuz in Babylonian). See Ezekiel 8:14–15; and see chap. 5 n. 54.

hours of midday.[37] Both rabbinic communities believed that the summer months were particularly dangerous. Yet it appears that the Palestinian rabbinic community tied that danger to the period between the two ritual fast days, while the Babylonian rabbinic community did not.

To successfully navigate one's daily existence, one must therefore be constantly aware of the time of day, time of week, time of year, and one's own personally propitious times as they relate to demons. This awareness was sometimes linked to the ritual calendar articulated in the Hebrew Bible and earlier rabbinic literature. Often it was not, and would therefore have required a new set of expert knowledge. At least theoretically, this expert knowledge shaped the way that one interacted with the passage of time from hour to hour, month to month, and year to year, creating a Babylonian rabbinic experience of time. And together with the rabbinic imbrication of the demonic with space and the body, these texts shaped the ways that a follower of the rabbis would, or at least should, move through a wider and much-contested world.

CONSTRUCTIONS OF SPACE

Like time, space does not exist outside of its interactions with humans and other beings. Doreen Massey argues that we must understand space as "the product of interrelations; as constituted through interactions, from the immensity of the global to the intimately tiny... [We must understand space] as always under construction. Precisely because space on this reading is a product of relations-between, relations which are necessarily embedded material practices which have to be carried out, it is always in the process of being made."[38] In a world that rabbinic Jews in Babylonia shared with non-rabbinic Jews, and also with Zoroastrians, Manichaeans, Mandaeans, Christians, and worshippers of ancient Mesopotamian gods,

37. How to define these midday hours is debated in this text. See *Lamentations Rabbah* 1:29.

38. Doreen Massey, *For Space* (London: Sage, 2005), 9. See also Michel de Certeau, "'Spaces' and 'Places,'" in *The Practice of Everyday Life*, trans. Steven Rendall (Berkeley: University of California Press, 1984), 117–30; Yi-Fu Tuan, *Space and Place: The Perspective of Experience* (Minneapolis: University of Minnesota Press, 1977).

space was never neutral but was always the site of multiple contested narratives and experiences. And, as with time, one way that the rabbis made space their own, privileging certain spaces and spatial experiences as uniquely rabbinic, was by using demons as their framing device.

The late antique Babylonian rabbis drew a map of their world using the presence of demons as its lines and points of interest. The rabbis used demons to mark both the peripheries and the centers of their world. These spaces were domestic (homes and hearths, and bathrooms), but they could also be communal or even global (bathhouses, study halls and rabbinic assemblies, and borders and distant lands). And using demons as their guide, they created a distinctive instruction manual on how to move through this world replete with communities visible and invisible.

Maximally, demons marked the distant, the peripheral. The anonymous voice in the *sugya* in b. *Pesaḥim* notes that fields are particularly dangerous spaces for drinking borrowed water; demonic dangers abound. The association of demons and fields was one that the rabbis shared with the professional ritual experts who wrote Babylonian incantation texts. These texts contained long lists of demons to be repelled—including many demons who "dwell in the fields."[39] Similarly, an anonymous discussion in b. *Berakhot* 3a–b explains that "demons (mazziqin) are commonly found" in fields, decrepit buildings, and ruins. Demons are found in areas isolated, distant, or abandoned. Although decrepit and abandoned buildings might be found anywhere, for the rabbis their very abandonment places them at the edge of human settlement.[40] B. *Berakhot* then offers a solution

39. Bo 38:3, ib 67:5, 100:5, 129:4, 130:2, in Michael Sokoloff, *A Dictionary of Jewish Babylonian Aramaic*, 313, s.v. דברא. See also Lorenzo Verderame, "Demons at Work in Ancient Mesopotamia," in *Demons and Illness from Antiquity to the Early-Modern Period*, ed. Siam Bhayro and Catherine Rider (Leiden: Brill, 2017), 67. These texts are discussed in more depth in chap. 6. See Sara Ronis, "Space, Place, and the Race for Power: Rabbis, Demons, and the Construction of Babylonia," *Harvard Theological Review* 110, no. 4 (2017): 588–603, 590–93 for a more extensive discussion of these texts.

40. In b. *Niddah* 17a, the anonymous voice associates cemeteries, another boundary of human settlement and life more generally, with a particular demon, *ruaḥ tum'ah* (lit: the demon of impurity). This teaching is likely based on t. *Terumot* 1:3, which describes one who sleeps in a cemetery as legally incompetent. The Babylonian Talmud appears to take a Tannaitic source about legal incompetence and turn it into a source about demonic harm. My thanks to Sahar Segal for suggesting this source. Curiously, this discussion in b. *Niddah* 17a is the only example I can find in the Babylonian Talmud in which a demon is explicitly

to the danger: traveling in groups of two or more, destabilizing the isolation of these spaces in order to traverse them safely.

Demons construct the boundaries of human settlement; they also construct the boundaries and character of rabbinic settlement. Twice in b. *Pesaḥim* 109–112a, the rabbis use the demonic to distinguish between the rabbinic community in Sasanian Babylonia and that of Roman Palestine. One instance amplifies the dangers of Roman Palestine while protecting the Babylonian community: "[the danger of demons who dwell in] 'the moon's shadow' applies only in the west [Palestine], but in the east [Babylonia], it is not harmful." The other instance locates demonic dangers almost exclusively in Sasanian Babylonia: "In the west, they are not particular about even numbers. In Nehardea, they are particular about even numbers . . . The general rule on the matter is: Anyone who is particular [about even numbers], [the demons] are particular about him. Anyone who is not particular, they are not particular about him." While according to this sugya, the Palestinian rabbis appear to be susceptible to a single type of demonic danger, the Babylonian rabbis have, by their very interest in the demonic, invited a much broader range of demonic attentions into their own home communities, especially into the rabbinic center at Nehardea. The prevalence of demonic attention is shaped by, and shapes in turn, the ways that the Babylonian rabbis integrate demons into their worldview; it constructs an exclusive set of dangers and potentialities inherent to the rabbis of Babylonia. The quality and quantity of demonic attention are thus important ways that the Babylonian rabbis distinguished themselves and their community from their Palestinian coreligionists.[41]

Within the borders of the Babylonian rabbinic community, demons are found in particular privileged places: the *be rabbanan* (a local place of advanced study associated with a particular rabbi), and the *kallah* (the periodic rabbinic assembly, which gathered rabbis from across Babylonia

associated with corpses and corpse impurity. See chap. 4 for a more sustained discussion of demons and corpse impurity in parallel Zoroastrian texts.

41. Notably, the Palestinian rabbis also distinguish between themselves and the Babylonian rabbis when it comes to invisible dangers, though this time it is the evil eye who attacks those in Babylonia, and spares those living in the Roman West. See p. *Shabbat* 14:3, 14c, and the discussion in Ronis, "Space, Place, and the Race for Power," 600.

for an extended communal study session). A narrative in b. *Qiddushin* 29b (discussed in depth in chapter 6) describes the destruction of a particularly malevolent demon who lived in the be rabbanan of Abaye, a fourth-generation Amora associated with the rabbinic center at Pumbedita.[42] In another conversation about demons, this same Abaye is reported to have taught that "the pressure at the kallah is from them, and the wearying of one's knees is from them, and the wearing out of the garments of scholars is from [the demons'] rubbing, and the bruising of one's feet is from them" (b. *Berakhot* 6a).[43] Demons are located at the center of the rabbinic world, in the very places where rabbis and their followers are found. The presence of demons in these rabbinic spaces affects the clothing and the very bodies of the rabbis who study there. These places are imbued with meaning both visible (Torah and community) and invisible (demons).

While demons are found at the communal center of the rabbinic world, they are also found at the domestic center of the rabbinic world, in the rabbinic home. Rabbinic discussions of demons and the rabbinic home pull in two directions. On the one hand, the home is a place of relative safety from demonic danger, as the requirement to stay home on Tuesday and Friday nights, discussed above, makes clear. Indeed, the rabbis insist in the extended b. *Pesaḥim* passage above [A3.2] that drinking an even number of drinks is only provocative to demons if one "intends to set off on a journey [after drinking the cups], but if he intends to stay home, it is not [harmful.]" This statement suggests that homes are places protected from the demonic dangers of even numbers. On the other hand, this statement is immediately undercut by statements that extend this very danger back into one's domestic life [A3.3, A3.4, and A3.2.1–2]. R. Zeira states that going to sleep immediately after drinking four cups is "like setting off on a journey." R. Papa insists that "going out to the privy is like setting off on a journey." As we will see, the privy or outhouse was also a danger-

42. See, e.g., b. *Pesaḥim* 52a; b. *Ketubot* 111a. This association is heightened in *Iggeret Rav Sherira Gaon*, which identifies Abaye as the *Nasi* of the yeshiva at Pumbedita. This identification may well be anachronistic.

43. On the development of the be rabbanan and the kallah, see David Goodblatt, "The History of the Babylonian Academies," in *The Cambridge History of Judaism*, ed. Steven T. Katz (Cambridge: Cambridge University Press, 2008), 4:821–39. This passage is discussed in depth in chap. 6.

ous place in its own right. These two rabbis extend the meaning of going on a journey and so open up demonic danger to even one who is staying home. Finally, the anonymous voice describes the practices of three Amoraim, Rava, Abaye, and R. Yitzḥak b. R. Yehuda, who took precautions against the dangers of even numbers inside their own homes, because "an important person is different [and more susceptible to harm]." A later statement that "a guest is not susceptible to even numbers" [A9.5] focuses even more fully on the dangers to individuals precisely within their *own* homes. Rabbinic discourse thus largely protects people from demonic danger inside their own homes (at least while awake), while at the same time insisting that rabbinic homes are more dangerous than non-rabbinic homes. When a rabbi lets his guard down, even in a place that should be safe, demons attack. Demonic attention is most targeted toward the most important people—the rabbis themselves. This demonic danger marks certain homes as rabbinic homes and requires an extra degree of attention and self-discipline within these powerful and powerfully fraught spaces.

Within the domestic sphere, as within rabbinic mapping more broadly, the rabbis use demons to mark both the center and the periphery. The rabbinic home is a center of domesticity and vulnerability, especially at one's table and in one's bed. As R. Papa suggests above, the privy is another key space of human domestic vulnerability more broadly. A semi-public space in which private bodily functions occur, the privy is a fraught location for the rabbis for two reasons: the absence of angelic protectors and the presence of privy demons.[44] B. *Berakhot* 60b offers two versions of a rabbinic prayer to the guardian angels who wait outside the privy while the person they guard relieves themself. The assumption is clearly that angels cannot or will not themselves enter this space.[45] While we might have assumed that people would have been grateful for the privacy, that privacy was not guaranteed. For the rabbis, another class of intermediary beings does join us in outhouses: the demons of the privy.[46] These demons

44. For an extensive discussion of this passage and the concept of guardian angels, see Gerald Septimus, "On the Boundaries of Prayer: Talmudic Ritual Texts with Addressees Other Than God" (PhD diss., Yale University, 2008), 24–91, esp. 50.

45. Septimus, "On the Boundaries of Prayer," 33–44.

46. Ibid., 50.

dwell both inside privies and also in the shadows cast by privies.[47] B. *Shabbat* 67a gives the privy demon a name, Bar-Širiqa Panda; according to a pseudo-baraita in b. *Gittin* 70a, he can cause a man to have epileptic children.[48] These demons cause real harm to unsuspecting excreters and their offspring. For the rabbis, then, going to the privy is a delicate balance of personal modesty and safety in numbers. According to b. *Berakhot* 62a,

> *R. Tanḥum b. Ḥanilai said: Anyone who behaves modestly in the privy is saved from three things: from snakes, from scorpions, and from demons (mazziqin). And some say: And also his dreams will be peaceful.* There were certain privies in Caesarea where, if two people entered together even during the day, they would be harmed. R. Ami and R. Assi used to enter one separately and they were not harmed. The rabbis said to them: Are you not afraid [to enter the privy alone]? They said to [the rabbis]: We have received a certain teaching. The mother of Rami b. Ḥama said to him: Do not allow another man to go with you to the privy. He said to them: I [too] have received a tradition. And what is the tradition that they [all] received? They received that the privy is a place of silence and modesty [and thus one must enter alone], and that sufferings are a time for silence and asking for mercy. The mother of Abaye raised a lamb. She told him to take it with him to the privy. Better she had raised a goat for him! [No, because] *a satyr [demon-goat, se'ir]* might transform *into a goat* [*se'ir*] [and attack Abaye]. Before he ascended to the head of the academy, when Rava used to go to the privy, R. Ḥisda's daughter used to rattle nuts in a bowl. When he became head of the academy, she made a window for him, and rested her hand on his head [so that he would not be alone].[49]

Only in the privy, a space where nudity and the public gaze intersect, might concerns for modesty override the general rule that there is safety in numbers (see above). But the danger still remains; it is women who provide the creative solutions that save the rabbis from these demonic dangers. Although the privy is a crucial space for rabbinic bodily functions, it is thus marked as peripheral to the rabbinic person: absent of guardian angels, absent of other rabbis, and even absent of rabbinic ingenuity.

As much as the rabbis used their understanding of demons to create

47. B. *Pesaḥim* 111b.

48. See the excellent discussion of this demon in Bamberger, "An Akkadian Demon in the Talmud."

49. My translation here is of MS Munich 95.

a particular kind of map of their world, they also used demons to create a blueprint for how rabbis should move within this mapped world. The prayers and practices required to safely negotiate the privy are one way that the rabbis conditioned a particular kind of ritual and bodily orientation to the spaces that they inhabited. In b. *Pesaḥim* 109b–112a, this orientation is further conditioned by the rabbinic discussion of trees and plants and their respective shadows. The Babylonian rabbis believed that some demons lived in trees and other flora. Specific demons were associated with specific plants, thus "the [demons] of caper shrubs are called ruḥe. The [demons] of zardata reeds are called šeda" [C4.2]. Interacting with particular trees in ways that could be interpreted as aggressive would lead these tree-dwelling demons to react and attack the perceived aggressor: "One who relieves himself on the stump of a date-palm tree, the demon (ruaḥ) Palga will seize him. One who rests his head on the stump of a date-palm tree, the demon (ruaḥ) Ẓreida will seize him" [C3.1–2]. These were apparently seen as aggressive acts, and the demons who are being urinated on and encroached upon are likely to lash out and harm the encroachers. And to be fair, even humans are likely to get aggressive if someone urinates on them.[50] If one has unintentionally interacted with

50. Human urine is seen as offensive or polluting in Zoroastrian tradition as well, but in a somewhat opposite way. As Mary Boyce notes, "The general theory concerning such defilements was that everything leaving the [human] body (such as blood, excrement, spit, breath), whether naturally or through illness or injury, was impure... One had to urinate squatting, so as to limit the area contaminated (*Vd.*, Pahl. *Vd.* 18.40–43; *Ṣad dar-e naṯr* 56), and great care was to be taken with hair combings and parings of nails" (Mary Boyce, "Cleansing. I. In Zoroastrianism," in *Encyclopædia Iranica Online* (1992, 2012 updated online), www.iranicaonline.org/articles/cleansing-i). According to the *Pahlavi Rivayat Accompanying the Dādestān ī dēnīg* 11.3, e.g., "(If) someone urinates standing, then (it is) one tanāpuhl sin for him; and (if) someone urinates one span and two inches across the sole of the foot, then (it is) one tanāpuhl sin for him" (in A. V. Williams, *The Pahlavi Rivayat Accompanying the Dādestān i Dēnīg* [Copenhagen: Royal Danish Academy of Sciences and Letters, 1990], 23). The goal was to limit the area in which urine might spray. Williams notes the specific demonic resonances of this prohibition: "According to Vd. 18.40–44 this is a sin which makes the demon Drug pregnant, because it pollutes the earth more than is necessary" (*Pahlavi Rivayat Accompanying the Dādestān i Dēnīg*, 144 n. 4). This attitude toward urine is specific to human urine; cow's urine, *gōmēz*, was understood to be a purificatory substance which repelled death-contamination, menstrual impurity, and the accompanying malicious demons. In Zoroastrian thought, bull urine is offensive to demons, while human urine serves as an attractant to them and a way to multiply the demonic forces. By contrast, the rabbis see human urine as offensive to demons (as it presumably would be to humans) and do not raise the possibility of animal urine at all.

a tree in one of these ways, there is only one remedy: "And what is the solution? Let him rest his feet upon it" [C3.4] This gesture presumably shakes off the seizing demon while demonstrating human superiority and control.

The rabbis also required their followers to leave a certain degree of distance from flora to appear nonthreatening to demons. According to a baraita associated with R. Shimon b. Laqish, turning aside between a palm tree and a wall to urinate and passing between two palm trees are both dangerous acts and the one who does them, "his blood is upon his head and he pays with his life" [B]. Even urinating too close to a tree was seen as aggressive and likely to provoke a response. Yet the anonymous gloss on these statements weakens the danger, explaining, "The statements '*One who turns aside between a palm tree and a wall to relieve oneself, and one who passes between two palm trees,*' applies only if there were fewer than four amot between them, but if there were four amot between them, then no [it is not harmful]" [B1]. Four amot is a common legal measurement in the Babylonian Talmud that often marks an individual's legal expectation of personal space.[51] According to this text, demons apparently also thought it was the smallest distance which signaled nonaggression. Trees and plants and their demonic inhabitants were dangerous and required a particular spatial awareness to negotiate. Where today we might imagine a walk in nature as peaceful and restorative, the rabbis' map of the world made it fraught, dangerous, and requiring continual hyperawareness of everything around them. No wonder, then, that the rabbis thought it was safer to just stay home, at least for most people most of the time.

Even the shadows cast by trees and other plants were understood to be part of a demon's personal space and thus demonically dangerous. According to the anonymous voice in b. *Pesaḥim*, "There are five shadows: the shadow of a single date-palm tree, the shadow of a lote tree, the

51. See "Arba Amot, Shi'ur," in vol. 2 of the *Encyclopedia Talmudit*. The importance of this unit of measurement is paralleled in the Zoroastrian *Šāyest nē Šāyest* 4:10, in Jehangir C. Tavadia, *Šāyast-Nē-Šāyast: A Pahlavi Text on Religious Customs* (Hamburg: Friederichsen, de Gruyter, 1930), 89, which discusses the unit of "four steps." The parallel is discussed in more depth by Kiel, "Redesigning *Tzitzit* in the Babylonian Talmud in Light of Literary Depictions of the Zoroastrian *Kustīg*," 199.

shadow of a fig tree, the shadow of a caper bush, and the shadow of a zardata reed. And some say also the shadow of a ship and the shadow of a willow tree" [C4.1]. The ship is the clear outlier in this list; perhaps the wood that ships were made of was imagined to bring its demons along with it. The rabbis expand the danger further: "The general rule of the thing is: any [tree] with many branches has harmful shadows. And any [bush] with many thorns has harmful shadows, except for the sorb tree." This same anonymous voice interweaves shadow-space and -time, "And they are common in morning shadows that are no shorter than a cubit. And [they are common in] evening shadows that are not a cubit long" [C4.5]. Trees with harmful shadows required continual care and avoidance; R. Ashi reports having seen R. Kahana "separate himself from all shadows" [C4.1.2]. Being expected to carefully navigate a world in which shadows were the extensions of demonic homes cultivated a constant and specific temporal-spatial awareness.

Paradoxically, while shadows were understood to be an extension of the tree itself, a marker of the demon's personal space, they were also understood to mark a demon's potential escape route from human aggression. R. Yitzḥak attributes particular danger to one who "sleeps in the shade of a single palm tree" [C2]. If demons live in trees and see shadows as an extension of their personal space, a single tree's shadow would leave nowhere for a demon to comfortably run when a human gets too close. This reading is supported by the continuation of the anonymous gloss: *"The shade of a single palm tree"* applies only when the shadow of its fellow did not fall upon it, but if the shadow of its fellow falls upon it, then no [it is not harmful]. And these words [regarding the palm tree being safe if its shadow overlaps with another's] apply only about the field" [C2.1–3]. If one shadow is dangerous, one might think that two overlapping shadows would double the danger. But instead, this passage suggests the opposite: that when a human encroaches upon demonic space, if the demon can easily flee from one tree to another by jumping from shadow to shadow, the demon will choose to do so rather than lash out in self-defense. When there is much room to escape, as in a field, a demon will attempt to avoid conflict and will instead flee, "but in the courtyard, even if the shadow of its fellow falls upon it, it is still harmful" [C2.3.1]. When demons are cramped and crowded together, there may not be room for one to flee safely, a fact that can lead to their self-defense through violence.[52] Demons are fundamental to rabbinic understandings of space, but we can begin to see how this construction of space also constructs demons as relatively shy, passive, and neutral unless provoked, a characterization discussed in more depth in the next chapter.

To paraphrase Massey, for the rabbis, space *was* always under construction, and demons were one of the tools that the rabbis used in this construction project.[53] The rabbis created a map in which spaces at the center and periphery were made meaningful through the presence and absence of demons. This rabbinic map was deeply embedded in a rabbinic worldview. Demons marked these spaces *as* rabbinic, and perhaps even exclusively rabbinic, in a diverse and multicultural world. Even the Ẓurva de-Rabbanan, someone belonging to a scholarly class that existed between the rabbis and non-rabbinic Jews, and whose name suggests that its members looked up to or affiliated with the rabbis, is not aware of all the demonic dangers and how to navigate them.[54]

In creating a particular understanding of space as shared by demons and human beings, with all the dangers attendant in such an understanding, the rabbis shaped a particular way of moving through the world: moving while continually aware of rabbinic teachings about demons and how to avoid provoking their aggression. In discussing Greece in the fifth-century B.C.E., Ruth Padel writes:

> For most people, the daemonic, like snakes in the house, was a basic fact of life, unexamined, shared by all in their own way while they got on with living... The fifth-century world is "naturally" charged with gods... as radically as ours is with pollutant chemicals, radioactivity, bacteria, electricity, television waves. We do not think continuously of these forces in the world around and in us, yet we know they are there.[55]

52. For an extended discussion of this passage, see Ronis, "Space, Place, and the Race for Power," 593–96.

53. Massey, *For Space*, 9.

54. N.m., meaning and etymology unclear, this word is found only in the phrase Ẓurva de-Rabbanan. See Sokoloff, *A Dictionary of Jewish Babylonian Aramaic*, 956–57, s.v. צורבא. For other Talmudic instances of the Ẓurva de-Rabbanan in which his intermediate class is evident, see b. *Baba Batra* 22a; b. *Beiẓah* 16b; b. *Bekhorot* 35b; b. *Berakhot* 16a; b. *Shabbat* 151b; b. *Ta'anit* 4a.

55. Padel, *In and Out of the Mind*, 139–40.

And yet, one thousand years later, the Babylonian rabbis did attempt to cultivate a continuous thought process which took seriously a demon-filled world and determined the ways that rabbinic followers could and indeed had to move through that world. It is not clear that the rabbis ever thought that this degree of knowledge was possible for the average Babylonian, or even the average Babylonian Jew. This was specialized knowledge, and it shaped a special kind of actor in the world—a rabbi.

CONSTRUCTIONS OF THE BODY

To take action based on specialized knowledge requires the production of a specialized body. And a specialized body is one partly formed through the bodily practice of eating and maintained though specific kinds of medical knowledge. Like excreting and sleeping, eating is another moment of human vulnerability. It is necessary for life but requires a degree of knowledge (in selecting nontoxic plants and nonspoiled meats and cheeses) and trust (in whoever prepared the food, whether enslaved people, women, or oneself). Jordan Rosenblum shows that the second- and third-century C.E. Tannaim created "rules that regulate what, with whom, and how one eats—and how one prepares that food" in order to "attempt to establish a discrete tannaitic identity."[56] Some of these rules are based on interpretation of the dietary laws in Leviticus 11, but they are in part efforts to create a distinctive community of men who eat together, separate from non-Jews and non-rabbinic Jews. The rabbis in late antique Babylonia continued to inculcate and elaborate the dietary restrictions established by the Tannaim. However, they also created a complementary body of traditions that regulated what and how one eats through the presence and absence of demonic danger.

Some foods and drinks are only demonically dangerous if consumed in a particular way. The most prominent rabbinic regulation around food and demons is the prohibition against eating or drinking in even numbers. As the pseudo-baraita that opens b. *Pesaḥim* 109b–112a states,

56. Jordan D. Rosenblum, *Food and Identity in Early Rabbinic Judaism* (Cambridge: Cambridge University Press, 2010), 2.

"One should not eat in even numbers, or drink in even numbers, nor wipe himself in even numbers, nor fulfill his [sexual] needs in even numbers" [A1]. This set of bodily practices provokes demonic attack. Beyond water, date beer, and a fermented asparagus drink called *ispargos* [A10.1–3], the b. *Pesaḥim* passage mentions eggs, cucumbers, and nuts as particularly dangerous when consumed in even numbers [A8.1].[57] In the next chapter, we will discuss this prohibition in some depth. For now, it is sufficient to note that an awareness of demons necessitates a total and complete alertness especially during the most bodily of moments.

For the rabbis, it was primarily in those moments that most remind us of our humanity that demonic danger abounded. Like urinating and excreting, drinking water is a natural act necessary for the function of human life, and yet, like these bodily acts, for the rabbis drinking water was another demonically fraught act requiring hyperawareness and particular modes of behavior. According to this same passage, water is dangerous when drunk from a river or lake at night [A′3], at all on a Tuesday or Friday night [A′2], if borrowed by a minor from someone else in a field [B2], drunk drop by drop [C5.1], or if drunk from a plate rather than a glass [c′5.2]. Indeed, regulations regarding the consumption of liquids are the enveloping structure of the entire b. *Pesaḥim* passage. These regulations are not marginal to the rabbinic construction of demons but constitutive.

Beyond the danger of consuming things in even numbers, some foods are also dangerous if consumed in other ways. According to a tradition attributed to R. Shimon b. Yoḥai in b. *Niddah* 17a, unpeeled garlic, eggs, and onions are potentially demonically dangerous, even fatal, to eat.[58]

57. Compare to the lists at b. *Berakhot* 57b and b. *Avodah Zarah* 29a, which are longer parallel lists of foods harmful to a sick person that include each of the foods mentioned here. Elman, "The World of the 'Sabboraim'" 405, argues that the author of b. *Pesaḥim* "limited the real danger, but explained the rabbinic warnings against the danger of demons as a public health measure, so to speak, and not as due to the danger of demons. And the three he chose were already known as constituting a danger to health." From the redactional context of the list in b. *Pesaḥim*, however, it is clear that the list is indeed demonically inflected.

58. The anonymous voice moderates this belief. Where the earlier tradition suggests that the act of eating these foods unpeeled is potentially fatal, the anonymous gloss limits this danger to when they are stored without their peels and roots. This limitation suggests a connection to the rabbinic laws about the dangers of exposing particular foods and beverages overnight.

Cress *(lepidium sativum)* is dangerous if one does not wash one's hands after eating it [B′1].[59] According to a statement by Abaye in b. *Ḥullin* 107b, one must feed a child with both hands to prevent demons from attacking.[60] In rabbinic discussions of demons, Abaye emerges as a particular expert in identifying demons and in preventing demonic attack. Here he suggests an important nuance to rabbinic constructions of eating: many foods are not themselves inherently dangerous; they only enable demonic harm if consumed in a rabbinically incorrect fashion.

For other foods, according to b. *Pesaḥim* 109b–112a, demonic danger is to be found in their storage. "Food and drink [stored] under the bed, even if they are covered with an iron utensil, a demon dwells upon them" [A′1]. If storing food and drink under the bed is dangerous, so is suspending bread from the roof beams: "[Foods] suspended in the house lead to poverty and this applies only to bread, but meat and fish are not harmful" [C5.2]. Bread was a staple food with ritual importance, but it was also a symbol of poverty, the food given to beggars. The connection between food storage and poverty is then further articulated in this same passage: "Bran in the house leads to poverty, crumbs in the house lead to poverty."[61] Like bread, bran was a food primarily eaten by the poor. A common saying in the Babylonian Talmud attributed to "the people" suggests that one should "be reimbursed by your debtor even in bran."[62] The symbolic association of bread and bran with poverty is made explicit in their functioning as a cause of poverty when suspended in the house. And indeed, these two statements bookend the explanation that "the genius appointed over food is named *Naqid* [clean, clear]. The genius

59. For the redactors of the Babylonian Talmud, cress is an herb which has both life-saving and life-harming qualities in combination with certain foods or actions. See b. *Shabbat* 109b, 113a; b. *Avodah Zarah* 28a; b. *Ketubot* 60b; and b. *Mo'ed Qatan* 11a.

60. See parallel at b. *Yoma* 77b.

61. Vatican 109 has the additional clause "דאמרי אינשי תלא סליה תלא מזוניה ולא אבל אמרן אלא בנהמא בבישרה וכוורי לית לו בה" (as people say, if he hangs up baskets, he hangs up his food, i.e., bread, but meat and fish are not harmful). This phrase appears a phrase later in MSS Munich 6, Munich 95, JTS Rab. 1608 (ENA 850), Oxford Opp. Add. Fol. 23, Vatican 134, Columbia X893T14a, and NY JTS 1623/2 Enelow Manuscript Collection 271. I have emended the text in light of MSS Munich 6, Munich 95, JTS Rab. 1608 (ENA 850), Oxford Opp. Add. Fol. 23, Vatican 134, Columbia X893T14a, NY JTS 1623/2 Enelow Manuscript Collection 271, and Cambridge T-S F1 (1) 116, which have the additional clause, "פארי בביתא קשי לעניותא נישוורא בביתא קשי לעניותא" (bran in the house leads to poverty, crumbs in the house lead to poverty).

62. See b. *Baba Batra* 92b, *Baba Meẓia* 118a, *Baba Qamma* 46b.

appointed over poverty is named *Navil* [defiled]."[63] Each name in some way points to aspects of their function—thus the poverty genie is named *Navil*, defiled, and the food genie is named *Naqid*, clean or clear.[64] Those who are clean are rewarded by the appropriate intermediary being with food; those who are dirty or otherwise defiled are punished with poverty. Intermediary beings can cause physical harm and death, but they can also wreak havoc with human lives in other ways.

Preparing, eating, and storing food were all fraught processes that required a distinctly rabbinic orientation toward food. The demonically related prohibitions described here are not based on interpretations of the dietary laws in Leviticus but, rather, are specialized rabbinic knowledge native to the rabbinic community in Sasanian Babylonia. Navigating these prohibitions safely and sustaining the rabbinic body required extensive rabbinic knowledge not only for the rabbi who was the intended audience of this corpus but also for his household—those who prepared, served, and stored the food. The rabbinic household itself was thus shaped by the presence and absence of demonic dangers inherent in food.

As already observed, food is only one of the ways that the rabbis thought demons could affect the human body. And indeed, for the rabbis, as for many in the ancient world, physical illness was one of the most common consequences of transgressing demonic norms. It is difficult to determine which diseases in the Babylonian Talmud were believed by the rabbis to be caused by demons. Modern readers might think of many of the treatments prescribed for diseases in the Talmud as magical in nature, filled with strange rituals, magical materials, and incantations. However, these treatments were part of the medical repertoire of trained health-care providers in late antique Sasanian Babylonia.[65] They do not neces-

63. The word נקידי appears in some MSS. of b. *Shabbat* 110b. See Shelomo Morag and Yechiel Kara, *Babylonian Aramaic in Yemenite Tradition: The Noun*, Edah Ve-Lashon, ed. A. Maman (Jerusalem: Magnes Press, 2002), 59, which suggests that this word refers to some form of bird in this context.

64. Neither of these beings, or the term איסרא, which is translated as "genius," appears elsewhere in the Bavli. Compare to b. *Ḥullin* 106a.

65. See, e.g., K. Codell Carter, "Causes of Disease and Death in the Babylonian Talmud," *Medizinhistorisches Journal* 26, no. 1/2 (1991): 94–104; M.J. Geller, "Akkadian Healing Therapies in the Babylonian Talmud," preprint 259, submitted to the *Max-Planck-Institut Für Wissenschafsgeschichte* in 2004.

sarily suggest a demonic cause for the illness to be treated.[66] Here I limit my discussion to those diseases which the rabbis explicitly associate with demons.

B. *Pesaḥim* 109b–112a names three explicitly demonic illnesses. First, "one who relieves himself on the stump of a date-palm tree, the demon (ruaḥ) Palga will seize him" [C3.1]. *Palga* is a term that refers to an apoplectic or paralytic episode.[67] This demon is also named in a number of the Babylonian incantation bowls.[68] Second, "one who rests his head on the stump of a date-palm tree, the demon (ruaḥ) Ẓreida will seize him" [C3.2]. The demon *Ẓreida*—the word refers to some kind of eye disease—appears as well in b. *Ḥullin* 105b, where he is known to attack someone when the table is cleared before everyone is finished eating.[69] The illnesses that these two demons cause are specified in their very names. The third demonic illness mentioned in this sugya is described in the case of a certain city official who relieves himself next to zardata reeds [C4.2.2.2]. The demons who live in these reeds lash out and here cause an unspecified illness since, as discussed, demons do not appreciate being urinated upon. Beyond b. *Pesaḥim*, a story in b. *Ketubot* 61a–b recounts that Mar Zutra and R. Ashi saw a demon (ruaḥ) of leprosy poised to attack King Yazdgird, after his food-preparer had (accidentally?) included some leprous meat in the dish. In b. *Yoma* 77b, the demon *Shibeta* [lit: serious illness] attacks

66. Carter points to Shmuel's statement in b. *Baba Meẓia* 107b that "all [disease] is caused by *ruaḥ*" to suggest the possibility of a demonic origin for all diseases. Shmuel's statement, however, appears with a definitive article *heh* across all extant manuscript traditions, meaning "the ruaḥ." This phrase never appears in connection with demons, only with the wind. Shmuel is actually attributing all disease to either a chill or bad air. See the excellent discussion in Bohak, "Conceptualizing Demons in Late Antique Judaism," 119–20, distinguishing between modern germ theory and ancient Jewish conceptions of demonic illness.

67. In Jewish Babylonian Aramaic, the word *palga* can also mean "half, waist," or "a portion of food." See Sokoloff, *A Dictionary of Jewish Babylonian Aramaic*, 910–11 s.v. #1 פלגא and #2. The term here seems to refer to some sort of attack on half the body or half the head. T. Kwasman, "The Demon of the Roof," in *Disease in Babylonia*, ed. Irving L. Finkel and Markham J. Geller (Leiden: Brill, 2007), 164, writes that "palga is quite clearly related to the Greek πληγη, blow or stroke, which has the meaning of paralysis in such English words as 'paraplegia' and 'hemiplegia.'"

68. Kwasman, "The Demon of the Roof," 163 n. 19–20. It is attested in Jewish Babylonian Aramaic in Bo 59:7, ib. 64:25, ib. 33:19, 105:2, listed according to Sokoloff's numbering in Sokoloff, *A Dictionary of Jewish Babylonian Aramaic*, 911, s.v. #2 פלגא.

69. Sokoloff, *A Dictionary of Jewish Babylonian Aramaic*, 971, s.v. #2 צרדא.

children whose food is served by an adult with unwashed hands.[70] And according to b. *Gittin* 70a, "*Our Rabbis taught: One who comes from a privy must not have sexual intercourse until he has waited the length of time it takes to walk half a mile, because the demon (šeid) of the privy is with him during that time; if he does, his children will be epileptic.*" In all these cases, demons do not cause disease capriciously or randomly, but only after one has done something that, however random it may appear to humans, is understood by demons as provoking a response.

The rabbis describe only a few illness-causing demons without mentioning an explicit provocation. The demon *Ben Nefalim* causes shortness of breath (b. *Bekhorot* 44b). B. *Shabbat* 66b–67a includes an extensive discussion of types of fevers, *eshata* in Aramaic, and their respective treatments. Yuval Harari has suggested that the word *eshata* is actually the proper name for a fever-causing demon,[71] but the Talmudic text does not include a discussion about what, if anything, feverish individuals did to be stricken with or by Eshata. The ways that one moves and feeds one's body can lead to particularly bodily effects caused by specific demons. The demons Ben Nefalim and Eshata remind us, however, that even the most careful among us can be laid low by a demonic illness. Specialized rabbinic knowledge is necessary to properly diagnose and treat these illnesses, and thereby maintain the rabbinic body.

A Note on Gender

Throughout this chapter, we have examined the ways that the rabbis thought with demons to construct particular kinds of normative rabbinic time, space, and bodies. Scholarship produced in a range of times and places has associated demons not with the normative but with the non-normative, the deviant, and by extension, the feminine.[72] While there is

70. Cf. b. *Ḥullin* 107b. Sokoloff, *A Dictionary of Jewish Babylonian Aramaic*, 1132, s.v. שיבתא defines Shibeta as the name of a demon personifying a serious illness. See also Bo 80:4, 82:3 114:9, in ibid.

71. Yuval Harari, *Jewish Magic before the Rise of Kabbalah*, trans. Batya Stein (Detroit: Wayne State University Press, 2017), 399.

72. For examples of scholars associating women and demons outside the late antique rabbinic world, see Dyan Elliot, *Fallen Bodies: Pollution, Sexuality and Demonology in the Middle Ages* (Philadelphia: University of Pennsylvania Press, 1999); J. H. Chajes, *Between Worlds: Dybbuks, Exorcists, and Early Modern Judaism*; Walter Stephens, *Demon Lovers:*

much evidence for this association in a number of textual corpora, it is worth noting that the association of demons and women is entirely absent in the Babylonian Talmud. B. *Pesaḥim* 109b–112a mentions two female demons: Agrat bat Maḥlat [C1.3] and the unidentified demon who is mother to a demon son [C4.1.1]. The vast majority of demons mentioned in the Talmud are male. Like men, women are susceptible to demonic dangers (such as those inherent in drinking in even numbers) and must take steps to avoid provoking demonic anger. In fact, in the discussion of the danger of privy demons, above, it is women who come up with the creative solutions that every day protect the rabbinic men in their lives.

Rabbinic literature did construct women as dangerous, but this danger was related to witchcraft. Although both demons and witchcraft were caused by invisible forces, for the Babylonian rabbis, these were two very different things. They manifested differently and were dealt with differently.[73] B. *Pesaḥim* 109b–112a highlights two of the many kinds of harm that witches cause: bringing danger to those who drink four, six, eight, or ten glasses; and cursing travelers on the road. Each of these challenges requires its own solution.

And yet, while both demons and witchcraft were dangerous, witchcraft was far more uncontrolled. As the passage in b. *Pesaḥim* 109b–112a demonstrates, witches could not be fully managed by rabbinic discourse; only a passing aside from an Arab on the road or internal information from the head of the witches could actually protect the unsuspecting from their harm. By contrast, rabbinic knowledge and education *could* effectively safeguard the rabbis from demonic harm. While the rabbis imagined that they understood demons and how to live in a world with them, they did not seem to imagine that they could fully understand the actual women with whom they shared their world.[74]

Witchcraft, Sex, and the Crisis of Belief (Chicago: University of Chicago Press, 2002); Ishay Rosen-Zvi, "Bilhah the Temptress: The Testament of Reuben and the 'Birth of Sexuality,'" *Jewish Quarterly Review* 96, no. 1 (2006): 65–94. I am not suggesting that these scholars are wrong, but rather only that this association does not appear to be a prominent part of the rabbinic discourse about demons found in the Babylonian Talmud.

73. See b. *Yoma* 83b; b. *Pesaḥim* 109b–112a; b. *Sanhedrin* 67b.

74. See longer discussion in Sara Ronis, "Gender, Sex, and Witchcraft in Late Antique Judaism," in *A Companion to Jews and Judaism in the Late Antique World, 3rd Century BCE–7th Century CE*, ed. Naomi Koltun-Fromm and Gwynn Kessler (Hoboken, NJ: Wiley-Blackwell, 2020), 391–404.

Constructing Demons, Constructing Rabbis

In *Demons and the Making of the Monk,* David Brakke argues that "the Christian monk was formed in part through imagining him in conflict with the demon."[75] Reading narratives of monastic encounters with demons, Brakke demonstrates that opposition to demons helped form the monastic self of late antique Egypt—as a Christian, male, renowned, renunciant self—as it also shaped demons as a particular kind of monastic opponent. The rabbinic self was also formed in connection to demons. While narratives are an important part of rabbinic discourse about demons, we have seen that the Talmud also constructs the rabbinic self through extensive discussions of law and practice as they relate to demons: the rabbinic self was a careful self, conditioned to move through space and time in particular and particularly careful ways; the rabbinic self was cultivated not only through eating specific foods but also through the preparing, serving, and storing of those foods in specific ways.[76] These practices shaped the rabbis as embodied actors constructing their own lived environment, and in so doing, constructing their own identities as rabbis.

Amoraic rabbis were not lone individuals in a solitary quest for safety; they were a scholastic religious community. Rosenblum argues that "identity is not a passive experience. Like the act of eating, it is an active social practice."[77] And indeed, here we see how the rabbis thought with demons to construct a particular kind of rabbinic community, one with its own map of the world privileging rabbinic sites and cultivating rabbinic ways of moving, its own calendar organizing their experience of time, and their own eating practices which went beyond the dietary laws theoretically incumbent on all Jews. The insistence that there was safety from demonic danger in numbers in most scenarios outside that of the privy was only the most explicit way of making clear that the rabbis

75. David Brakke, *Demons and the Making of the Monk: Spiritual Combat in Early Christianity* (Cambridge, MA: Harvard University Press, 2006), 5.

76. Mira Balberg, *Purity, Body, and Self in Early Rabbinic Literature* (Berkeley: University of California Press, 2014), 46, argues that "the rabbinic discourse of purity and impurity not only constitutes a picture of the lived world, but constitutes—and prescribes—a way of being in the world." The rabbis clearly use as many tools as are available to them to create a totalizing discourse which constructs the world as rabbinic and conditions a totalizing way of being in the world.

77. Rosenblum, *Food and Identity in Early Rabbinic Judaism,* 7.

were a group who moved together, through time, space, and the rigors of everyday life.[78]

Rabbinic discourse about living with demons does not explicitly lead to wider recognition or to an increased sense of power over non-rabbinic Jews. While it was likely that others might notice one's scrupulosity in walking near trees and plants (particularly for those rabbis who lived in a more agricultural environment), or in drinking the appropriate number of beverages, rabbinic discourse about these practices does not engage with the concept of public recognition. Instead, the benefits appear internal. In most of the rabbis' legal discussions about demons, the society that the rabbis engage with here is entirely their own, with borders and boundaries that created a particularly rabbinic self. Even a Ẓurva de-Rabbanan could not completely access the rabbinic way of life. And if being a member of the rabbinic movement, with its claims to elite knowledge and a unique connection to the divine, were the carrot of being a member of this group, then demonically induced illness, poverty, and even death were the stick of not adhering to its practices.

Rabbinic discourse insisted that demons could be dangerous, uncontrolled, and even fatal. But they also insisted that demons mostly respond to human provocation and are unlikely to initiate harm. And so, as the rabbis think with demons to construct a rabbinic self, they are also constructing a demonic self, one which is often neutral and passive, though territorial and violent when encroached upon. The rabbis insist that they know the minutiae of what is provoking to demons; the corollary of this insistence is that they also imagined that demons were aware of the minutiae of rabbinic legislation and had bought into rabbinic demarcations of space, time, and the body. And as the next chapter explores in more depth, the rabbis make these discursive moves specifically through rabbinic legal discourse.

78. See b. *Qiddushin* 29b; b. *Berakhot* 3a–b, 62a.

4 Legal Demons

When Almighty God, to beautify the nature of the world, willed that that earth should be visited by angels, when they were sent down they despised His laws . . . Being contaminated, they could not return to heaven. Rebels from God, they uttered words against Him. Whence wandering they now subvert many bodies, and it is these especially that ye this day worship and pray to as gods.

Commodianus, mid-third century C.E.

Drink not the third glasse, which thou canst not tame,
when once it is within thee.

George Herbert

Like so many in the late antique world, the Babylonian rabbis believed that demons not only existed but also actively engaged with humankind in tangible ways. When faced with the threat of visible and invisible demons with the capacity to commit great harm, the rabbis made a very rabbinic choice, which is to say that the rabbis chose to deal with demons using legal discourse. By *legal discourse*, I mean both the explicit use of law to control and regulate and the implicit embedding of legal language, concepts, and rhetorical structures in discussions about demons across genres.

Epigraphs: Commodianus, *The Instructions of Commodianus in Favour of Christian Discipline*, in Phillip Schaff, *Ante-Nicene Fathers*, vol. 4 (Grand Rapids, MI: Christian Classics Ethereal Library), 458; George Herbert, "The Church-porch," found at www.logoslibrary.org/herbert/temple/porch1.html.

The last chapter examined the ways that the rabbis thought with demons to construct rabbinic time, space, and bodies. As that discussion made clear, the rabbis did not think with demons only in their biblical interpretations (midrash) and narratives (aggadata). The rabbis thought extensively with demons using legal discourse. This phenomenon is part of a wider trend in rabbinic thought; many scholars have shown how the rabbis of Sasanian Babylonia used legal discourse to engage with and systematize the full range of their own human experience: time, space, the life cycle, the body, and more.[1] The decision to treat these topics legally meant that the rabbis imagined that the whole world was subject to rabbinic jurisprudence.[2] Rabbis constructed rabbinic law, and rabbinic law

1. See chap. 3. On time, see also Sarit Kattan Gribetz, "Conceptions of Time and Rhythms of Daily Life in Rabbinic Literature, 200–600 C.E." (PhD diss., Princeton University, 2013); Lynn Kaye, *Time in the Babylonian Talmud: Natural and Imagined Times in Jewish Law and Narrative* (Cambridge: Cambridge University Press, 2018), especially 56–85; Sacha Stern, "The Rabbinic Concept of Time from Late Antiquity to the Middle Ages," in *Time and Eternity: The Medieval Discourse*, ed. Gerhard Jaritz and Gerson Moreno-Riaño (Turnhout, Belgium: Brepols, 2003), 129-45; Jacob Neusner, "Telling Time in Rabbinic Judaism: Correlating the Lunar-Solar Calendar with the Lectionary Cycle," *Miscelánea de Estudios Árabes y Hebraicos* 53 (2004): 231–48. On space, see e.g., Charlotte Elisheva Fonrobert, "The Political Symbolism of the Eruv," *Jewish Social Studies* 11, no. 3 (2005): 9–35; David Kraemer, *Rabbinic Judaism: Space and Place* (London: Routledge, 2015), Ronis, "Space, Place, and the Race for Power." On the life cycle, see e.g., Yitzchak D. Gilat, *Prakim be-Hishtalshelut Ha-Halakhah* (Ramat-Gan, Israel: Bar-Ilan University Press, 1992), Nissan Rubin, *Time and Life Cycle in Talmud and Midrash: Socio-Anthropological Perspectives* (Boston: Academic Studies Press, 2008); David Kraemer, *The Meanings of Death in Rabbinic Judaism* (London: Routledge, 1999), 14–35. On the body, see, Charlotte Elisheva Fonrobert, *Menstrual Purity: Rabbinic and Christian Reconstructions of Biblical Gender* (Stanford: Stanford University Press, 2000); "The Semiotics of the Sexed Body in Early Halakhic Discourse," in *How Should Rabbinic Literature be Read in the Modern World?*, ed. Matthew Kraus (Piscataway, NJ: Gorgias Press, 2006), 79–104; Daniel Boyarin, *Carnal Israel: Reading Sex in Talmudic Culture* (Berkeley: University of California Press, 1993); Shai Secunda, "The Construction, Composition and Idealization of the Female Body in Rabbinic Literature and Parallel Iranian Texts: Three Excursuses," special issue: The Jewish Woman and Her Body, ed. Rachel S. Harris, *Nashim: A Journal of Jewish Women's Studies & Gender Issues* 23 (Spring–Fall 2012): 60–86.

2. This includes the world of the imagined past, where major biblical figures and Second Temple institutions become rabbinized as the rabbis retroject their presence and importance into the immediate and mythic pasts. For sustained examination of this phenomenon, see Jeffrey L. Rubenstein, *Stories of the Babylonian Talmud* (Baltimore: Johns Hopkins University Press, 2010); *Talmudic Stories: Narrative Art, Composition, and Culture*; Richard Kalmin, "Holy Men, Rabbis, and Demonic Sages in Late Antiquity," in *Jewish Culture and Society under the Christian Roman Empire*, ed. Richard Kalmin and Seth Schwartz (Leuven, Belgium: Peeters, 2003), 213–49; *Migrating Tales*. Over time, rabbinic legal discourse became more sophisticated and abstract. Leib Moscovitz, *Talmudic Reasoning: From Casu-*

constructed the rabbis as those most able and authorized to understand it in all its complexity. And as rabbis—a scholastic elite focused on legal interpretation and dialectic as much as on communal and theological development—they used the law and their status as lawmakers to define, restrict, and prevent demonic harm.

The first half of this chapter explores two case studies that demonstrate how the authors of the Babylonian Talmud integrated the demonic into the rabbinic legal system in order to both neutralize the threat of the demonic and present themselves, the rabbis, as those empowered to control these possible threats. We will see that many of the rabbis' discursive moves were part of wider conversations across cultural lines in late antiquity, with parallels to ancient Greek, Mesopotamian, and Zoroastrian ideas as well as to the Babylonian magic bowls. The rabbis' legalizing approach to demons was part of a broader legalizing trend in Sasanian Babylonia, but the rabbis take this trend one step further than many of their non-Jewish and non-rabbinic peers in the region. For the rabbis, when demons are subjugated to rabbinic law, the very nature of what it means to *be* a demon changes. The second half of this chapter maps those changes. Rather than appearing exclusively or even primarily as malevolent beings controlled by the legal powers of the rabbis, demons are integrated into the law as subjects, agents, and even as rabbinic teachers. Commodianus thought that demonic origins were rooted in their hatred for divine law; for the rabbis, however, demons lived by and perhaps even loved the law. Through the legal discourse of the Babylonian Talmud, demons become followers of the rabbis and members of the rabbinic community.

DEMONS IN THEIR CUPS

The last chapter discussed the ways that the rabbis' belief in the demonic danger of "even numbers" conditioned particularly rabbinic ways of eating, drinking, and behaving. Let us now return to this idea, and to b.

---

istics to Conceptualization (Tübingen: Mohr Siebeck, 2002), 343–66, has argued that, over the course of the Amoraic and Stammaitic projects, the Babylonian rabbis demonstrate increased conceptualization in their discussion of rabbinic law.

Pesaḥim 109b–112a as a whole, to examine how the rabbis enacted this belief through legal discourse in the opening claims of the sugya.

As we have already seen, the tenth chapter of tractate *Pesaḥim* examines the ritual meal on the first night of the holiday of Passover. The first mishnah of the tenth chapter of *Pesaḥim* opens with the dictate, "*One should have no fewer than four cups of wine.*" The four cups structure the ritual meal, grounding different ritual and didactic moments over the course of the evening. Reading this mishnah in fourth-century Roman Palestine, the rabbis of the Palestinian Talmud ask a series of questions relating to the four cups: How large should each cup be? How much of the wine in the cup must a person drink each time? What biblical verses do these cups correspond to?[3]

Reading this exact same mishnah, the rabbis of Sasanian Babylonia produced a very different set of questions. The anonymous voice of the Talmud immediately asks, "How could our Rabbis institute something that would ultimately lead to danger? For surely it was taught in a baraita: *One should not eat* in even numbers, *or drink* in even numbers, *nor wipe himself* in even numbers, *nor fulfill his [sexual] needs* in even numbers." The rabbis' concern with the mishnah in *Pesaḥim* is directly related to the even number of cups that one must consume on the first night of Passover; it has nothing to do with public drunkenness or private dissolution. In fact, one very real possible solution might be to simply drink *five* cups of wine instead of four. This numerical concern then leads the rabbis to delimit these demonic dangers through legal interpretation. Three named rabbis propose different solutions to the problem of the four cups.

Underlying their concerns is the Babylonian rabbinic belief that consuming certain foods or performing certain acts an even number of times is deliberately provoking to demons and could cause demons to lash out in retaliation. This belief is made explicit in the first rabbinic attempt to solve the problem posed by the Mishnah.

The fourth-generation Amora R. Naḥman bar Yitzḥak performs an exegetical reading of a verse in Exodus that describes the night of the first Passover in Egypt. "*R. Naḥman bar Yitzḥak said: "It is a night that*

3. P. *Pesaḥim* 10:1 (68b) and following.

is guarded" (Exod. 12:42). It is a night that is guarded from the demons (mazziqin)."[4] R. Naḥman bar Yitzḥak's reading argues for the exceptionalism of the first night of Passover as a night where God guards Israel from demons directly. According to R. Naḥman bar Yitzḥak, then, the first night of Passover is the only night when demonically provoking acts can be performed.

R. Naḥman bar Yitzḥak's peer Rava then performs his own complicated math: "*Rava said: The cup of blessing [the third cup of the ritual meal, upon which the Grace after Meals is recited] combines for good things but not for bad things.*" Rava divides the four cups into a grouping of three and a grouping of one, two odd numbers. While a modern reader may note that three plus one usually equals four, in this context, Rava insists that this math is entirely inappropriate. Rava's suggestion can be read together with a larger legal discussion in tractate *Berakhot* 51a about the cup over which the Grace after Meals is recited. There, the rabbis insist—because of the danger of drinking an even number of drinks—that this cup must be an odd-numbered cup to be ritually appropriate.[5] Belief in the danger of even numbers can be found, explicitly and implicitly, in a number of halakhic contexts undergirding laws about food, drink, and ritual obligations to God.

Finally, the redactors of b. *Pesaḥim* 109b–112a cite the opinion of the sixth- (or seventh) generation Amora Ravina: "*Ravina said: Each cup is a separate commandment [and thus they do not combine at all].*" Like Rava's answer, Ravina's answer is deeply imbricated in the halakhic structures which undergird the Bavli as a whole. As an example, the legal

4. This teaching is paralleled in b. *Rosh HaShanah* 11b, where it is unattributed.

5. B. *Berakhot* 51a: "*R. Assi said: One must not speak over the cup of blessing. R. Assi said: One should not say Grace after meals over the cup of divine punishment.* What is the cup of divine punishment? R. Naḥman b. Yitzḥak said: A second cup. It has been taught similarly in a baraita: "*One who drinks an even number [of drinks] should not say Grace because it says, 'Prepare to meet your God, O Israel,' (Amos 4:12) and he must fix his eyes upon it* so that he should not take his mind off it *and he must send it around to his household as a gift.*" There, the cup's susceptibility to demonic danger is heightened by an interpretation of Amos 4:12 that suggests that one who has consumed an even number of cups is a dead man walking unprepared to engage with God. Only those who are properly prepared to encounter the divine can lead the ritual blessings over wine after a meal. The prohibition on even numbers is thus built into the halakhic fabric of the cup of blessing. See also b. *Sotah* 38b.

separation of ritual acts into individual commandments with the specific language of "*each . . . is a separate commandment*" also appears in Talmudic discussions about the religious rituals commanded on the holiday of Sukkot.[6] It is a standard legal mode of explaining the presence of multiple blessings over one seemingly continuous ritual performance.

All three of the rabbinic solutions to the problem of the four cups of wine on Passover are context-specific, relating to the particular ritual setting of the first night of the holiday. Underlying all these interpretations is the belief that drinking an even number of drinks at any other time is dangerous, if not fatal. Ultimately, what this Talmudic passage *says* is that one is actually permitted to consume the four cups of wine on Passover. What it *does* is use Amoraic exegetical and legal authority to uphold the mishnah and protect its followers from demonic attack in this one time and space each year. And at least Rava and Ravina imply that demons are able to do the complex acts of (dis)counting that lead to counting an odd number of cups on the first night of Passover and beyond.

As we have already seen, the discussion of demons and the law in b. *Pesaḥim* continues for another seven pages, a tremendous length for a single sugya in the Talmud. In this extended redacted literary text, the rabbis deploy biblical exegesis, case studies, and legal debate about intentionality to expand protection for their followers. In so doing, the rabbis increase the amount of rabbinic legal knowledge that demons are assumed to possess. For example, one rabbinic informant, discussed in depth below, explains that with two cups of liquid, one is punished by the demons regardless of intentionality, but with four one is liable only if one drank intentionally. Distinguishing between accidental and intentional action is a legal approach evident as early as the Hebrew Bible's criminal law codes and developed in great depth in the later rabbinic corpus.[7] Here it is the responsibility of the demon, not a rabbinic judge, to determine a person's intentions and then take appropriate action. The rabbis' legal approach assumes that demons need to know as much as the rabbis themselves in order to behave in demonically and rabbinically appropriate ways.

6. See b. *Sukkah* 45b, b. *Beiẓah* 30b.

7. See Exod. 21:12–14; Num. 21. And see Strauch Schick, "Intention in the Babylonian Talmud," 19–29.

According to the rabbinic imagination, this kind of legal knowledge is exclusive to the rabbinic community. The sugya in b. *Pesaḥim* has an elliptical reference to "the case of Rabbah b. Naḥmani." That case is explained in B. *Baba Meẓia.* According to b. *Baba Meẓia* 86a, Rabbah b. Naḥmani fled from Persian officials and took shelter in an inn near a marsh. A Persian official was sent in search of him and happened to eat at the same inn:

> They [the inn attendants] brought a table before [the official] and offered him two cups, and then took the table from before him. [The official's] face turned backwards. They said to [Rabbah b. Naḥmani], "What should we do to this man? He is the king's messenger!" He said to [the inn attendants], "Bring the table before him again and offer him another cup and then take the table from him, and he will be healed." They did thus and [the official] was healed. [The official] said, "I indeed know that the man I am seeking is here." He searched for [Rabbah b. Naḥmani] and found him.

Rabbah b. Naḥmani was again forced to flee and eventually died. Much scholarship has been devoted to this passage, and in particular, to its evidence on the rabbinic relationships to the Sasanian state.[8] However, here I call attention to the delicate choreography of drinks that causes and solves the problem of the Persian royal messenger. The royal messenger is unaware of the potential dangers of drinking an even number of drinks and drinks two drinks during his meal. Like a character out of *The Exorcist,* the royal messenger's face spins around. Only the incognito rabbinic sage recognizes the true roots of the problem. According to the rabbis, non-Jewish Persians are susceptible to the danger of even numbers though they are unaware of that fact. Only the rabbis can accurately diagnose the problem and prescribe the appropriate solution. Once the Persian messenger has been healed, even this non-Jew realizes that his healer must be a great rabbi.

8. See, e.g., Moshe Beer, "Concerning the Deposal of Rabbah Bar Naḥmani from the Headship of the Academy: A Chapter in the History of the Relationship between the Sages and the Exilarchs," *Tarbiz* 33 (1964): 349–57; E. E. Urbach, "Concerning Historical Insight into the Account of Rabbah Bar Naḥmani's Death," *Tarbiz* 34 (1965): 156–61; Eliezer Segal, "Law as Allegory? An Unnoticed Literary Device in Talmudic Narratives," *Prooftexts* 8, no. 2 (1988): 245–56; Richard Kalmin, "Saints or Sinners, Scholars or Ignoramuses? Stories About the Rabbis as Evidence for the Composite Nature of the Babylonian Talmud," *AJS Review* 15, no. 2 (1990): 195–96.

Within the sugya found at b. *Pesaḥim* 109b–112a, the rabbis eventually designate the concern with even numbers a *halakhah le-moshe mi-sinai,* a law given to Moses at Sinai: "When R. Dimi came [to Babylonia from Roman Palestine], he said: *Two eggs, two cucumbers, two nuts, and something else are a halakhah from Moses at Sinai.* And the identity of the something else was doubtful to the rabbis, and so they decreed [that the law of evens applies] in all things" (b. *Pesaḥim* 110b). In rabbinic thought, a *halakhah le-moshe mi-sinai* has the force of written biblical law, though transmitted orally. Christine Hayes notes that designating something a *halakhah le-moshe mi-sinai* "may be a device for conferring authority upon a law of unstable authority." [9] In this instance, the designation serves to give authority to a teaching with no biblical or Tannaitic basis, a teaching that the Talmudic redactors are aware is contested, while justifying their stringent application of the ambiguity of "something else" to all even numbers.

In the previous chapter, we examined how the Babylonian rabbis used demons to create and regulate rabbinic time, space, and bodies in Babylonia. The designation of the danger of even numbers as a *halakhah le-moshe mi-sinai* applies its danger evenly across the rabbinic world.[10] The Talmud tells us that R. Dimi brought this tradition from Roman Palestine to Sasanian Babylonia. The Babylonian concern with even numbers is

9. For a more in-depth discussion of the term *halakhah le-moshe mi-sinai* in rabbinic literature, and a discussion of the relevant bibliography on the subject, see Christine Hayes, "'Halakhah Le-Moshe Mi-Sinai' in Rabbinic Sources: A Methodological Case Study," in *The Synoptic Problem in Rabbinic Literature*, ed. Shaye Cohen (Providence, RI: Brown University Press, 2000), 70. Hayes characterizes the use of *halakhah le-moshe mi-sinai* in the Talmuds as marking a teaching as (1) "not open to change or abolition," (2) the possible "basis for legal analogies," (3) having "no logical justification," and (4) "decidedly stringent in cases of doubt" (ibid., 82). The use of *halakhah le-moshe mi-sinai* in b. *Pesaḥim* 110b aligns closely with these characteristics.

10. R. Dimi is believed to have been one of the *naḥotei,* rabbinic travelers who played a crucial role in the transmission of rabbinic teachings between Roman Palestine and Sasanian Babylonia. On the naḥotei, see Marcus Mordecai Schwartz, "As They Journeyed from the East: The Nahotei of the Fourth Century and the Construction of the Rabbinic Diaspora," *Hebrew Union College Annual* 86 (2015): 63–99; and see the productive critique of this reading in James Adam Redfield, "Redacting Culture: Ethnographic Authority in the Talmudic Arrival Scene," *Jewish Social Studies* 22, no. 1 (Fall 2016): 29–80; ibid., "'When X Arrived, He Said . . .': The Historical Career of a Talmudic Formula," unpublished work, accessed 6 December 2019, www.academia.edu/29627483/_When_X_Arrived_he_said_The_Historical_Career_of_a_Talmudic_Formula_appendix_to_Redacting_Culture_.

thus presented as having originated in the west with the authority and importance of the land of Israel, while being given the further force of a law given to Moses at Sinai. And yet, as we have already seen, though the danger may apply across the rabbinic world, and perhaps even the Jewish world more broadly, according to the Babylonian rabbis, it is only the Babylonian rabbis who have the expert knowledge and insight to deal with the problem appropriately.

UNDERSTANDING EVEN NUMBERS

Why do the rabbis believe that even numbers are especially provoking to demons? Over the course of the Bavli sugya, the scope of the harm is contested but the assumption itself is always allowed to stand. This tradition is not found in the Bible or Second Temple literature—so how did it develop? The introduction discussed early scholars' attempts to dismiss the demonic in the Babylonian Talmud as an external corruption of an internally pure Judaism. Attempts to situate rabbinic demonic discourse in the non-rabbinic world continue to occur, particularly in relation to the rabbinic prohibition of "even numbers."[11] While I resist the urge to attribute demonology to foreign cultures as a means of rescuing "authentic" or "pure" rabbinic thought, demonology is a useful lens through which to understand the kinds of cross-cultural conversations that the rabbis may have participated in within the ancient world.

Some scholars have looked to geographically proximate cultures for evidence of an association between even numbers and demons. Michael Baris has suggested that the prohibition of even numbers was a negative

11. Elman, "The World of the 'Sabboraim'" 398–412. For a survey of Greco-Roman uses of the number three specifically, see Euguene Tavenner, "Three as a Magic Number in Latin Literature," *Transactions and Proceedings of the American Philological Association* 47 (1916): 117–43. Elman is correct in noting that Tavenner does not distinguish between harmful and positive conceptions of the number three. Certainly, like rabbinic culture, non-rabbinic cultures were engaged in assigning meaning to particular numbers, but there is no evidence that the rabbis knew of the poet Virgil's valorization of the number three, and the nature and limits of their shared cultural world is still unknown. For preliminary attempts to articulate this relationship, see Levinson, "Enchanting Rabbis," 57 n. 9; Bohak, *Ancient Jewish Magic: A History*, 360.

response to Zoroastrian dualism. According to Baris, the fear of even numbers "represents a dualistic world view, fraught with theological danger."[12]

Indeed, there is clearly some numerical overlap with Zoroastrian demonology, though ironically, it is most prominent in the shared idea that people are safer in pairs than alone when it comes to demonic dangers. We see this belief play out in the laws preserved in the Zoroastrian *Pahlavi Vīdēvdād*. The *Vīdēvdād*, which literally translates to "The Law Repudiating the Demons," is a composite text written in Avestan. As William Malandra notes, it was likely redacted "after Avestan ceased to be a live medium of communication, yet was still understood in its general contours," during the Parthian (247 B.C.E.–224 C.E.) or early Sasanian period (224–651 C.E.).[13] The *Vīdēvdād* was later glossed and interpreted by commentators who spoke and wrote in Pahlavi. This even-more-composite text is called the *Pahlavi Vīdēvdād*. Establishing the relative dates of the commentators cited in the *Pahlavi Vīdēvdād* allows us to date some of its discussions to the fourth-sixth centuries C.E., though the text continued to be edited and glossed for centuries.[14] According to the *Pahlavi Vīdēvdād*, a corpse must be carried by at least two people in order to prevent the attack of *Nasuš*, the corpse demon. The presence of two people sharing the weight of the corpse prevents a full-throated demonic attack on either.[15] And as we saw in chapter 3, going to fields or ruins in pairs also works to protect rabbinic followers from demonic harm.[16]

The idea that there is safety in numbers is an instance in which the rabbis and Zoroastrian elites seem to share a tradition, though whether that sharing was intentional or the result of commonsense human experi-

12. Michael Baris, "'I Am the One': A Monist Looks at the Double Death and Life of Rabba Bar Naḥmani," *Review of Rabbinic Judaism* 23, no. 1 (2020), 36.

13. William W. Malandra, "Vendīdād," in *Encyclopædia Iranica Online* (2000, 2006 updated online), www.iranicaonline.org/articles/vendidad.

14. Malandra, "Vendīdād"; Elman, "The Other in the Mirror. Part One," 15; Prods Oktor Skjærvø, "The Videvdad: Its Ritual-Mythical Significance," in *The Age of the Parthians*, ed. Vesta Sarkhosh Curtis and Sarah Stewart (London: I. B. Tauris, 2007), 112–15; Mahnaz Moazami, *Wrestling with the Demons of the Pahlavi Widēwdād* (Leiden: Brill, 2014), 4–8.

15. Pahlavi Vīdēvdād 8.10. See Moazami, *Wrestling with the Demons of the Pahlavi Widēwdād*, 225.

16. See b. *Berakhot* 3a–b; and see the outlier to this tradition in b. *Qiddushin* 29b, discussed in chap. 6.

ences around dangers and safety is not clear. Regardless, it is not a subtle critique of Zoroastrian dualism. Is it possible that rabbinic beliefs around even numbers represent a divergent attitude toward a different aspect of Zoroastrian demonology? Certainly. Yet the rabbis are rarely so subtle in their critiques of their contemporaries.

M. J. Geller associates the fear of even numbers with earlier ancient Near Eastern traditions. According to Geller, "The reason for this fear of 'pairs' comes directly from Babylonian extispicy, which was an elaborate system in which 'right' and 'left' were used to indicate 'good' or 'bad' respectively, although it depended upon a point of reference, i.e. 'left' is bad for the subject but 'good' if it refers to his enemy. It seems probable that 'left' as unlucky or 'sinister' could refer to an 'even' number if one counts with one's hands, starting with the right hand."[17] While the parallel is intriguing, the genealogical relation between the two concepts remains unproven. Extispicy and the rabbinic concept of even numbers are quite different, both in modes of practice—the ritual specialist's use of animal entrails to predict the future and the rabbinic drinking of cups of wine—and in modes of conceptualization, distinguishing between subjective evil and certain demonic harm. And it is worth noting that, were one to count with one's hands starting with the left hand, an entirely different set of numbers might be seen as demonically provocative and therefore dangerous. As we will see in chapters 5 and 6, rabbinic demonic discourse aligns in content with ancient Mesopotamian discourse in significant ways. However, as of yet, the prohibition of even numbers does not seem to be one of them.

A more likely parallel is found in Greek philosophy. Plato associates even numbers with inferior things, ill omens, and the gods of the underworld. Even numbers are the less optimal, and so are unworthy of being offered to the Olympian gods on high.[18] The later philosopher Plutarch, discussed in chapter 2, reports Plato's position, but shades it further toward the *daimonic*. Plutarch writes that "Plato assigns to the Olympian gods right-hand qualities and odd numbers, and to the *daimones* the opposite of these."[19] Plutarch then links Plato's association of daimones

17. Geller, "Akkadian Healing Therapies in the Babylonian Talmud," 56–57.

18. Plato, *Laws*, 717A, in Plato, *Laws*, trans. R. G. Bury, vol. 1 (Cambridge, MA: Harvard University Press, 1929), 296–97.

19. Translation adapted from Plutarch, *On Isis and Osiris* 361B, in Plutarch, *Moralia*, vol. 5, 62–63. See discussion of this passage in Martin, *Inventing Superstition*, 103.

with even numbers to an assumption that the daimones have "a complex and inconsistent nature and purpose."[20] Plutarch continues by reporting an otherwise unknown position attributed to the Greek philosopher Xenocrates (c. 396–314 B.C.E.).

> Xenocrates also is of the opinion that such days [that are even-numbered] are days of ill omen, and such festivals as have associated with them either beatings or lamentations or fastings or scurrilous language or ribald jests have no relation to the honors paid to the gods or to worthy daimones but he believes that there exist in the space about us certain great and powerful natures, obdurate, however, and morose, which take pleasure in such things as these, and, if they succeed in obtaining them, resort to nothing worse.[21]

Plutarch's writings attest to an association between even numbers and daimones, though we must remember that Plutarch himself was unsure that daimones were evil; Plutarch saw daimones as subordinate to the gods but largely morally superior to human beings.[22] Yet in his juxtaposition of Plato's opinion with that of Xenocrates, who combines even-numbered days with natures who take pleasure in the dismal, the violent, and the vulgar, we begin to see an association between even numbers, daimones, and potential danger. Although there is little evidence that this association enjoyed wide currency in late antiquity, it is the most likely conversation partner with rabbinic demonology. This association was perhaps amplified and made more important to rabbinic demonology as a result of the Sasanian cultural world in which the rabbis lived, a world with a strong sense of dangerous demons all around, ideas of demons and numbers being in some way connected, and competing claims about how to protect oneself and one's community. And this likely conversation partner may also explain why the belief that even numbers provoke demonic harm largely appears in rabbinic traditions after the fourth century C.E. when, as discussed in chapter 2, Greek and Roman traditions began to be translated and transmitted in the Sasanian East.[23]

This genealogy is particularly striking given the rabbis' insistence that "in the west, they are not particular about demons," discussed in the previ-

20. Plutarch, *On Isis and Osiris* 361A, in Plutarch, *Moralia,* vol. 5, 62–63.
21. Adapted from Plutarch, *On Isis and Osiris* 361B, in Plutarch, *Moralia,* vol. 5, 62–63.
22. See discussion in chap. 2.
23. See Kalmin, *Jewish Babylonia between Persia and Roman Palestine,* 174–75.

ous chapter. At least in Plato's time, and again in Plutarch's, in the west they *were* particular about even numbers. The rabbis' spatial claims should not be read as an accurate geography of ideas, but rather as doing important discursive work for the rabbinic construction of self and community.

The rabbis as a community existed in a world shaped by two major empires with a range of diverse understandings of demons. Rabbinic demonology reflects the rabbis' position at the intersection of these competing worldviews. It is clear that the rabbis are in conversation with many diverse demonological discourses, but in their bricolage of different elements together, and their reframing of them all in light of rabbinic beliefs about the creation of the world, the celestial hierarchy, and what it means to be a person in the (rabbinic) world, the rabbis create something entirely new. Regardless of potential parallels between rabbis and other cultures relating to the fear of even numbers, the notion of even numbers as explicitly *provoking* to demons appears to be entirely rabbinic in its conception. Yet the rabbis do not name these rabbinic origins; instead they root this belief in the biblical past and in Moses, the original Jewish sage. In so doing, they argue that their beliefs are older than and superior to the beliefs found in both the west *and* the east. From its constructed origins at Sinai, to its spatial and temporal articulations, to its regulation through halakhic discourse, to the names of the sages who appear in this sugya, the Talmudic concern with even numbers as a means of avoiding demonic attack is thus deeply rooted in the rabbinic project and worldview.

WATER, WATER, EVERY WHERE

A similar rabbinic concern with demons and beverages can be seen in the second of our two cases studies, which forms the closing bookend of this extended sugya (A and A′ in my numbering of b. *Pesaḥim* 112a). Like the opening bookend, this passage deals with the particular dangers that come with drinking liquids. The passage is organized as a series of three Tannaitic or pseudo-Tannaitic statements in Hebrew. The first statement is relatively simple: "*Food and drink under the bed, even if they are covered with an iron utensil, an evil demon (ruaḥ ra'ah) dwells upon them.*" Iron was a material used primarily for weapons of war; as such, many ancient demonologies contain a belief that iron is a material that protects against and vanquishes evil demons. This Tannaitic teaching suggests that even the act of guarding one's food and drink with tools made of such *materia magica* does not protect it from evil spirits if it is placed under the bed overnight. The second and third statements are each introduced with the formula marking a Tannaitic teaching: 'our rabbis taught' *(tanu rabbanan)*. These are followed by Aramaic glosses. The structure—a baraita and anonymous commentary—is a familiar one in the Babylonian Talmud. The second statement reads,

> *Our rabbis taught: A man should not drink water on Tuesday nights and Friday nights, and if he did drink, his blood is upon his head.* And if he is thirsty, what [should he do]? Let him say *seven kolot* (Ps. 29) and then drink. And if not, let him say thusly: *Lul Shafan, Anigron, Anirdefai* [meaning obscure].[24] I dwell between the stars, I become fat among the thin ones

24. This incantation varies much across manuscripts, making translation difficult. I have chosen to translate it as "Lul Shafan, Anigron, Anirdefai. I dwell between the stars; I become fat among the thin ones / the superior ones between the chasms." The first four words remain obscure in this context. Sokoloff, *A Dictionary of Jewish Babylonian Aramaic*, 144, s.v. אניגרון does not translate these words, defining *anigron*, e.g., as a "word in a charm formula." However, each of these words does have some degree of meaning in ancient Hebrew texts. In Biblical Hebrew, a *lul* is a winding pathway or staircase. (See Francis Brown, S.R. Driver, and Charles A. Briggs, "לול," in *The Brown-Driver-Briggs Hebrew and English Lexicon* [Peabody, MA: Hendrickson, 1906], 533). Similarly, in Biblical Hebrew, *shafan* is a rock hyrax ("שפן," in *The Brown-Driver-Briggs Hebrew and English Lexicon*, 1050–51). The Yemenite manuscripts read the second word as *shapaz*, leading to translations such as a golden night (MS Columbia X893T14a) and a golden staircase (MS NY JTS 1623/2 Enelow Manuscript). Both of these make sense in the context of the heavens and cosmos illuminated in the second part of the incantation. *Anigron* appears in the Babylonian Talmud in several instances and means beet-juice. In b. *Shabbat* 109b, anigron is specified along with artichoke and theriac as particularly efficacious against the dangers of exposed beverages and witchcraft. The word also appears in B. *Berakhot* 35b–36a, in MSS Paris 671, Oxford Opp. Add. fol. 23, Munich 95, and in the Spanish Print edition, London BL Harl. 5508, and NY JTS 1623/2 Enelow Manuscript Collection 271 of b. *Yoma* 76a. According to Sokoloff, *A Dictionary of Jewish Babylonian Aramaic*, 144, s.v. אניגרא an *anigra* is a type of coin. *Anirdaphon* could be related to *indrafta*, which appears to be a type of bird (b. *Ḥullin* 62b; and see Jastrow, *A Dictionary of Targumim, Talmud, and Midrashic Literature*, 82 s.v. אנדרפטא). However, while each of these words can be assigned a linguistic meaning, it is unclear how they all fit together. Given the garbled nature of these words in the manuscripts, it may be impossible to recover their original meaning, if there ever was one. These may also have been *voces magicae*, magical words with no particular meaning ascribed to them; some of their power may have even come from their perceived obscurity or mystery. On *voces magicae*, see Hans Dieter Betz, "Jewish Magic in the Greek Magical Papyri (PGM VII. 260–71),"

> [or: the superior ones] between the chasms. And if not, if there is another person lying next to him, let him wake him up and say: Ploni son of Plonita, I am thirsty for water, and then let him drink. And if [there is no other person there], let him rattle the cover of the pitcher, and then let him drink. And if not, let him spit into [the waters], and then let him drink.

This text presents some of the major ways that the rabbis respond to demons: a combination of physical actions and incantations, the presentation of alternatives, and the marking of times and locations. The Hebrew teaching is followed by a structured series of five possible ways around the prohibition of drinking on these nights. Each possibility is introduced by the phrase "and if not." The expression "and if not" is used in legal discussions in the Babylonian Talmud to demarcate multiple (though ranked) options in properly observing halakhic strictures.[25] If, for some unstated reason, the actor did not perform the previously suggested action, the rabbis present another option. The chain of five "and if not" statements sets our sugya apart from other sugyot where the statement appears only once or twice. Here, the enchainment suggests an amplification of the normal features of halakhic discourse, providing an increased number of a posteriori options for a legal actor.

The first two options proposed are verbal formulas, the last two are ritual gestures, and the middle possibility mixes ritual speech and gesture. They run the gamut from reciting biblical verses (Ps. 29 includes the relevant verse, "The voice of the Lord is over the waters; the God of glory thunders, the Lord, over the mighty waters" (NJPS)), to reciting an otherwise unknown incantation, to partnering with someone else, to physical gestures. These remedies are meant to invoke protection or to startle the demons presumed present before the act of drinking occurs, such that any

---

in *Envisioning Magic: A Princeton Seminar and Symposium*, ed. Peter Schafer and Hans G. Kippenberg (Leiden: Brill, 1997), 45–63; and W. M. Brashear, "The Greek Magical Papyri: An Introduction and Survey; Annotated Bibliography (1928–1994)," in *Aufstieg und Niedergang der Romischen Welt* (Berlin: Walter de Gruyter, 1995).

25. The expression is used over 150 times in the Bavli. While sometimes it is explicitly followed by a referent, "and if [he does] not do X," most often the referent is only implied based on the previous action articulated. For examples in which the referent is explicit, see b. *Sukkah* 38a, 47b. For examples in which the referent is implied, see b. *Beiẓah* 11a, 20a, b. *Berakhot* 51b already discussed above, b. *Ḥagigah* 13a, b. *Eruvin* 76a.

demons who are resting upon the water will flee. These acts are preventative in nature, rather than meant to treat the effects of a demonic attack.

A striking parallel can be found in a Babylonian incantation bowl, Moussaieff 164, where the ritual specialist gives six "and if not" options to persuade a demon to leave a household alone:[26]

> (1) If you appear as a dog I adjure and put you under oath by means of "I am that I am."
>
> (2) And if you do not depart and go out of the house of Abandad son of Batgada and from the dwelling of Sami daughter of Parsita I shall bring against you the shard of a fortunate man and I shall defile you.
>
> (3) And if not, I shall bring against you the staff of a leprous man and I shall strike you.
>
> (4) And if not I shall bring against you a rod of seven pieces that seven sorcerous women are riding and their eight ghosts.
>
> (5) And if not I shall bring against you water from the mouths of seven people with gonorrhea/discharge and I shall pour [it] on you and I shall remove you.
>
> (6) And if you do not flee and go out from the house of Abandad son of Batgada and from the dwelling of Sami daughter of Parsita his wife, you demons and afflictions and satans and shadows, you shall all be under the ban of Rabbi Joshua bar Peraḥia, amen amen selah.[27]

To my knowledge, these are the only two texts with a substantial enchainment of "and if not" clauses extant from late antique Babylonia. But the structural similarity between this incantation text and the Talmudic text above highlights the significant differences between the ways that their authors use this structure to create a particular relationship between one or more humans and a demon. In the incantation text, the speaker addresses a demon directly, warning him to flee after he has appeared to the bowl's clients. In the Babylonian Talmud, the anonymous redactor speaks to a human actor, advising him on ways to prevent exposure to demonic harm. In the incantation text, demons are the enemy, and must be compelled to

26. See discussion of these bowls in chap. 6.

27. Text and translation from Dan Levene, "'If You Appear as a Pig': Another Incantation Bowl (Moussaieff 164)," *Journal of Semitic Studies* 52, no. 1 (2007): 61–62.

obey through the use of magical objects and historiolae, brief narratives found in incantations that offer authority for acts of ritual power when written or recited.[28] The clauses amplify the threat while they simultaneously suggest that the ritual expert is not confident in his or her innate ability to control the demon. The incantation text assumes that the demon is recalcitrant and will need multiple incentives to leave his victims alone. By contrast, the Talmudic text assumes that any one method will work, but that humans are fundamentally lazy and need a range of increasingly simple options to protect themselves. In the Talmudic text, demons follow rabbinic protocol when asked. Ironically, the incantation text agrees with this conclusion. The final option provided by the incantation text names a rabbi—R. Joshua b. Peraḥia—renowned in the incantation bowls for his exorcistic abilities, who is apparently the only strong enough threat to conclude the incantation. [29] The bowl text invokes a rabbinic authority without the rabbis' confidence that their rituals will work the first time.[30] As these two texts imagine demonic dangers, they also imagine human communities with distinct relationships to these otherworldly beings. The rabbis are confident in their own abilities to control demons and demonic dangers; all it takes is a little (rabbinic) human effort.

The Talmudic text concludes with a third Hebrew teaching and its Aramaic glosses.

> *Our rabbis taught: One should not drink water from the rivers or the lakes at night, and if he does, his blood is upon his head, because of the danger.* What is this danger? The danger of *shavriri* [translated roughly as day and night blindnesses]. And if he is thirsty, what [should he do]? If he has a friend with him, let him say: [Ploni son of Plonit, I am thirsty for water]. And if not, let him say to himself: Ploni son of Plonit, *your mother told you to be careful of shavriri vriri riri iri ri* in an unglazed cup.[31]

28. David Frankfurter, "Narratives That Do Things," in *Narrating Religion*, ed. Sarah Iles Johnston (New York: MacMillan Reference USA, 2016), 95–106; Bohak, *Ancient Jewish Magic*, 312.

29. See Markham J. Geller, "Joshua B. Perahia and Jesus of Nazareth: Two Rabbinic Magicians" (PhD diss., Brandeis University, 1974), 87.

30. This bowl is also notable for its citation of a mishnah—m. *Shevuot* 4:3—in its incantation. Although many bowls name R. Joshua b. Peraḥia, only this one pairs a rabbinic authority with a rabbinic text.

31. This text is paralleled at b. *Avodah Zarah* 12b, where it is organized differently.

The conversation moves out of the home with its drawn water to the great outdoors and its natural bodies of water. The modes of getting around the prohibition include both familiar possibilities—speaking to a friend—and a new approach, a strange incantation recited to oneself.

This incantation shares several classic features with other late antique magical incantations. The vocal permutations of the word *shavriri* call to mind the third-century Roman physician Quintus Serenus Sammonicus's prescription that those ill with a particular kind of fever wear an amulet at their neck containing the word Abracadabra repeated over and over again with more letters removed each time.[32] The similarity of the *shavriri vriri riri iri ri* incantation to this Greco-Roman one points to a shared belief in the efficacy of this kind of verbal manipulation on disease prevention and management. The demon's power over its human victim is erased as the demon's name vanishes one letter at a time. Beyond the shared content of specific gods, angels, and demons, the late antique world shared structures of incantation. This Greco-Roman incantation form is primarily found in medical treatises and magical recipe books. In the Babylonian Talmud, however, the incantation is part of a legal discussion of the ways that one who is thirsty can drink water safely and halakhically.

The Babylonian rabbis' legal interest in demonology has been dismissed as folklore or narrative. While much could be said about the assumption that such labels are in fact dismissive, an even more focused objection to these labels here is that the Talmudic text itself signals the legal nature of the rabbis' discussion of demons. The rabbis treat these shared ideas using the same dialogic forms and structures, the same emphasis on intention, and the same conceptual thinking that they use to regulate laws about the Sabbath, festivals, and dietary practice. And just as the rabbis were not alone in thinking about and with demons, they were not alone in deciding to treat these beliefs legally in late antique Sasanian Babylonia.

32. Quintus Serenus Sammonicus, *Liber Medicinalis*, 935ff, *PHI Latin Texts*, at http://latin.packhum.org/loc/1515/1/0#0. On this parallel, see Bohak, *Ancient Jewish Magic*, 266–270, esp. 266 n. 109–110; Christopher A. Faraone, "Magic and Medicine in the Roman Imperial Period: Two Case Studies," in *Continuity and Innovation in the Magical Tradition*, ed. Gideon Bohak et al. (Leiden: Brill, 2011), 146.

ZOROASTRIAN INTERSECTIONS

We have already seen that the rabbis are in conversation with Second Temple and Tannaitic rabbinic traditions about demonic origins. We have also seen how they align discursively with Greco-Roman taxonomies and attitudes toward even numbers. But the rabbis lived in a Sasanian Babylonia that was also socially and culturally complex on a more local level. Sasanian Babylonia was home to a variety of religious groups: Jews, Christians, Manichaeans, Mandaeans, followers of indigenous Babylonian religious traditions, and the ruling Zoroastrian elite. The writings produced by the Zoroastrian ruling class have proved to be a fruitful comparanda to rabbinic literature. Like the rabbis, Zoroastrian elites were in the process of creatively composing oral texts. Like rabbinic texts, Zoroastrian texts took the form of independent traditions as well as commentaries on earlier texts newly understood to be canonical. Scholars such as Yaakov Elman, Yishai Kiel, and Shana Strauch Schick have shown that the increased rabbinic interest in legal conceptualization and an increased degree of abstraction were part of a wider legalizing trend in Sasanian Babylonia that occurred in conversation with the Zoroastrian elite.[33] The Babylonian rabbis' interest in treating concerns about demons through extensive legal discourse is not found in earlier Jewish approaches to the demonic, but it is closely paralleled in contemporaneous Zoroastrian legal texts.

Zoroastrian texts demonstrate this legalizing trend with their modes of interpretation, glossing, and dialogic interplay. As part of this larger trend, increased legalization is evident in those rituals relating to demons, as seen in texts such as the *Pahlavi Vīdēvdād*. The *Pahlavi Vīdēvdād's* approach to demons clearly demonstrates this increasing interest in legal conceptualization and legalization. Let us look at one example, a passage

33. Elman, "The Other in the Mirror. Part One"; Yishai Kiel, "In the Margins of the Rabbinic Curriculum: Mastering *'Uqṣin* in the Light of Zoroastrian Intellectual Culture," *Journal for the Study of Judaism* 45 (2014):1–31; "Shaking Impurity: Exegesis and Innovative Traditions in the Babylonian Talmud and Pahlavi Literature," in *Encounters by the Rivers of Babylon: Scholarly Conversations between Jews, Iranians, and Babylonians in Antiquity*, ed. Shai Secunda and Uri Gabbay (Tübingen: Mohr Siebeck, 2014), 413–34; Strauch Schick, "Intention in the Babylonian Talmud." See also Leib Moscovitz, "Between Casuistics and Conceptualization: On the Term *Ameru Davar Ehad* in the Palestinian Talmud," *Jewish Quarterly Review* 91, no. 1/2 (2000): 101–42; *Talmudic Reasoning: From Casuistics to Conceptualization*, 343–66.

found at *Pahlavi Vīdēvdād* 5.38 which discusses the demonic attacks associated with death and dead bodies. The passage discusses whether a Zoroastrian can be polluted by the corpse of a non-Zoroastrian, and whether a non-Zoroastrian can be polluted by the corpse of a Zoroastrian. In the *Pahlavi Vīdēvdād*, corpse pollution is caused by an attack of the *druj ī Nasuš*, the female demon of defilement and dead matter; so the question becomes, does Nasuš attack non-Zoroastrians? The first paragraph is a Pahlavi translation of the Avestan *Vīdēvdād* with Pahlavi glosses in square brackets; the following paragraphs are a later commentary on that text.

> For alive, Spitama Zarathustra, the sinful, two-footed rogue [non-Iranian] and thus the unrighteous heretic, carries away from the righteous man enough food, clothing, wood, felt, and iron, not so when dead [not polluted].
>
> This is known from the Avesta: The non-Iranian always becomes *margazān*, a sinner deserving of death, like (a member of) an evil religion.
>
> Sōšāns said: We may not become unclean by their (corpses), for they are evil when alive and (sinners) deserving of death when dead; they may become unclean through our (corpses), for they do not count Nasuš in their law.
>
> Gōgušnasp said: They may not become polluted through our (corpses), for Nasuš does not rush on to anyone who does not have it in their law. But we may become polluted with their (corpses), because men of any religious law may become righteous; that is known from (the passage) *tuiriianąm daxiiunąm* (The [Law] of the Turanian Lands).[34]

The late fourth-century or early fifth-century jurist Sōšāns argues that Nasuš only attacks the corpses of right-thinking and right-behaving Zoroastrians, but the resulting corpse pollution can affect anyone who is not careful, including non-Zoroastrians. His contemporary Gōgušnasp inverts this position: any righteous person's corpse might be polluted by Nasuš after death, regardless of religious affiliation. However, only Zoroastrians are susceptible to the pollution spread by these corpses, as "Nasuš does not rush on to anyone who does not have it in their law."[35]

34. Translation adapted from Pahlavi *Vīdēvdād* 5.38, in Moazami, *Wrestling with the Demons of the Pahlavi Widēwdād*, 146–50.

35. See Elman, "The Other in the Mirror. Part One," for an extended and clarifying discussion of this passage of the Pahlavi *Vīdēvdād* in its Sasanian context.

The legal debate in the *Pahlavi Vīdēvdād* constructs Nasuš as aware of religious affiliation and as acting in ways that can be legally understood and quantified by the Zoroastrian jurists. While Nasuš is not subject to the sages' debate, according to Gōgušnasp and reminiscent of the Babylonian rabbis' claim that "anyone who is particular [about even numbers], [the demons] are particular about him," their very act of debating draws her attention and interest.

The *Pahlavi Vīdēvdād* also describes Nasuš rushing from the North into a corpse "in the form of a repelling fly, with knees crooked, with projecting buttocks, (having) unlimited phlegm... like the most sinful [the most polluted] evil animal."[36] Nasuš is repulsed and exorcised by exposing the corpse to the gaze of a dog or, according to some, a bird.[37] The *Pahlavi Vīdēvdād* interrogates this ritual legalistically:

> The dogs that smite the demon of dead matter are these: sheepdog, house dog, hunting dog (and) young dog.
>
> Sōšāns said: The crow also smites her (the demon of dead matter) and the blind dog when it lays its snout over (the dead boy), the mountain buzzard, the black crow and the lammergeyer when it casts its shadow over (the dead body); that is, when (its shadow) falls on (the dead body). It thus goes over (the dead body) if there is no cloud; then it casts its shadow over (the dead body) and will smite it. It smites (the demon of dead matter) through everything except through glass.
>
> There is one who says thus: It will not smite in the water or (when it is) covered; this too, when the dog looks up the back of the head of the man in contact, it will smite [the demon].[38]

Later Zoroastrian texts further develop their temporal, spatial, and ritual definitions of demonic attack and exorcism, and they mandate the isolation and restriction of dead bodies to the *daxma*, a circular burial chamber built far from human settlement.[39] These texts testify to a continuing

36. *Vīdēvdād* 7.2, in Moazami, *Wrestling with the Demons of the Pahlavi Widēwdād*, 185. See also *Dādestān ī Dēnīg* 16.6–7, in Mahmoud Jaafari-Dehaghi, *Dādestān Ī Dēnīg*, pt.1 (Paris : Association Pour L'Avancement des Études Iraniennes, 1998), 68–69.

37. See also S. K. Mendoza Forrest, *Witches, Whores, and Sorcerers: The Concept of Evil in Early Iran* (Austin: University of Texas Press, 2011), 50–51.

38. Pahlavi *Vīdēvdād* 7.2C–E, in Moazami, *Wrestling with the Demons of the Pahlavi Widēwdād*, 185.

39. The daxma appears to be a post-Islamic adaptation of Zoroastrian practice, when the public exposure of corpses would have been more difficult. See Pahlavi *Vīdēvdād* 7.53–58,

legal interest in preventing and regulating the attacks of demons such as Nasuš.

The rabbis' use of increasingly complex legal thinking about demons to undergird their legal system was part of a specific trend in late antique Sasanian Babylonia. In the late antique world, demonic discourses functioned primarily through narratives: cosmological epics, poems, and hagiographies. Only the Babylonian rabbis and the Zoroastrian commentators turned primarily to law as a way to construct, control, and avoid demons.

Although the rabbis and Zoroastrians share a discursive *form*, their demonologies were fundamentally different because demons functioned in different ways in their broader worldviews. For Zoroastrians, demons were the evil creations of the evil god Ahriman.[40] Jurists could create laws to avoid demonic attack and protect their followers. But demons and jurists existed in two fundamentally different conceptual realms, and never the twain shall meet. By contrast, the rabbis of Sasanian Babylonia were believers in a messy monotheism that left room for a range of intermediary beings all subjugated to a single, mostly benevolent Supreme Being. This theological context can partly explain the rabbis' intertwined interests in subjugating demons to rabbinic law and in integrating demons into the rabbinic world. What is particularly striking about this comparison is that both groups use similar terminology (Zoroastrians used *ŠDYA*, pronounced *dēw*, while a key rabbinic term was *šeid*) to describe two very different sorts of beings who were controlled in strangely similar ways.

DEMONS AS WITNESSES, WARNERS, AND DEFENDANTS IN THE RABBINIC COURT

Rabbinic discourse insisted that demons adhered to rabbinic constructions of time, space, and the body and were able to track the rabbis' convoluted math around even numbers. Through rabbinic legal discourse,

in Moazami, *Wrestling with the Demons of the Pahlavi Widēwdād*, 210–13; James R. Russell, "Burial. III. In Zoroastrianism," in *Encyclopædia Iranica Online* (2011), www.iranicaonline.org/articles/burial-iii.

40. A.V. Williams, "Dēw," in *Encyclopædia Iranica Online* (1994, 2011 updated online), www.iranicaonline.org/articles/dew. Note, however, that the intermediary being *Way* is depicted as neutral. My thanks to Yishai Kiel for pointing out *Way's* neutrality.

demons were subordinated to rabbinic authority and rabbinic law. The rabbinic use of demons to bolster rabbinic authority and motivate compliance with rabbinic law was only one part of a broader effort to incorporate demons fully into the rabbinic legal system. The rabbis complemented this stance with a discursive move unlike anything seen in the extant evidence from contemporaneous cultures: within the rabbinic system, demons could also function as subjects and agents. In the context of purity laws, Mira Balberg argues that "one does not actively become a person, as far as the rabbis are concerned, until one subordinates oneself to the law."[41] By emphasizing that demons were subjects and agents of rabbinic law, the rabbis insist on the personhood of demons, a personhood which, as we have already begun to see, could be neutral or even positively marked. Demons functioned as subjects and agents precisely in those areas that the rabbis recognized as having the most to do with demons: questions of identity and issues of space. At times, demonic actors are integrated into the legal system as a method of last resort. But at other times they are considered a priori participants in legal proceedings in the rabbinic court.

Demons appear in discussions of how to identify legitimate legal actors and witnesses. Thus, according to a mishnah in *Gittin* 6:6 and *Yevamot* 16:6, "If a man has been thrown into a pit and calls out, anyone who hears his voice should write a divorce document for the man's wife, those [who hear his voice] should write a divorce document and give it [to his wife]." A woman may be given permission to remarry based on a voice affirming that she is divorced, or a voice stating that her husband has died, *even if* the person whose voice it is remains unseen. In chapter 3, we examined the difficulty in distinguishing between demonic and human bodies when visibility is obscured. In b. *Gittin* 66a, the anonymous voice of the Babylonian Talmud raises this same concern: perhaps the voice, if not visibly attached to an identifiably human body, might belong to a demon? According to the anonymous voice in b. *Gittin* 66a,

> But should we not worry that he is a demon (šeid)? *R. Judah said: This is a case where he was seen to have the appearance of a human.* But [demons] can also look like men? This is a case where they can also see his shadow.

41. Balberg, *Purity, Body, and Self*, 132–33.

> But demons can also have a shadow? This is a case where they also saw the shadow of his shadow. And should you say that [demons] also have [a shadow of a shadow],[42] didn't R. Ḥanina say: My son[43] Jonathan taught me that they do have a shadow but they do not have a shadow of a shadow . . . A Tanna of the school of R. Ishmael taught: *In the time of danger, they write and give [the divorce document] even when they do not recognize the speaker.*[44]

In this Talmudic text, the difference between humans and demons is difficult to perceive visually and impossible to detect aurally. When the rabbis do not have the time to effectively gather and interrogate all witnesses, and with the confusion possible between the demonic and humankind, a demon can actually effect a legal divorce between a man and his wife. The rabbis do not allow the fear that a particular speaker is a demon to derail the legal process—a posteriori, demons can effect divorce. The demon's role as de facto legal actor is also supported by a statement attributed to Rava in b. *Makkot* 6b, that, in the case of the legal warning before a crime that leads to legal liability, "*the warning stands even if it was uttered by the actor himself, or even if it came from a demon (šeid).*" While Rava's statement may well be meant as a rhetorical device, the rhetoric works because of an underlying assumption that, in some situations, demons will turn out to have been effective legal actors with the potential to participate in the judicial system. These legal teachings imagine demons involving themselves in human legal matters, not only witnessing legal situations but also participating in them.

In the rabbinic imagination, demons could serve not only as witnesses and warners in legal contexts but also as defendants in court cases. A remarkable text in b. *Ḥullin* 105b contains the story of one such court case.

> Abaye said: At first, I thought the reason why one should not sit under a rain spout is because water pours out there. The master told me it was [actually] because demons (mazziqin) are common there.
>
> Certain porters were once carrying a barrel of wine. Wanting to rest, they placed the barrel under a rain spout. The barrel burst. They went before Mar

42. Emended according to MS Arras 889.

43. All the extant manuscripts read בני, yet the print edition of the exact parallel at b. *Yevamot* 122a reads שידא.

44. MS Arras 889.

> b. R. Ashi. He banned [the demon].[45] [The demon] came before [Mar b. R. Ashi] and said to him: What should I have done to those men? For they placed [the barrel] on my ear! [Mar b. R. Ashi] said to him: Even so, in a place where people are commonplace, you did not have the right! You acted improperly, now go and pay [for the barrel of wine]. [The demon] said to him: I do not have the money. Set a date on which I will pay. He set a date but [the demon] did not come on that day [to pay for the barrel.] When he came [at a later date], [Mar b. R. Ashi] said to him: Why did you not come on time? [The demon] said to him: We have no right to take anything that is tied up, sealed, collected, or counted, so we can only take things that are in a state of ownerlessness [and thus it took me longer to collect the money].

Certain spaces are marked as demonic, and this demarcation means that they are spaces that are safe for demons to occupy. This demon was not looking for humans to attack—he was sitting quietly (so quietly he could not be heard!) and minding his own business. It is only when the porters ignominiously place a barrel on his ear that he reacts with violence. Even then, the demon displaces the violence from the porters who have harmed him to the barrel itself, causing not physical but financial harm. For this response, Mar b. R. Ashi excommunicates the unnamed demon, an act which the demon resists. Although presumably the demon was originally invisible (otherwise, why would they have placed the barrel on top of him?), he now literally appears before the court of Mar b. R. Ashi to explain himself. Mar b. R. Ashi rules that the demon should have been more aware of humans in a public space and finds him financially liable. We might expect the demon to reject the court's ruling and its deadline for repayment, but the demon himself testifies to his respect for the limitations on how and what demons can collect from humankind. The demon's presumed membership in the rabbinic community is highlighted in Mar b. R. Ashi's initial excommunication of the demon; you can only expel from your community someone who was already a member. The demon's response—rushing to the court to defend himself—suggests that this pre-

45. This expression, "שמתיה" (he banned him), has parallels in both verb and noun forms in reference to demons to Bo. 82:6, 14:9, 106:4, 90:2, in Sokoloff, *A Dictionary of Jewish Babylonian Aramaic*, 1162–63, s.v. שמת and שמתא. See also Geller, "Joshua B. Perahia and Jesus of Nazareth," 87. In the Babylonian Talmud, it can also refer to the ban or excommunication of a person from the rabbinic community. See, e.g., b. *Baba Meẓia* 108b, b. *Baba Qamma* 15b, b. *Megillah* 16b, b. *Ḥullin* 18a, b. *Qiddushin* 70b.

sumption of membership is mutual. According to the logic of the narrative, the demon is a law-abiding citizen with all the rights and all the responsibilities that this identity entails.

As we have seen in the last chapter, human beings are usually cautioned to take care in times and places where demons are common. In b. *Ḥullin* 106a, however, the inverse is true; demons are cautioned to take care in places where humans are common. Demons are liable for disobeying rabbinic teachings because they are understood to be responsible, legally competent agents and subjects of the law. In this account, as in the pseudo-baraita in b. *Pesaḥim* discussed above, demons do not generally occupy themselves with thinking about humans or harming humans; they would rather be left alone and leave others alone in turn. Demons only attack when they are first attacked themselves, when they are explicitly provoked by actions understood to be generally harmful or particularly provoking to demons. The rabbis' depiction of demons is not in accord with modern perceptions of ancient demonology that imagines demons as malevolent and aggressive to unsuspecting humans.[46] On this point, it is also not in accord with contemporaneous Zoroastrian demonology.

The rabbis control demons through rabbinic law and concomitantly integrate demons into the rabbinic legal system as witnesses, warners, and even as defendants. This act of integration allows demons to succeed and even flourish according to the rabbinic metrics of success. Indeed, some demons even become rabbinic teachers themselves.

DEMONS AS RABBINIC TRADENTS AND TEACHERS

At least one Talmudic demon developed a reputation as a rabbinic teacher in his own right—Joseph the demon (šeida). Joseph the demon appears in both legal texts and legal contexts; he is consistently presented as teaching the rabbis about issues both demonic and nondemonic.

46. See discussion of this phenomenon in Sara Ronis, "A Demonic Servant in Rav Papa's Household: Demons as Subjects in the Mesopotamian Talmud," in *The Aggada of the Babylonian Talmud and Its Cultural World*, ed. Geoffrey Herman and Jeffrey L. Rubenstein (Providence, RI: Brown Judaic Studies, 2018), 3–21.

Joseph the demon appears as an important informant in the same extended text about even numbers discussed above. Although to be fair, if one wants insight into the world of the demonic, who better to ask than a demon himself?

> R. Joseph said: Joseph the demon (šeida) told me: Ashmedai the king of the demons (šeidei) is appointed over even numbers, and a king is not called a demon (mazziq, lit: harmer). And some say, on the contrary, a king has the authority in his hands [to harm whomever he pleases].
>
> R. [Papa] said: Joseph the demon (šeida) told me: For two we kill, for four we [only harm]. With two, [we punish] whether it was accidental or intentional [to drink an even number]; with four, if it was accidental, no, but if it was intentional yes. And if he happens to go out [having drunk even numbers], let him hold his straight right arm [sleeve] in his left arm [sleeve] and that of the left in his right arm [sleeve], and let him say: You (pl.) and I are three. And if he hears someone say [You and I are] four, let him say, [You and] I are five. And if he hears someone say [You and I are] six, let him say, [You and I are] seven.
>
> This once happened and when they reached one hundred and one, the demon (šeida) burst.

Two different Babylonian sages transmit Joseph the demon's teachings, and they cite him using a citation formula that rabbis traditionally use to quote their own rabbinic teachers.[47] Thus the rabbis themselves introduce the demonic informant Joseph as a teacher of rabbis.

Joseph's first teaching neutralizes demonic dangers by defanging the king of demons and his followers. His teaching is a pun on the word *mazziq*, which means both "harmer" and "demon." Joseph the demon suggests that Ashmedai king of the demons is, in fact, not a harmful demon at all, and so even numbers cannot cause harm to human beings. Joseph the demon protects humanity from demonic forces by organizing the demonic world along the same monarchical lines as the human world. We will further discuss the rabbinic characterization of Ashmedai later in

47. A cursory search through the Bar Ilan Responsa database shows eight instances of this citation formula in the Mishnah and one hundred and two instances of this citation formula in the Babylonian Talmud. In the overwhelming majority of these instances, an Amora cites another Amora of the previous generation, referring to a teaching that he apparently personally received.

this chapter. An anonymous voice challenges Joseph's interpretation, not on the basis of Ashmedai's demonic nature but because of the everyday realities inherent in an absolute monarchy. The exegetical uncertainty is immediately resolved by Joseph's second teaching.

Joseph's second teaching aligns more neatly with broader rabbinic legal strategies. In distinguishing between the accidental and intentional consumption of an even number of drinks, Joseph the demon continues a strategy first employed by the Torah and then by the Mishnah in a variety of legal and ethical spheres. Categorizations based on intent can be found, for example, in sacrificial law and the laws governing sexual relationships, murder, and the desecration of God's name.[48] As Strauch Schick has demonstrated, the Palestinian and Babylonian Talmuds apply the category of intent to an even wider legal sphere, using it as a basic building block to determine liability in a wide range of violations of halakhah.[49] Joseph the demon's recourse to intentionality is another example of how demons are constructed together with halakhic terms, concepts, and literary structures. The demonic is not outside the halakhic system; it is understood and regulated through the halakhic categories that organize rabbinic law more generally.

Joseph is treated as a reliable tradent who proposes the successful solution if one has drunk an even number of drinks.[50] By grasping one's arms,

48. For Torah, see Exod. 21:12–14; Num. 21, 35. For the Mishnah, see, e.g., m. *Yevamot* 6:1; m. *Qiddushin* 2:8; m. *Zevaḥim* 8: 12; m. *Avot* 4:4. The Tosefta also uses these categories in discussions of Sabbath observance. See t. *Shabbat* 10: 19.

49. See, e.g., p. *Gittin* 5:5 (46a–b); p. *Demai* 4:1 (23d–24a); p. *Yevamot* 6:1 (7b); p. *Ketubot* 3:1 (27b–c); p. *Nedarim* 2:2 (37b); b. *Gittin* 53a; b. *Baba Qamma* 32b, 85a; b. *Megillah* 15b; b. *Sanhedrin* 8b, 76b; b. *Eruvin* 68b; b. *Shabbat* 38a, 68b. See also Strauch Schick, "Intention in the Babylonian Talmud."

50. Veltri, "The Rabbis and Pliny the Elder," 72, quotes Pliny writing that one who sits with his fingers interlaced in the presence of pregnant women or patients being treated for illness is guilty of witchcraft. Veltri suggests that the binding of the hands together symbolizes the binding of someone else's witchcraft or evil intents from achieving their intended effect. In the case of b. *Pesaḥim* 110a, it has the additional effect of asserting "oddness." The physical action is paralleled in b. *Berakhot* 55b, where the same gesture of the hands in combination protects against the evil eye when performed together with the statement, "I, P son of P come from the seed of Joseph, over whom the evil eye does not rule, as it is said, 'Joseph is a fruitful bough, a fruitful bought *alei ayin*' (Gen. 49:22)." For a discussion of this passage and the evil eye, see Richard Kalmin, "The Evil Eye in Rabbinic Literature of Late Antiquity," in *Judaea-Palaestina, Babylon and Rome: Jews in Antiquity*, ed. Benjamin Isaac and Yuval Shahar (Tübingen: Mohr Siebeck, 2012), 116–17. It thus appears to be a posture meant to protect against unseen harms.

the subject becomes the essence of "oddness," with his (now conjoined one) arm and (two) legs equaling only three limbs. The speaker must then maintain his assertion of "oddness" even though a demonic voice attempts to join with him to create an even number.[51] In the context of the sugya, Joseph the demon's teaching is immediately put into practice: the anonymous voice tells us that this very scene once occurred and not only was the human saved but also the demon burst and was destroyed. Joseph's teaching proves its effectiveness. One demon's danger is neutralized by another demon's rabbinic teaching.

Joseph the demon appears again in b. *Eruvin* 43a, where his role as teacher to the rabbis is made even more explicit.

> Come and listen: Who was it that said seven legal traditions on a Sabbath morning in front of R. Ḥisda at Sura and [then again] on the same Sabbath late afternoon in front of Rabbah at Pumbedita? Some say that it was Elijah who said them, which proves that *the law of Sabbath limits [the distance one can travel outside a city on the Sabbath] does not apply above ten tefaḥim* [i.e., handsbreadths from the ground and therefore Elijah could travel this distance on the Sabbath because he flew in his flying chariot (See 2 Kings 2)]. No, perhaps the demon (šeida) Joseph said them [and demons move great distances in the blink of an eye].[52]

It would take thirty-seven hours to walk from the rabbinic center of Sura to the rabbinic center of Pumbedita on twenty-first-century roads.[53] Presumably, it would have taken even longer in late antiquity. The challenge of delivering rabbinic lectures in both places within the same twenty-five-hour span of a single Sabbath could only be met by a being with superhuman powers—Elijah or Joseph the demon. The parallels between the two figures—both liminal figures, at times outsiders and at times at the center of the rabbinic world, both dangerous but also mainly using their power for good—are a provocative and informative window into how this teach-

51. Veltri, "The Rabbis and Pliny the Elder," 72, suggests that the binding of the hands together symbolizes the binding of someone else's witchcraft or evil intents from achieving their intended effect. See discussion in chap. 6.

52. Interestingly, the Soncino translation of this text glosses Joseph the demon's name with the phrase "who would break the Sabbath laws with impunity." When Joseph is placed into his proper context in rabbinic demonology, however, we see that Joseph is not a Sabbath-breaker at all; he uses his supernatural abilities to facilitate rabbinic Torah learning on the Sabbath.

53. According to Google Maps.

ing's anonymous author imagined the nature and role of demons. Like the prophet Elijah, Joseph the demon has been chosen to uphold the rabbinic movement. Joseph the demon has become the rabbinic teacher par excellence; he uses his ability to move large distances in the blink of an eye to further the rabbinic project by teaching legal traditions to rabbis at both hearts of the Babylonian rabbinic world.[54]

Even Joseph the demon's name is remarkable. In contrast to Christian and Zoroastrian demons whose names often translate to human failings (Lust, Wrath, Sloth, Gluttony, etc.) Joseph has a righteous biblical name. The manuscript tradition is extremely corrupted, but it is possible that other Talmudic texts reference demons named Jonathan and Yoḥanan, names also drawn from biblical and Jewish history.[55]

Joseph the demon's relationship to the rabbis and rabbinic teachings is also recognized outside the text of the Babylonian Talmud. One Aramaic incantation bowl includes "Rabbi Joseph the demon (šeda)" in a list of rabbis who issued a historic ban against demonic threat.[56] Here Joseph is not simply a teacher of rabbis but a titled rabbi himself.

Joseph's participation in the rabbinic movement as a tradent and teacher sheds light on a text we have already encountered in chapter 3, from b. *Berakhot* 6a:

> It was taught in a baraita: *Abba Benjamin said: If the eye had been given permission to see them, no creature could withstand the demons (mazziqin).* R. Joseph said: They are more numerous than we are, and they stand around us like a mound to a furrow. R. Huna said: Each of us has one thousand [demons] to his left and one thousand to his right. Abaye said: The pressure at the kallah (the periodic rabbinic public study session in Babylonia)[57]

54. The idea of rabbinically erudite demons who observe Jewish law as laid out by the rabbis is expanded into an entire realm of halakhically observant demons in the medieval *Tale of the Jerusalemite*. See discussion in chap. 5. See also Joseph Dan, "Five Versions of the Story of the Jerusalemite," *Proceedings of the American Academy for Jewish Research* 35 (1967): 99–111; David Stern, "The Tale of the Jerusalemite," in *Rabbinic Fantasies: Imaginative Narratives from Classical Hebrew Literature*, ed. David H. Stern and Mark J. Mirsky (New Haven, CT: Yale University Press, 1998), 121–42. Although Dan argues that demons are first imagined to be Jews in the medieval period, it is clear from the discussion above that at least *some* demons were imagined as rabbinic Jews in Talmudic times.

55. See b. *Yevamot* 122a. The identity of this demon remains uncertain. See chap. 2, n. 71.

56. JBA 26 (MS 1928/43), in Shaul Shaked et al. *Aramaic Bowl Spells: Jewish Babylonian Aramaic Bowls*, vol. 1 (Leiden: Brill, 2013), 153.

57. For discussions of the kallah, see chap. 3.

> is from them, and the wearying of one's knees is from them, and the wearing out of the garments of scholars is from [the demons'] rubbing, and the bruising of one's feet is from them.[58]

Demons are found everywhere, but they are so packed in at the rabbinic kallah that they have physical effects on the rabbis present. Chapter 3 examined how the rabbis used the presence of demons to mark the domestic and intellectual centers of the rabbinic world. But how did they understand the demonic interest in these centers? What did they think demons were *doing* in these spaces? If demons are malevolent and seek to do only evil, then perhaps they attend the kallah to harm the rabbis. But this interpretation is unlikely given the broader characterizations of demons in the Bavli. In fact, this text is remarkably neutral about demons; the rabbis are overwhelmed by their sheer numbers, but their character is not discussed. Yet given the ways that the rabbis construct demons as subordinated to rabbinic law, and as tradents and teachers of the rabbis, it makes sense that demons, like all other members of the rabbinic community, would attend the annual assembly of the rabbis and their followers. The overcrowding at the kallah is thus an unpleasant but unintentional side effect of being part of a robust community with members both visible and invisible.

DEMONIC RULERS AND RABBINIC ANXIETIES

The integration of demons into rabbinic law and the rabbinic legal system functioned to neutralize demonic threats and incentivize compliance with rabbinic laws. But, as demons were understood to be a distinct creation with superhuman abilities, this integration also created the opportunity for new rabbinic anxieties. If demons had more power than the rabbis, and demons could become rabbis, what was to stop demons from becoming *better* rabbis than the rabbis themselves? This anxiety comes to the fore in a long narrative passage in b. *Gittin* 68a–b.

The story is attached to a broader discussion in b. *Gittin* 66a about a

58. My thanks to Natalie Polzer for bringing this text to my attention and for being my conversation partner on it.

specific demon, *kordiakos*, who attacks those who drink new wine.[59] Following this discussion, the redactors of the sugya attach a story which also juxtaposes a particular demon and wine. The story is set in the biblical past, when King Solomon began to build the First Temple in Jerusalem. 1 Kings 6:7 prohibits using any metal implements in quarrying and cutting the stones needed for construction, and so, according to the talmudic story, Solomon is uncertain how to go about building the Temple. Solomon asks the rabbis, here retrojected back into the biblical period, what to do. The rabbis inform Solomon that there is something called the *shamir* which can cut stones without metal, and they suggest that Solomon seek out a male and female demon in order to ask them how to find it.[60] The male and female demon captured by Solomon do not know the location of the shamir but suggest that "Ashmedai king of the demons (šeidim) would know." When Solomon asks them where Ashmedai is to be found, the demons reply,

> He is on such-and-such mountain. [Solomon asked:] How will I recognize it? [They responded:] He has dug a well, and filled it with water [to drink], and covered it with a large flint rock, and sealed it with his seal. Every day he ascends to the heavenly academic session and learns the heavenly Torah lesson, and then descends to the earthly academic session and learns the earthly Torah lesson and inspects his seal and uncovers [the well] and drinks and covers it and leaves.[61]

59. This demon is an example of hyperdemonization in the Babylonian Talmud. M. Gittin 7:1 states that "*one who was seized by a kordiakos and said: Write a get for my wife, it is as if he has said nothing*." In the context of the mishnah, kordiakos appears to be a medical condition, and indeed, translators and scholars have identified a number of medical conditions that could be at the root of this phrase. See Sara Ronis, "'Do Not Go Out Alone at Night': Law and Demonic Discourse in the Babylonian Talmud" (PhD diss., Yale University, 2015), 201–02, for a summary of these interpretations. The verb *A.H.Z.*, translated here as "to seize," is used in the Mishnah more broadly to describe physiological actions with physiological responses. See, e.g., m. *Bekhorot* 5:2; m. *Shabbat* 16:5; m. *Yoma* 8:6. Although there is no consensus on the word's meaning, this mode of interpretation of the mishnah in Gittin is continued by the Palestinian Talmud in p. *Gittin* 7:1 (48c) which treats this phrase as a marker of mental incompetence. B. *Gittin* 67b, however, is either unaware or uninterested in what modern readers might call a medical interpretation, and instead turns to the demonic.

60. According to m. *Avot* 5:6, the Shamir was created at sundown on the sixth day of creation, just like demons were. Perhaps their affinity to each other stems from this shared genesis.

61. Following MS Vatican 130.

According to this account, the demon king spends his day studying Torah in rabbinic academies, first in heaven, and then, presumably with actual rabbis, on earth. Perhaps aware of rabbinic prohibitions against drinking water that has been "exposed" overnight, he takes extensive precautions to drink only covered, uncontaminated water.[62] To capture Ashmedai, King Solomon's messenger Benayahu b. Yehoyada uses the power of gravity to sneakily empty the well and fill it with wine while leaving the seal undisturbed. When the demon king uncovers his well and discovers the wine,

> He said: It is written, "*Wine is a scoffer, strong drink a roisterer, [he who is muddled by them will not grow wise]*" (Prov. 20:1, NJPS); and it is written, "*Lechery, wine, and new wine destroy the mind [of My people]*" (Hos. 4:11, NJPS). I will not drink. When he got thirsty, he could not [hold himself back]. [He said: It is written, "[You (God) make . . .] *Wine that cheers the heart of men*" (Ps. 104:15, NJPS)].[63]

Ashmedai's ability to cite and manipulate biblical verses to achieve particular aims is remarkably rabbinic. His manipulation of these verses reminds us that wine—like demons—can be positive or negative forces in a man's life. Inevitably, Ashmedai falls into a drunken stupor and Benayahu binds him with chains inscribed with the Tetragrammaton, God's holy four-letter name. When Ashmedai awakes and struggles with the chains, Benayahu tells him, "The name of your Master is upon you, the name of your Master is upon you." Ashmedai immediately calms; he recognizes God as his master and subjugates himself to divine authority.[64]

62. See m. *Terumot* 8:4–5; b. *Ḥullin* 9b–10a.

63. See Kalmin, *Migrating Tales,* 99 n. 13, for a discussion of the inclusion of this line.

64. To this point, the narrative partly parallels the account in the *Testament of Solomon,* discussed in chap. 2. There demons interfere with Solomon's building of the Temple, until Solomon prays to God in the Temple (?) and the angel Michael gives Solomon a ring with a sacred seal to "imprison all the demons, both female and male, and with their help you shall build Jerusalem when you bear this seal of God" (1:5 in Duling, "Testament of Solomon," 962). At this point, the demon Ornias appears in order to attack a small boy, and Solomon instructs the boy to throw the ring at the demon and shout, "Come! Solomon summons you." The boy effectively traps the demon and brings Ornias to Solomon, who then takes command of the demon. With the support of the angel Ouriel, Solomon forces Ornias and his demonic minions to work on the Temple while also interrogating each of the demons about their powers, abilities, and weaknesses. The story ends with all the demons controlled, the Temple built, and Solomon in power and being led astray by foreign women. The two stories are clearly related, most likely as different articulations of oral stories that circulated about

The next part of the story follows standard folkloric tropes. On their journey back to Solomon's palace, Ashmedai and Benayahu meet a series of stock characters. In each case, Ashmedai is able to see beyond these characters' present circumstances to their true natures and destinies. For example, Ashmedai laughs when he sees a man ask a shoemaker for shoes that will last seven years. He later explains that the man is destined to die within the next seven days, making his desire for long-lasting shoes ludicrous. After several such encounters, Ashmedai is brought to Jerusalem. There, he is made to wait for a number of days because of Solomon's drunkenness and gluttony. Eventually, when Solomon sobers up, Ashmedai tells him how to find the shamir. With the help of the shamir, Solomon's workers then build the Temple, but even when the work is completed, the human king continues to enslave the demon king.

One day, Solomon asks Ashmedai a question. "*It is written, "[God who freed them from Egypt is for them] like the to'afot re'em" (Num. 24:8) [lit: eminences of an ox]*,[65] and we explained: "*Like the to'afot*," those are the ministering angels; "*re'em*," those are the demons (*šedim*)." Solomon's interpretation of the verse parallels angels, demons, and God Goddself. But the verse appears to contrast these three with humans. Solomon inquires about this contrast: "How are you greater than [humans]?" Ashmedai cunningly replies, "Take the chain [with the Tetragrammaton inscribed upon it] off of me and give me your seal-ring [inscribed with the Tetragrammaton]—I will show you how I am greater." Although at this point, even a less-than-savvy reader might be shouting, "It's a trap!" Solomon seems unaware of any possible ulterior motives. He removes the chain and gives Ashmedai the royal ring of power. Immediately, Ashmedai "swallowed it, placed one wing in heaven and the other wing on earth [to brace himself] and hurled [Solomon] four hundred miles [away]." With Solomon gone, the demon king steals the human king's identity, imper-

Solomon. These stories have an even older origin; see Josephus, *Antiquities of the Jews*, 8.45; and see extensive discussion in Torijano, *Solomon the Esoteric King*. These tropes are shaped by each cultural context and do distinct work: the demons in the *Testament of Solomon* prophesy the coming of Jesus and their eventual destruction, while the demon in B. *Gittin* serves to uphold the authority of the rabbis and express rabbinic anxieties around their construction of the demonic. The association of Solomon and the demonic continues into the Qur'an, discussed in chap. 5.

65. See NJPS translation, note on Num. 23:22.

sonating Solomon and ruling in his stead. He even has sex with some of the women in Solomon's harem. This act is what leads to his downfall; it is his insistence on wearing socks during coitus that allows the rabbis to realize that he is not the king but a demon with chicken feet, a common demonic feature discussed in chapter 2.[66] Solomon makes his way back to Jerusalem and presents himself to the rabbis. They give Solomon another ring inscribed with God's name on it and another set of chains, to help him expose Ashmedai and eject the demon king from the palace. But all is not well, for Solomon remains traumatized by the experience and must develop new coping mechanisms, "and thus it is written, *'There is Solomon's couch encircled by sixty warriors of the warriors of Israel, all of them trained in warfare, skilled in battle, each with sword on thigh [because of terror by night]'* (Song of Sol. 3:7–8, NJPS)."

The story is capped by a debate attributed to the third-generation Amoraim Rav and Shmuel: "*One said: [Solomon was first] a king and [later] a commoner, and the other said: [First] a king and [later] a commoner and [then again] a king.*" The story ends on a note of uncertainty about whether Solomon ever regains his throne.

The story's opening leads the reader to believe that this will be a narrative in which Solomon is both the main character and the hero. But as the narrative progresses, it becomes clear that, in fact, Ashmedai is at the center of the tale. And he is a sympathetic center at that. It is Ashmedai who embodies rabbinic values: study in the rabbinic academies, knowledge of Torah, wisdom, and political power. As Kalmin argues, Solomon is here depicted as "a magician who fails because he is deficient in rabbinic learning."[67] The Talmud's version of Solomon—with his inability to understand the biblical text without recourse to demonic insight, his various excesses, his ability to be fooled—is remarkably unimpressive.[68] Even in the eventual reversal of the power relations, Ashmedai remains sym-

66. It is unclear whether the rabbis are characterizing Ashmedai as distinctively lustful, as in Tobit, or if they imagine that he is merely keeping up appearances.

67. Kalmin, *Migrating Tales*, 97.

68. Kalmin, *Migrating Tales*, 114, argues that "it is possible that the audience is meant to think more highly of Ashmedai than of Solomon." I concur, but it is not only possible but also probable given the narrative flow of the story.

pathetic in his desire for revenge. Narratively, Ashmedai works with the rabbis to critique Solomon's behaviors and problematize his reputation.

Scholars have examined this extended narrative through the lens of source-criticism, folklore studies, and Jewish mysticism.[69] Ashmedai's name is originally derived from the Young Avestan demon *aēšmō.daēva*, the Zoroastrian demon of Wrath.[70] Ashmedai actually appears in an earlier Jewish text, the second-century B.C.E. apocryphal book of Tobit, where he is depicted as the lustful, jealous, and murderous demon Asmodeus. But while the Talmudic demon king thus emerges out of a long literary tradition, his representation in this rabbinic narrative is distinct from earlier depictions. Here, the demon king is decidedly not characterized by wrath or lust; the rabbis treat the name Ashmedai as a proper name not a statement of character.[71]

Ashmedai king of the demons also appears in the text of Moussaieff 164, the incantation bowl discussed above. There, he is invoked—together with Metatron, the signet-ring of Solomon, and other beings and objects of power—in order to expel a demon from the house of Abandad son of Batgada and Sami daughter of Parsita.[72] Both the Bavli and this incantation bowl text depict Ashmedai positively. In the incantation text, Ashmedai's power comes from his position in the heavenly court; in the rabbinic

69. For a source critical reading of this text, see Kalmin, *Migrating Tales*, 95–129. For a folkloric approach, see Eli Yassif, *Sipur Ha-Am Ha-Ivri: Toldotav, Sugav U-Mashma'uto* (Jerusalem: Mossad Bialik, 1994), 102–03. For a reading of the text through a later mystical lens, see Raphael Patai, "Lilith," *Journal of American Folklore* 77 (1964): 295–314. Patai cites a medieval midrash which names Ashmedai's father as David himself: "One night, David was asleep in the camp in the desert, and in his dream Igrath coupled with him and bore Adad [identical with Hadad the Edomite]. And when they asked him, "What is your name?" he answered, "My name is Ad, Ad is my name" (*Ad sh'mi* in Hebrew), and they called him Ashm'dai. He is Ashmodai, the King of the demons who deprived Solomon of his kingdom" (307, and see n. 62). This midrash reframes the Talmudic story as a legitimate dynastic struggle for the throne between two of the king's sons, Ashmedai (the older brother—and thus perhaps the legitimate king?), and Solomon (the younger). This dynamic, where the younger brother Solomon takes the throne when he perhaps should not have, mirrors the biblical narrative of Solomon's ascent to the throne in 2 Sam.

70. J. P. Asmussen, "Aēšma," in *Encyclopædia Iranica Online* (1983, 2011 updated online), www.iranicaonline.org/articles/aesma-wrath.

71. Although, at the end of the story, the Talmudic Ashmedai may be understood to be just as vengeful as the apocryphal Asmodeus.

72. Levene, "'If You Appear as a Pig': Another Incantation Bowl (Moussaieff 164)," 61.

text, it apparently comes from his rabbinic knowledge, some of which is learned in the heavenly yeshiva.

The Babylonian Talmud's Ashmedai is not simply a Zoroastrian demon in rabbinic garb. Kalmin compellingly describes Ashmedai in this story as a "rabbinized Jewish holy man;" for much of the story, Ashmedai is a remarkably effective though somewhat antisocial rabbi.[73] Where Christian writers had taken Greek daimones and turn them into malevolent demons, here the rabbis take a Zoroastrian demon and turned him into a rabbinic sage.

But the rabbinic depiction of Ashmedai and his actions is not all positive. Ashmedai's behavior takes a sinister turn when he outsmarts Solomon and usurps his throne. Kalmin and Reuven Kiperwasser have both argued that this tonal shift is evidence of the seams between two or more earlier sources that have been combined and recombined.[74] This source-critical observation is persuasive. On the level of the text as redacted and transmitted to the reader, however, Ashmedai's characterization highlights rabbinic anxieties about demons—both the anxiety that demons might remain partially uncontrollable and the anxiety that, when part of the rabbinic system, these intermediary beings might out-rabbi the rabbis. Ashmedai, with his manifold abilities—his abilities to study in the academies in heaven and on earth, to manipulate biblical verses for various ends, and to perceive the truth of reality in a way no human could—might end up being smarter than the rabbis themselves. Ashmedai certainly outsmarts King Solomon, whose abilities to summon and control the natural and supernatural world open the tale. Thus, this narrative concludes by upholding rabbinic ingenuity against non-rabbinic expertise such as that of Solomon. It takes targeted and collective rabbinic investigation to discover that the king is now an impostor and then to

73. Kalmin, *Migrating Tales*, 116. As Kalmin argues, "the story also domesticates the king of the demons by depicting him as a danger to no one and a source of no disruption as long as human beings make no attempt to rule over him or confine him to civilization. He possesses esoteric information that it is occasionally important for human beings to acquire, but once that information has been supplied the relationship should end. Trouble ensues when Solomon refuses to allow Ashmedai to return to his mountaintop" (ibid., 119).

74. Kalmin, *Migrating Tales*, 95–129; Reuven Kiperwasser, "Solomon, Ashmedai and Other Friends," unpublished work, 2016.

take action to expel him from the palace.[75] This not-entirely-controllable intermediary being poses a potential challenge to rabbinic supremacy at the same time as he upholds studying Torah in rabbinic houses of study and rabbinic modes of thinking as the most worthwhile ways in which to spend one's time.

The integration of demons into rabbinic space, time, and law creates tremendous opportunities for rabbinic creativity, holistic legal thinking, and self-authorization. Like their Zoroastrian contemporaries, the rabbis used the law and legal discourse to circumscribe and control demonic forces. But this legal discourse is paired with a characterization of the demonic as subjects, agents, and tradents of the rabbinic legal system in ways that have no parallels to contemporaneous religious practices and beliefs. This rabbinic characterization points to a distinctive way of understanding the nature and function of demons. As the narrative about Ashmedai and Solomon shows, however, this rabbinic "solution" to the problem of demons created new problems and anxieties of its own. The next chapter explores one way that the rabbis attempt to solve this problem of their own making.

75. See Kalmin, *Migrating Tales*, 125. Kalmin identifies the rabbinic action here as an exorcism. I take up this topic in chap. 6.

5 Serving the Rabbinic Project

What praise is more valuable than the praise
of an intelligent servant?

Jane Austen, *Pride and Prejudice*

Everyone in late antique Babylonia agreed—demons were dangerous. For the Babylonian rabbis, demons posed particularly dangers related to space, time, and the human body. But as we have seen, for the rabbis, demons were also dangerous because the rabbinic construction of demons' superhuman abilities—their physical abilities, and their intellectual abilities as applied to the study of Torah—posed a direct challenge to rabbinic intellectual supremacy. The rabbis feared that demons could and *would* out-rabbi the rabbis. One way that the rabbis dealt with this problem of their own making was to subordinate demons to rabbinic authority, making demons servants of the rabbinic project and making at least one demon the literal servant of a rabbi. In making these moves, the rabbis prove to be aligned with much older Mesopotamian religious traditions.

The last two chapters have explored the ways that the rabbis used demons to discursively condition their followers to live rabbinically as they eat, drink, go to the bathroom, have sex, sleep, and move through the public and private domains. There are multiple demonic discourses at play. The rabbis acknowledge demonic danger as they undermine it for

Epigraph: Jane Austen, *Pride and Prejudice* (London: Wordsworth Editions, 1999), 167.

their own followers: if you follow rabbinic dicta, you are largely safe from demonic attack; but if you disobey rabbinic dicta, you will be attacked by demons. This type of totalizing discourse, whether or not it was ever actually enacted in particular rabbis' lived experiences, involved both rewards (the proud lineage, spiritual fulfillment, and prestige of belonging to the rabbinic class) and punishment (dangerous demons). The rabbis control and neutralize capricious, dangerous intermediary beings; at the same time, the rabbis construct demons as enforcers of rabbinic law.

The first part of this chapter expands on the ways that the rabbis use demons positively to affirm rabbinic superiority: to mark important people in the community, to gain exclusive access to supernatural information, and to build themselves up as literal masters of demonic servants. In the second part of the chapter, the rabbis' positive construction of demons is diachronically situated in a thick cultural web dating back to ancient Mesopotamia. I demonstrate the continued relevance of this discursive move from ancient Sumer and Akkad into the medieval period, pointing to the importance of positive demon servants to a range of religious traditions and their understandings of the world, their own power, and their privileged relationship to the divine.

AN IMPORTANT MAN IS DIFFERENT

Constructing demons as subordinate to the rabbis and the rabbinic project requires affirming that demons recognize rabbinic prestige. The rabbis perform this affirmation by insisting that demons are more likely to attack those who provoke them if the provokers are important, that is, elite rabbis, than if they are common folk.[1] When one anonymous voice in b. *Pesaḥim* 109b asserts that people are free from the danger of even numbers if they drink in their own homes with no intention of leaving, this position is immediately contradicted by the examples of Rava, Abaye, and

1. The phrase appears fourteen times in the Bavli and functions consistently throughout. See Zvi Aryeh Steinfeld, "Adam Ḥashuv Shani," *Dine Israel* 13–14 (1987): 196, which notes that this expression does not appear in the parallel sugyot in the Yerushalmi, when such parallels exist.

R. Yitzḥak [b. R. Yehuda], who were (necessarily) careful of even numbers in their own homes because the danger still existed in these domestic sanctuaries. To resolve the contradiction, the anonymous voice insists that "an important man is different."[2] The anonymous voice introduces personal status as a factor in the susceptibility to demonic danger, a factor which is amplified throughout the course of the discussion. These illustrious sages are susceptible to demonic attack when others are not precisely *because* these sages are more important than everyone else. Demons pay rabbis more attention and expect more caution and care from them because, to demons, rabbis are important people.

In a curious parallel, in discussing women and the danger of even numbers, the same sugya insists that demons only attack women who are important. The idea that important or prominent women are in a different halakhic category than nonimportant women is not unique to this sugya.[3] The rabbis thought that important women's honor and prestige had practical implications for the laws relating to their dress and behavior in the public sphere.[4] The exemption of ordinary women from the dangers of even numbers is evidence that, for the rabbis, susceptibility to demonic activity is a marker of high status. Since only important people are the focus of demonic attention, this attention is neither embarrassing nor shameful. Instead, it is a status symbol.[5]

2. The anonymous voice thus upholds the original law and validates the examples which appear to contradict it.

3. The concept appears in multiple locations in the Bavli, though it does not appear in the rabbinic literature of late antique Palestine. Its usage supports Richard Kalmin's contention that the Babylonian rabbis were significantly more concerned about class and prestige than the Palestinian rabbis were. See Richard Kalmin, *The Sage in Jewish Society of Late Antiquity* (London: Routledge, 1999) 7–12.

4. See, e.g., b. *Shabbat* 59b, which discusses women's adornments on the Sabbath. Important women are permitted to wear elaborate hair decorations on the Sabbath because "important women do not remove their hair ornaments [in public and so there is no fear of carrying on the Sabbath]." Similarly, some manuscripts of b. *Baba Meẓia* 9b state that an important woman acquires an animal even without leading it because it would be beneath her dignity to do so in the marketplace. See also b. *Pesaḥim* 108a, b. *Avodah Zarah* 25b, and b. *Ketubot* 71b.

5. Read against this background, the Babylonian rabbinic belief that demons are interested only in the rabbis of the Babylonian East and not those of the Palestinian West, discussed in chap. 4, is yet another subtle way that the Babylonian rabbis construct themselves as superior to their western colleagues.

IF I AM IMPORTANT IN HEAVEN

But it was not enough to argue that demons pronounced at least some rabbis to be superior to common folk. Constructing demons as subordinate to the rabbis and the rabbinic project required demonic affirmation that the rabbis were superior to demons themselves—in knowledge, power, and divine approbation. This affirmation is found in b. *Pesaḥim* 112b.

We have already seen in chapter 4 that b. *Pesaḥim* 112b lists three things that R. Judah commanded Rav: "Do not go out alone at night, and do not stand naked before a lamp, and do not go into a new bathhouse, lest it cave in." The anonymous redactors gloss the first clause:

> *"Do not go out alone [at night]"* as it is taught in a baraita*: One should not go out alone at night on Tuesday or Friday nights because Agrat bat Maḥlat goes out, and eighteen thousand myriads of destructive angels [malakhei ḥabalah] go out with her. And each of these [destructive angels] has individual permission to destroy [anything].*

Agrat bat Maḥlat also appears earlier in tractate *Pesaḥim*, where she is named in an incantation meant to protect against witchcraft, "Agrat disappear! Asya Blusya, let them be slain! Receive this in your bosom!"[6] These passages seem to indicate that she is a powerful leader of demonic forces.[7] However, as the anonymous voice of b. *Pesaḥim* 112b makes clear, her power is not limitless.

6. B. *Pesaḥim* 111a. MSS Oxford Opp. Add. fol. 23 and NY JTS 1623/2 Enelow Manuscript Collection 271 both make the connection even clearer by naming Agrat more precisely in the incantation: "Agrat bat Maḥlat disappear!" Agrat may also appear in a Babylonian incantation bowl. Gordon Bowl L has a reference to אגרתא, which he translates as "letter." See Cyrus H. Gordon, "Aramaic and Mandaic Magical Bowls," *Archiv Orientalni* 9 (1937): 93–95. However, based on the research of E. S. Drower, Gordon retranslates this word as a written (personified?) curse in "Aramaic Incantation Bowls," in *Orientalia* n.s. 10 (1941): 358. The relationship of this curse and the demon Agrat remains yet to be explored.

7. This narrative has a mystical afterlife in the Zohar. According to *Zohar Song of Songs* 69a, "on every second day and fourth day an evil spirit—woman of whoredom (Hosea 1:2)—goes about the Garden of Eden. Some garments are lured by that evil spirit, and the evil spirit craves them." *The Zohar: Pritzker Edition*, vol. 11, ed. Daniel C. Matt, trans. Joel Hecker (Stanford, CA: Stanford University Press, 2016), 449. My thanks to Joel Hecker for bringing this text to my attention. See also b. *Ta'anit* 27b, which notes a concern that on Wednesday, croup will attack children. See also p. *Ta'anit* 4:3; m. *Soferim* 17:5; Rashi on Gen. 1:14.

They used to be found [outside] every night. One time, she met R. Ḥanina b. Dosa and said to him: If they did not announce concerning you in heaven, "Be careful of R. Ḥanina b. Dosa, my son," I would certainly have put you in danger! He said to her: And if I am important in heaven, I decree upon you that you never pass through settled regions. She said to him: I beg you, leave me room! He left her Tuesday nights and Friday nights. Another time, she met Abaye. She said to him: If they did not announce concerning you in heaven, "Be careful of Naḥmani, my son," I would certainly have put you in danger! He said to her: If I am important in heaven, I decree that you never pass through settled regions.

But we see that they do pass through! Those are the female gezita [demons] whose horses fell out from under them.[8]

Agrat bat Maḥlat is controlled and subordinated by two powerful rabbis of different generations: the Tanna R. Ḥanina b. Dosa and the Amora Abaye.[9] R. Ḥanina b. Dosa appears across rabbinic literature as a charis-

8. B. *Pesaḥim* 112b–113a, translation of MS Vatican 125. This phrase could mean that these demons are out looking for their horses, or that they are lost in the public arena and cannot find their way home.

9. Fascinatingly, the beginning of the narrative is paralleled in part in an incantation bowl (AIT 42) published by Montgomery, *Aramaic Incantation Texts from Nippur* (Philadelphia: University of Pennsylvania Museum, 1913), 258–64: "Elijah the prophet was walking in the road and he met the wicked Lilith and all her band. He said to her: Where are you going, impure one and spirit (ruaḥ) of impurity, with all your impure band walking along? And she answered and said to him: My lord Elijah, I am going to the house of the woman in childbirth who is in pangs(?), of So-and-so daughter of Such-a-one, to give her the sleep of death and to take the child she is bearing, to suck his blood and to suck the marrow of his bones and to devour his flesh. And said Elijah the prophet—his memory for a blessing! With a ban from the Name—bless it!—shalt you be restrained and like a stone! And she answered and said to him: For the sake of YYY postpone the ban and I will flee, and I will swear to thee in the name of YYY God of Israel that I will let go this business in the case of this woman in childbirth and the child to be born to her and every inmate so as do no injury" (translation adapted from ibid., 259–60). Recognizing the danger Elijah poses to her life and activities, Lilith next offers a series of incantations and secret names that people in labor can use to ward off her attacks. Montgomery there notes the commonness of the trope of the holy person encountering a demon on the road and forcing them to offer up names that will afford those who know them protection. The Talmud's story is clearly part of the broader trope that this incantation text represents. But the bowl has some key differences from the rabbinic narrative: rather than Agrat, the demon is Lilith. Instead of a rabbi, the demon encounters the biblical prophet Elijah. Yet in the bowl too she recognizes his superiority, naming him "my lord." Curiously, b. *Pesaḥim* appears to be the only such story extant in which the demon does not offer conditional protection but instead is convinced by the holy man—here two wonder-working rabbis—to stay away completely. The rabbis' reputations and negotiations are effective in a way that even the prophet Elijah's may not be.

matic wonder-worker with power over demons, snakes, and other dangerous beings.[10] R. Ḥanina b. Dosa's fame as a wonder-worker extends beyond rabbinic literature: he appears in a historiola found in a number of Babylonian incantation bowls. This common historiola describes a meeting between R. Ḥanina b. Dosa and the demon Agag bat Baroq, at which R. Ḥanina b. Dosa is said to have ordered the demon to stop causing migraines and other illnesses.[11] Here, too, R. Ḥanina b. Dosa uses his rabbinic power to control a powerful female demon.[12] Though R. Ḥanina b. Dosa appears in the Mishnah, Tosefta, Talmuds, and the incantation texts, Kalmin notes that only in the Babylonian Talmud is R. Ḥanina b. Dosa depicted as "engaging in the study of Torah, the height of human endeavor according to the rabbinic system of values."[13] For the Babylonian rabbis, his identities as Torah scholar and controller of demons are interconnected.

While R. Ḥanina b. Dosa can thus protect his fellow humans five nights a week, Abaye goes even further; he blocks Agrat from roaming settled regions entirely. According to the final statement of the Bavli passage, the few demons who do appear in settled regions are there accidentally, because they have gotten lost or are out looking for their horses. As I discussed in chapter 4, Abaye is a master of avoiding demonic attack, thanks in part to the expert advice of his female family members. Here, Agrat bat Maḥlat is explicitly and divinely subordinated to the rabbis' authority—God has unambiguously declared that extra care must be taken around these two important rabbis. The story of Agrat bat Maḥlat thus provides divine affirmation of rabbinic superiority to demons and of the rabbis' ability to use their superior status to control and constrain the demon horde.

10. P. *Berakhot* 5:1 (38a), e.g., includes a cycle of stories about R. Ḥanina b. Dosa in which the Roman archon, proconsul, and General Ursicinus all affirm R. Ḥanina b. Dosa's affinity to Torah, the angels, and divine power. See Baruch Micah Bokser, "Wonder-Working and the Rabbinic Tradition: The Case of Ḥanina B. Dosa " *Journal for the Study of Judaism* 16, no. 1 (1985): 52–60. See also t. *Berakhot* 3:20, b. *Berakhot* 33a.

11. See Shaked et al., *Aramaic Bowl Spells*, 52–92; Dan Levene, *A Corpus of Magic Bowls: Incantation Texts in Jewish Aramaic from Late Antiquity* (London: Kegan Paul, 2003), 115–20.

12. See also b. *Ta'anit* 22b–23a.

13. Richard Kalmin, "Christians and Heretics in Rabbinic Literature of Late Antiquity," *Harvard Theological Review* 87, no. 2 (1994): 158.

The Babylonian Talmud's quasi-divine discursive subordination of the demonic to rabbinic authority is paralleled in part in a discourse found in a number of Syriac Christian texts. One fifth-century Syriac Christian account offers a story in which a demon recognizes the individual authority of particular Christian holy men. Theodoret of Cyrrhus, in his *Life of James of Cyrrhestica* (XXI.15), tells the following story:

> They [monastic Marcionites, followers of the theologian Marcion who was rejected by many early Church fathers as a heretic] tried to make war invisibly by using magic spells and having recourse to the cooperation of evil demons. Once by night there came a wicked demon, who exclaimed in Syriac, 'Why Theodoret, do you make war on Marcion? Why on earth have you joined battle with him? What harm has he ever done to you? End the war, stop your hostility, or you will learn by experience how good it is to stay quiet. Know well that I would long ago have pierced you through, if I had not seen the choir of the martyrs with James [of Cyrrhestus] protecting you.[14]

In the continuation of the story, Theodoret realizes that the "choir of martyrs" that the demon referred to is a holy flask of oil blessed by "very many martyrs" that the author has hung by his bed, and that the power of James of Cyrrhestus is present in the form of a cloak that the saint himself had given Theodoret to use as a pillow.[15] The demon in this story recognizes that Theodoret is protected by powerful ritual objects imbued with demon-repelling Christian holiness and thus cannot be harmed.

As in the Talmudic story above, this demon affirms the protection and power of a holy man. And as in the Talmudic story above, the holy man has done nothing in the moment to invoke this protection: his decor (or a voice in heaven) intervene on his behalf. Yet unlike the Talmudic account above, in the *Life of James of Cyrrehstica,* demons are primarily associated with sectarian conflict. Demons are connected to heretical Marcionites and are opposed to righteous Syriac monks. This association is consistent with early Christian demonology more broadly, in which demons are

14. Theodoret of Cyrrhus, *A History of the Monks of Cyrrhus,* trans. R. M. Price (Kalamazoo, MI: Cistercian Publications, 1985), 139. My thanks to Nell Champoux bringing this text to my attention.

15. Ibid., 140.

evil beings who serve Satan and oppose the good, that is, the orthodox.[16] There is no evidence, however, that demons are used aggressively in intra-Jewish sectarian debates during this period. According to the rabbis, different Jewish groups (such as the Ẓurva de-Rabbanan) may be more or less expert at dealing with demons, but, while demons might cause harm to various groups' claims to totalizing expertise, they are not deployed by specific groups to cause physical harm to others.

The sixth-century Syriac *Acts of Mār Mārī the Apostle* also includes a number of instances in which Christian holy men force demons to stop interacting with human beings, this time outside the context of sectarian debate.[17] In one instance, the apostle Mār Mārī attempts to convert Shahgirad, king of the city of Shahqirt, by convincing him that the statues that the king worships are in fact evil demons. He sends a disciple to compel the demons to leave the statues and make themselves visible to the populace.

> "Thus says Mār Mārī the apostle of Jesus Christ: 'In the living word of our Lord Jesus Christ, you have no right to come into the presence of all the people except in a hideous appearance!'" And in the presence of the king and all the people who were gathered there, the demons came out in various likenesses, such as unclean beasts and insects. They were seventy-two in number, and screamed in lament and said: "Oh! You, son of Mary! Lo! You have filled the whole world with your teaching, and you will not desist before you drive us out into the wilderness and desolate places! We do not know where to go now!" The blessed Mār Mārī shouted at them, saying: "You have no right, in the word of our Lord, to let us hear your voices! Go to gehenna, for the fire is ready for you and for your worshipers!"... Our father, the Apostle Mār Mārī, ordered the demons to go to the abyss. He baptized the king and the city in the name of the Father, the Son, and the Holy Spirit."[18]

Here too, a demonic horde recognizes the authority of a holy man and is geographically constrained by his commands. Here too, the demonic

16. See discussion in chap. 3.

17. On the dating of this text, see Amir Harrak, *The Acts of Mār Mārī the Apostle* (Atlanta: Society of Biblical Literature, 2005), xv–xvii.

18. Harrak, 30–33. My thanks to David Brodsky for suggesting the text's relevance to this discussion.

horde's retreat creates space and safety for humankind. And here too, demons are associated with ruins and wilderness.

These similarities are paired with a number of key discursive differences between this early Christian narrative and that of the Babylonian rabbis. Although Mār Mārī invokes his own authority in the *Acts of Mār Mārī* ("thus says Mār Mārī the apostle of Jesus Christ..."), the demons recognize only the "son of Mary," a synonym for Jesus, as an authority with power over demons. Mār Mārī is only effective to the extent that he represents Jesus in his commands. By contrast, in the rabbinic narrative, the authority *is* actually in the hands of R. Ḥanina b. Dosa and Abaye. This authority is recognized by heaven, that is, God, but it is the rabbis themselves who force Agrat and her minions to leave humankind alone. This difference is entirely rhetorical—in both accounts, the demons are forced by the holy men to leave particular communities alone—and yet they model two different relationships to the demonic—that of Mār Mārī is mediated through Jesus; that of R. Ḥanina b. Dosa and Abaye is direct and immediate. A second key difference is that of the demons' relationship to human and divine space. In the Talmudic narrative, Agrat is associated with two geographic spheres: abandoned and inhabited spaces on particular nights of the week, and heaven, where she hears God discussing specific rabbinic figures. By contrast, in the *Acts of Mār Mārī,* the demons are originally associated with human spaces, but eventually are all sent to Gehenna, or hell.[19] These two differences can also be found in the third-century C.E. Syriac *Acts of Thomas,* where the apostle Thomas invokes Jesus to send a range of demons to Gehenna.[20] This is an important point; in the Syriac Christian text demons are associated with hell and the devil. In no extant rabbinic text are demons associated with either, a fact which makes sense in the context of the demonic origin stories and taxonomies discussed in chapters 1 and 2.

These late antique Syriac Christian texts testify to the phenomenon of demons recognizing the power and saintliness of particular holy men and

19. For its use in a Christian context, see Matt. 5:30 and 10:28, and Mark 9:43.

20. See, e.g., *The Acts of Thomas* 73–74, in Albertus Frederik Johannes Klijn, *The Acts of Thomas: Introduction, Text, and Commentary,* 2nd rev. ed. (Leiden: Brill, 2003), 152–53. For the date, see ibid., 15.

responding accordingly to the benefit of individuals or communities. The rabbinic narrative must be understood within a broader context in which such stories circulated and were made a meaningful part of communal identity formation. However, these Syriac Christian texts also highlight ways that the rabbinic construction of demons differs: demons engage directly with humans; are associated with heaven, not hell; and are part of the normative community, not the heretical other. The Talmudic story of Agrat bat Maḥlat is part of a broader trend in the Babylonian Talmud that sees demons as members of the rabbinic community and subordinates demons to the rabbis and rabbinic authority.

RABBINIC/DEMONIC EXPERTISES

In the stories of Agrat bat Maḥlat above, rabbis come upon demons outdoors and use these serendipitous encounters for good.[21] Yet, if demons are legally subordinated to rabbinic authority, then the rabbis must imagine some way to initiate communication with them. One of the markers of particularly illustrious rabbis is the ability to speak the language of demons. The Talmud records that both Hillel and R. Yoḥanan b. Zakkai were able to speak "*the speech of demons (šeidim).*"[22] This ability is part of their rabbinic expertise over all spheres of knowledge and is a crucial element of rabbinic prestige and exceptionalism. But how does one find a demon to speak to?

B. *Sanhedrin* 67b suggests that demons can and do appear to help particular human beings when invoked. In this extended sugya, the rabbis attempt to define and categorize forbidden and permitted magical acts.

21. See also b. *Berakhot* 3a–b, discussed in chap. 3.

22. B. *Sukkah* 28a, and its parallel in b. *Baba Batra* 134a. In both texts, the speech of demons is followed by "שיחת דקלים" (the speech of palm trees). The association between demons and palm trees, discussed in chap. 3, may explain this juxtaposition. See also *Massekhet Soferim,* whose list excludes the speech of palm trees. Solomon's expertise over demons is found in Josephus, *Antiquities of the Jews* 8.44–45 and Targum Eccles. 2:5. Muslim literature attributes to Solomon the ability to speak the language of demons; in Jewish literature, it first appears in *Targum Sheni to Esther* on 1 Kings 4:33, likely a post-Islamic text. These Talmudic texts thus appear to be the earliest instance in which the rabbis suggest that demons spoke their own demonic language.

The fourth-generation Palestinian Amora R. Ayvu b. Nagri insists in the name of R. Hiyya b. Abba that the Egyptian sorcerers in the time of the Exodus performed some of their magical acts with the help of demons. Abaye then adds that *any* sorcerer who is careful to use "particular tools works through demons; the one who is not careful [to use particular tools works] through *kishuf* [forbidden witchcraft]." Apparently, demons can be invoked and used to perform supernatural acts with the help of specialized tools. While the sugya is clear that kishuf is biblically forbidden, the question of whether it is halakhically permitted to work through demons is left unresolved.

If demons can be invoked, can the rabbis be the ones doing the invoking? Are rabbis permitted to use their social capital to force demons to serve them? An ostensibly earlier baraita from a passage in b. *Sanhedrin* 101a provides one answer.[23]

> *Our rabbis taught: One may oil and massage the intestines [of a sick person] on Shabbat, and one may recite charms over snakes and scorpions on Shabbat, and a utensil may be passed over the eye on Shabbat [in some sort of healing ritual]. R. Simeon b. Gamaliel said: To what situation is this teaching referring? To using a utensil that can be used [on Shabbat], but it is forbidden [to pass a utensil over the eye on Shabbat] if the utensil cannot be used [on Shabbat]. And one cannot interrogate demons (šeidim) on Shabbat. R. Yose says: Even on weekdays, this is forbidden. R. Huna said: The halakhah is not according to R. Yose. And even R. Yose only forbade it because of danger, for R. Isaac b. Joseph was swallowed up by a cedar tree.*[24]

The subject of this legal discussion is not how humans can avoid demons in specific locations or time periods, but if and when humans can deliberately seek out demons in order to achieve particular aims. The medieval commentator Rashi suggests that the purpose of this interrogation is to ask a demon about the location of a lost object. The expression *šoalim ba-davar*, which I have translated as "interrogated," could also more generally refer to a form of augury or future-telling. The rabbis do not question whether they have the ability or authority to summon demons and interrogate them on the Sabbath. The ability and the authority to do so

23. See discussion on dating rabbinic traditions in the introduction.
24. MS Florence II-I-9.

are assumed. The question is whether the act of summoning demons on the Sabbath violates Sabbath law. The more stringent opinion of R. Yose is rejected and explained away as being motivated by the sad story of R. Isaac b. Joseph. Perhaps desiring a happy ending, the Vilna print edition of the Talmud concludes the story with the lines: "and a miracle was performed for [R. Isaac b. Joseph] and the tree split open and spat him out." However, none of the earlier manuscripts contains this clause; it seems likely that the redactors meant the story to end unhappily with the death or disappearance of the rabbi who summoned demons.[25] And yet the sugya insists that, though risky, summoning demons is possible and even permissible, at least six days of the week.[26]

The baraita found in b. *Sanhedrin* 101a is paralleled in Tosefta *Shabbat* 7:23. Here, the first speaker in the text states: "*One may whisper [an incantation] over an eye, a serpent, or a scorpion, but one cannot whisper incantations over demons (šeidim).*[27] R. *Yose says: Even on a weekday, one cannot whisper incantations [over a demon].*" The parallel continues in a different direction: "*And thus did R. Yose used to say: There are no regions worse than the Sodomite regions, for as long as a man is evil, he is referred to as a (Silmi)[Sodomite]. There is no one among the nations who is harsher than the Amorites, for as long as a man is harsh, he is referred to as an Amorite.*" Three important differences can be noted between the

25. The parallel text in the Palestinian Talmud does not mention demons but rather focuses on the dangers caused by the evil eye and the ways that the Palestinian rabbis acted to counter its effects. This baraita might suggest an underlying connection between healing on the Sabbath and unseen potentially malevolent forces that are interpreted in different ways by the Palestinian Amoraim and their Babylonian colleagues. For a discussion of this baraita, see Kalmin, "The Evil Eye in Rabbinic Literature of Late Antiquity," 126–28; Harari, *Jewish Magic before the Rise of Kabbalah*, 420–31.

26. It is worth noting, however, that offering incense to a demon in order to enchant him is apparently forbidden according to Rava's understanding of the *Ba'al Ov* in Lev. 19:31. See b. *Keritot* 3b for the discussion. Perhaps offering incense is something that can only be done in the Temple as part of divine service. Soncino translates the verb חבר there as "exorcise." The term more accurately refers to enchanting or charming something in order to control it. See M. J. Geller, "Four Aramaic Incantation Bowls," in *The Bible World: Essays in Honor of Cyrus H. Gordon*, ed. Gary Rendsburg et al. (New York: KTAV and the Institute of Hebrew Culture and Education, 1980), 49–50; Sokoloff, *A Dictionary of Jewish Babylonian Aramaic*, 429, s.v. חברא suggests that at least in the noun form, the word can refer to a charmer or magician.

27. "ואין לוחשין בדבר שדים." The verb LḤŠ refers to whispering an incantation over something. See Sokoloff, *A Dictionary of Jewish Babylonian Aramaic*, 623, s.v. לחש.

baraita in the Bavli and the baraita in the Tosefta. First, in the Tosefta, R. Yose's prohibition against demonic interaction is allowed to stand; in the Bavli, R. Yose's prohibition is struck down by R. Huna. Second, the Tosefta's text is concerned with incantations *over* demons that are presumably meant to repel a demonic force paralleled to the other dangers listed; the Bavli's text is concerned with attempts to invoke and interrogate demons. Unlike the Tosefta, the Bavli presents the human person as enlisting the demon to serve the person's own needs. Third, the Tosefta associates these incantations with *darkhei Emori*, the foreign and forbidden "ways of the Amorites." By contrast, in b. *Sanhedrin*, invoking demons is permitted during the week, and integrated into the rabbinic system. Rabbis can summon demonic forces to serve them during the work week.

DEMONIC SERVANTS IN RABBINIC HOUSEHOLDS

The domestication of the demonic reaches its heights in the Bavli tractate *Ḥullin* when one demon becomes the actual domestic servant of an exceptional rabbi. B. *Ḥullin* 105b–106a is made up of a series of eight statements by the fourth-generation Babylonian Amora Abaye.[28] The statements have a parallel structure: Abaye explains the rationale he "used to think" was behind a particular practice, and then explains what the "Master," likely Rabbah b. Naḥmani, then taught him was the actual reason for the practice. The majority of Abaye's statements are followed by anonymous stories that support the Master's interpretation against Abaye's initial understanding. The following statement and story appear within this context:

> Abaye said: At first I thought the reason why one pours off [a little water] from the mouth of the jug [before drinking] was flotsam [i.e., fibers floating on the surface of the water] but now my Master has told me: It is because there is evil water.

28. This sugya has already been examined by Shamma Friedman, "Mivneh Sifruti Be-Sugyot Habavli," in *Sugyot Be-Heker Ha-Talmud Ha-Bavli: Mehkarim Be-Inyanei Mivneh, Herkev Ve-Nusah* (New York: Jewish Theological Society of America, 2010), 136–48. See Ronis, "A Demonic Servant in Rav Papa's Household," 4 n. 6.

> A certain demon (šeida) in the household of R. Papa once went to fetch water from the river but was away a long time. When he returned he saw them pouring off [a little water] from the mouth of the jug. He exclaimed: Had I known that you were in the habit of doing this, I would not have been away so long![29]

The story is vague as to what makes evil water so evil; regardless, the demon servant acts in concert with and in place of the rest of the rabbi's household to avoid the potential harm.[30] Although we have already seen how the rabbis thought water could be demonically dangerous, here the demon is not the source of the problem but an agent working toward a solution.[31] This nameless demon cannot be dismissed as mere metaphor or symbol; at the story's end, the rabbi's household has water that it did not have at the beginning. But what is a demon doing as a servant in the household of the great Babylonian sage? Why is he so strict about following rabbinic dicta? The rabbis' subordination of demons to rabbinic halakhah and rabbinic authority here takes its final step: a demon who not only obeys the rabbis but also formally serves a rabbi's household, who takes responsibility for the rabbi and his family's safety and allegiance to rabbinic practice. The demon's supernatural knowledge is now in service, both intellectually and also physically, to the rabbi's needs.

This shift in the construction of the demonic solves a number of problems posed by the existence of a powerful and capricious class of intermediary beings. In chapters 3 and 4, we examine the ways that the rabbis

29. My translation here is of MS Vatican 123b.

30. I have translated the term used here to describe the demon "דהוה בי רב פפא" (who was of the household of Rav Papa) as "servant." The term appears in two different Talmudic contexts: in the first context, it describes students who are part of a particular rabbi's disciple circle; in the second, it describes someone or something attached to his home. See Sokoloff, *A Dictionary of Jewish Babylonian Aramaic*, 208, 218, s.v. ביתא and בי רב. See b. *Baba Qamma* 35a, where the expression is used of an ox, and b. *Ḥullin* 53b, where it is used of a duck. The overlap between these two meanings might point to the function of a disciple circle as the training ground for future members of the rabbinic class, a training in part carried out by acting as the body servant of the rabbinic master. See Goodblatt, "The History of the Babylonian Academies." See Ronis, "A Demonic Servant in Rav Papa's Household," for further discussion of the possible meanings of evil water.

31. Medieval interpreters later suggest that the danger is itself demonic. However, in its original context, the text suggests that it is the demon who mitigates the harm; he does not cause it.

constructed demons as dangerous and used that danger to cultivate particular modes of rabbinic being. But in this story, a similar aim is achieved in a different way: rabbinic law and practice are affirmed and rabbinic authority is maintained by neutralizing the demonic danger entirely and marking the demon as a positive member of the rabbinic community. This story is the only time in the Babylonian Talmud that a demon is referred to as a member of a rabbinic household. But rather than being understood as exceptional, it must be understood as the most extreme iteration of a larger discursive trend on the part of the Babylonian rabbis of late antiquity to neutralize and domesticate demonic beings. This shift does not happen in a vacuum.

ANCIENT MESOPOTAMIAN DEMONS

When trying to properly locate the Babylonian rabbis in their cultural context, it makes sense to first look to the rabbis' contemporaries. And demons are indeed depicted as subordinate to holy men and their invocations of Jesus and the saints in Syriac Christianity. But in these instances, demons can only obey the commands to flee, to avoid harming the faithful, and to literally go to hell. Yet demons are not depicted as faithful servants to a holy man in contemporaneous Zoroastrian, Syriac Christian, or Manichaean texts from late antique Babylonia. In these traditions, demons are the malevolent agents of the ultimate forces of evil (Ahriman, Satan, or the world of darkness); they function as adversaries and foils for holy men and women, and their location in a holy person's home could only be imagined as nefarious.[32] However, demons *are* depicted as neutral servants to authority figures in much earlier Mesopotamian texts. Among the many other contemporaneous traditions in circulation, Babylonian rabbis

32. There is one example from a late antique Greek philosophical text in which a female philosopher, Sosipatra, is apprenticed to daimones and serves them in exchange for learning the secrets of the universe. See Eunapius, *Lives of the Philosophers*, 46671, quoted in Naomi Janowitz, *Magic in the Roman World: Pagans, Jews and Christians*, (London: Routledge, 2001), 96. Notably, in the case of Sosipatra, the power relations are inverted—it is the female philosopher who is the servant and the daimones who are the masters. See also Martin, *Inventing Superstition*, 182. For further details on daimones as they relate to early Christian and rabbinic demons, see chap. 2.

were also the heirs to much older Sumerian and Akkadian constructions of demons as servile and servants.

Tracing the reception of ancient Mesopotamian traditions forward in history is a difficult task. The enormous time span covered by the term "ancient Mesopotamia" means that dynamism and diversity are fundamental characteristics of its traditions. From the beginnings of Sumerian civilization in the Tigris-Euphrates Valley between 5500 and 4000 B.C.E., this region was home to new technologies, new forms of governance, and new systems of belief. In the late third millennium B.C.E., the Akkadian empire developed north of Sumer between the Tigris and Euphrates rivers. This was the first Semitic-speaking empire in the region. The Amorites migrated into the region from Syria in the second millennium. This migration, together with a substantial population decline in Sumer, led new powers to emerge in the region—Babylonia in the south and Assyria in the north. The death of the Assyrian king Ashurbanipal in 627 B.C.E. and the resulting political instability in Assyria led to outbreaks of conflict; eventually, the Babylonians emerged victorious and expanded their empire northward.[33] Regional and chronological specificity plays an important role in the study of ancient Mesopotamia: many significant narratives and themes are specific to only one city-state, civilization, or century. Others appear in multiple forms across civilizations, or even within a single empire. However, many older ideas survive in some form in the Babylonian, Achaemenid, Parthian, and then Sasanian worlds.

Intermediary beings appear across a number of ancient Mesopotamian narrative genres: disputations between animate and/or inanimate objects;[34] lists (of gods, temples, temple personnel, and religious language); prayer requests and incantations; hymns; wisdom literature; inscriptions; and mythological accounts. These texts describe various gods both major and minor, personal protective deities, and a wide range of intermediary beings. As with early Greek philosophical texts, the authors of these works do not clearly and consistently distinguish between minor

33. Tammi J. Schneider, *An Introduction to Ancient Mesopotamian Religion* (Grand Rapids, MI: William B. Eerdmans, 2011), 18–25, 29.

34. Such as *The Debate Between Bird and Fish* c.5.3.5, in ibid., 92.

gods, intermediary beings, and monsters.[35] To complicate things even further, some later Babylonian incantations also do not clearly distinguish between evil demons and evil men.[36]

The absence of a precise taxonomy should not imply, however, that ancient Mesopotamian demonology was simplistic or underdeveloped. Demons were understood to be the creation of the gods: created through the sexual intercourse of one or more gods, or built out of a range of building materials and then given life.[37] Many demons were gendered male or female. Their bodies were often described in writing and images as hybrid, incorporating humanoid physical elements as well as elements from wild animals and snakes.[38] With features combined in unnatural ways, these demonic bodies could look monstrous. To add to the difficulty in categorizing demons, many ancient Mesopotamian demons could alter their appearances.[39] Some demons are given individual names and characteristics. Many others are classed together in groups with collective names, such as the *Aḫḫazu* (seizers), *Alû, Lilû, Lilîtu,* and *Ardat Lilî, Ekimmu* (ghosts), *Gallû, Ilu* (deities), *Labaṣu,* LAMA/*Lamassu,*

35. In the *Enuma Elish* Tablets 4–5, the goddess Tiamat gives birth to eleven creatures meant to fight with her against Marduk and the younger gods. These eleven are alternately categorized as monsters, demons, and deities themselves. See W. G. Lambert, *Babylonian Creation Myths* (Winona Lake, IN: Eisenbrauns, 2013), 84–107; Stephanie Dalley, trans., *Myths from Mesopotamia: Creation, the Flood, Gilgamesh, and Others* (Oxford: Oxford University Press, 2009), 252–61.

36. See, e.g., R. Campbell Thompson, *The Devils and Evil Spirits of Babylonia: Being Babylonian and Assyrian Incantations against the Demons, Ghouls, Vampires, Hobglobins, Ghosts, and Kindred Evil Spirits, Which Attack Mankind,* vol. 1, *Evil Spirits* (London: Luzac, 1903), 129–39.

37. See, e.g., *Enki and Ninmah* 69–71; *Enuma Elish* Tablet 1 in Dalley, *Myths from Mesopotamia,* 237–38.

38. Snakes were associated with demons, but evidence of beneficent snake god cults also exists. See W. Farber, "Lamastu," in *Reallexikon der Assyriologie und Vorderasiatischen Archäologie,* ed. Erich Ebeling (Berlin: W. de Gruyter, 1984), 6:442; R. Pientka-Hinz, "Schlange. A. In Mesopotamien," ibid. (2009) 12:202–218.

39. "Anzu II.i [Standard Babylonian Version]," in Dalley, *Myths from Mesopotamia,* 213. Scholars of the ancient Near East such as Black and Green (*Demons and Symbols of Ancient Mesopotamia,* 63) have distinguished between demons and monsters by labeling as *demonic* any bipedal hybrid creature and as *monstrous* anything depicted as walking on all fours. This distinction, however, is a modern invention; I have found no evidence that it is a taxonomic schema that was meaningful within ancient Mesopotamia. The present study therefore examines both types of beings later classified as either demons or monsters.

Lamaštu, Rābiṣu (lurkers), *Šêdu*, and UDUG.[40] These names are in a variety of ancient Mesopotamian languages: Babylonian scribes continued to use Sumerian and Akkadian names for demons, while adding new names of their own.

Some of these beings, such as the UDUG, LAMA, and *Gallû*, were imagined to be neutral intermediary beings. Scribes and ritual experts marked these demons with the adjectives *evil* and *good* depending on the context in which they were invoked.[41] Thus, King Gudea of Lagaš described himself as being blessed with having a good UDUG demon who went before him, and a good LAMA demon who followed him.[42] One common Akkadian formula asks, "Get out, evil *rābiṣu*; come in, good *rābiṣu*!"[43] Similarly, the scribe in one Old Babylonian text requests: "May the evil UDUG and the evil galla stand aside. May the good UDUG and the good galla be present." An even later incantation prays that "the good *sédu* and the good *lamassu* daily walk by my side."[44] These creatures can be good or bad; given their duality, humans must be precise in specifying which should come close and which should stay away.

Many demons served as the servants and emissaries of specific gods. Anne Marie Kitz shows that the Akkadian *rābiṣu,* traditionally interpreted as an evil demon, is in fact a "neutral being that is nothing other than a current of wind dispatched by the deities to perform certain

40. Thompson, *The Devils and Evil Spirits of Babylonia*, vol. 1, *Evil Spirits*, xxiv–xxv; Black and Green, *Gods, Demons and Symbols of Ancient Mesopotamia.*

41. Gina Konstantopoulos, "Shifting Alignments: The Dichotomy of Benevolent and Malevolent Demons in Mesopotamia," in *Demons and Illness from Antiquity to the Early-Modern Period*, ed. Siam Bhayro and Catherine Rider (Leiden: Brill, 2017), 19–38,

42. Gudea Cylinder B ii.9–10 in Dietz Otto Edzard, *Gudea and His Dynasty* (Toronto: University of Toronto Press, 1997), 89; Black and Green, *Gods, Demons, and Symbols of Ancient Mesopotamia,* 179.

43. Anthony Green, "Neo-Assyrian Apotropaic Figures: Figurines, Rituals and Monumental Art, with Special Reference to the Figurines from the Excavations of the British School of Archaeology in Iraq at Nimrud," *Iraq* 45, no. 1 (1983): 91 n. 40, discussed in Anne Marie Kitz, "Demons in the Hebrew Bible and the Ancient Near East," *Journal of Biblical Literature* 135, no. 3 (2016): 454–55. Green notes that the formula "Go out, X; Come in Y" apears in several iterations in Assyiran inscriptions (92).

44. Graham Cunningham, *"Deliver Me from Evil": Mesopotamian Incantations 2500–1500 BC* (Rome: Editrice Pontificio Instituto Biblico, 1997), 128.

duties."[45] The rābiṣu is a neutral being; its characterization as positive or negative depends on the "nature of the assignment it receives from the deity who sends it forth."[46] And yet the association of the demonic and the negative is so strong that the rābiṣu's real nature has been overlooked by most translators. Kitz argues that this neutral understanding of the rābiṣu implies that it is not a demon[47]; I would suggest, however, that this understanding requires us to rethink what we mean (hostile, angry, violent) when we use the word *demon*.[48] Demons' characterizations as "good" or "bad" depended on the nature of the god they served and the kinds of tasks they were assigned.

Let us look at one example of demons who function as servants to divine beings, found in the Sumerian stories of Inana and Ereškigal.[49] In this narrative cycle, Inana, the goddess of love and warfare, goes into her older sister Ereškigal's domain—the underworld—to attend the funeral of Ereškigal's husband. For reasons that are not entirely clear (the teasing of a younger sister? An attempted coup?), Inana sits on Ereškigal's throne. Ereškigal sees this act as a threat of usurpation, turns Inana into a corpse, and displays her body on a hook. Three other gods, Enlil, Nanna, and Enki, then descend deep into the underworld to negotiate Inana's rescue. As part of the negotiations with Ereškigal, Inana agrees to send someone else to the underworld in her stead and is then freed. Ereškigal sends some of her demonic minions to accompany her sister and ensure that Inana upholds her end of the bargain. Inana and her demonic companions

45. Kitz, "Demons in the Hebrew Bible and the Ancient Near East," 447. Kitz connects the rābiṣu with the spirit being referred to as a *ruah* and argues that "the רעה [evil] attributed to a divine רוח [spirit] actually references its mission and not its moral standing" (ibid.). This adjectival qualification is paralleled in Akkadian texts that modify rābiṣu with the adjective *lemnu* (evil).

46. Ibid., 455.

47. Ibid., 462.

48. Rita Lucarelli, "Illness as Divine Punishment: The Nature and Function of the Disease-Carrier Demons in the Ancient Magical Texts," in *Demons and Illness from Antiquity to the Early-Modern Period*, ed. Siam Bhayro and Catherine Rider (Leiden: Brill, 2017), 53–60, has made the same argument about the role and nature of disease-carrier demons in ancient Egypt. Lucarelli argues that the main distinction between demon and deity in ancient Egypt is that demons were not the foci of cultic practices.

49. The narrative appears in *Dumuzi and Ĝeštin-ana*: c.1.4.1.1, *Dumuzi and his Sisters*: c.1.4.1.3, and *Inana's Descent to the Nether World*: c.1.4.1.

pass some of Inana's courtiers on their journey from the underworld. The demons suggest that the courtiers would be fit replacements for Inana in the underworld, but she rejects their suggestion. But when Inana comes upon her lover Dumuzi, all dressed up and sitting on a throne under an apple tree, apparently not missing her at all, she insists that he be her replacement in the underworld. Against his protests, the demons then take him to the underworld, where he remains.[50]

Within the logic of the story, Dumuzi must have experienced demons as frightening beings who appear out of nowhere, and, unprovoked, drag him into the underworld. However, from the perspective of the omniscient narrator and his audience, the demons are simply obeying the orders of the goddesses who command them. They are not independent agents, but are, in themselves, neutral. The demons are aware of their role and characterization in the narrative. In one variant of the story, during the hunt for a replacement victim, several of the demons declare: "Demons have no mother; they have no father or mother, sister or brother, wife or children... Demons are never kind, they do not know good from evil."[51] Demons do not act with mercy or compassion; they do not recognize family relationships or love. They are characterized by obedience, and their description as either good or evil by storytellers depends on what deity they serve and how that deity's divine will supports or contradicts human desires. The emissaries of a complex, capricious pantheon made up of different gods with different agendas are themselves complex, capricious, and contradictory. Depending on their mission, they can cause illness or drag you down

50. This story continues to be told into the later Babylonian period, where the deities are named Ištar, Ereškigal, and Tammuz. There was likely was an annual festival of mourning for Dumuzi (Tammuz in Babylonian) to mark his entry into the underworld that continued to be observed into the Sasanian period. See O. R. Gurney, "Tammuz Reconsidered: Some Recent Developments," *Journal of Semitic Studies* 7, no. 2 (1962): 147–60; Thorkild Jacobsen, "Towards the Image of Tammuz," *History of Religions* 1, no. 2 (1962): 189–213; Edwin M. Yamauchi, "Additional Notes on Tammuz," *Journal of Semitic Studies* 10, no. 5 (1966): 10–15; JoAnn Scurlock, "Images of Tammuz: The Intersection of Death, Divinity, and Royal Authority in Ancient Mesopotamia," in *Experiencing Power, Generating Authority: Cosmos, Politics, and the Ideology of Kingship in Ancient Egypt and Mesopotamia*, ed. Jane A. Hill et al. (Philadelphia: University of Pennsylvania Museum of Archaeology and Anthropology, 2013), 151–84; J. A. Scurlock, "K 164 ("Ba" 2, P. 635): New Light on Mourning Rites for Dumuzi?," *Revue d'Assyriologie et d'archéologie orientale* 86, no. 1 (1992): 53–67.

51. *Dumuzi and Ĝeštin-ana*: c.1.4.1.1.

into hell; but they can also protect and shepherd those who have the favor of the gods.

These ideas find their way, in nascent form, into the Hebrew Bible. In 1 Samuel 16:14, for example, Saul is terrified by an "evil spirit from the LORD" (NJPS), suggesting that this spirit is sent to do evil to Saul at the command of God, who is in the process of revoking Saul's kingship.[52] Of course, here it is not a pantheon of capricious gods, but a single (ethical) God who commands these intermediary forces. Notably, though the Bible is unambiguous that God sends an evil spirit to attack Saul, the late antique rabbis never interpret these biblical stories in ways that make this reading explicit.

Ancient Sumerian and Akkadian traditions had long afterlives in Assyrian and Babylonian culture. Many traditions circulated even into the Achaemenid (c. 550–330 B.C.E.), Parthian (150 B.C.E.–226 C.E.), and Sasanian (224–651 C.E.) periods. The Achaemenids used the Babylonian lunar calendar to celebrate ancient Mesopotamian cultic festivals.[53] Archaeologists have found fragmentary Sumerian and Akkadian cuneiform texts written, possibly as scribal exercises, in the second and early-third centuries CE.[54] That these languages were still valued and taught in the Parthian and early Sasanian periods suggests another vector for the transmission of traditions and literature. Late antique Syriac Christian writers in Edessa denounced named Babylonian gods and their worshippers in their writings, which suggests that communities that worshipped these deities were still present and active in the region.[55] And indeed, members of the court of the late Sasanian king Xusrow I (531–579 C.E.) were aware

52. Kitz, "Demons in the Hebrew Bible and the Ancient Near East," 459–60. See also 1 Sam. 18:10.

53. Stephanie Dalley, "Occasions and Opportunities. 2. Persian, Greek, and Parthian Overlords," in *The Legacy of Mesopotamia*, ed. Stephanie Dalley et al. (Oxford: Oxford University Press, 1998), 35.

54. Joachim Oelsner, "Incantations in Southern Mesopotamia—From Clay Tablets to Magical Bowls: Thoughts on the Decline of the Babylonian Culture," in *Officina Magica: Essays on the Practice of Magic in Antiquity*, ed. Shaul Shaked (Leiden: Brill, 2005), 36–41; Dalley, "Occasions and Opportunities 2. Persian, Greek, and Parthian Overlords," 41–42.

55. See, e.g., Jacob of Sarug, *Fall of the Idols* 11.51–62; *Doctrina Addai* 15b–16a in George Howard, *The Teaching of Addai* ed. Robert L. Wilken et al. (Chico, CA: Scholars Press, 1981), 48–49. For further instances of this survival, and a broader discussion of this phenomenon, see H. J. W. Drijvers, *Cults and Beliefs at Edessa*, ed. M. J. Vermaseren (Leiden: Brill, 1980), 40–75. My thanks to Shana Zaia for bringing these texts to my attention.

of the Babylonian epic of creation, the *Enuma Elish*. Certain Babylonian narrative tropes even persist into Zoroastrian literature that was first written down and interpreted during the early medieval period.[56] Filtered through progressive empires with their own distinctive cultures and contexts, elements of early Mesopotamian culture survived well beyond the advent of Islam.

The portrayal of a demon as a servant-member of R. Papa's household makes sense within the rich cultural matrix of late antique Babylonia. Unlike Inana and Ereškigal, R. Papa is human. But like these goddesses, R. Papa is presented as worthy of being able to command demons. A rabbi is important enough—and powerful enough—to include demonic subordinates in his household. And these demons are punctilious in doing what they are commanded to: Inana's replacement is sent to the underworld, and the rabbi's household gets its water from the river.

In the last fifteen years, scholars of rabbinic literature have begun to investigate intersections between Babylonian rabbinic literature and ancient Mesopotamian medicine and demonology with very fruitful results.[57] Avigail Manekin Bamberger, for example, has convincingly demonstrated that the privy demon Bar-Širiqa Panda, discussed in chap-

56. Dalley, "The Sassanian Period and Early Islam, C.A.D. 224–651," in *The Legacy of Mesopotamia*, ed. Stephanie Dalley et al. (Oxford: Oxford University Press, 1998), 172, points to Yasht 19 and the *Vīdēvdād* as examples. Although parts of these texts cannot be definitively dated to late antiquity, the appearance of these traditions in texts that may in part be early medieval testifies to their continued survival. For an example of a Babylonian narrative trope that survives in Zoroastrian literature, see the Zoroastrian tale of King Jamshid (Yima), which notes that Jamshid ruled the entire world in peace but on three occasions had to expand the world due to overpopulation (*Yašt* 19). In the earlier Babylonian *Epic of Atrahasis*, Atrahasis, too, must expand the world's borders on three occasions due to overpopulation. See Dalley, "The Sassanian Period and Early Islam, C.A.D. 224–651," 172–73, for further analysis of the parallels between these two texts.

57. See Geller, "Akkadian Healing Therapies in the Babylonian Talmud"; Mark J. Geller, "An Akkadium Vademecum in the Babylonian Talmud," 13–32. Scholars have noted that the Israelites first formally encountered Mesopotamian beliefs and culture in the Babylonian Exile (586–516 B.C.E.). See Stephanie Dalley, "The Influence of Mesopotamia upon Israel and the Bible," in *The Legacy of Mesopotamia*, ed. Dalley et al. (Oxford: Oxford University Press, 1998), 60–79; Charles E. Carter, *The Emergence of Yehud in the Persian Period: A Social and Demographic Study* (Sheffield, UK: Sheffield Academic Press, 1999), 300–16. See especially J.B. Pritchard, ed. *Ancient Near Eastern Texts Relating to the Old Testament* (Princeton, NJ: Princeton University Press, 1950), which was critical to scholarship on Mesopotamian parallels in the Hebrew Bible. Pritchard there describes an 1872 lecture by George Smith as the foundational moment of the study of Assyriology and the Hebrew Bible, but the field continued to grow and expand through the twentieth century.

ter 3, can be identified with the Babylonian privy demon Šulak, both of whom are lion-faced demons associated with epilepsy.[58] My reading of R. Papa's demon servant, and demonic subservience to the rabbinic project in general, is part of this same project. But here it is not a specific demon or medical practice but a much larger discursive trend that survived thousands of years and found its way into the Bavli. But this is not an unthinking transposition or borrowing. What we see here is an alignment in perspective and discourse that emerges in a culture in which multiple demonic discourses interact.

However, this alignment is not complete. The demon in b. *Ḥullin* 105b–106a is not neutral and dependent on the gods for instruction; he is a positive independent actor, an autonomous servant of the rabbinic community who is scrupulous in observing rabbinic traditions and protecting his rabbinic household, even when he is not asked to do so. The demon's scrupulosity only makes sense against the backdrop of the rabbis' broader discursive move to integrate demons into the halakhic system, making demons subject to rabbinic halakha and the rabbis who teach it. Within the rabbinic imagination, this move is so successful that the demon's scrupulosity is enacted even without rabbinic surveillance.

MUSLIM, CHRISTIAN, AND JEWISH AFTERLIVES

While the Babylonian rabbis appear to be unique in late antiquity in their adoption and adaptation of early Mesopotamian understandings of demons as neutral servants of powerful forces, this construction of the demonic has an important afterlife in medieval Muslim, Christian, and Jewish contexts. In all of these later traditions, at least some demons are positively marked, with lives dedicated in service to religious ideas and ideals. A brief discussion of the medieval depictions of neutral and positively marked demons testifies to the continued importance of this discursive move to a range of religious traditions and communities.

It is in the Muslim world of the seventh through tenth centuries that the narrative depiction of demons as servants of both God and the holy

58. Bamberger, "An Akkadian Demon in the Talmud."

man flowers in full.[59] The Qur'an is full of references to *jinn*, the Arabic word for demons. According to the Qur'an, the jinn were created to worship God.[60] Indeed, they affirm the superiority of the Qur'an, as Mohammed declares: "It was revealed unto me that a group of jinn listened, and said 'truly we have heard a wondrous Qur'an that guides to sound judgment; so we believe in it and will ascribe none as partner unto our Lord.'"[61] Although jinn have supernatural powers, such as the ability to move from place to place "in the blink of an eye," the Qur'an insists that they are not all-knowing; only God has true omniscience.[62] Any problematic or troubling elements of their characterization as also God's creations have been elided.[63] And like all God's creations, they, too, are destined to be judged in the Final Judgment; those jinn who are found worthy will enter Paradise.[64]

In the Qur'an, jinn serve God's designs, but they also serve God's holy men, specifically Solomon, who is described as having large numbers of jinn as personal servants.[65] This characterization is particularly noteworthy given the depiction of Solomon in b. *Gittin* 67b–68a, discussed in chapter 4. The Talmud describes Solomon as able to control minor demons, but he is ultimately overpowered by the demon king Ashmedai

59. My thanks to Nerina Rustomji and Sarit Kattan Gribbetz for suggesting this parallel.

60. Q 51:56 in Seyeed Hossein Nasr et al., eds., *The Study Quran: A New Translation and Commentary* (New York: Harper One, 2015), 1280.

61. Q 72:1 in ibid., 1428.

62. See Q 15:18; 27:39–40 on movement; Q 34:14 on *jinn*'s lack of omniscience.

63. I am not arguing that there is a direct relationship between the Qur'an and the Babylonian Talmud. It is certainly possible that the Qur'anic construction of demons is a direct outgrowth of the Talmudic construction of demons. It is also possible, however, that both the Talmud's depiction of demons and that of the Qur'an are different articulations of common stories that circulated orally and were popular in a range of settings in both the Roman West—as testified to by Josephus and the *Testament of Solomon*—and in the Sasanian East, as evidenced by the Babylonian Talmud and the Qur'an. It is possible that the Qur'an's understanding of how demons must fit into their monotheistic worldview aligned with that of the rabbis and led to similar outcomes, without the Qur'an relying directly on the Babylonian Talmud. Yet even still, it is noteworthy that the Qur'an describes demons as being compelled (by Allah) to serve King Solomon (and only King Solomon), whereas in the Babylonian Talmud, there is no evidence that Rav Papa's demon servant is being compelled to serve the rabbi and his household.

64. Q 37:158. And see Jacqueline Chabbi, "Jinn," in *Encyclopaedia of the Qur'an*, ed. Jane Dammen McAuliffe (Leiden: Brill, 2003) for an extended discussion of jinn in the Qur'an.

65. Q 27:17, 39; 34:12.

and his superior wit. By contrast, the Qur'anic jinn are indeed subordinate to Solomon and do his will.

In the medieval period, jinn are portrayed as followers of Muslim law and are understood to be liable to penalties for breaking these laws. D. B. MacDonald and his coauthors argue that jinn's "legal status in all respects was discussed and fixed, and the possible relations between them and [hu]mankind, especially in questions of marriage and property, were examined."[66] As individuals subordinated to the law, jinn begin to appear as students of Muslim teachers in medieval Muslim literature: they are depicted as learning the Qur'an, Muslim philosophy, Arabic grammar, and Arabic poetry; they even write their own Arabic poetry.[67] Much like the ancient Greek Muses, jinn also inspire human poetry and other creative pursuits; the eleventh-century poet Abu 'Amir ibn Shuhayd describes a jinn who functions as a sort of servant-muse, helping the human poet travel to meet other poets and find inspiration.[68] Because jinn are not innately evil, they can be integrated into Muslim legal and narrative texts with some degree of ease, though as always, the danger inherent in their power and abilities still remains. In this way, medieval Islam's demonology aligns significantly with that of the Babylonian Talmud.

In the eleventh through thirteenth centuries, Syriac Christian texts introduce the motif of a "penitent" demon who serves holy men.[69] In one

66. Duncan B. MacDonald et al., "Djinn," in *Encyclopaedia of Islam* (Brill Online, 2012), http://referenceworks.brillonline.com/entries/encyclopaedia-of-islam-2/djinn-COM_0191.

67. See texts cited in Amira El-Zein, *Islam, Arabs, and the Intelligent World of the Jinn* (Syracuse, NY: Syracuse University Press, 2009), 28–31. Although the work conflates historical periods and writings, it contains a number of primary sources from medieval Muslim thinkers which describe and discuss the jinn's subjugation to Muslim belief and law.

68. *The Treatise of Familiar Spirits and Demons*, in ibid., 125. According to El-Zein, ibid., 126, a similar account is described by Abu Zaid al-Qurashi (d. 786) three hundred years earlier, but with less detail. El-Zein notes a poem attributed to a pre-Islamic poet: "I am a man whose follower is a jinni / I befriended him, and he befriended me for life / He drinks from my cup / And I drink from his cup / Thanks Be to God who gave him to me!" (175–76). If correctly identified as pre-Islamic, this poem may serve as evidence that at least one other community or individual had a demonology similar to that of the rabbis during the period contemporaneous with the Babylonian Talmud. More work needs to be done on late antique discourse about demonology in the Arabian Peninsula.

69. This is different from, for example, the mid-fifteenth-century story cycles of the eleventh-century St. John of Novgorod, who subdued a malevolent demon and forced the demon to take him from Novgorod to Jerusalem and back in one night. This demon remains malevolent but is forced by the saint to serve him for one night. See Serge A. Zenkovsky,

remarkable narrative in Mingana Syriac Manuscript 205, a demon reveals himself to a servant at an Egyptian monastery, saying, "I am a traitor to God, one of the *jinn*. I want to offer repentance to God before his rule and his harsh judgment overtake me, so that he might do mercy with me."[70] The demon's description of himself as a jinn suggests a familiarity with at least the language of Muslim demons, but his description of himself as evil and requiring repentance is better aligned with early Second Temple and Christian texts. This demon then presents himself as a human postulant at the monastery, and is welcomed in.[71] In the earlier *Sayings of the Desert Fathers,* a late antique collection of Egyptian Christian monastic teachings, demons present themselves as human to monks in order to tempt these ascetics to sin.[72] But unlike the demons described in the *Sayings of the Desert Fathers,* in this Syriac manuscript, the demon's presentation as human is motivated by piety and a sincere desire to repent. At the monastery, he becomes exceptional in his fasting, diligence, and punctiliousness. The demon uses his ability to travel huge distances in the blink of an eye—by now a familiar demonic ability—to perform tasks for the monastery; in one notable episode, he brings a fishing boat complete with fishermen and their daily catch to the monastery courtyard to meet the monks' desire for fresh fish. But the human servant eventually discloses the postulant's demonic nature; the monks respond with shock and fear. At this point, the demon expresses his true repentance to the monks, and together they all pray for the demon to be saved. Both the story and the crisis at the monastery are resolved when "a voice came to them saying: 'I have accepted his repentance through your prayers.' And it happened that immediately he rose up to the merciful Lord and the most high God, to be with the angels of the first rank forever and ever, Amen."[73] This demon is a monastic postulant and a servant at the monastery; he uses his demonic

---

Medieval Russia's Epics, Chronicles, and Tales (New York: Dutton, 1974), 310–14. My thanks to Erik Potter for bringing this text to my attention.

70. Liza Anderson, "Story of a Demon Who Repented and Was Accepted by God, from Mingana Syriac Manuscript 205, 159a–164b," unpublished translation, accessed 21 July 2015 at www.academia.edu/2151969/Story_of_a_Demon_who_Repented_and_was_Accepted_by_God.

71. Ibid.

72. See, e.g., discussion in Brakke, *Demons and the Making of the Monk,* 160–70.

73. Ibid.

powers for the good of the monastery. He is the Christian equivalent of a demon serving the rabbis, or a demon becoming a rabbi himself. But the Christian discomfort with this idea is apparent; the demon cannot be comfortably integrated into monastic life. The only happy ending possible is the demon's assumption into the angels, for demons can only truly be integrated into the community in heaven.

Demons are more comfortably depicted as part of a religious community in the medieval Jewish "Tale of the Jerusalemite."[74] This tale, which Moses Gaster calls "one of the earliest fairy-tales accessible to European readings," portrays an entire community of rabbinically observant demons.[75] The story begins with an unnamed young man vowing to his dying father never to travel by sea. Predictably, ten years later he breaks his vow, swayed by the promise of distant treasures. Eventually he finds himself lost in a province at the ends of the earth, which is inhabited by demons. These demons attend synagogue daily, recite the morning prayers properly, study diligently with the synagogue's rabbi, and, when they discover the human interloper and the circumstances that brought him to their province, seek to appropriately punish the oath-breaker according to rabbinic law.[76] Their king, our old friend Ashmedai, tests the man's knowledge of Bible, Mishnah, and Talmud, and, impressed with the extent of the man's knowledge, decides to spare the man on condition that he stay and instruct Ashmedai's son in Torah. Through a series of fairy-tale misadventures, the man marries Ashmedai's daughter and has a child with her, whom they name Solomon. But the man eventually returns to his human life, abandoning his demon wife and child for a human wife and family that we now learn he had left behind. The demon community is appalled,

> "But you are a scholar of Torah! They said to him. "How can you break your oath? The time has passed that you yourself stipulated. Not only are you transgressing the prohibition, 'You shall not swear falsely by My name' (Lev. 19:12); but you are also forfeiting the positive injunction, 'If a man marries

74. See Stern, "The Tale of the Jerusalemite," 121, for a discussion of the text's date. Stern is most convinced by Jehuda Zlotnik's argument dating the text to Geonic Babylonia, in the ninth or tenth century. See also Dan, "Five Versions of the Story of the Jerusalemite," for a discussion of the text's history.

75. Folklore 42 [1931]:157 in Stern, "The Tale of the Jerusalemite," 121.

76. Stern, "The Tale of the Jerusalemite," 127–30.

> another [wife], he must not withhold from [his first wife] her food, clothing, or her conjugal rights' (Exodus 21:10)."[77]

They criticize him both for the original act of abandoning his first wife and family and for lying. Polygamy is biblically (and apparently demonically) permitted, but abandonment and lying are forbidden. Eventually the demon princess follows the man to his hometown and compels the man to issue her a rabbinic divorce; at the moment of divorce, she kisses him goodbye and strangles him to death. The story concludes with their half demon son being made ruler over the human city and being accepted by the human townsfolk.

As in the story of Ashmedai and King Solomon in b. *Gittin* 68a–b, discussed in the previous chapter, the demons in the "Tale of the Jerusalemite" are more righteous than the young Jew. Again, we have someone named Solomon, and sexual misadventures. But here it is not the demon king but the human man who has violated sexual mores and treated wives badly. And here we are introduced not just to a single exceptional demon king but to an entire land of demons who are subject to rabbinic law, observe it diligently, are immersed in its forms of argumentation, and enforce it zealously. The demonic community welcomes the human man into their community and honors his Torah-knowledge, though he ultimately turns out to be undeserving of their honor. The human community welcomes the half-demon son as a member of their own community and as their leader. The demons pose a threat only because the man is faithless and deceitful. The moral of the story is made clear at the tale's conclusion: "Accordingly a son should always obey his father's commands and never break an oath."[78] Sea travel was never meant to be in this man's future.

The Babylonian Talmud is the earliest and perhaps only late antique text which evidences the survival or revival of the ancient Mesopotamian idea of demons as integrated into the community as neutral servants to powerful figures. This idea is developed even more fully in early medieval narratives. The trope's afterlife testifies to the continued importance of depicting demons as positive servants of the divine and of religious leaders—to understandings of authority, the religious community, and the world more broadly.

77. Ibid., 137.
78. Ibid., 141.

WRAPPING UP

In the Babylonian Talmud, this depiction is part of a larger rabbinic discourse about demons that constructs demons as passive, neutral, integrated into the halakhic system, and part of a monotheistic cosmology. In rabbinic discourse about demons, negative, neutral, and positively marked demons affirm rabbinic superiority, enforce rabbinic laws and boundaries, participate in the rabbinic legal system, answer rabbis' calls, and, in one exceptional case, serve rabbinic households. This discourse about demons is very much a part of the rabbinic project more broadly: a project of legal thinking, the transmission and analysis of earlier traditions, a particular kind of identity formation, and theological world building. While there are certainly Talmudic texts that insist that demons are dangerous and even, at times, fatal, these texts are juxtaposed with other discussions in which demons are positively marked as teachers, students, and servants of the rabbinic project. We see a range of rabbinic approaches to the demonic, approaches which are at times at odds with one another though they are deeply interconnected by the rabbinic worldview and rabbinic legal discourse. Like so many other aspects of rabbinic literature, rabbinic demonology is multivocal and hard to characterize.

The Babylonian rabbis adapt and reshape existing cultural elements as they continue to create unique cultural elements of their own;[79] in so doing, they challenge, complicate, and affirm the rabbinic system as a whole. This construction of the demonic undermines contemporaneous—and modern—Christian depictions of demons as malevolent intermediary beings who attack human beings. But if demons are not only, or even mostly, malevolent attackers, then what did the rabbis make of the most prominent way that ancient peoples engaged with demons: exorcism?

79. This is a model that Yaron Eliav calls "filtered absorption." See Yaron Z. Eliav, "The Roman Bath as a Jewish Institution: Another Look at the Encounter between Judaism and the Greco-Roman Culture," *Journal for the Study of Judaism* 31, no. 4 (2000): 426–27. For an alternative though complementary model, see Michael L. Satlow, "Beyond Influence: Toward a New Historiographic Paradigm," in *Jewish Literatures and Cultures: Context and Intertext*, ed. Anita Norich and Yaron Z. Eliav (Providence: Brown Judaic Studies, 2008), 53.

6 Exorcising Demons

For I have seen a certain man of my own country, whose name was Eleazar, releasing people that were demoniacal in the presence of Vespasian, and his sons, and his captains, and the whole multitude of his soldiers.

Josephus, *Antiquities of the Jews* 8.42

Hollywood horror movies have shaped how many in the United States think about demons today. Demonic possessions and exorcisms play a starring role in horror films like *The Exorcist, The Babadook, Insidious, The Evil Dead, The Amityville Horror*, and many more. These modern narratives of demonic possession play on fears about bodily autonomy, bodily integrity and permeability, and the fear that people you love and trust may be corrupted by forces outside their—and your—control. The sheer number of spinoffs to these movies (these five films have had a collective count of thirty prequels, sequels, and television adaptions as of 2018) testifies to the popularity of this film genre.[1]

These fears are by no means exclusive to modernity; in late antiquity too, much of the anxiety about demons focused on demonic possessions and how to treat them. In what follows, I distinguish between *attacks*—in which demons attack the human from outside the human body—and

Epigraph: Flavius Josephus, *The Works of Flavius Josephus*, trans. William Whiston (Auburn: John E. Beardsley, 1895), http://data.perseus.org/citations/urn:cts:greekLit:tlg0526.tlg001.perseus-eng1:8.42.

1. Based on a cursory search of the Wikipedia pages for each film franchise.

possessions—in which demons attack from within. Second Temple Jewish literature offers extensive literary evidence of many Jews' preoccupation with demonic attacks, possessions, and exorcisms. Demons could attack or possess human beings, but they could also attack or possess particular spaces. Many ancient Jews believed that both demonic attacks and possessions were life-threatening. They also believed that such events could be treated by ritual experts we would call exorcists.[2] These exorcists gained prestige, power, payment, and more work from the public recognition of their successful exorcisms.

Over the course of this book I have argued that the Babylonian Talmud contains at least two interconnected discourses around demons: one which admits to demons' capriciousness and capacity for harm, and one which neutralizes demons and paints them as subjects of and participants in the rabbinic project. These two discourses cannot be plotted along a chronological narrative of either evolution or corruption; they exist side by side within the multivocality of rabbinic literature. Rabbinic narratives of demonic attack and exorcism fall along a spectrum between these two distinctive modes of characterization, from demons as absolutely malevolent and harmful to demons as rabbinic allies and friends.

Given the prominence of demons to rabbinic discourse in a wide range of areas and given the ways that stories of exorcism were used to bolster individuals' authority and reputation, we might expect to see numerous narratives of demonic possession and exorcism in rabbinic literature. But rabbinic literature subverts this expectation.

EXORCISING THE DEMON IN THE HOUSE OF STUDY

There is only one narrative in the entire Babylonian Talmud in which an unequivocally malevolent demon engages in an act of possession, and there it possesses not a person but a place. As part of a discussion about how to prioritize one's limited resources for Torah study in a family unit, b. *Qiddushin* recounts that,

2. This terminology is by no means consistent across Second Temple period Jewish texts from Josephus, Qumran, and the synoptic Gospels.

> the [son] of R. Aḥa b. Jacob was sent by his father [to study] before Abaye. When he returned [home], [his father] saw that his legal traditions were not honed. [R. Aḥa b. Jacob] said to him: I am better than you. You remain here, and I will go [to study]. Abaye heard that he was coming. There was a certain demon [in] the *be rabbanan* [place of advanced study,[3] such that [even] when two entered, even during the day, they would be injured. Abaye said to them, "Let no man offer him hospitality [so he is forced to stay in the be rabbanan], for perhaps a miracle will take place through him." When [R. Aḥa b. Jacob] stayed the night in that be rabbanan, [the demon] appeared to him as a seven-headed serpent. Each time that [R. Aḥa b. Jacob] bowed down, one head fell off. [R. Aḥa b. Jacob] said to them: If there had not been a miracle on my behalf, you would have endangered me!

As discussed in chapter 5, Abaye's expertise on issues relating to the demonic is well attested through the Babylonian Talmud, but it appears that there are limits to what he himself can accomplish; he is unable to exorcise the demon from his own be rabbanan. Instead, R. Aḥa b. Jacob successfully vanquishes the seven-headed serpent demon through his acts of exorcistic bowing, and makes Abaye's be rabbanan safe to use again for its proper purposes.[4]

Although this is the only depiction of such a malevolent demon in the Bavli, the negative characterization of this demon participates in the broader rabbinic discourse about demons discussed in previous chapters. The physical mutability of demons explored in chapter 2 is hinted at in the way that the text describes the demon as "appearing" as a seven-headed serpent. Chapter 3 examined the ways that the rabbis constructed space by linking demons to particular physical locations at both the periphery and the center of the Jewish world.[5] What is more central than the be rabbanan of one of the greatest rabbinic minds of his generation? And indeed, demonic integration into the rabbinic legal system (see chapter 4) may itself be implied by the demon's location in the be rabbanan.

And yet, the broader rabbinic discourse about demons also serves to heighten the ways that this particular demon is an outlier. Although we

3. Sokoloff, *A Dictionary of Jewish Babylonian Aramaic*, 218–19, s.v. בי רבנן.

4. This text is treated in substantially more depth in Sara Ronis, "A Seven-Headed Demon in the House of Study: Understanding a Rabbinic Demon in Light of Zoroastrian, Christian, and Babylonian Textual Traditions," *AJS Review* (2019).

5. Ronis, "Space, Place, and the Race for Power."

saw in chapter 3 that the rabbis insist that humans are particularly susceptible to demonic attack at night, this demon attacks even during the day.[6] According to an anonymous statement in b. *Berakhot* 3a–b, entering dangerous spaces with a colleague is one way to protect oneself from demonic harm. There is supposed to be safety in numbers, and yet the demon in Abaye's be rabbanan does not hesitate to attack, even when the people enter in pairs. The demon's utter malevolence establishes R. Aḥa b. Jacob as a particularly sharp rabbinic hero whose prowess in studying the traditions translates into exorcistic powers that surpass even those of his teacher, Abaye.

Although this demon is clearly shaped by rabbinic discourse, this story also participates in broader cultural discourses about demons. Narratives where heroes defeat multiheaded serpents or dragons are found throughout Indo-European mythologies. In Greek mythology, Hercules vanquishes the nine-headed Hydra with his powerful club; in Zoroastrian literature, Frēdōn (in Pahlavi) or Θraētaona (in Avestan) destroys the primeval dragon Azdahāg (in Pahlavi) or Aži Dahāka (in Avestan) with his sword and club.[7] According to *Yašt* 14, the hero "*s*mashed the giant dragon [Aži Dahāka] with three mouths, three heads, six eyes, a thousand tricks, the mighty strong, deceiving Lie, that evil (affecting) the living beings, possessed by the Lie: the mighty strong Lie that the Evil Spirit whittled forth, against the bony world of the living, for the destruction of the living beings of Order."[8] These stories describe dragons or serpents, with nine and three heads respectively, being destroyed by strong heroes using military might.

More closely parallel to this Talmudic demon, however, are much older Mesopotamian traditions of seven-headed supernatural serpents. The Babylonian epic of creation tells us that, at the beginning of creation,

6. See, e.g., b. *Megillah* 3a; b. *Pesaḥim* 112b–113a.

7. On the Greek Hydra, see Ps.-Apollodorus, *Library* 2.5.2. On Azdahāg, see *Yašt* 14; *Forrest, Witches, Whores, and Sorcerers*, 131; Prods Oktor Skjærvø, "Aždahā. I. In Old and Middle Iranian," in *Encyclopædia Iranica* (2011). There is a single possible reference to a seven-headed dragon in a Zoroastrian manuscript of the *Bundahišn* 22.10, in Behramgore T. Anklesaria, *Zand-Ākāsīh: Iranian or Greater Bundahišn* (Bombay: Dastur Framoze A. Bode, 1956), 184–85. Found neither in the parallel *Indian* or *Lesser Bundahišn*, this reference appears substantially later than the Talmudic narrative.

8. Translation from S. K. Mendoza Forrest, *Witches, Whores, and Sorcerers*, 131.

the primordial goddess Tiamat battled the other gods for supremacy and survival. Tiamat created monsters to fight by her side, including a seven-headed serpent she called the Mušmaḫḫu.[9] Unfortunately for her and her monstrous creations, Tiamat lost the war and the Mušmaḫḫu was destroyed. Sumerian texts praise Ninurta, god of war and scribes, for defeating "the seven-mouthed mušmah serpent."[10] To the west in Ras al-Sham (today's northern Syria), the Ugaritic Ba'al Cycle also testifies to the prominence of a narrative in which a seven-headed serpent, here called Lotan, is defeated by a god. The war goddess Anat brags: "Surely I lifted up the dragon, I overpowered him? I smote the writhing serpent, Encircler-with-seven-heads!"[11] Echoes of this primordial battle survive in the Hebrew Bible with the Leviathan. This Biblical Hebrew name is linguistically related to the Ugaritic Lotan. Hints of this myth can also be seen in Psalm 74:14, in which God is depicted as the hero who "crushed the heads [note the plural] of the Leviathan."[12] Though the biblical authors do not specify here the number of heads that the Leviathan had, this number does survive elsewhere. In first-century C.E. Asia Minor, the author of the New Testament book of Revelation describes a seven-headed dragon who is also Satan.[13] There is no evidence that the rabbis were aware of Revelation,

9. See Lambert, *Babylonian Creation Myths*, 230–32, 443–44; Dalley, *Myths from Mesopotamia*, 252–61.

10. *Ninurta's Return to Nibru: A Šir-gida to Ninurta*, available at The Electronic Text Corpus of Sumerian Literature, Faculty of Oriental Studies, University of Oxford, 2003–06, http://etcsl.orinst.ox.ac.uk/. See also Amar Annus, *The God Ninurta in the Mythology and Royal Ideology of Ancient Mesopotamia* (Helsinki: Neo-Assyrian Text Corpus Project, 2002), 109–123.

11. Elsewhere in the Ugaritic Ba'al Cycle, the god Mot claims that Ba'al was the one to kill this seven-headed serpent, who he calls both Lotan and Shalyat. See Wayne T. Pitard, "Voices from the Dust: Tablets from Ugarit and the Bible " in *Mesopotamia and the Bible: Comparative Explorations*, ed. Mark W. Chavalas and K. Lawson Younger Jr. (London: Continuum, 2003), 261; Adam E. Miglio, "A Study of the Serpent Incantation KTU 1.82: 1–7 and Its Contributions to Ugaritic Mythology and Religion," *Journal of Ancient Near Eastern Religions* 13 (2013): 30–48.

12. See also Isa. 27:1; Ps. 104:26. See Calvert Watkins, *How to Kill a Dragon: Aspects of Indo-European Poetics* (Oxford: Oxford University Press, 1995), 313–20, 464-70; Adela Yarbro Collins, *The Combat Myth in the Book of Revelation* (Missoula: Scholars Press for Harvard Theological Review, 1976), 101–56; Avigdor Shinan and Yair Zakovitch, *From Gods to God: How the Bible Debunked, Suppressed, or Changed Ancient Myths and Legends*, trans. Valerie Zakovitch (Philadelphia: Jewish Publication Society, 2012), 11–16.

13. See Rev. 12.

but the seven-headed dragon's survival in one context suggests it may well have survived in another. The previous chapter discussed evidence that the late Sasanian king Xusrow I (531–579 C.E.) knew of the Babylonian epic of creation, the *Enuma Elish.* If these traditions were still in circulation in the Sasanian Empire, the rabbis could well have drawn on them directly. But whether or not the rabbis drew directly from ancient Near Eastern traditions, we have already seen demonstrated the ways that rabbinic discourse aligned with some ancient Near Eastern discourse about demons; the physical description of the demon in b. *Qiddushin* 29b is another example of this phenomenon.[14]

And yet the mode by which R. Aḥa b. Jacob vanquishes the demon has no parallels in these ancient Near Eastern texts; in these earlier texts, divine warriors vanquish the seven-headed serpent in battle with weapons of war. In b. *Qiddushin* 29b, a rabbi defeats the demon through the act of bowing, which as early as the Mishnah became a rabbinic synecdoche for embodied prayer.[15]

This narrative turn is consistent with broader trends in late antiquity. Accounts of holy men defeating demons through prayer appear with increasing frequency in the fourth and fifth centuries across the Roman and Sasanian Empires. In the west, Athanasius's fourth-century *Life of Anthony* and the fifth-century *Life of Daniel the Stylite*—both Christian hagiographies—depict ascetic monks destroying demons through prayer and bowing.[16] In fact, Philip Keisman points out remarkable parallels between the literary depictions of Daniel the Stylite's exorcism of the demons dwelling in a particular church and the story of R. Aḥa b. Jacob in B. *Qiddushin* 29b. These parallels include the demon's location in a sacred space, the involvement of the local community, and the phrase, "If there had not been X on my behalf, you would have endangered me!"[17]

14. Bamberger, "An Akkadian Demon in the Talmud," has made a similar argument about the survival of the Akkadian demon Šulak as the privy demon Bar Širiqa in b. *Gittin* 70a.

15. See M. *Yoma* 3:9, b. *Yoma* 53b, b. *Berakhot* 31a, 34b; b. *Megillah* 22b; b. *Shevuot* 16b.

16. *Life of St. Anthony* 22–23, 39, 48; *Life of St. Daniel the Stylite,* 14–20. See also Daniel Ogden, *Dragons, Serpents, and Slayers in the Classical and Early Christian Worlds: A Sourcebook* (Oxford: Oxford University Press, 2013), 194–237. See also Eli Yassif, *The Hebrew Folktale: History, Genre, Meaning* (Bloomington: Indiana University Press, 2009), 153.

17. Philip Keisman, "'If a Miracle Hadn't Happened for Me . . .': Daniel the Stylite and Rav Acha as Parallel Protagonists," unpublished work, 2017.

As noted, Kalmin identifies a substantial increase in Babylonian rabbinic awareness of traditions from the Roman West beginning in the fourth century C.E.[18] Closer to home in the east, Zoroastrian legal texts record prayer formulas to be used against demonic foes; the Christian *Acts of the Persian Martyrs* describe how the eponymous martyrs used prayers and the sign of the cross to vanquish demons.[19] It is not surprising then that b. *Qiddushin* depicts an ancient Near Eastern demon being killed by late antique exorcistic practices.

This account demonstrates the manifold ways in which rabbinic discourse about demons participated in broader intercultural conversations with a wide range of textual traditions and ritual practices. The rabbis adopt and adapt new cultural elements in a creative bricolage that serves to further the rabbinic project. It is perhaps unsurprising then that the demon—unique among demons in the Babylonian Talmud—is so unabashedly malevolent, just like the demons in the Christian hagiographies. A late antique exorcism requires a particular kind of late antique demon. And yet here, the wandering Christian holy man has become a rabbi famous for his honed rabbinic knowledge.

USING YOUR WORDS AND GESTURES TO REPEL DEMONS

Although the narrative of R. Aḥa b. Jacob and the seven-headed serpent demon is the only narrative in the Babylonian Talmud of a rabbi killing an unabashedly evil demon who has possessed either a person or a place, there exist both legal and narrative passages which depict the expulsion or repulsion of demonic attackers through verbal formulas, ritual gestures and the writing of amulets.

The Talmud prescribes verbal formulas to prevent particular forms of

18. Richard Kalmin, *Jewish Babylonia between Persia and Roman Palestine*, 9–10.

19. On Zoroastrian examples, see *Vīdēvdād* 8.79, 9.46, 10.1–18, 11.9–14, 18.30–49; 19.2 in Moazami, *Wrestling with the Demons of the Pahlavi Widēwdād*; and see the extensive discussion in Ronis, "A Seven-Headed Demon in the House of Study," n. 49. On the Syriac Acts of the Persian Martyrs, see, e.g., *The History of the Holy Mar Ma'in*, 77–82, in Sebastian P. Brock, *The History of the Holy Mar Ma'in, with a Guide to the Persian Martyr Acts* (Piscataway, NJ: Gorgias Press, 2009), 48–54.

demonic attack. Some verbal formulas quote or reference the Bible. To prevent an attack of the demon (ruaḥ) *Znunim* [Immorality], one must say, *"He pours contempt on great men, and makes them lose their way in trackless deserts" (Ps. 107:40, NJPS).*[20] Other formulas are apparently unconnected to scripture. For the privy demon, one should say: "On the heads of lions and on the nostrils of lion-cubs you found the demon Bar-Širiqa Panda; in a garden bed he is purified, I have enfolded him."[21] A verbal formula for use against generic demons (šeida) reads: "You were cursed, you were cursed. Cursed, broken and banned be Bar Tit, Bar Tama, Bar Tina like Shamgaz, Merigaz, and Istamei."[22] The generic demon appears to be named Bar Tit, Bar Tama, and Bar Tina; the powers invoked to curse and ban him are obscure. In fact, these verbal formulas often have obscure phrasing and hapax legomena; it is not always clear if the words would have been readily understood at the time, if the words were intended to be obscure, or if the manuscript tradition is particularly corrupt.

At times, verbal formulas could be replaced by ritual gestures. A passage in b. *Pesaḥim* 112a already discussed in chapter 4 provides a range of options for protecting oneself from the demonic attack provoked by drinking water on Tuesday and Thursday nights:

> And if he is thirsty, what [should he do]? Let him say *seven kolot* (Ps. 29) and then drink. And if not, let him say thusly: Lul Shafan, Anigron, Anirdefai. I dwell between the stars,[23] become fat among the thin ones.
>
> And if not, if there is another person lying next to him, let him wake him up and say: Ploni son of Plonita, I am thirsty for water, and then let him drink. And if [there is no other person there], let him rattle the cover of the pitcher, and then let him drink.
>
> And if not, let him spit into [the waters], and then let him drink.

20. B. *Pesaḥim* 111a.

21. B. *Shabbat* 67a, in MS Munich 95.

22. B. *Shabbat* 67a, following Sokoloff, *A Dictionary of Jewish Babylonian Aramaic*, 348, s.v. דפקוק. See also b. *Pesaḥim* 111a. The manuscript versions of this text have slight differences in the names of the demons cursed.

23. So Sokoloff, *A Dictionary of Jewish Babylonian Aramaic*, 212, s.v. בי כוכבי. Another possible translation is: I dwell among the great chasms.

The first option is to recite Psalm 29, a particularly appropriate biblical text to use against water-dwelling demons. Psalm 29:3 proclaims that "the voice of the Lord is over the waters; the God of glory thunders, the Lord, over the mighty waters" (NJPS). The God who is over the water is invoked to protect the drinker from the unseen dangers of drinking water on these nights. The second option offers an obscure verbal formula. The third option involves speaking to another human being—perhaps it is the act of vocalization which in some sense warns the demon of one's presence. The fourth and fifth options offer ritual gestures designed to ward off any demons near the water. Verbal formulas and ritual gestures are equally effective, and indeed interchangeable, in making this water safe for human consumption.

In some cases, ritual gestures combined *with* verbal formulas were the most effective means of protection. As we have already discussed in chapter 3, b. *Pesaḥim* 110a has the demonic informant Joseph the demon telling the rabbis what to do if they accidentally drink an even number of drinks: "let him hold his straight right arm in his left arm [sleeve] and that of the left in his right arm [sleeve], and let him say: You (pl.) and I are three. And if he hears someone say [You and I are] four, let him say, [You and] I are five. And if he hears someone say [You and I are] six, let him say, [You and I are] seven."[24] The demon Joseph's instructions are followed by a brief validating story: "This once happened and when they reached one hundred and one, the demon burst." For the rabbis, ritual gestures had the ability to repel and even destroy demonic attackers.

So did amulets. Amulets had to be highly precise to function effectively, and therefore required specialized (rabbinic) knowledge. Thus, the anonymous voice in b. *Gittin* 67b asks, "What is kordiakos? Shmuel said: One who is bitten by the new wine of the wine press. Then why did it not say, *one who has been bitten by new wine*? It comes to teach us that this demon (ruḥa) is called kordiakos. What is the relevance of this [fact]? For amulets." The rabbis must know the demon's proper name in order to successfully repel it, and to pass the technique on to the next generation.

Similarly, when b. *Pesaḥim* discusses the precise names and quantities of a variety of demons, it links this discussion explicitly to the need to write

24. See discussion of this gesture in chap. 4.

precise amulets: “The [demons] of zardata reeds are called šeda. These zardata reeds that are close to the city have no fewer than sixty demons (šeidei). What is the relevance of this [fact]? For the writing of amulets” (b. *Pesaḥim* 111b). In b. *Pesaḥim*, this rabbinic fact is immediately supported with a story: “A certain city official went and relieved himself near zardata reeds near a city.” As discussed in chapter 3, demons take particular exception to people urinating on them; the city official thus suffers demonic retaliation for this perceived act of aggression. “He became seriously ill,” and sought a cure. “A certain one of the rabbis who didn’t know that zardata reeds are infested with sixty demons (šeidei) went and wrote an amulet for one [demon].” This man who called himself a rabbi made a critical mistake and wrote an amulet for the wrong number of demons. This mistake is both ineffective at curing the city official and the source of much mockery on the part of the sixty demons: “He heard that they had suspended a hinga [a musical instrument common in Babylonia] within [the reeds] and sang: That man’s soudarion [neck cloth] is like that of our Rabbis, but when they examined him, [they discovered that] he did not [even] know ‘*Blessed art Thou*.’” Though the man dresses like a rabbi with a rabbinic handkerchief, he is made aware—by the demons themselves—of his own ignorance of basic rabbinic teachings. The story gives the demons of the reeds a voice that musically valorizes the rabbis with demonical knowledge and devalues pretenders to that title. Finally, “a certain one of our Rabbis who did know that the zardata reeds are infested by sixty demons (šeidei) wrote an amulet for sixty demons (šeidei). He heard them say: All of you, remove yourselves from here!”[25]

The story underlines the ignorance of both non-Jewish officials and unlearned rabbinic Jews to the true nature of demonic harm, and the unique authority of the learned rabbis to expel demons and prevent such harm. Even demons know that for true expertise in the demonic, one needs a rabbi—not just someone who *dresses* like a rabbi. Rabbinic knowledge of demons works because, for the demons as for the rabbis themselves, truly knowledgeable rabbis are “our rabbis.” Demons may cause harm to

25. The story’s conclusion here implies that the rabbi’s command is effective. Nevertheless, it is curious that the text does not make this effectiveness explicit.

the ignorant, but rabbinic sages are protected from harm and are able to protect others through the writing of amulets.

Amulets and other apotropaic objects were used across the ancient Near East to ward off illness, demonic dangers, and social curses. Jews in the First and Second Temple periods used metal and clay amulets on which were inscribed various ritual formulas to invoke protection.[26] Even the Mishnah, which rarely mentions demons, is aware of amulets and regulates their production and use on Shabbat.[27] The association of Jews and amulets was known well enough that, in fourth-century Antioch, the early church father John Chrysostom publicly criticized Jews for using amulets to effect healing, though this critique was largely rhetorical.[28] Much closer to home in Sasanian Babylonia, many Jews and others spent a lot of time trying to use one specific kind of ritual object as protection against a range of unseen forces.

INSCRIBING PROTECTION TO WARD OFF EVIL: THE BABYLONIAN INCANTATION BOWLS

The most common type of ritual object for protection from demons that has survived from Sasanian Babylonia is the incantation bowl. Babylonian incantation bowls were made up of incantations written on the insides of clay bowls by professional bowl scribes. These incantation bowls were meant to protect named clients from harm both specific and general. After being written, they were most likely buried upside down; there is

26. See B. A. Mastin, "The Inscriptions Written on Plaster at Kuntillet 'Arjud," *Vetus Testamentum* 59, no. 1 (2009): 99–115; Gideon Bohak, "Jewish Magic in the First and Second Temple Periods," in *Angels and Demons: Jewish Magic through the Ages*, ed. Filip Vukosavovic (Jerusalem: Bible Lands Museum, 2010), 12–15, for a summary of scholarship on these amulets.

27. M. *Shabbat* 6:2, 8:3; m. *Sheqalim* 3:2. See also m. *Keilim* 23:1; m. *Miqva'ot* 10:2. Altogether, amulets are mentioned in the Mishnah five times, nine times in the Palestinian Talmud, and forty-six times in the Babylonian Talmud. Note the enormous growth (820% relative to the Mishnah, and 411% relative to the Palestinian Talmud) in the Babylonian Talmud. This phenomenon should not surprise us given the Babylonian rabbis' increased interest in unseen dangers.

28. John Chrysostom, *Against the Jews,* Homily 8.6, quoted in Bohak, *Ancient Jewish Magic*, 315.

evidence that they were found at the four corners of the clients' homes. The incantations were not meant to be copied or read by human beings, instead they may have functioned as demonic "mouse-traps" meant to capture demons and neutralize demonic aggression.[29] Bowls were mass-produced and inscribed with incantations in a variety of languages for a wide range of clients; archaeologists have found bowls written in Syriac, Mandaic, and Jewish Babylonian Aramaic, for clients across the religious spectrum.[30] These bowls reflect a particular culture of practices related to demons, a culture not limited to a single religious community.[31] Like the rabbinic texts described above, the bowl texts are characterized by their specificity, but they are also characterized by their apparent attempts at comprehensiveness; bowl scribes often included as comprehensive a list of threats as possible to increase the likelihood that their incantations would work. The majority of named threats are demons, such as the frequently mentioned "spirit (ruḥa) whose name is Agag daughter of Baroq, daughter of Baroqta, daughter of Naqor, daughter of Namon, daughter of the evil eye."[32] The scribe names the demon and records her lineage, lest there be any confusion about who exactly is being warded off.

The demons named by the bowls are described as attacking humans, possessing human dwellings, and, at times, possessing human bodies to cause disease. The bowls use a range of techniques for dealing with these demonic dangers: statements of divorce, excommunication, calling on

29. Naveh and Shaked, *Amulets and Magic Bowls*, 15; Levene, *Corpus of Magic Bowls*, 2. The source texts must have circulated in written form, however, as we see not only parallel incantations but also parallel drawings. See also Gideon Bohak, "Babylonian Incantation Bowls—Past, Present and Future," review of *A Corpus of Magic Bowls: Incantation Texts in Jewish Aramaic from Late Antiquity*, by Dan Levene, *Pe'amim* 105/106 (2005–06): 257.

30. Syriac bowls have been found written in Manichaean, Nestorian, and Estrangello script. Several bowls appear to be written in Pahlavi, but these have yet to be published or interpreted. See Shaul Shaked, "Magical Bowls and Incantation Texts: How to Get Rid of Demons and Pests," *Qadmoniot* 129 (2005): 5; Naveh and Shaked, *Amulets and Magic Bowls*, 17.

31. Levene, *Corpus of Magic Bowls*, 6; Bohak, "Babylonian Incantation Bowls," 254.

32. Agag's genealogy is usually followed by a list of her aliases: "They call you blinder, smiter, sightless; they call you lame, they call you itchy, they call you crawler." JBA 1 (MS 1927); JBA 2 (MS 1927/1929); JBA 3 (MS 1927/45); JBA 4 (MS 1927/1947); JBA 5 (MS 1927/64); JBA 6 (MS 2053/10); JBA 7 (MS 2053/12); JBA 8 (MS 2053/55); JBA 9 (MS 2053/183); JBA 10 (MS 2053/185); JBA 11 (MS 2053/79); JBA 12 (MS 2053/178), in Shaked et al. *Aramaic Bowl Spells*, 56–88, 91–96.

powerful human or intermediary protectors, citing biblical verses seen as effectively exorcistic, and invoking particular ritual items—seals, rings, lances, and so on.[33] These techniques enacted *through* writing were paired with the ritual acts *of* writing and burying the incantation bowl itself. The bowls name a number of important figures who serve as either authority for the act of expulsion or as an authority involved in the expulsion itself. R. Joshua b. Peraḥia is the most common figure invoked; the incantation texts describe him as having written an effective divorce decree against evil demons at some point in history, which serves as a precedent and historiola for future acts of divorce against evil demons.[34] Often, the bowls invoke angelic protection, opposing angels to demons in a way that should be familiar to us from Christian taxonomies of intermediary beings (see chapter 2).[35] Given the bowl scribes' assumption that demons are opposed by angels, at least one bowl scribe may have thought that Ashmedai himself was an angel with his ability to prevent and heal demonic attacks, writing an incantation asking for healing "by the name of the angel Ashmedai, Amen, Amen, Selah."[36] And yet one fascinating incantation text invokes R. Agzar bar Dibšata, R. Joseph the Demon, and the demons and dark ones that are in Babylonia for protection.[37]

The demonology of the Babylonian incantation bowls resists systematization. Across linguistic types and religious lines, in the bowls, demons can be both anonymous collectives and named individuals with distinct genealogies. Demons can be male or female and take on a variety of appearances in the human world. Demons attack from within the human body and from without. They dwell in specific locations in the home and on the outskirts of human habitation. While several bowls threaten to

33. Shaked et al., *Aramaic Bowl Spells*, 9–12. On statements of divorce, see Ahuvia, "Israel among the Angels," 175–83. The statements of divorce are not replicas of the rabbinic divorce, but rather they appropriate and adapt rabbinic language and figures to enhance the power of their ejection of a particular demonic threat from a household or individual. See Avigail Manekin Bamberger, "Jewish Legal Formulae in the Aramaic Incantation Bowls," *Aramaic Studies* 13 (2015) 69–81.

34. JBA 42 (MS 2053/190), in Shaked et al., *Aramaic Bowl Spells*, 198.

35. See Ronis, "'Do Not Go Out Alone at Night,'" 363–66. See Ahuvia, "Israel among the Angels," for a comprehensives analysis of angels in the Babylonian incantation bowls.

36. JBA 58 (MS 2053/166), in Shaked et al., *Aramaic Bowl Spells*, 258. See also JBA 26 (MS 1928/43) in ibid., 153.

37. JBA 26 (MS 1928/43) in ibid.

send demons to the Netherworld or the Abyss, demons do not seem to originate in hell or the underworld.[38] Most demons listed are evil, but the insistence on linguistically marking such demons with the adjective *evil* suggests that other demonic forces may not be malevolent. Demons are legal actors bound by rabbinic divorce decrees, and yet their malevolence must also be dealt with through acts of ritual power, objects of ritual power, and physical destruction at the hands of angelic protectors. Demons are scared of rabbinic figures and remain controlled by the acts of R. Joshua b. Peraḥia, and yet this control does not extend to preventing demonic attacks in the first place.[39]

The Babylonian incantation bowls have been found in the same regions of Sasanian Babylonia where the Babylonian rabbis lived.[40] The bowls written in Jewish Babylonian Aramaic shed light on a community of bowl producers who spoke and wrote in Jewish Babylonian Aramaic but who were either not part of elite rabbinic culture or whose activities were not valorized in its central text, the Babylonian Talmud. There is only one possible reference to incantation bowls in the Babylonian Talmud, appearing in two anonymous incantations which end with the phrase: "Ploni son of Plonit, *your mother told you to be careful of shavriri [day and night blindness] vriri riri iri ri* in an unglazed cup/bowl."[41] The vast majority of Babylonian incantation bowls are unglazed, and the incantation texts themselves refer to the bowls as *kasa* or *kosa,* a cup or bowl.[42] This expression may suggest that the authors of the anonymous layer of the Babylonian Talmud did in fact know about and reference incantation bowls, if only exceedingly rarely and obliquely.

38. 088M BM 91724; 1881-7-14, 5 in Segal, *Catalogue of the Aramaic and Mandaic Incantation Bowls in the British Museum* (London: British Museum Press, 2000), 117; JBA 55 (MS 1928/1), in Shaked et al. *Aramaic Bowl Spells,* 246.

39. See Ronis, "'Do Not Go Out Alone at Night,'" 344–69.

40. Gordon, "Aramaic Incantation Bowls," 356.

41. B. *Avodah Zarah* 12b; b. *Pesaḥim* 112a. The word *ḥyv'ry* which I have translated as "unglazed," means "white, silvered, translucent, unglazed, light." Sokoloff, *A Dictionary of Jewish Babylonian Aramaic,* 450–51, s.v. חיור. The color white is often used in antidemonic incantations and rituals (see, e.g., b. *Shabbat* 109, b. *Avodah Zarah* 14b, b. *Gittin* 69b), but in this context, the word should most likely be translated as "unglazed."

42. Philip S. Alexander, "Jewish Elements in Gnosticism and Magic, c. CE 70–c. CE 270," in *The Cambridge History of Judaism,* ed. W. Horbury et al. (Cambridge: Cambridge University Press, 1999), 3:1069; Montgomery, *Aramaic Incantation Texts from Nippur,* 43.

The bowl writers and their clients should be situated within a complex world of cultural interpretation, interaction, and synthesis. Within this broader world, demons are largely malevolent, fixated on attacking human beings, and expelled by means of the verbal statements and ritual gestures of powerful experts. This is a characterization consistent with the rabbinic narrative of the demon in Abaye's *be rabbanan,* discussed above.

PERFORMING POSSESSION

I have argued, however, that a prominent rabbinic discursive trend constructed demons as neutral or even positively marked participants in the rabbinic project. It should thus not surprise us to see narratives in which rabbinic exorcistic powers are deployed in strange or surprising ways as part of positive relationships with specific demons. A Palestinian rabbinic tradition found in *Leviticus Rabbah* 24:3 demonstrates this phenomenon clearly with a story in which the rabbis join forces together with a local demon to expel a demon who is new in town.

> R. Berekhiah said in the name of R. Simon: *It happened in our town that Abba Yose, a man of Ẓaytor would sit and study [Torah] at the mouth of a spring,* and a certain spirit (ruḥa) who dwelled there revealed himself to [Abba Yose] and said: You know how many years I have lived here, and you [pl.] and your wives come and go in the morning and the afternoon and are never harmed. Now you should know that a certain evil spirit (ruaḥ bish) wants to live here and he will harm people. [Abba Yose] said to him: What should we do? [The demon] said to him: Go and inform the people of the town, and say to them: Whoever has a hammer, whoever has a shovel, and whoever has a spade, bring them here tomorrow at dawn and watch the surface of the water. And when they see a disturbance on the water, let them rattle with the iron tools and say: Ours wins! And let them not leave this place until they see a blood clot rise on the face of the water. [Abba Yose] went and informed the townspeople and said to them: Whoever has a hammer, whoever has a shovel, and whoever has a spade, bring them here tomorrow at dawn and watch the surface of the water. And when they saw a disturbance on the water, they rattled with the iron tools and said: Ours wins! Ours wins! And they did not leave this place until the time that they saw a blood clot rise on the face of the water.

The local demon's goodness is both implicit—in that Abba Yose studies next to the demon's spring constantly without harm—and explicit—as the demon himself reminds the people of Ẓaytor of their safety with him over their many years together. Abba Yose and the townspeople believe "their" demon without question. Although in the story, there are harmful demons who seek to injure human beings, there are also demons actively engaged in keeping the peace, who participate in networks of positive relationships with individuals and communities. The story implies that good humans and good demons can band together to fight evil.[43] As in the Babylonian rabbinic halakhic sugya relating to Joseph the demon in b. *Pesaḥim*, discussed in chapter 4, here the demon is construed as the expert informant in how to deal with demonkind.

The procedure described in *Leviticus Rabbah* to exorcise the encroacher is the only extant description of an exorcism in Palestinian rabbinic midrash. The mode of exorcism entails using iron implements, which in late antiquity were often understood to be resistant or even repellant to demons,[44] loud noises, and claims of ownership over the spring and the local demon of the town. Demonic embodiment is emphasized: the demon's death or banishment is marked by his physical bleeding, the iron implements achieve their aims. This narrative is an exorcistic account, but the exorcists in question include another demon.

Another Palestinian Rabbinic account in which a friendly intermediary being allies with the rabbis against an evil force is found in *Genesis Rabbah* 63:8. According to this account, the Emperor Diocletian wanted to take revenge against the rabbis for disrespecting him before he became the emperor. Seeking a pretext to punish the rabbis, Diocletian intentionally summons R. Yehuda Nesiah to the imperial court at Banias without leaving him enough time to travel there. The plan is for R. Yehuda Nesiah

43. The midrash concludes, "Now, a fortiori, if demons, who were not created in order to receive help, need help, how much more so do we humans, who were created to receive help, need it. Therefore, '*Send forth your help from the sanctuary*' (Ps. 20:2)." Demons are mean to be independent, but still sometimes need help from human beings. For the authors of this midrash, this need is an important heuristic device to impart proper moral behavior to human beings.

44. For this belief in rabbinic thought, see b. *Pesaḥim* 109b–112a, b. *Berakhot* 6a; and see discussion in chap. 4. For a discussion of this belief in late antique Christian contexts, see Russell, *Satan*, 139–40.

to be late, snub the emperor, and give Diocletian a pretext to bring the full force of the empire against the rabbis as a consequence for this disrespect. R. Yehudah Nesiah and R. Shmuel b. Naḥman discuss the problem in a bathhouse in Tiberias, where a bathhouse being named Arginiton overhears their discussion. Where the Babylonian rabbis associated demonic dangers with the privy, this being is located in a bathhouse; Palestinian midrash identifies the public bathhouse as a particularly magically fraught location.[45] Arginiton decides to help the rabbis arrive in time by essentially teleporting them to Banias in the blink of an eye. Arginiton then helps the rabbis enter through the gates of the city, which Diocletian has had locked to bar their way. When Diocletian further schemes to kill R. Yehuda Nesiah by forcing him to bathe in scalding water, Arginiton cools the water down so the rabbi can survive his bath. With Arginiton's aid, the rabbis undermine Diocletian's nefarious attempt to punish and kill rabbis, even though the rabbinic narrator concludes by faulting the rabbis for their initial acts of disrespect. The text does not explicitly name Arginiton a demon, but the narrative includes many of the hallmarks of rabbinic demonology: the association with a dangerous location (here a bathhouse), the ability to travel large distances quickly, and as we have seen in the story of Rabbah b. Naḥmani and the Persian royal messenger (see chapter 5), the ability to subvert gentile authority while bolstering rabbinic power.[46] Rather than expelling a demon from a specific place, the rabbis here enter the demon's space in Tiberias. Unlike the danger the invasive evil demon poses in the tale from *Leviticus Rabbah*, the danger here is human. Together, the rabbis and Arginiton repel Diocletian and thwart his machinations. While thwarting the emperor's terrible plan is not the same thing as exorcising a demon, this midrash echoes the general

45. In Palestinian rabbinic literature, the bathhouse was often the site of contests between rabbis and either heretics or magicians. See Levinson, "Enchanting Rabbis."

46. Jastrow, *Dictionary of Targumim, Talmud and Midrashic Literature* 116, defines the Arginiton as "*helper of sailors, Arogonautes*, a demon." Michael Sokoloff, *A Dictionary of Jewish Palestinian Aramaic of the Byzantine Period* (1990; Ramat-Gan, Israel: Bar-Ilan University Press, 1992), 73 s.v. ארגינט defines it as a demon, of uncertain origin. See also Yaron Z. Eliav, "A Scary Place: Jewish Magic in the Roman Bathhouse," in *Man near a Roman Arch: Studies Presented to Prof. Yoram Tsafrir*, ed. Leah Di Segni et al. (Jerusalem: Israel Exploration Society, 2009), 88–97; Katherine Dunbabin, "Baiarum Grata Voluptas: Pleasures and Dangers of the Baths," *Papers of the British School at Rome* 57 (1989): 6–46.

themes of salvation and aid from demonic figures in the face of malevolent external actors found in other rabbinic texts.[47]

In both of the Palestinian midrashic narratives discussed, the demon's location in a particular space, and indeed a space associated with water (see chapter 4), allows the demon to share knowledge and skills with rabbinic visitors. Rabbinic powers are bolstered by demonic figures who protect the rabbis from external dangers. Although Palestinian rabbinic discourse about demons is substantially less developed than that of their Babylonian colleagues, these accounts share many characteristics with Babylonian rabbinic discourse about demons. Demons are depicted as positive supporters of humankind, the Jewish community, and specifically of the rabbis who (at least in rabbinic theory) lead the Jewish people.

This trend is at its most heightened in a narrative found in the Babylonian Talmud in tractate *Me'ilah*.[48] B. *Me'ilah* 17a–b is a sugya which ostensibly aims to discover the source for the tradition that the blood of reptiles is impure. Over the course of the discussion about impurity, the redactor introduces an only partially related narrative. According to the Talmudic tale, the Roman government decrees that it is forbidden to keep the Sabbath and circumcise infants, and also obligates men to have sexual intercourse with menstruant women. After their first strategy of appeasement fails, a small group of rabbis journey to Rome to beg the emperor to reconsider his decree. On the road from Galilee to Rome, "*Ben Talamion*[49] *came out to greet [R. Shimon]: Ben Talamion said to them, "Do you want me to go with you? R. Shimon cried out and said: An angel was designated for the maidservant of my father three times [i.e., even the maidservant of my ancestor was worthy of the intervention of an intermediary being],*

47. See Moshe Simon-Shoshan, "Did the Rabbis Believe in Agreus Pan? Rabbinic Relationships with Roman Power, Culture, and Religion in *Genesis Rabbah* 63," *Harvard Theological Review* 111, no. 3 (July 2018): 425–50, for a thorough analysis of this text in its cultural contexts.

48. Kalmin, *Migrating Tales*, 53–79, notes that this narrative is composite and made up of several traditions, some from Palestine, which were stitched together imperfectly. The seams are visible in the shifts between Hebrew and Aramaic, and between the singular and the plural in describing the narrative's actors. The section of interest here is the episode which involves Ben Tamalion/Talamion.

49. The name appears spelled both Ben Talamion and Ben Tamalion. I have attempted to be faithful to the Hebrew/Aramaic text in my translation, though Kalmin, *Migrating Tales*, 57, notes that Talamion is the more likely original spelling.

and I not even once. Nevertheless, may the miracle occur." Though Ben Talamion is not identified, R. Shimon's response points to Ben Talamion's supernatural identity, an identity made even clearer in the rest of the story. "[Ben Talamion] went ahead and entered the body of the emperor's daughter." Ben Talamion uses the classic demonic ability to move large distances in the blink of an eye to run ahead of the rabbis. "When [R. Shimon] arrived there, *he said: Ben Tamalion, leave! Ben Tamalion, leave!* And when they called him, he came out and left." The story ends in typical folktale fashion: "[The emperor] said to them: Ask for whatever you want, and go into the treasure house and take whatever you want. They went and found that letter [on which the decrees against the Jews were written]. They took it and ripped it up. *And this is what R. Eleazar b. Yose said: I saw [the written decree] in Rome and on it were several drops of blood.*"[50]

While R. Shimon is the main character of this narrative, Ben Talamion is the true hero of the episode. We never learn R. Shimon's original plan for the annulment of the Roman decree upon his arrival in Rome; it is not clear that he has one. Ben Talamion is the one who offers a successful strategy, who prompts R. Shimon to literally "perform" an exorcism. Where narratives of demonic possession and exorcism are popular and widespread in the late antique Roman world, we have already seen that they are largely absent from rabbinic literature of this period. In fact, this is the only account of a demon possessing a human body in the Bavli corpus, and even here it is a staged possession performed for an imagined Roman audience. Yet the Babylonian rabbis are clearly aware not only of the popularity of demonic possession and exorcism in the Roman West, but also of the specific formula often used to perform them: "Name of demon, leave!" Eli Yassif has argued that this account is "mimicking the ritual then widely used by the Christian saints to banish spirits."[51] But the rabbis are not mimicking; they are purposefully absorbing and appropriating.[52] The rabbis deploy and even amplify the differences between western and Babylonian rabbinic demonologies to construct themselves

50. Translation adapted from Kalmin, *Migrating Tales*, 56–58.

51. See Yassif, *The Hebrew Folktale*, 154–55.

52. Yuval Harari notes that it is not actually the technical aspects of the ritual performance that are effective here. See Harari, *Jewish Magic before the Rise of Kabbalah*, 406–07.

as the religious elite most capable of dealing with demons across both empires.

The rabbis' appropriation is deeply embedded in both the Roman and the Sasanian worlds. In the nineteenth century, Israel Levi identified the demon Ben Talamion/Tamalion with the apostle Bartholomew.[53] In Christian tradition, St. Bartholomew has a special connection to demons. Late antique accounts of Bartholomew's exorcistic practices survive in Greek, Arabic, Coptic, and Latin.[54] The late sixth-century C.E. text Pseudo-Abdias offers an important Christian parallel to this particular rabbinic narrative. Pseudo-Abdias tells the story of Bartholomew's mission to a province in India ruled by a king named Polymius, where many of the residents, including the king's own daughter, are possessed by demons. Hearing of Bartholomew's arrival in town and his power as an exorcist, the king summons Bartholomew and asks him to exorcise his daughter, which Bartholomew does. Polymius seeks to reward the apostle with gold, silver, gems, and clothing, but Bartholomew cannot be found. In the dead of night under cover of darkness, Bartholomew then appears in Polymius's private chambers and begins to teach the king about Christianity. After more evangelization and the performance of even more exorcistic acts, the king converts to Christianity together with his family, his men-at-arms, and everyone else in his kingdom.[55] Kalmin has traced the migration of the Bartholomew motifs from the Latin east to Sasanian Babylonia through Christian Armenia.[56] The possible western origin of the tale of Ben Talamion emphasizes the ways that the Babylonian rabbis select from a range of cultural elements in constructing and adapting their own traditions.

53. Israel Levi, "Légendes Judeo-Chrétiennes," *REJ* 8 (1884): 197–205; and see Kalmin, *Migrating Tales*, 74 n. 55.

54. See Kalmin, *Migrating Tales*, 73 for a discussion of the linguistic range of narratives. For examples of these narratives, see *Passion de Barthélemy*, and *Prédication de Barthélemy dans la Ville de L'Oasis et Martyre de Barthélemy*, in Pierre Geoltrain and Jean-Daniel Kaestli, eds., *Écrits Apocryphes Chrétiens*, vol. 2 (Paris: Gallimard, 2005), 795–808 and 875–99.

55. *Passion de Barthélemy* 7–8, in ibid., 798. See Kalmin, *Migrating Tales*, 74 n. 55, for a history of scholarship on this parallel.

56. *Migrating Tales*, 74–79. The search for the origins of this tradition is not complete, but it promises to shed light on the broader cultural networks within which the rabbis lived and operated.

This narrative has been studied fruitfully both as a model of shared folkloristic motifs and as an example of rabbinic interaction with non-rabbinic traditions.[57] This narrative, however, should also be contextualized within broader rabbinic discourse about demons. Where the apostle gains authority by exorcising demons, the Babylonian rabbis gain authority by integrating demons into the rabbinic system. In the rabbinic construction of Ben Talamion, the demon is a rabbinic ally who only "performs" the role of a malevolent demon to aid the rabbis in their quest to annul the harmful decrees. Ben Talamion implements a plan, and the rabbis follow his lead. His actions lead to the amelioration of life for the Jewish people. The demon is embedded in a sugya in which the rabbis discuss the origins of the impurity laws as they relate to reptilian blood. The halakhic discussion is mentioned throughout, and its language is picked up at the end of the narrative with the mention of the drops of blood on the imperial decree. The subjugation of the demonic to halakhah and the resultant integration of demons into the halakhic system are made manifest through this narrative's content and form. Ben Talamion is embedded into the survival of rabbinic Judaism in his actions and in his presence in the tradition. The demon is not merely neutralized but rendered a crucial rabbinic ally.

The story of the rabbis' performance of an exorcism for the daughter of the Roman emperor emphasizes rabbinic difference and the power that this difference gives them over those Romans who falsely believe that power is theirs. The rabbis can play the game according to Roman rules, but even then, they are destined to win because the Romans are fundamentally wrong, not just about the rules but about the essence of the game itself.

This assertion is one that appears to cross imperial lines. A contemporaneous narrative in *Pesiqta de-Rav Kahana*, a Palestinian rabbinic work, also recognizes that non-Jews believe in demonic possession and exorcism, but insists that this idea is patently ridiculous. According to *Pesiqta de-Rav Kahana*, a non-Jew asks R. Yoḥanan b. Zakkai how the ritual of

57. See, most recently, Kalmin, *Migrating Tales*; Ephraim Nissan, "Thematic Parallels in the Rabbinic Aggadah vs. Christian Hagiography: Modes of Convergence, and Sample Tales," special issue: Life-worlds and Religious Commitment: Ethnographic Perspectives on Subjectivity and Islam, *La Ricerca Folklorica* 69 (2014): 161–72; Harari, *Jewish Magic before the Rise of Kabbalah*.

the red heifer worked in the time of the Temple. R. Yoḥanan b. Zakkai explains that it functioned like an exorcism: the sacrifice paralleled the act of burning herbs under the nose of a possessed person, and the ritual ablution paralleled the act of pouring of water, acts which are both meant to force the demon to flee from the possessed person. R. Yoḥanan b. Zakkai explains to the non-Jew that the "*spirit (ruaḥ) of impurity*" is like any other malevolent spirit. But when the non-Jew leaves, satisfied with his answer, the rabbi's students say to him, "*You passed him off with a reed [something relatively simple and easy to rebut]! What will you say to us?*" The rabbi responds with a different rationale for both corpse-impurity and the ritual of the red heifer: the divine will.[58] The author of this story is clearly familiar with exorcistic practices in this period, and yet the story associates non-Jews with possession and exorcism while suggesting that both are patently ridiculous. Possession and exorcism may be a necessary part of the lingua franca of dealing with non-Jews, but they do not reflect the truth that the rabbis know underlies everything: namely, that of God's absolute power and authority.

All these narratives should not obscure the fact that the rabbis admit that demons can be dangerous and even fatal. The rabbis include only one narrative of a malevolent demon possessing a space; but the number of rabbinic teachings designed to prevent demonic harm and cure it once it has occurred make clear that the rabbis are very aware of the dangers that demons can inflict on the unwary and the unknowing. The exorcistic narratives discussed here highlight, however, that this demonic danger does not lie in the possibility of demonic possession—in hijacking a human body and piloting it for nefarious aims—except in the account of b. *Me'ilah*, where it is clearly performative and linked explicitly to Roman culture and beliefs. In the other accounts, demons are physically linked to a particular space but never to the interiority of a particular human body.[59] True demonic possession is entirely absent from rabbinic literature.

58. *Pesiqta de-Rav Kahana* 4:7. See discussion of this story and the broader trope in which a rabbi gives one "logical" answer to a non-Jew before giving a "radical, rabbinic exegetical" answer to his own rabbinic community, in Kalmin, *Jewish Babylonia*, 96–97.

59. The words used by the Babylonian Talmud to describe demonic attack emphasize this externality. In particular, the verb *A.H.Z.*, to seize, discussed above, is used consistently to describe demonic attack from without. See, e.g., b. *Shabbat* 151b (where the attacker is the

A STRIKING ABSENCE

The absence of demonic possession in rabbinic literature distinguishes rabbinic exorcism both from contemporaneous Christian exorcistic practices and from the texts of the Babylonian incantation bowls. The absence of stories of bodily exorcisms in rabbinic texts is all the more striking when compared with earlier Jewish exorcistic traditions from the Second Temple period. Found at Qumran, the *Genesis Apocryphon* (1Q20) depicts the biblical Abraham expelling a demon from a possessed Pharaoh through prayer and the laying of hands.[60] The first-century Jewish historian Josephus tells the story of an exorcist named Eleazar, who draws a demon out of the body of a possessed person through his nostrils by means of a powerful ring associated with King Solomon.[61] The synoptic Gospels, which are at least partial exemplars of first-century Jewish literature, are full of stories of Jesus exorcising people who have been possessed by demons. In one episode that appears in all three synoptic Gospels, for example, Jesus exorcises a Gerasene man possessed by a legion of demons. He casts the demons out of the man and into a herd of pigs who subsequently stampede into the sea and die.[62] Second Temple Jewish texts

demon Lilith); b. *Pesaḥim* 111b (where the attackers are the demons *Palga* and *Ẓreida*); and a similar tradition in p. *Shabbat* 14:3 (14c), where R. Akiva is seized by the evil eye. This usage is corroborated by the incantation bowls written in Jewish Babylonian Aramaic. Thus, for example, in JBA 26 (MS 1928/43), the exorcist states, "Some of their hair [שערהון] . . . , some of their blood [דמיהון שקלית לחתמיהון] I have taken for sealing them; and some of their skin [גלדיהון שקלית לרקאה ברון] I have taken for patching them; seven times seven it is seized by its tufts of hair," in Shaked et al., *Aramaic Bowl Spells*, 153. See also JBA 55 (MS 1928/1) in ibid., 246.

60. 1Q20 20, in Martinez and Tigchelaar, *The Dead Sea Scrolls Study Edition*, 43. See also Eshel, "Demonology in Palestine," 148–50. Some might include Tobit in this list. In Tobit 6–8, the hero successfully exorcises the malevolent and lustful demon Asmodeus with angelic help; in this case, however, the demon is not explicitly described as attacking from *within* the human body.

61. *Antiquities of the Jews* 8.2.5. See also Eshel, "Demonology in Palestine," 214–16.

62. Mark 5:1–5:13; Matthew 8:28–32; Luke 8:26–33. See also Matthew 9:32–33, 12:22–23; Mark 7:24–30, 9:14–29 Luke 4:33–37, 9:37–43. This phenomenon continues after Jesus's death, when some appear to attempt exorcism in Jesus's name. See, e.g., Acts 19:13. For a discussion of this trope's relative absence in the Gospel of John, see Eric Sorensen, *Possession and Exorcism in the New Testament and Early Christianity*, Wissenschaftliche Untersuchungen Zum Neuen Testament 2. Reihe 157 (Tübingen: Mohr Siebeck, 2002), 118–19, 166. Sorensen contrasts the Hellenistic Jewish context of the synoptics, and the important role that demon possession and exorcism played in first century Judea, with the Gospel of

describe bodily exorcism and prescribe against it. An exorcistic incantation formula against demons found at Qumran adjures beings who "en] ter into the body, to the male Wasting-demon and the female Wasting-demon."[63] Second Temple Jewish demons were dangerous, possessive, and highly mobile, moving in and out of human bodies as they—and powerful exorcists—pleased.

In all these texts, demons attack humans to cause harm. They do so by entering into the bodies of unsuspecting humans and causing havoc and disease from within. Exorcism is understood to force the demons out of their corporeal homes and to prevent their return. Exorcisms happen publicly; the ability to successfully exorcise demonic possession is a key mode of performing authority and power to a broader population—a community, a public populace, and the future readers of these texts.

Early Christianity picks up on the ritual power and rhetorical force of bodily exorcism in Second Temple Judaism(s). Across the Mediterranean world, the early church fathers expand the role of exorcism and integrate it into their nascent theological system. Accounts of bodily exorcism are found in the apocryphal *Acts of Thomas* and *Acts of Peter*.[64] Exorcisms take on even more importance in the various hagiographical *Lives* of holy men and women.[65] We have already seen how descriptions of exorcism were essential to the construction of the apostle Bartholomew.[66] David

John's alignment with the Greco-Roman West, in which demon possession and exorcism were much less prominent means of interaction with intermediary beings in this period.

63. 4Q560 1:3, translation from Douglas L. Penney and Michael O. Wise, "By the Power of Beelzebub: An Aramaic Incantation Formula from Qumran (4Q560)," *Journal of Biblical Literature* 113, no. 4 (1994): 632. See also 4Q510–511, 11Q11. See Eshel, "Demonology in Palestine," 284–86; Ida Fröhlich, "Demons and Illness in Second Temple Judaism: Theory and Practice," in *Demons and Illness from Antiquity to the Early-Modern Period*, ed. Siam Bhayro and Catherine Rider (Leiden: Brill, 2017), 81–96, for discussion of this text.

64. *Acts of Thomas* 12, 20, in Bart D. Ehrman, *Lost Scriptures: Books That Did Not Make It into the New Testament* (Oxford: Oxford University Press, 2003), 126, 29; *Acts of Peter* 11, in ibid., 142. See also the *Ascension of Isaiah*, where Manasseh is possessed by Sammael Malchira. In this instance it appears that Manasseh remains possessed until his death.

65. Cyrrhus, *A History of the Monks of Cyrrhus* III.9, 22; IX.4, 9, 10; XIII.10. See also Sebastian P. Brock and Susan Ashbrook Harvey, *Holy Women of the Syriac Orient* (Berkeley: University of California Press, 1987), 176, for the example of a deceased Christian holy woman who revives to offer her tooth to male bishops for use in their exorcistic practices.

66. *Passion de Barthélemy*, and *Prédication de Barthélemy dans la Ville de L'Oasis et Martyre de Barthélemy*, in Geoltrain and Kaestli, *Écrits Apocryphes Chrétiens*, 795–808 and 875–899.

Brakke has described the ways that the *Life of Anthony* and the *Sayings of the Desert Fathers* also testify to the importance of demonic exorcism to the formation of the holy man in late antique Egypt.[67] In Syria, Theodoret of Cyrrhus describes the monks Marcianus, Peter the Galatian, and Macedonius as renowned for their exorcisms.[68] Bodily exorcism takes on an important role in more formalized Christian ritual as well; beginning in the early third century, exorcism is integrated into the sacrament of baptism.[69] The operative assumption is that all non-Christians are possessed by demons; Christian baptism is the only way to successfully and permanently exorcise these malevolent forces. Demonic attacks and their repulsions become so associated with early Christianity that in the fourth century, the emperor Julian stated about Christians that "these two things are the quintessence of their theology, to hiss at demons and make the sign of the cross on their [own] forehead."[70]

Given the existence of this trope in earlier Jewish tradition, its prominence in contemporaneous Christianity, and the important theological, polemical, and discursive work that demonic possession and exorcism perform in both Second Temple Judaism and early Christianity, why *don't* the rabbis tell stories of bodily exorcism?

DEMONIC POSSESSION AND RABBINIC ANTHROPOLOGY

Understandings of the body as possessed or "possessable" depend on particular cultural constructions of the body and the self. Second Temple Jewish anthropology lent itself to such an understanding. Many Second Temple Jews adopted a Platonic binary between body and soul. This binary was not neutral: the soul was the locus of the self, and the body a

67. Brakke, *Demons and the Making of the Monk*, 35–36; 81–83, 153, 223–39.
68. See the *Lives* of these monks in Theodoret of Cyrrhus, *A History of the Monks of Cyrrhus*.
69. Henry Ansgar Kelly, *The Devil at Baptism: Ritual, Theology, and Drama* (Ithaca, NY: Cornell University Press, 1985), 81, 110, 124–25. See also Kalleres, "Demons and Divine Illumination," 183–85.
70. Julian, *Epistle* 19, in Wilmer C. Wright, ed., *Julian*, vol. 3, *Letters; Epigrams; Against the Galilaeans; Fragments* (Cambridge, MA: Harvard University Press, 1923), 52, quoted in Russell, *Satan*, 167.

container or even prison made of flesh.[71] This anthropology differs substantively from that of the rabbis. Alon Goshen-Gottstein suggests that, for the rabbis, "metaphysically soul and body form a whole, rather than a polarity."[72] Daniel Boyarin situates this discursive move in a broader cultural context, explaining that "for rabbinic Jews, the human being was defined as a body—animated, to be sure, by a soul—while for Hellenistic Jews (such as Philo) and (at least many Greek-speaking) Christians (such as Paul), the essence of a human being is a soul housed in a body."[73] Unlike those Jewish writers that came before them, the rabbis imagined the human being as a single, animated being whose body and soul worked and lived in harmony.[74]

The rabbis' construction of the human as an animated body can be seen in rabbinic discussions across a range of issues. Perhaps most well known is the rabbinic prayer recited after using the bathroom, which blesses God "who has created the human being with wisdom and created in *him* [emphasis added] orifices and hollows."[75] Human beings are identified with their bodies—orifices and hollows and all. For the rabbis of the Talmud, the human person remains all these things even after death; the Talmud depicts the future resurrection of the dead as a resurrection of radically embodied persons; according to B. *Sanhedrin,* the dead are even resurrected with their clothes on.[76] The rabbinic human being is an animated body, from the beginning of time to beyond its inevitable end.[77]

71. See, e.g., 2 Cor. 5:1–4; and see Boyarin, *Carnal Israel,* 31–32.

72. Alon Goshen-Gottstein, "The Body as Image of God in Rabbinic Literature," *Harvard Theological Review* 87, no. 2 (1994): 176–77. I first encountered this text in Boyarin, *Carnal Israel,* 33.

73. Boyarin, *Carnal Israel,* 5. Mira Balberg has productively shown the ways that the rabbis specifically located certain aspects of what it means to be human in the body or in the soul; these rabbinic locations do not undermine the essential unity of the human being as a unified body-soul. See Balberg, *Purity, Body, and Self,* 50–51.

74. According to Goshen-Gottstein (in "The Body as Image of God," 178), "the final severance of soul and body, however, occurs only when Hellenistic anthropology enters Judaism through the philosophical masters of the Middle Ages."

75. B. *Berakhot* 60b; and see Boyarin, *Carnal Israel,* 34.

76. B. *Sanhedrin* 91a.

77. Rosen-Zvi, *Demonic Desires,* 7, argues that the rabbinic *yeẓer* is a "fully internalized entity that resides inside the human heart." Rosen-Zvi notes that the yeẓer comes to explain human sinfulness: "The rabbis did not accept the attribution of sin to external cosmological entities. Rabbinic 'classic' demonology—rather developed in and of itself—lost its traditional

The rabbinic construction of the human being as an animated body foreclosed the possibility of bodily possession. For the body to be possessed by a demon, the soul must be evicted or suppressed to create room for the demonic attacker. If the soul is inextricably integrated with the body, there is no space for a demon to enter. Even more so, there is no human body for the demon to control; the body is not a separate force which can be operated remotely or by a different type of spirit. The metaphor of hijacking works effectively here. For a car to be hijacked, there must be a car, and there must be a driver. These two things must be separate; a hijacker must be able to replace the driver by displacing them from the driver's seat. One could theoretically hijack a Honda Civic in a busy American city (though I wouldn't recommend trying it), but one could never hijack one of the animated cars in Pixar's Cars—what would that even look like? It is only in a Roman world with a different understanding of the human person that there is room for a rabbinic demon to stage a demonic possession by playing on the anthropological assumptions of the imperial household.

Rabbinic anthropology and its interrelationship with rabbinic models of demonic attack also align with earlier ancient Mesopotamian anthropology. Martin Stol insists that "there is no Babylonian evidence for possession at all." According to Stol, in ancient Mesopotamian demonology, "a spirit 'reaches' or 'seizes' a human being and he is closest when he is 'tied' to his victim... Demons and diseases 'overthrow' the patient, or 'cover' him like a garment."[78] The language of possession does not accurately describe demonic attack in ancient Mesopotamia. But while demons may not possess their human victims and pilot their victims' bodies, they can

function as an explanation for human sinfulness" (ibid., 128). As the present work argues, rabbinic demonology lost this function as a result of a new construction of demons as neutral enforcers of rabbinic law and as rabbinic subjects themselves. Rosen-Zvi is absolutely correct in his reading of this phenomenon against a background of Second Temple and Tannaitic Jewish literatures. However, the figure of the yeẓer as demonic remains to be contextualized against the backdrop of Babylonian rabbinic literature, a task to which, I hope, the present work contributes. The yeẓer as described by Rosen-Zvi is a permanent part of the human person, though conceptualized as separate. It is not a malevolent force that attacks only *some* people but is part of what it means to be an animated human being. Thus, if Rosen-Zvi is correct, it, too, does not quite fit the model of demonic possession; instead, if the yeẓer is an internalized "demonic" entity, for the rabbis, to be human is actually to be part demon.

78. Marten Stol, *Epilepsy in Babylonia* (Groningen, Netherlands: STYX Publications, 1993), 52.

and do attack from within, though only rarely.[79] One incantation against the demon Lamaštu describes her attack thus: "She entered the door of the house, / Slipping through the door socket. / Once slipped through the door socket, she saw the boy: / She seized him seven times in his abdomen."[80] Ancient Mesopotamian demons can in fact enter the body and cause disease, but this disease is caused by the demon attacking the organs externally from within, not by displacing the soul and causing the body to act erratically or harm itself. This ancient Mesopotamian anthropology offers important parallels to that of the late antique rabbis.

Curiously, the rabbinic insistence on the unity of the body and soul, with its concomitant rejection of demonic possession, is found in both Babylonian rabbinic literature, where we might expect to find Mesopotamian echoes, and in Palestinian rabbinic literature, which generally has less awareness of or interest in ancient Mesopotamian ideas. Is this a case where an ancient Mesopotamian idea first made its way to Roman Palestine during the time of the Mishnah? Or is this a case of the rabbis independently developing an anthropological understanding which happened to align with a much earlier model of human anthropology? Causation is still impossible to determine. What we *can* determine is that this model became integral to rabbinic understandings of the self, and their understandings of what made the rabbinic community—even the rabbis in the west—distinctive from other late antique groups.

Rabbinic anthropology informs rabbinic demonology and, concomitantly, rabbinic demonology becomes inextricably linked to the rabbis' construction of what it means to be a human being, a Jew, and a member of the rabbinic community. The rabbinic self is a preventative self, conditioned in ways that prevent demonic attack and constructed in ways that prevent the possibility of demonic possession. It is also a powerful self, a self with power over demons, gentiles, and even the Roman imperial family.

79. Verderame, "Demons at Work in Ancient Mesopotamia," 71. Sorensen quotes a ritual in the *Udug-hul* in which Enki tells his son to "calm the patient, and bring out the censer and torch for him, / so that the Namtar demon existing in a man's body, may depart from it" (*Udug-hul* 7.669–74; trans. Geller in Sorensen, *Possession and Exorcism*, 31–32). This is a rare case in the extant ancient Mesopotamian literature. See also Stol, *Epilepsy in Babylonia*, 52, which describes a spirit entering a man through his ears and causing pain in his head; Konstantopoulos, "Shifting Alignments," 36–37.

80. Lorenzo Verderame, "Demons at Work in Ancient Mesopotamia," 66.

Conclusion

THE DEMON'S IN THE DETAILS

The Talmud contains much that is immaterial and frivolous, of which it treats with great gravity and seriousness; it further reflects the various superstitious practices and views of its Persian birthplace, which presume the efficacy of demoniacal medicines, of magic, incantations, miraculous cures, and interpretations of dreams, and are thus in opposition to the spirit of Judaism.

Heinrich Graetz, *History of the Jews*

I began this book by describing some of the ways that demons remain a fascinating fiction in twenty-first century American discourse. For many modern readers of the Babylonian Talmud, rabbinic demons, too, remain a fascinating fiction, a strange footnote in an otherwise elevated, philosophical, legally complex, or inspirational corpus. The perception that demons are a fiction is often paired with the suspicion that belief in demons smacks of superstition and cannot comfortably be understood to be a part of the religious tradition.

My hope is that, over these many chapters, this book has shown that Talmudic demons are neither superstition nor fiction. For the authors and earliest students of these texts, demons were all too real; rabbinic thinking about demons was a major locus of identity formation, world building, and theological imagination. As a result, the laws and narratives dealing with demons are some of the most fascinating and engaging in the Baby-

Epigraph: Graetz, *History of the Jews*, vol. 2, 633.

lonian Talmud. The rabbis of late antique Sasanian Babylonia thought with demons to condition a particular way of *being* a rabbi in the world at the same time as they constructed demons as essential to rabbinic power, authority, and law. The rabbinic authors of the Babylonian Talmud used demons to construct a rich world filled with social and cultural boundaries both visible and invisible; only full immersion in rabbinic tradition could allow participants to really see and navigate these boundaries. To be a rabbi was to be constantly thinking about demons and their dangers, to live a life with ever-present attention to the dangers that demons posed to the ignorant or unwary. To be non-rabbinic was to be constantly in demonic danger; to be a rabbi was to be in productive community with rabbinic demons. But in classical rabbinic fashion, we must still ask, *mai nafka minah?* What is the practical application of this fact? And indeed, what are the broader implications of exploring rabbinic demonology?

This project has been bounded largely by a time period—late antiquity—and a religious community—the rabbis of Sasanian Babylonia. These limitations have given the work a focus and delimited a realistic corpus of study. But as much as these limits have aided this project, I hope that this project has also complicated and expanded what we mean when we talk about late antiquity as a time period and the rabbis of Sasanian Babylonia as a particular kind of religious community.

WHAT IS LATE ANTIQUITY?

The last thirty years have seen scholars interrogate the meaning and utility of the term "late antiquity." Within the field of religious studies, Peter Brown first popularized the term late antiquity as a way of expanding the scholarly focus beyond fourth-through-sixth-century Christian Patristics, toward a more religious and socially diverse understanding of the period.[1] Brown's work successfully located particular religious communi-

1. Elizabeth A. Clark, "From Patristics to Late Antiquity at *The Catholic Historical Review*," *Catholic Historical Review* 101, no. 2 (2015): 28. See also Peter Brown, *The Making of Late Antiquity* (Cambridge, MA: Harvard University Press, 1978). Averil Cameron notes that "this heyday of late antique studies has disrupted the old certainties about our own historical development. It has substituted new questions for old ones and subverted tradi-

ties in this period within a broader society, both socially and temporally, an expansion that requires greater breadth and more extensive training for scholars of the period. And indeed, Averil Cameron notes that many scholars have retreated from late antiquity back to a more manageable focus.[2] Yet in *Interpreting Late Antiquity: Essays on the Post-Classical World,* several senior scholars of this period advocate for further expanding the time period demarcated by the term late antiquity: "The time has come for scholars, students, and the educated public in general to treat the period between around 250 and 800 as a distinctive and quite decisive period of history that stands on its own" as an age of empires.[3] The traditional periodization has been even further challenged by Garth Fowden, who argues that events during this period must be properly contextualized not only within a few centuries but also within the entire "First Millennium from Augustus to Bīrūnī's contemporary and correspondent, Ibn Sīnā (Avicenna)," a millennium that saw the rise of three major world religions.[4] Some scholars are slowly expanding the context in which to place events, ideas, and debates in the late antique world even further. While no one scholar can realistically be an expert at all aspects of life in this entire period, when we work together as a scholarly community, this expansion can only enrich our understandings.

This work has argued that properly contextualizing rabbinic discourse requires looking not only to the first centuries of the first millennium but much further back in time. Late antiquity was a rich and complex time, and understanding it requires understanding the very "antiquity" against which late antiquity is defined. To study late antiquity is also to study the afterlives of much older narratives, practices, and ideas emerging both from the Greco-Roman world and from the world of ancient Mesopota-

tional assumptions about the classical and medieval worlds" (Averil Cameron, "The "Long" Late Antiquity: A Late Twentieth-Century Model," in *Classics in Progress: Essays on Ancient Greece and Rome,* ed. T. P. Wiseman [Oxford: Oxford University Press, 2002], 191).

2. Cameron, "The 'Long' Late Antiquity," 171.

3. G.W. Bowersock, Peter Brown, and Oleg Grabar, "Introduction," in *Interpreting Late Antiquity: Essays on the Post-Classical World,* ed. G. W. Bowersock et al. (Cambridge, MA: Belknap Press of Harvard University Press, 2001), ix; and see Garth Fowden, *Before and after Muḥammad: The First Millennium Refocused* (Princeton, NJ: Princeton University Press, 2014), 49–50.

4. Fowden, *Before and after Muḥammad,* 5.

mia, with attention to how traditions are changed and made newly relevant across space and time. In arguing against a more limited definition of late antiquity, the editors of *Interpreting Late Antiquity* hoped that "readers . . . begin the 21st century with fewer artificial barriers in their minds, erected between periods and regions which have proved, in the light of modern research, to be more continuous with each other than we had once thought."[5] These continuities can certainly be seen in rabbinic literature.

THE RABBIS IN THEIR SASANIAN CONTEXT

This book has sought to expand the cultural, religious, and historical contexts of late antique rabbinic demonology. When I began my research for this project, I was expecting rabbinic demonology to be in conversation with Christianity and Zoroastrianism, and indeed, much of rabbinic demonology does testify to interactions with contemporaneous approaches to demonology. At times rabbinic interactions with Christians and Zoroastrians are clear from rabbinic demonic discourse. At other times what is most striking is those elements of Zoroastrian or Christian demonology that are decidedly absent from the rabbis' demonology. Like for Zoroastrians, for the rabbis in late antique Sasanian Babylonia, demons were a part of normative religious discourse and the normative religious world that the rabbis cultivated. But unlike the Zoroastrians, though the rabbis mark women and religious and ethnic outsiders as peripheral, demons are found at the heart of the rabbinic community—spatially, temporally, and bodily. The rabbis shared tropes about demons and powerful holy men with contemporaneous Christians, but unlike Christian demons, rabbinic demons were more likely to serve as powerful allies than as dangerous enemies. The Qur'an further testifies to the continued importance of this framing of demons in late antiquity. The rabbis were selective in adapting other religious communities' beliefs about demons and integrating them into the rabbinic framework, and we can learn as much from what the rabbis ignored of their contemporaries as we can from what the rabbis adopted.

5. Bowersock et al. "Introduction," x.

And yet as I researched, I was continually surprised by the ways that my research inexorably pulled me further and further back in time. Much of rabbinic demonology is actually discursively aligned with the demonologies of communities whose members thought and wrote and lived long before the rabbis' own lifetimes—demonologies found in Sumerian and Akkadian texts and in the work of Plato and other Greek philosophers. Like the authors of ancient Mesopotamian texts, the rabbis understood demons as capricious servants of the gods who attack—when they attack—from without. Much like Plato, the rabbis understood demons to be most often morally neutral, if not positively marked. Some of these older ideas flourished in scholastic communities conventionally thought of as relatively insular. Others survived and were transmitted by scribes in royal archives, though evidence of a wider distribution is lacking. And some ancient ideas and practices seem to have survived in local indigenous communities only now being understood as rabbinic conversation partners.

Late antique Sasanian Babylonia was a place where different religious communities interacted, and diverse religious traditions were transmitted across the generations. Within this complicated, expanded understanding of late antiquity, the rabbis engaged with a wealth of ideas, adopting, adapting, and rejecting a range of beliefs and practices related to demons. Mapping the rabbis in their cultural conversations about demons allows us to understand the broader discourses the rabbis participated in and to see which rabbinic discourses are unparalleled in the extant literature. Babylonian rabbinic texts demonstrate awareness of Second Temple and Tannaitic beliefs about demons, ancient Babylonian and contemporaneous Zoroastrian discourses, and, beginning in the fourth century, Christian and Greco-Roman ideas as well. As the Bavli story of Ben Talamion discussed in chapter 6 highlights, this awareness was mediated by the rabbis' critical assessments of these diverse demonic discourses.

The rabbis imagined a universe filled with intermediary beings that was subordinated to a profoundly rabbinic understanding of the world. This rabbinic worldview was an explicitly *Babylonian* rabbinic worldview. The rabbis name and even amplify the differences between their demonology and those of the Romans, Zoroastrians, and the rabbis' own Palestinian colleagues in order to situate themselves as the true experts in all things demonic. The rabbis do not undermine the widespread belief in demons;

such an undermining may never have occurred to them as a possibility. Indeed, the rabbis made sense of the world by both affirming that their coreligionists' lived experiences of demons was real and by reinterpreting those experiences in light of rabbinic scholastic traditions.

At the forefront of the Babylonian rabbinic worldview was a belief in monotheism, a single God who created the world and the Torah, and who chose Israel as God's special people. Rabbinic monotheism was a messy monotheism; the world was filled with many kinds of intermediary beings—angels, demons, and also the hypostasized evil eye and evil inclination. Yet the insistence that all beings are subordinated to the will of an ethical God limited the degree of malevolence that intermediary beings could be thought to have. From their very origins, demons are not the creation of a malevolent deity or a primeval act of sin, but are instead an intentional part of the global community, and perhaps more importantly, the rabbinic community. Where today, many dismiss demons as non-normative superstition, for the rabbis demons were profoundly normative and fundamental to rabbinic religion. Boundaries between religion and magic, and the normative and the non-normative, are porous and ever shifting, moving at times to exclude and at times to selectively include a wide range of beliefs, attitudes, and peoples.

The rabbinic integration of relatively neutral demons within their normative religious system aligns most closely with the treatment of demons in Greco-Roman and Sumerian and Akkadian polytheistic discourses. We might have thought that monotheistic systems of thought would have more in common with one another than they do with dualistic or polytheistic ones. Given numerical affinities, we might have even thought that monotheists and dualists have more in common with each other than either do with polytheism. But not all monotheisms are the same. Although Christians and Jews both insisted on a single omniscient, omnipotent divine creator, Christian monotheism in this period made space for an independently acting Satan with his own evil minions. It appears that the Jewish bowl scribes also had room for independent malevolent forces in their own complex, highly syncretistic theology of the world. Rabbinic monotheism did not. Instead, the rabbis' understanding of a single all-powerful God whose ways transcend human understanding had many parallels to the aggregated all-powerful nature of the capricious gods in a sprawling pantheon. The very category of monotheism, and what that category means to the lives, beliefs, and worldviews of those who espouse it, is itself complex, messy, and diverse—just like late antique demonologies. And this messiness is brought to light in new ways when we recognize the important role the rabbinic demonology played in creating a particular kind of monotheism and a particular understanding of God.

Demons *are* real. Demons are real not necessarily, in the sense of embodied independent forces acting on the world but, rather, in the sense of doing real discursive work in real people's lives, both in ancient societies and in our own. For communities that believe in demons and that see those demons as interacting with humankind, demons are a real force to be reckoned with. These communities do important cultural work and theological thinking through reckoning with demons. As we have seen, many ritual experts try to understand a world in which demons play an active role, while also trying to build in safeguards for their own complicated communities. Demons are not separate from ritual experts' understandings of the world and of their places in it, and demons are not separate from the ways that non-experts then interact with their communal leaders and create their own understandings of the world. To pay particular attention to creatures and creations long understood to be at the margins of religion, rational thought, and human society, then, is to explore anew what it means to be a person in community and in the world, both in late antiquity and in our own time.

Bibliography

Adelman, Rachel. *The Return of the Repressed: Pirqe De-Rabbi Eliezer and the Pseudepigrapha*. Supplements to the Journal for the Study of Judaism, edited by Hindy Najman. Leiden: Brill, 2009.

Ahuvia, Mika. "Israel among the Angels—A Study of Angels in Jewish Texts from the Fourth to Eighth Century C.E." PhD diss., Princeton University, 2014.

Alexander, Philip S. "Contextualizing the Demonology of the Testament of Solomon." In *Die Dämonen—Demons: Die Dämonologie der Israelitisch-Jüdischen und Frühchristlichen Literatur im Kontext ihrer Umwelt*, edited by A. Lange, H. Lichtenberger, and K. F. Diethard Römheld, 613–35. Tübingen: Mohr Siebeck, 2004.

———. "The Demonology of the Dead Sea Scrolls." In *The Dead Sea Scrolls after Fifty Years: A Comprehensive Assessment*, edited by Peter W. Flint and James C. Vanderkam, 331–53. Leiden: Brill, 1999.

———. "Jewish Elements in Gnosticism and Magic, c. CE 70–c. CE 270." In *The Early Roman Period*, edited by W. Horbury, W. D. Davis, and John Sturdy, 1052–78. Vol. 3 of *The Cambridge History of Judaism*. Cambridge: Cambridge University Press, 1999.

———. "Targumim and Early Exegesis of 'Sons of God' in Genesis 6." *Journal of Jewish Studies* 23, no. 1 (1972): 60–71.

Amsler, Monika. "Medical Theory + Grammar = *Voces Magicae.*" Paper presented at the Association for Jewish Studies annual meeting, San Diego, December 2019.

Anderson, Liza, trans. "Story of a Demon Who Repented and Was Accepted by God, from Mingana Syriac Manuscript 205, 159a–164b." Unpublished work. Available at www.academia.edu/2151969/Story_of_a_Demon_who_Repented_and_was_Accepted_by_God.

Anderson, Sonja. "Idol Talk: The Discourse of Idolatry in the Early Christian World." PhD diss., Yale University, 2016.

Anklesaria, Behramgore T. *Zand-Ākāsīh: Iranian or Greater Bundahišn.* Bombay: Dastur Framoze A. Bode, 1956.

Annus, Amar. *The God Ninurta in the Mythology and Royal Ideology of Ancient Mesopotamia.* State Archives of Assyria Studies. Helsinki: Neo-Assyrian Text Corpus Project, 2002.

"Arba Amot, Shi'ur–." In *Encyclopedia Talmudit,* edited by Shlomo Yosef Zevin, vol. 2, 157–59. Jerusalem: Yad HaRav Herzog.

Aristotle. *Parts of Animals; Movement of Animals; Progression of Animals.* Translated by A. L. Peck and E. S. Forster. Loeb Classical Library. Cambridge, MA: Harvard University Press, 1937.

Asmussen, J. P. "Aēšma." In *Encyclopædia Iranica Online.* 1983, updated and published online in 2011. www.iranicaonline.org/articles/aesma-wrath.

———. "Christians in Iran." In *The Selucid, Parthian and Sasanian Periods,* edited by E. Yarshater, 924–48. Vol. 3, Pt. 2 of *The Cambridge History of Iran.* Cambridge: Cambridge University Press, 1983.

Aubin, Melissa Margaret. "Gendering Magic in Late Antique Judaism." PhD diss., Duke University, 1998.

Balberg, Mira. *Purity, Body, and Self in Early Rabbinic Literature.* Berkeley: University of California Press, 2014.

Bamberger, Avigail Manekin. "An Akkadian Demon in the Talmud: Between Šulak and Bar-Širiqa." *Journal for the Study of Judaism* 44 (2013): 282–87.

———. "Jewish Legal Formulae in the Aramaic Incantation Bowls." *Aramaic Studies* 13 (2015): 69–81.

Baris, Michael. "'I Am the One': A Monist Looks at the Double Death and Life of Rabba Bar Naḥmani." *Review of Rabbinic Judaism* 23, no. 1 (2020): 19–50.

Becker, Adam Howard. *Fear of God and the Beginning of Wisdom: The School of Nisibis and Christian Scholastic Culture in Late Antique Mesopotamia.* Philadelphia: University of Pennsylvania Press, 2006.

———. "Martyrdom, Religious Difference, and 'Fear' as a Category of Piety in the Sasanian Empire: The Case of the Martyrdom of Gregory and the Martyrdom of Yazdpaneh." *Journal of Late Antiquity* 2, no. 2 (2009): 300–36.

Beer, Moshe. "Concerning the Deposal of Rabbah Bar Naḥmani from the Headship of the Academy: A Chapter in the History of the Relationship between the Sages and the Exilarchs [in Heb.]." *Tarbiz* 33 (1964): 349–57.

Berkowitz, Beth A. *Animals and Animality in the Babylonian Talmud.* Cambridge: Cambridge University Press, 2018.

Betz, Hans Dieter. "Jewish Magic in the Greek Magical Papyri (PGM VII. 260–71)." In *Envisioning Magic: A Princeton Seminar and Symposium*, edited by Peter Schafer and Hans G. Kippenberg, 45-63. Leiden: Brill, 1997.

Biale, David. *Gershom Scholem: Kabbalah and Counter-History*. Cambridge, MA: Harvard University Press, 1979.

Black, Jeremy, and Anthony Green. *Gods, Demons and Symbols of Ancient Mesopotamia: An Illustrated Dictionary*. London: British Museum Press, 1992.

Blau, Ludwig. *Das altjüdische Zauberwesen*. Strasbourg: K. Trübner, 1898.

Bohak, Gideon. *Ancient Jewish Magic: A History*. Cambridge: Cambridge University Press, 2008.

———. "Babylonian Incantation Bowls—Past, Present and Future [in Heb.]." Review of *A Corpus of Magic Bowls: Incantation Texts in Jewish Aramaic from Late Antiquity*, by Dan Levene. *Pe'amim* 105/106 (2005–06): 253–65.

———. "Conceptualizing Demons in Late Antique Judaism." In *Demons and Illness from Antiquity to the Early-Modern Period*, edited by Siam Bhayro and Catherine Rider, 111–33. Leiden: Brill, 2017.

———. "Demons, Demonology. V. Judaism. A. Second Temple and Hellenistic Judaism." In *Dabbesheth-Dreams and Dream Interpretation*, edited by Hans-Josef Klauck, Volker Leppin, Bernard McGinn, Choon-Leong Seow, Hermann Spieckermann, Barry Dov Walfish, and Eric J. Ziolkowski, 546–49. Vol. 6 of *Encyclopedia of the Bible and Its Reception*. Berlin: De Gruyter, 2013.

———. "Jewish Magic in the First and Second Temple Periods." In *Angels and Demons: Jewish Magic through the Ages*, edited by Filip Vukosavovic, 12–15. Jerusalem: Bible Lands Museum, 2010.

———. "Jewish Myth in Pagan Magic in Antiquity." In *Myths in Judaism: History, Thought, Literature*, edited by I. Gruenwald and Moshe Idel, 97–122. Jerusalem: Zalman Shazar Center, 2004.

Bokser, Baruch Micah. "Wonder-Working and the Rabbinic Tradition: The Case of Ḥanina B. Dosa." *Journal for the Study of Judaism* 16, no. 1 (1985): 42–92.

Bowersock, G. W., Peter Brown, and Oleg Grabar. "Introduction." In *Interpreting Late Antiquity: Essays on the Post-Classical World*, edited by G. W. Bowersock, Peter Brown, and Oleg Grabar, vii–xiii. Cambridge, MA: Belknap Press of Harvard University Press, 2001.

Boyarin, Daniel. *Carnal Israel: Reading Sex in Talmudic Culture*. Berkeley: University of California Press, 1993.

Boyce, Mary. "Cleansing. I. In Zoroastrianism." In *Encyclopædia Iranica Online*. 1992, updated 2012. www.iranicaonline.org/articles/cleansing-i.

———. *A History of Zoroastrianism*. Vol. 1, *The Early Period*. 2nd impression with corrections. Leiden: Brill, 1989. First published in 1975.

Brakke, David. *Demons and the Making of the Monk: Spiritual Combat in Early Christianity*. Cambridge, MA: Harvard University Press, 2006.

Brand, Miryam T. "Demons and Dominion: Forcing Demons into the Divine Order in Jubilees and the Dead Sea Scrolls." In *From Scrolls to Traditions: A Festschrift Honoring Lawrence H. Schiffman*, edited by Stuart S. Miller, Michael D. Swartz, Steven Fine, Naomi Grunhaus, and Alex P. Jassen, 18–37. Leiden: Brill, 2020.

——. *Evil Within and Without: The Source of Sin and Its Nature as Portrayed in Second Temple Literature.* Edited by Armin Lange, Bernard M. Levinson, and Vered Noam. Journal of Ancient Judaism Supplements. Göttingen, Germany: Vandenhoeck & Ruprecht, 2013.

Brashear, W. M. "The Greek Magical Papyri: An Introduction and Survey; Annotated Bibliography (1928–1994)." In *Aufstieg und Niedergang der Romischen Welt*, 3380–684. Berlin: Walter de Gruyter, 1995.

Brenk, Frederick E. "'A Most Strange Doctrine.' *Daimon* in Plutarch." *Classical Journal* 69, no. 1 (1973): 1–11.

Breytenbach, C., and P. L. Day. "Satan." In *Dictionary of Deities and Demons in the Bible*, edited by Karel van der Toorn, Bob Becking, and Pieter W. Van der Horst, 726–32. Leiden: Brill, 1999.

Brock, Sebastian P. *The History of the Holy Mar Ma'in, with a Guide to the Persian Martyr Acts.* Piscataway, NJ: Gorgias Press, 2009.

Brock, Sebastian P., and Susan Ashbrook Harvey. *Holy Women of the Syriac Orient.* Transformation of the Classical Heritage. Berkeley: University of California Press, 1987.

Brodsky, David. *A Bride without a Blessing: A Study in the Redaction and Content of Masskhet Kallah and Its Gemara.* Tübingen: Mohr Siebeck, 2006.

Brody, Robert. "Judaism in the Sasanian Empire: A Case Study in Religious Coexistence." In *Irano-Judaica II: Studies Relating to Jewish Contacts with Persian Culture Throughout the Ages*, edited by Shaul Shaked and Amnon Netzer, 52–62. Jerusalem: Yad Izak Ben-Zvi and the Hebrew University of Jerusalem, 1990.

——. "Stam Ha-Talmud ve-Divrei Ha-Amoraim." In *The Bible and Its World, Rabbinic Literature and Jewish Law, and Jewish Thought*, edited by Baruch J. Schwartz, Abraham Melamed, and Aharon Shemesh, 213–32. Vol. 1 of *Iggud: Selected Essays in Jewish Studies.* Jerusalem: World Union of Jewish Studies, 2008.

Brown, Francis, S. R. Driver, and Charles A. Briggs. *The Brown-Driver-Briggs Hebrew and English Lexicon.* Peabody, MA: Hendrickson, 1906.

Brown, Peter. *The Making of Late Antiquity.* Cambridge, MA: Harvard University Press, 1978.

Cabezón, José Ignacio. "Introduction." In *Scholasticism: Cross-Cultural and Comparative Perspectives*, edited by José Ignacio Cabezón, 1–8. Albany: State University of New York Press, 1998.

Cameron, Averil. "The 'Long' Late Antiquity: A Late Twentieth-Century Model." In *Classics in Progress: Essays on Ancient Greece and Rome*, edited by T. P. Wiseman, 165–91. Oxford: Oxford University Press, 2002.

Carter, Charles E. *The Emergence of Yehud in the Persian Period: A Social and Demographic Study*. Sheffield, UK: Sheffield Academic Press, 1999.

Carter, K. Codell. "Causes of Disease and Death in the Babylonian Talmud." *Medizinhistorisches Journal* 26, no. 1/2 (1991): 94–104.

Chabbi, Jacqueline. "Jinn." In *Encyclopaedia of the Qur'an*, edited by Jane Dammen McAuliffe, 43–50. Leiden: Brill, 2003.

Chadwick, Henry. *Origen: Contra Celsum*. Cambridge: Cambridge University Press, 1965. First published in 1953.

Chajes, J. H. *Between Worlds: Dybbuks, Exorcists, and Early Modern Judaism*. Philadelphia: University of Pennsylvania Press, 2003.

Chidester, David. *Savage Systems: Colonialism and Comparative Religion in Southern Africa*. Studies in Religion and Culture. Charlottesville: University of Virginia Press, 1996.

Clark, Elizabeth A. "From Patristics to Late Antiquity at *The Catholic Historical Review*." *Catholic Historical Review* 101, no. 2 (2015): 27–71.

Collins, Adela Yarbro. *The Combat Myth in the Book of Revelation*. Missoula, MT: Scholars Press for Harvard Theological Review, 1976.

Coulot, C. "L'Instruction Sur Les Deux Esprits (1QS III, 13–IV, 26)." *Religious Studies Review* 82 (2008): 147–60.

Cunningham, Graham. *"Deliver Me from Evil": Mesopotamian Incantations 2500–1500 BC*. Rome: Editrice Pontificio Instituto Biblico, 1997.

Cyrrhus, Theodoret of. *A History of the Monks of Cyrrhus*. Translated by R. M. Price. Cistercian Studies Series. Kalamazoo, MI: Cistercian Publications, 1985.

Dalley, Stephanie. "The Influence of Mesopotamia upon Israel and the Bible." In *The Legacy of Mesopotamia*, edited by Stephanie Dalley, A. T. Reyes, David Pinree, Alison Salvesen, and Henrietta McCall, 57–84. Oxford: Oxford University Press, 1998.

———. trans. *Myths from Mesopotamia: Creation, the Flood, Gilgamesh, and Others*. Oxford World's Classics. Oxford: Oxford University Press, 2009.

———. "Occasions and Opportunities. 2. Persian, Greek, and Parthian Overlords." In *The Legacy of Mesopotamia*, edited by Stephanie Dalley, A. T. Reyes, David Pinree, Alison Salvesen, and Henrietta McCall, 35–56. Oxford: Oxford University Press, 1998.

———. "The Sassanian Period and Early Islam, c. A.D. 224–651." In *The Legacy of Mesopotamia*, edited by Stephanie Dalley, A. T. Reyes, David Pinree, Alison Salvesen, and Henrietta McCall, 163–81. Oxford: Oxford University Press, 1998.

Dan, Joseph. *The Esoteric Theology of Ashkenazi Hasidism [in Heb.]*. Jerusalem: Bialik Institute, 1968.

———. "Five Versions of the Story of the Jerusalemite." *Proceedings of the American Academy for Jewish Research* 35 (1967): 99–111.

Daryaee, Touraj. *Sasanian Persia: The Rise and Fall of an Empire.* London: I. B. Tauris, 2009.

de Certeau, Michel. "'Spaces' and 'Places.'" In *The Practice of Everyday Life*, 117–30. Translated by Steven Rendall. Berkeley: University of California Press, 1984.

de Lange, N. R. M. *Origen and the Jews: Studies in Jewish-Christian Relations in Third-Century Palestine.* Cambridge: Cambridge University Press, 1976.

Devereux, Georges. *Essais D'Ethnopsychiatrie Générale.* Paris: Gallimard, 1970.

———. *Ethnopsychoanalysis: Psychoanalysis and Anthropology as Complementary Frames of Reference.* Berkeley: University of California Press, 1978.

Dillon, John, and Sarah Klitenic Wear. *Dionysius the Areopagite and the Neoplatonist Tradition: Despoiling the Hellenes.* Ashgate Studies in Philosophy and Theology in Late Antiquity. Farnham, UK: Ashgate, 2007.

Dirks, Nicholas B. *Castes of Mind: Colonialism and the Making of Modern India.* Princeton, NJ: Princeton University Press, 2001.

Doody, Aude. "Pliny's *Natural History*: *Enkuklios Paideia* and the Ancient Encyclopedia." *Journal of the History of Ideas* 70, no. 1 (2009): 1–21.

Drijvers, H. J. W. *Cults and Beliefs at Edessa.* Edited by M. J. Vermaseren. Études Préliminaires aux Religions Orientales dans L'Empire Romain. Leiden: Brill, 1980.

Duling, D. C. "The Testament of Solomon." In *The Old Testament Pseudepigrapha*, edited by James H. Charlesworth, 935–88. Garden City, NY: Doubleday, 1983.

Dunbabin, Katherine. "Baiarum Grata Voluptas: Pleasures and Dangers of the Baths." *Papers of the British School at Rome* 57 (1989): 6–46.

Edzard, Dietz Otto. *Gudea and His Dynasty.* Toronto: University of Toronto Press, 1997.

Ehrman, Bart D. *Lost Scriptures: Books That Did Not Make It into the New Testament.* Oxford: Oxford University Press, 2003.

Eliav, Yaron Z. "The Roman Bath as a Jewish Institution: Another Look at the Encounter between Judaism and the Greco-Roman Culture." *Journal for the Study of Judaism* 31, no. 4 (2000): 416–54.

———. "A Scary Place: Jewish Magic in the Roman Bathhouse." In *Man near a Roman Arch: Studies Presented to Prof. Yoram Tsafrir*, edited by Leah Di Segni, Yizhar Hirschfeld, Joseph Patrich, and Rina Talgam, 88–97. Jerusalem: Israel Exploration Society, 2009.

Elior, Rachel. *Dybbuks and Jewish Women in Social History, Mysticism and Folklore.* Jerusalem: Urim Publications, 2008.

Elliot, Dyan. *Fallen Bodies: Pollution, Sexuality, and Demonology in the Middle Ages.* Philadelphia: University of Pennsylvania Press, 1999.

Elman, Yaakov. "Middle Persian Culture and Babylonian Sages: Accommodation and Resistance in the Shaping of Rabbinic Legal Tradition." In *The Cambridge Companion to the Talmud and Rabbinic Literature,* edited by Elisheva Charlotte Fonrobert and Martin S. Jaffee, 165–97. New York: Cambridge University Press, 2007.

———. "Order, Sequence, and Selection: The Mishnah's Anthological Choices." In *The Anthology in Jewish Literature,* edited by David Stern, 53–80. New York: Oxford University Press, 2004.

———. "The Other in the Mirror: Iranians and Jews View One Another: Questions of Identity, Conversion, and Exogamy in the Fifth-Century Iranian Empire. Part One." *Bulletin of the Asia Institute,* n.s. 19 (2005): 15–25.

———. "The World of the 'Sabboraim': Cultural Aspects of Post-Redactional Additions to the Bavli." In *Creation and Composition: The Contribution of the Bavli Redactors (Stammaim) to the Aggada,* edited by Jeffrey L. Rubenstein, 383–415. Tübingen: Mohr Siebeck, 2005.

El-Zein, Amira. *Islam, Arabs, and the Intelligent World of the Jinn.* Syracuse, NY: Syracuse University Press, 2009.

Epstein, Jacob Nahum. *Mavo Le-Nusakh Ha-Mishnah.* 2nd ed. 2 vols. Jerusalem: Y. L. Magnes, 1999. First published in 1948.

Eshel, Esther. "Demonology in Palestine during the Second Temple Period [in Heb.]." PhD diss., Hebrew University of Jerusalem, 1999.

Eshleman, Kendra. *The Social World of Intellectuals in the Roman Empire: Sophists, Philosophers, and Christians.* Greek Culture in the Roman World. Cambridge: Cambridge University Press, 2012.

Evans-Pritchard, E. E. *Witchcraft, Oracles and Magic among the Azande.* Oxford: Clarendon Press, 1939.

Faraone, Christopher A. "Magic and Medicine in the Roman Imperial Period: Two Case Studies." In *Continuity and Innovation in the Magical Tradition,* edited by Gideon Bohak, Yuval Harari, and Shaul Shaked, 135–58. Leiden: Brill, 2011.

Farber, W. "Lamastu." In *Reallexikon der Assyriologie und Vorderasiatischen Archäologie,* edited by Erich Ebeling, vol. 6, 439–46. Berlin: W. de Gruyter, 1984.

Fonrobert, Charlotte Elisheva. *Menstrual Purity: Rabbinic and Christian Reconstructions of Biblical Gender.* Contraversions. Stanford, CA: Stanford University Press, 2000.

———. "The Political Symbolism of the Eruv." *Jewish Social Studies* 11, no. 3 (2005): 9–35.

———. "The Semiotics of the Sexed Body in Early Halakhic Discourse." In *How*

Should Rabbinic Literature be Read in the Modern World?, edited by Matthew Kraus, 79–104. Piscataway, NJ: Gorgias Press, 2006.

Forrest, S. K. Mendoza. *Witches, Whores, and Sorcerers: The Concept of Evil in Early Iran.* Austin: University of Texas Press, 2011.

Foucault, Michel. *The Archaeology of Knowledge.* Translated by Alan Sheridan. New York: Pantheon, 1972.

———. *Discipline and Punish: The Birth of the Prison.* Translated by Alan Sheridan. New York: Random House, 1977, 1995.

———. "Truth and Power." In *Power/Knowledge: Selected Interviews and Other Writings, 1972–1977,* edited by Colin Gordon, 109–33. New York: Pantheon, 1980.

Fowden, Garth. *Before and after Muḥammad: The First Millennium Refocused.* Princeton, NJ: Princeton University Press, 2014.

Fraade, Steven D. "Hearing and Seeing at Sinai: Interpretive Trajectories." In *The Significance of Sinai: Traditions about Sinai and Divine Revelation in Judaism and Christianity,* edited by George J. Brooke, Hindy Najman, and Loren T. Stuckenbruck, 247–68. Leiden: Brill, 2008.

———. *Enosh and His Generation: Pre-Israelite Hero and History in Post-Biblical Interpretation.* Society of Biblical Literature Monograph. Chico, CA: Scholars Press, 1984.

———. "Rabbinic Polysemy and Pluralism Revisited: Between Praxis and Thematization." *AJS Review* 31, no. 1 (2007): 1–40.

Frankfurter, David. *Evil Incarnate: Rumors of Demonic Conspiracy and Ritual Abuse in History.* Princeton, NJ: Princeton University Press, 2006.

———. "Narratives That Do Things." In *Narrating Religion,* edited by Sarah Iles Johnston, 95–106. New York: MacMillan Reference USA, 2016.

Freudenthal, Gad. "Maimonides' Philosophy of Science." In *The Cambridge Companion to Maimonides,* edited by Kenneth Seeskin, 134–66. Cambridge: Cambridge University Press, 2005.

Friedman, Shamma. "Mivneh Sifruti Be-Sugyot Habavli." In *Sugyot Be-Heker Ha-Talmud Ha-Bavli: Mehkarim Be-Inyanei Mivneh, Herkev Ve-Nusah,* 136–48. New York: Jewish Theological Society of America, 2010.

———. "'Wonder Not at a Gloss in Which the Name of an *Amora* Is Mentioned': The Amoraic Statments and the Anonymous Material in the Sugyot of the Bavli Revisited." In *Melekhet Mahshevet: Studies in the Redaction and Development of Talmudic Literature,* edited by Aharon Amit and Aharon Shemesh, 101–44. Ramat-Gan, Israel: Bar-Ilan University Press, 2011.

———. "Pereq Ha-isha Rabba Ba-Bavli: Be-Ẓiruf Mavo Klali al Derekh Ḥeker Ha-Sugya." In *Texts and Studies: Analecta Judaica,* edited by H. Z. Dimitrovsky, 277–321. New York: Jewish Theological Seminary of America, 1977.

Fröhlich, Ida. "Demons and Illness in Second Temple Judaism: Theory and

Practice." In *Demons and Illness from Antiquity to the Early-Modern Period*, edited by Siam Bhayro and Catherine Rider, 81–96. Leiden: Brill, 2017.

Frye, Richard N. "Minorities in the History of the Near East." In *A Green Leaf: Papers in Honour of Professor Jes P. Asmussen*, edited by W. Sundermann, J. Duchesne-Guillemin, and F. Vahman, 461–71. Leiden: Brill, 1988.

Gafni, Isaiah. "The Political, Social, and Economic History of Babylonian Jewry, 224–638 CE." In *The Late Roman-Rabbinic Period*, edited by Steven T. Katz, 792–820. Vol. 4 of *The Cambridge History of Judaism*. Cambridge: Cambridge University Press, 2008.

Gager, John. "The Social Place of Magic in the Graeco-Roman World." Paper presented at the Philadelphia Seminar on Christian Origins, Williams Hall, University of Pennsylvania, 5 October 1976. Minutes available at http://ccat.sas.upenn.edu/psco/archives/psco14-min.htm#b1.

Garb, Jonathan. "Mysticism and Magic: Objections, Doubts, Accommodation." *Mahanayim* 14 (2002): 97–109.

Geller, Markham J. "Akkadian Healing Therapies in the Babylonian Talmud." Preprint 259, submitted to the Max-Planck-Institut Für Wissenschafsgeschichte in 2004. https://www.mpiwg-berlin.mpg.de/Preprints/P259.PDF.

———. "An Akkadium Vademecum in the Babylonian Talmud." In *From Athens to Jerusalem: Medicine in Hellenized Jewish Lore and in Early Christian Literature*, edited by Samuel Kottek and Manfred Horstmanshoff, 13–32. Rotterdam: Erasmus, 2000.

———. "Four Aramaic Incantation Bowls." In *The Bible World: Essays in Honor of Cyrus H. Gordon*, edited by Gary Rendsburg, Ruth Adler, Milton Arfa, and Nathan H. Winter, 47-61. New York: KTAV and the Institute of Hebrew Culture and Education, 1980.

———. "Joshua B. Perahia and Jesus of Nazareth: Two Rabbinic Magicians." PhD diss., Brandeis University, 1974.

Geoltrain, Pierre, and Jean-Daniel Kaestli, eds. *Écrits Apocryphes Chrétiens*. Vol. 2. Paris: Gallimard, 2005.

Gilat, Yitzchak D. *Prakim be-Hishtalshelut Ha-Halakhah*. Ramat-Gan, Israel: Bar-Ilan University Press, 1992.

Goldin, Judah. *The Fathers According to Rabbi Nathan [Version A]*. New Haven, CT: Yale University Press, 1955.

Goodblatt, David. "The History of the Babylonian Academies." In *The Late Roman-Rabbinic Period*, edited by Steven T. Katz, 821–39. Vol. 4 of *The Cambridge History of Judaism*. Cambridge: Cambridge University Press, 2008.

Gordon, Cyrus H. "Aramaic and Mandaic Magical Bowls." *Archiv Orientalni* 9 (1937): 84–106.

———. "Aramaic Incantation Bowls." *Orientalia* n.s. 10 (1941): 116–41, 272–89, 339–60.

Goshen-Gottstein, Alon. "The Body as Image of God in Rabbinic Literature." *Harvard Theological Review* 87, no. 2 (1994): 171–95.

Graetz, Heinrich. *History of the Jews.* 5 vols. Vol. 2, *From the Reign of Hyrcanus (135 BCE) to the Completion of the Babylonian Talmud.* Philadelphia: Jewish Publication Society of America, 1967. First published in 1893.

Green, Anthony. "Neo-Assyrian Apotropaic Figures: Figurines, Rituals and Monumental Art, with Special Reference to the Figurines from the Excavations of the British School of Archaeology in Iraq at Nimrud." *Iraq* 45, no. 1 (1983): 87–96.

Gross, Simcha. "Empire and Neighbors: Babylonian Jewish Identity in Its Local and Imperial Context." PhD diss., Yale University, 2017.

Gurney, O. R. "Tammuz Reconsidered: Some Recent Developments." *Journal of Semitic Studies* 7, no. 2 (1962): 147–60.

Halivni, David Weiss. *The Formation of the Babylonian Talmud.* Translated by Jeffrey L. Rubenstein. Oxford: Oxford University Press, 2013.

Harari, Yuval. *Jewish Magic before the Rise of Kabbalah.* Translated by Batya Stein. Raphael Patai Series in Jewish Folklore and Anthropology. Detroit: Wayne State University Press, 2017.

———. "Leadership, Authority, and the 'Other' in the Debate over Magic from the Karaites to Maimonides." In *Journal for the Study of Sephardic and Mizrahi Jewry* 1/2 (2007): 79–101.

———. "The Sages and the Occult." In *The Literature of the Sage,* edited by Shmuel Safrai, Zeev Safrai, Joshua Schwartz, and Peter J. Tomson, 521–66. Assen, Netherlands: Royal van Gorcum, 2006.

———. "What Is a Magical Text? Methodological Reflections Aimed at Redefining Early Jewish Magic." In *Officina Magica: Essays on the Practice of Magic in Antiquity,* edited by Shaul Shaked, 91–124. Leiden: Brill, 2005.

Harrak, Amir. *The Acts of Mār Mārī the Apostle.* Atlanta: Society of Biblical Literature, 2005.

Harrington, Daniel J. "The Original Language of Pseudo-Philo's *Liber Antiquitatum Biblicarum.*" *Harvard Theological Review* 63 (1970): 503–14.

Hayes, Christine. "'Halakhah Le-Moshe Mi-Sinai' in Rabbinic Sources: A Methodological Case Study." In *The Synoptic Problem in Rabbinic Literature,* edited by Shaye Cohen, 61–117. Providence, RI: Brown University Press, 2000.

Hempel, Charlotte. "The *Treatise on the Two Spirits* and the Literary History of the Rule of the Community." In *Dualism in Qumran,* edited by Geza G. Xeravits, 102–20. London: T&T Clark, 2010.

Herman, Geoffrey. "'One Day David Went Out for the Hunt of the Falconers': Persian Themes in the Babylonian Talmud." In *Shoshannat Yaakov: Jewish and Iranian Studies in Honor of Yaakov Elman,* edited by Shai Secunda and Steven Fine, 111–36. Leiden: Brill, 2012.

Hesiod. *Theogony; Works and Days; Testimonia.* Translated by Glenn W. Most. Loeb Classical Library. Cambridge, MA: Harvard University Press, 2007.

Hezser, Catherine. "Rabbis as Intellectuals in the Context of Graeco-Roman and Byzantine Christian Scholasticism." Paper presented at the School of Oriental and Asian Studies, University of London, 2017.

Hoffman, David. *The First Mishnah and the Controversies of the Tannaim.* New York: Maurosho Publications of Cong. Kehillath Yaakov, 1977. First published in German in 1881.

Horbury, William. "Origen and the Jews: Jewish-Greek and Jewish-Christian Relations." *The Jewish-Greek Tradition in Antiquity and the Byzantine Empire,* edited by James K. Aitken and James Carleton Paget, 79–90. Cambridge: Cambridge University Press, 2014.

Horden, Peregrine. "Afterword: Pandaemonium." In *Demons and Illness from Antiquity to the Early-Modern Period,* edited by Siam Bhayro and Catherine Rider, 412–18. Leiden: Brill, 2017.

Howard, George. *The Teaching of Addai.* Edited by Robert L. Wilken, William R. Schoedel, and Roberta Chestnut. Texts and Translations; Early Christian Literature Series. Chico, CA: Scholars Press, 1981.

Hunter, Erica C. D. "Aramaic-Speaking Communities of Sasanid Mesopotamia." *ARAM* 7 (1995): 319–35.

Hutter, Manfred. "Manichaeism in the Early Sasanian Empire." *Numen* 40, no. 1 (1993): 2–15.

Iamblichus. *De Mysteriis.* Translated by Emma C. Clarke, John M. Dillon, and Jackson P. Hershbell. Writings from the Greco-Roman World. Atlanta: Society for Biblical Literature, 2003.

Idel, Moshe. "Jewish Magic from the Renaissance Period to Early Hasidism." In *Religion, Science, and Magic in Concert and in Conflict,* edited by Jacob Neusner, Ernest S. Frerichs, and Paul Virgil McCracken Flesher, 82–117. New York: Oxford University Press, 1989.

Ilan, Tal. *Massekhet Ta'anit: Text, Translation, and Commentary.* Feminist Commentary on the Babylonian Talmud. Tübingen: Mohr Siebeck, 2008.

Isaac, E. "1 (Ethiopic Apocalypse of) Enoch." In *The Old Testament Pseudepigrapha,* edited by James H. Charlesworth, 5–90. Garden City, NY: Doubleday, 1983.

Jaafari-Dehaghi, Mahmoud. *Dādestān Ī Dēnīg.* Pt. 1. Studia Iranica. Paris: Association pour l'Avancement des Études Iraniennes, 1998.

Jacobs, Andrew S. *Remains of the Jews: The Holy Land and Christian Empire in Late Antiquity.* Divinations: Rereading Late Ancient Religion. Stanford, CA: Stanford University Press, 2003.

Jacobs, Louis. "Are There Fictitious Baraitot in the Babylonian Talmud?" *Hebrew Union College Annual* 42 (1971): 185–96.

Jacobsen, Thorkild. "Towards the Image of Tammuz." *History of Religions* 1, no. 2 (1962): 189–213.

Jacobson, Howard. *A Commentary on Pseudo-Philo's "Liber Antiquitatum Biblicarum": With Latin Text and English Translation*. Vol. 1. Leiden: Brill, 1996.

Janowitz, Naomi. *Magic in the Roman World: Pagans, Jews and Christians*. London: Routledge, 2001.

Janowski, B. "Jackals." In *Dictionary of Deities and Demons in the Bible,* edited by Karel van der Toorn, Bob Becking, and Pieter W. van der Horst, 459. Leiden: Brill, 1999.

Jastrow, Marcus. *Dictionary of Targumim, Talmud and Midrashic Literature*. London: Luzac, 1903.

Jolly, Karen. "Medieval Magic: Definitions, Beliefs, Practices." In *Witchcraft and Magic in Europe: The Middle Ages,* edited by Bengt Ankarloo and Stuart Clark, 1–72. Philadelphia: University of Pennsylvania Press, 2002.

Josephus. *The Jewish War*. Translated by Martin Hammond. Oxford World's Classics. Oxford: Oxford University Press, 2017.

Kalleres, Dayna S. "Demons and Divine Illumination: A Consideration of Eight Prayers by Gregory of Nazanzus." *Vigiliae Christianae* 61 (2007): 157–88.

Kalmin, Richard. "Christians and Heretics in Rabbinic Literature of Late Antiquity." *Harvard Theological Review* 87, no. 2 (1994): 155–69.

———. "The Evil Eye in Rabbinic Literature of Late Antiquity." In *Judaea-Palaestina, Babylon and Rome: Jews in Antiquity,* edited by Benjamin Isaac and Yuval Shahar, 111–38. Tübingen: Mohr Siebeck, 2012.

———. "The Formation and Character of the Babylonian Talmud," in *The Late Roman-Rabbinic Period,* edited by Steven T. Katz, 840–76. Vol. 4 of *The Cambridge History of Judaism*. Cambridge: Cambridge University Press, 2006.

———. "Holy Men, Rabbis, and Demonic Sages in Late Antiquity." In *Jewish Culture and Society under the Christian Roman Empire,* edited by Richard Kalmin and Seth Schwartz, 213–49. Leuven, Belgium: Peeters, 2003.

———. *Jewish Babylonia between Persia and Roman Palestine*. Oxford: Oxford University Press, 2006.

———. *Migrating Tales: The Talmud's Narratives and Their Historical Context*. Berkeley: University of California Press, 2014.

———. *The Sage in Jewish Society of Late Antiquity*. London: Routledge, 1999.

———. *Sages, Stories, Authors, and Editors in Rabbinic Babylonia*. Atlanta: Scholars Press, 1994.

———. "Saints or Sinners, Scholars or Ignoramuses? Stories about the Rabbis as Evidence for the Composite Nature of the Babylonian Talmud." *AJS Review* 15, no. 2 (1990): 179–205.

———. "Talmudic Portrayals of Relationships between Rabbis: Amoraic or Pseudepigraphic?" *AJS Review* 18, no. (1993): 165–197.

Kapferer, Bruce. *A Celebration of Demons: Exorcism and the Aesthetics of Healing in Sri Lanka.* Bloomington: Indiana University Press, 1983.

Kattan Gribetz, Sarit. "Conceptions of Time and Rhythms of Daily Life in Rabbinic Literature, 200–600 C.E." PhD diss., Princeton University, 2013.

———. "Time, Gender, and Ritual in Rabbinic Sources." In *Religious Studies and Rabbinics: A Conversation,* edited by Elizabeth Shanks Alexander and Beth A. Berkowitz, 139–57. London: Routledge, 2017.

Kaye, Lynn. *Time in the Babylonian Talmud: Natural and Imagined Times in Jewish Law and Narrative.* Cambridge: Cambridge University Press, 2018.

Keisman, Philip. "'If a Miracle Hadn't Happened for Me . . .': Daniel the Stylite and Rav Acha as Parallel Protagonists." Unpublished work. 2017.

Kelly, Henry Ansgar. *The Devil at Baptism: Ritual, Theology, and Drama.* Ithaca, NY: Cornell University Press, 1985.

———. *Satan: A Biography.* Cambridge: Cambridge University Press, 2006.

Kidd, Ian. "Some Philosophical Demons." *Bulletin of the Institute of Classical Studies* 40 (1995): 217–24.

Kiel, Yishai. "Creation by Emission: Recreating Adam and Eve in the Babylonian Talmud in Light of Zoroastrian and Manichaean Literature." *Journal of Jewish Studies* 66, no. 2 (2015): 295–316.

———. "In the Margins of the Rabbinic Curriculum: Mastering *ʿUqṣin* in the Light of Zoroastrian Intellectual Culture." *Journal for the Study of Judaism* 45 (2014): 1–31.

———. "Redesigning *Tzitzit* in the Babylonian Talmud in Light of Literary Depictions of the Zoroastrian *Kustīg.*" In *Shoshannat Yaakov: Jewish and Iranian Studies in Honor of Yaakov Elman,* edited by Shai Secunda and Steven Fine, 185–202. Leiden: Brill, 2012.

———. "Shaking Impurity: Exegesis and Innovative Traditions in the Babylonian Talmud and Pahlavi Literature." In *Encounters by the Rivers of Babylon: Scholarly Conversations between Jews, Iranians, and Babylonians in Antiquity,* edited by Shai Secunda and Uri Gabbay, 413–34. Tübingen: Mohr Siebeck, 2014.

Kiperwasser, Reuven. "Solomon, Ashmedai and Other Friends." Unpublished work. 2016.

Kister, Menahem. "Avot De-Rabbi Nathan: Studies in Text, Redaction and Interpretation." PhD diss., Hebrew University of Jerusalem, 1993.

Kitov, Eliyahu. *The Book of Our Heritage: The Jewish Year and Its Days of Significance.* Translated by Nachman Bulman and Ruth Royde. Revised by Dovid Landesman. Adapted and expanded ed. Jerusalem: Feldheim, 1997. First published in 1968.

Kitz, Anne Marie. "Demons in the Hebrew Bible and the Ancient Near East." *Journal of Biblical Literature* 135, no. 3 (2016): 447–64.

Klijn, Albertus Frederik Johannes. *The Acts of Thomas: Introduction, Text, and Commentary.* 2nd rev. ed. Leiden: Brill, 2003.

Klingenschmitt, Gordon. *The Demons of Barack H. Obama: How the Gift of Discerning of Spirits Reveals Unseen Forces Influencing American Politics.* Self-published, CreateSpace, 2012.

Kohler, George Y. "Judaism Buried or Revitalized? '*Wissenschaft des Judentums*' in Nineteenth-Century Germany—Impact, Actuality, and Applicability Today." In *Jewish Thought and Jewish Belief,* edited by Daniel J. Lasker, 27–63. Beer Sheva, Israel: Ben-Gurion University of the Negev Press, 2012.

Kohut, Alexander. *Ueber die jüdische Angelologie und Daemonologie in ihrer Abhängigkeit vom Parsismus.* Leipzig: Brockhaus, 1866.

Konstantopoulos, Gina. "Shifting Alignments: The Dichotomy of Benevolent and Malevolent Demons in Mesopotamia." In *Demons and Illness from Antiquity to the Early-Modern Period,* edited by Siam Bhayro and Catherine Rider, 19–38. Leiden: Brill, 2017.

Kraemer, David. *The Meanings of Death in Rabbinic Judaism.* London: Routledge, 1999.

———. "On the Reliability of Attributions in the Babylonian Talmud." *Hebrew Union College Annual* 60 (1989): 175–90.

———. *Rabbinic Judaism: Space and Place.* London: Routledge, 2015.

Kuhn, Thomas S. *The Structure of Scientific Revolutions.* Fiftieth Anniversary Edition (4th ed). Chicago: University of Chicago Press, 2012.

Kwasman, T. "The Demon of the Roof." In *Disease in Babylonia,* edited by Irving L. Finkel and Markham J. Geller, 160–86. Leiden: Brill, 2007.

Lambert, W. G. *Babylonian Creation Myths.* Winona Lake, IN: Eisenbrauns, 2013.

Lerner, M. B. "The External Tractates." In *The Literature of the Sages,* edited by Shmuel Safrai, 367–409. Philadelphia: Fortress Press, 1987.

Levene, Dan. *A Corpus of Magic Bowls: Incantation Texts in Jewish Aramaic from Late Antiquity.* London: Kegan Paul, 2003.

———. "'If You Appear as a Pig': Another Incantation Bowl (Moussaieff 164)." *Journal of Semitic Studies* 52, no. 1 (2007): 59–70.

Levi, Israel. "Légendes Judeo-Chrétiennes." *REJ* 8 (1884): 197–205.

Levinson, Joshua. "Enchanting Rabbis: Contest Narratives between Rabbis and Magicians in Rabbinic Literature of Late Antiquity." *Tarbiz* 75 (2006): 295–328.

Licht, Jacob. "An Analysis of the Treatise on the Two-Spirits in DSD." In *Aspects of the Dead Sea Scrolls,* edited by Chaim Rabin and Yigael Yadin, 88–100. Jerusalem: Magnes Press, 1958.

Liddell, Henry George, and Robert Scott. *A Greek-English Lexicon.* Oxford: Clarendon Press 1996.

Lincoln, Bruce. *Gods and Demons, Priests and Scholars: Critical Explorations in the History of Religions.* Chicago: University of Chicago Press, 2012.

Löhnert, A, and A. Zgoll. "Schutzgott. A. In Mesopotamien." In *Reallexicon der Assyriologie und Vorderasiatischen Archäologie,* vol. 12, edited by Michael P. Streck, 311–14. Berlin: W. de Gruyter, 2009–11.

Lucarelli, Rita. "Illness as Divine Punishment: The Nature and Function of the Disease-Carrier Demons in the Ancient Magical Texts." In *Demons and Illness from Antiquity to the Early-Modern Period,* edited by Siam Bhayro and Catherine Rider, 53–60. Leiden: Brill, 2017.

Luibhéid, Colm, and Paul Rorem, eds. *Pseudo-Dionysius: The Complete Works.* Rev. ed. Classics of Western Spirituality. New York: Paulist Press, 1987.

MacDonald, Duncan B., H. Massé, P.N. Boratav, K.A. Nizami, and P. Voorhoeve. "Djinn." In *Encyclopaedia of Islam,* edited by P. Bearman et al. 2nd edition. Brill Online, 2012. http://referenceworks.brillonline.com/entries/encyclopaedia-of-islam-2/djinn-COM_0191.

Malandra, William W. "Vendīdād. I. Survey of the History and Contents of the Text" In *Encyclopædia Iranica Online.* 2000, updated and published online 2006. www.iranicaonline.org/articles/vendidad.

———. "Zoroastrianism. I. Historical Review up to the Arab Conquest." In *Encyclopædia Iranica Online.* 2005. www.iranicaonline.org/articles/zoroastrianism-i-historical-review.

Martin, Dale B. *Inventing Superstition: From the Hippocratics to the Christians.* Cambridge, MA: Harvard University Press, 2004.

———. "When Did Angels Become Demons?" *Journal of Biblical Literature* 129, no. 4 (2010): 657–77.

Martinez, Florentino Garcia, and Eibert J. C. Tigchelaar. *The Dead Sea Scrolls Study Edition.* 2 vols. Leiden: Brill, 1997.

Marx-Wolf, Heidi. *Spiritual Taxonomies and Ritual Authority: Platonists, Priests, and Gnostics in the Third Century C.E.* Divinations: Rereading Late Ancient Religion. Philadephia: University of Pennsylvania Press, 2016.

Massey, Doreen. *For Space.* London: Sage, 2005.

Mastin, B. A. "The Inscriptions Written on Plaster at Kuntillet 'Arjud." *Vetus Testamentum* 59, no. 1 (2009): 99–115.

Metso, Sarianna. *The Textual Development of the Qumran Community Rule.* Leiden: Brill, 1997.

Meyer, Michael A. "Two Persistent Tensions within Wissenschaft Des Judentums." *Modern Judaism* 24, no. 2 (2004): 105–19.

Miglio, Adam E. "A Study of the Serpent Incantation KTU 1.82: 1–7 and Its Contributions to Ugaritic Mythology and Religion." *Journal of Ancient Near Eastern Religions* 13 (2013): 30–48.

Moazami, Mahnaz. *Wrestling with the Demons of the Pahlavi Widēwdād*. Leiden: Brill, 2014.

Mokhtarian, Jason Sion. *Rabbis, Sorcerers, Kings, and Priests: The Culture of the Talmud in Ancient Iran*. Oakland: University of California Press, 2015.

Montgomery, James A. *Aramaic Incantation Texts from Nippur*. Philadelphia: University of Pennsylvania Museum, 1913.

Morag, Shelomo, and Yechiel Kara. *Babylonian Aramaic in Yemenite Tradition: The Noun*. Edah Ve-Lashon. Edited by A. Maman. Jerusalem: Magnes Press, 2002.

Moscovitz, Leib. "Between Casuistics and Conceptualization: On the Term *Ameru Davar Ehad* in the Palestinian Talmud." *Jewish Quarterly Review* 91, no. 1/2 (2000): 101–42.

———. *Talmudic Reasoning: From Casuistics to Conceptualization*. Tübingen: Mohr Siebeck, 2002.

Muehlberger, Ellen. *Angels in Late Ancient Christianity*. Oxford: Oxford University Press, 2013.

Murphy, Frederick James. *Pseudo-Philo: Rewriting the Bible*. Oxford: Oxford University Press, 1993.

Murphy, Trevor Morgan. *Pliny the Elder's "Natural History": The Empire in the Encyclopedia*. Oxford: Oxford University Press, 2004.

Nasr, Seyeed Hossein, Caner K. Dagli, Maria Massi Dakake, Joseph E. B. Lumbard, and Mohammed Rustom, eds. *The Study Quran: A New Translation and Commentary*. New York: Harper One, 2015.

Nathan, Tobie. *Du Commerce avec les Diables*. Paris: Les Empêcheurs de Penser en Rond, 2004.

———. *Nous Ne Sommes Pas Seuls au Monde: Les Enjeux de l'Ethnopsychiatrie*. Paris: Points, 2007.

Naveh, Joseph, and Shaul Shaked. *Amulets and Magic Bowls: Aramaic Incantations of Late Antiquity*. Jerusalem: Magnes Press, 1985.

Neis, Rachel. *The Sense of Sight in Rabbinic Culture: Jewish Ways of Seeing in Late Antiquity*. Cambridge: Cambridge University Press, 2013.

Neusner, Jacob. *Development of a Legend: Studies on the Traditions Concerning Yoḥanan Ben Zakkai*. Leiden: Brill, 1970.

———. *In Search of Talmudic Biography: The Problem of the Attributed Saying*. Chico, CA: Scholars Press for Brown Judaic Studies, 1984.

———. *A Life of Rabbi Yohanan Ben Zakkai*. Leiden: Brill, 1962.

———. "Telling Time in Rabbinic Judaism: Correlating the Lunar-Solar Calendar with the Lectionary Cycle." *Miscelánea de Estudios Árabes y Hebraicos* 53 (2004): 231–48.

Nissan, Ephraim. "Thematic Parallels in the Rabbinic Aggadah vs. Christian Hagiography: Modes of Convergence, and Sample Tales." Special issue: Life-

Worlds and Religious Commitment: Ethnographic Perspectives on Subjectivity and Islam. *La Ricerca Folklorica* 69 (2014): 161–72.
Oelsner, Joachim. "Incantations in Southern Mesopotamia—From Clay Tablets to Magical Bowls: Thoughts on the Decline of the Babylonian Culture." In *Officina Magica: Essays on the Practice of Magic in Antiquity*, edited by Shaul Shaked, 30–51. Leiden: Brill, 2005.
Ogden, Daniel. *Dragons, Serpents, and Slayers in the Classical and Early Christian Worlds: A Sourcebook*. Oxford: Oxford University Press, 2013.
Origen. *Homilies on Luke; Fragments on Luke*. Translated by Joseph T. Lienhard. The Fathers of the Church. Washington, DC: Catholic University of America Press, 1996.
Orlov, Andrei A. *Dark Mirrors: Azazel and Satanael in Early Jewish Demonology*. Albany: State University of New York Press, 2011.
——. *The Enoch-Metatron Tradition*. Tübingen: Mohr Siebeck, 2005.
Padel, Ruth. *In and Out of the Mind: Greek Images of the Tragic Self*. Princeton, NJ: Princeton University Press, 1992.
Pagels, Elaine. *The Origin of Satan*. New York: Random House, 1995.
Panaino, Antonio, Reza Abdollahy, and Daniel Balland. "Calendars." In *Encyclopædia Iranica Online*. 1990. www.iranicaonline.org/articles/calendars.
Patai, Raphael. "Lilith." *Journal of American Folklore* 77 (1964): 295–314.
Payne, Richard E. *A State of Mixture: Christians, Zoroastrians, and Iranian Political Culture in Late Antiquity*. Oakland: University of California Press, 2015.
Penney, Douglas L., and Michael O. Wise. "By the Power of Beelzebub: An Aramaic Incantation Formula from Qumran (4Q560)." *Journal of Biblical Literature* 113, no. 4 (1994): 627–50.
Pientka-Hinz, R. "Schlange. A. In Mesopotamien." In *Reallexikon der Assyriologie und Vorderasiatischen Archäologie*, edited by Erich Ebeling, vol. 12, 202–218 (Berlin: W. de Gruyter, 2009).
Pitard, Wayne T. "Voices from the Dust: Tablets from Ugarit and the Bible." In *Mesopotamia and the Bible: Comparative Explorations*, edited by Mark W. Chavalas and K. Lawson Younger Jr., 251–75. London: Continuum, 2003.
Plato. *Laws*. Translated by R. G. Bury. Loeb Classical Library. Vol. 1. Cambridge, MA: Harvard University Press, 1929.
——. *Timaeus*. Translated by Donald J. Zeyl. Indianapolis: Hackett, 2000.
Ployd, Adam. "Participation and Polemics: Angels from Origen to Augustine." *Harvard Theological Review* 110, no. 3 (2017): 421–39.
Plutarch. *Moralia*. Vol. 2, *How to Profit by One's Enemies; On Having Many Friends; Chance; Virtue and Vice; Letter of Condolence to Apollonius; Advice about Keeping Well; Advice to Bride and Groom; The Dinner of the Seven Wise*

Men; Superstition. Translated by Frank Cole Babbitt. Loeb Classical Library. Cambridge, MA: Harvard University Press, 1928.

——. *Moralia.* Vol. 5, *Isis and Osiris; The E at Delphi; The Oracles at Delphi No Longer Given in Verse; The Obsolescence of Oracles.* Translated by Frank Cole Babbitt. Loeb Classical Library. Cambridge, MA: Harvard University Press, 1936.

——. *Moralia.* Vol. 7, *On Love of Wealth; On Compliancy; On Envy and Hate; On Praising Oneself Inoffensively; On the Delays of the Divine Vengeance; On Fate; On the Sign of Socrates; On Exile; Consolation to His Wife.* Translated by Phillip H. De Lacy and Benedict Einarson. Loeb Classical Library. Cambridge, MA: Harvard University Press, 1959.

Pourshariati, Parvaneh. *Decline and Fall of the Sasanian Empire: The Sasanian-Parthian Confederacy and the Arab Conquest of Iran.* London: I. B. Tauris in association with the Iran Heritage Foundation, 2008.

Pritchard, J. B., ed. *Ancient Near Eastern Texts Relating to the Old Testament.* Princeton, NJ: Princeton University Press, 1950.

Ravitzky, Avishur. "Maimonides and His Disciples on Linguistic Magic and 'the Madness of the Writers of Amulets' [in Heb.]." In *Jewish Culture in the Eye of the Storm: A Jubilee Book in Honor of Yosef Ahituv,* edited by Aviezer Sagi and Nahem Ilan, 431–58. Tel Aviv: Ha-Kibbutz Ha-Meukhad, 2002.

Redfield, James Adam. "Embedding, Sublation, Ambivalence: Ethnographic Techniques in Early Rabbinic Law." Article circulated for a seminar at the annual conference of the Association for Jewish Studies, Washington, DC, December 2017.

——. "Redacting Culture: Ethnographic Authority in the Talmudic Arrival Scene," *Jewish Social Studies* 22, no. 1 (Fall 2016): 29–80.

——. "'When X Arrived, He Said . . .': The Historical Career of a Talmudic Formula," Unpublished work. Accessed 6 December 2019. Available at www.academia.edu/29627483/_When_X_Arrived_he_said.

Reed, Annette Yoshiko. *Fallen Angels and the History of Judaism and Christianity: The Reception of Enochic Literature.* Cambridge: Cambridge University Press, 2005.

Ronis, Sara. "A Demonic Servant in Rav Papa's Household: Demons as Subjects in the Mesopotamian Talmud." In *The Aggada of the Babylonian Talmud and Its Cultural World,* edited by Geoffrey Herman and Jeffrey L. Rubenstein, 3–21. Providence, RI: Brown Judaic Studies, 2018.

——. "'Do Not Go Out Alone at Night': Law and Demonic Discourse in the Babylonian Talmud." PhD diss., Yale University, 2015.

——. "Gender, Sex, and Witchcraft in Late Antique Judaism." In *A Companion to Jews and Judaism in the Late Antique World, 3rd Century BCE–7th Century CE,* edited by Naomi Koltun-Fromm and Gwynn Kessler, 391–404. Hoboken, NJ: Wiley-Blackwell, 2020.

———. "Imagining the Other: The Magical Arab in Rabbinic Literature." *Prooftexts* 39, no. 1 (2021): 1–28.

———. "Intermediary Beings in Late Antique Judaism: A History of Scholarship." *Currents in Biblical Research* 14, no. 1 (2015): 94–120.

———. "A Seven-Headed Demon in the House of Study: Understanding a Rabbinic Demon in Light of Zoroastrian, Christian, and Babylonian Textual Traditions." *AJS Review* 43, no. 1 (April 2019): 125–42.

———. "Space, Place, and the Race for Power: Rabbis, Demons, and the Construction of Babylonia." *Harvard Theological Review* 110, no. 4 (2017): 588–603.

Rosen-Zvi, Ishay. *Demonic Desires: Yetzer Hara and the Problem of Evil in Late Antiquity.* Philadelphia: University of Pennsylvania Press, 2011.

———. "Bilhah the Temptress: The Testament of Reuben and the 'Birth of Sexuality,'" *Jewish Quarterly Review* 96, no. 1 (2006): 65–94.

Rosenblum, Jordan D. *Food and Identity in Early Rabbinic Judaism.* Cambridge: Cambridge University Press, 2010.

Rubenstein, Jeffrey L. *Stories of the Babylonian Talmud.* Baltimore: Johns Hopkins University Press, 2010.

———. *Talmudic Stories: Narrative Art, Composition, and Culture.* Baltimore: Johns Hopkins University Press, 1999.

Rubin, Nissan. *Time and Life Cycle in Talmud and Midrash: Socio-Anthropological Perspectives.* Boston: Academic Studies Press, 2008.

Russell, James R. "Burial. III. In Zoroastrianism." In *Encyclopædia Iranica Online.* 2000. www.iranicaonline.org/articles/burial-iii.

Russell, Jeffrey Burton. *Satan: The Early Christian Tradition.* Ithaca, NY: Cornell University Press, 1981.

Sacks, Steven Daniel. *Midrash and Multiplicity: Pirke De-Rabbi Eliezer and the Renewal of Rabbinic Interpretive Culture.* Berlin: De Gruyter, 2009.

Said, Edward W. *Orientalism.* New York: Vintage Books, 1978.

Satlow, Michael L. "Beyond Influence: Toward a New Historiographic Paradigm." In *Jewish Literatures and Cultures: Context and Intertext,* edited by Anita Norich and Yaron Z. Eliav, 37–53. Providence, RI: Brown Judaic Studies, 2008.

———. *Jewish Marriage in Antiquity.* Princeton, NJ: Princeton University Press, 2001.

Schaff, Phillip. *Ante-Nicene Fathers.* Vol. 4. Grand Rapids, MI: Christian Classics Ethereal Library, 1885.

Schmitt, Rüdiger. "Demons, Demonology. II. Hebrew Bible/Old Testament." In *Dabbesheth–Dreams and Dream Interpretation,* edited by Hans-Josef Klauck, Volker Leppin, Bernard McGinn, Choon-Leong Seow, Hermann Spieckermann, Barry Dov Walfish, and Eric J. Ziolkowski, 536–39. Vol. 6 of *Encyclopedia of the Bible and Its Reception.* Berlin: De Gruyter, 2013.

Schneider, Tammi J. *An Introduction to Ancient Mesopotamian Religion.* Grand Rapids, MI: William B. Eerdmans, 2011.

Schofer, Jonathan Wyn. *Confronting Vulnerability: The Body and the Divine in Rabbinic Ethics.* Chicago: University of Chicago Press, 2010.

Scholem, Gershom. *Major Trends in Jewish Mysticism.* New York: Schocken Books, 1941.

Schwartz, Howard. *Miriam's Tambourine: Jewish Folktales from around the World.* New York: Seth Press, 1986.

Schwartz, Marcus Mordecai. "As They Journeyed from the East: The Nahotei of the Fourth Century and the Construction of the Rabbinic Diaspora." *Hebrew Union College Annual* 86 (2015): 63–99.

Schwartz, Sarah L. "Building a Book of Spells: The So-Called *Testament of Solomon* Reconsidered." PhD diss., University of Pennsylvania, 2005.

———. "Reconsidering the *Testament of Solomon.*" *Journal for the Study of Pseudepigrapha* 16, no. 3 (2007): 203–37.

Scurlock, JoAnn. "Images of Tammuz: The Intersection of Death, Divinity, and Royal Authority in Ancient Mesopotamia." In *Experiencing Power, Generating Authority: Cosmos, Politics, and the Ideology of Kingship in Ancient Egypt and Mesopotamia,* edited by Jane A. Hill, Philip Jones, and Antonio J. Morales, 151–84. Philadelphia: University of Pennsylvania Museum of Archaeology and Anthropology, 2013.

———. "K 164 ("Ba" 2, P. 635): New Light on Mourning Rites for Dumuzi?" *Revue d'Assyriologie et d'archéologie orientale* 86, no. 1 (1992): 53–67.

Secunda, Shai. "The Construction, Composition and Idealization of the Female Body in Rabbinic Literature and Parallel Iranian Texts: Three Excursuses." Special issue: The Jewish Woman and Her Body, ed. Rachel S. Harris. *Nashim: A Journal of Jewish Women's Studies and Gender Issues* 23 (Spring–Fall 2012): 60–86.

———. "Reading the Bavli in Iran." *The Jewish Quarterly Review* 100, no. 2 (2010): 310–42.

Segal, Eliezer. "Law as Allegory? An Unnoticed Literary Device in Talmudic Narratives." *Prooftexts* 8, no. 2 (1988): 245–56.

Segal, J. B. *Catalogue of the Aramaic and Mandaic Incantation Bowls in the British Museum.* London: British Museum Press, 2000.

Septimus, Gerald. "On the Boundaries of Prayer: Talmudic Ritual Texts with Addressees Other Than God." PhD diss., Yale University, 2008.

Shahbazi, A. Shapur. "Sasanian Dynasty." In *Encyclopædia Iranica Online.* 2005. www.iranicaonline.org/articles/sasanian-dynasty.

Shaked, Shaul. "Magical Bowls and Incantation Texts: How to Get Rid of Demons and Pests [in Heb]." *Qadmoniot* 129 (2005): 2–13.

Shaked, Shaul, James Nathan Ford, and Siam Bhayro. *Aramaic Bowl Spells: Jewish Babylonian Aramaic Bowls.* Vol. 1. Leiden: Brill, 2013.

Shinan, Avigdor, and Yair Zakovitch. *From Gods to God: How the Bible Debunked, Suppressed, or Changed Ancient Myths and Legends*. Translated by Valerie Zakovitch. Philadelphia: Jewish Publication Society, 2012.

Sigalow, Emily. "Towards a Sociological Framework of Religious Syncretism in the United States." *Journal of the American Academy of Religion* 84, no. 4 (2016): 1029–55.

Simon-Shoshan, Moshe. "Did the Rabbis Believe in Agreus Pan? Rabbinic Relationships with Roman Power, Culture, and Religion in *Genesis Rabbah* 63." *Harvard Theological Review* 111, no. 3 (July 2018): 425–50.

Skjærvø, Oktor, "Pahlavi Primer," unpublished workbook with periodic updates (2016).

Skjærvø, Prods Oktor. "Aždahā. I. In Old and Middle Iranian." In *Encyclopædia Iranica* Online 1987, updated and published online 2011. www.iranicaonline.org/articles/azdaha-dragon-various-kinds#pt1.

———. "Counter-Manichean Elements in Kerdir's Inscriptions. Irano-Manichaica II." In *Atti Del Terzo Congresso Internazionale Di Studi "Manicheismo E Oriente Cristiano Antico," Arcavacata Di Rende-Amantea 31 Agosto—5 Settembre 1993*, edited by L Cirillo and A. V. Tongerloo, 314–42. Leuven, Belgium: Brepols, 1997.

———. "Iran. VI. Iranian Languages and Scripts. (3) Writing Systems." In *Encyclopædia Iranica Online*. 2006, updated 2012. www.iranicaonline.org/articles/iran-vi3-writing-systems.

———. "Kartir." In *Encyclopædia Iranica Online*. 2011, updated 2012. www.iranicaonline.org/articles/kartir.

———. *The Spirit of Zoroastrianism*. New Haven, CT: Yale University Press, 2011.

———. "The Videvdad: Its Ritual-Mythical Significance." In *The Age of the Parthians*, edited by Vesta Sarkhosh Curtis and Sarah Stewart, 105–41. London: I. B. Tauris, 2007.

———. "Zoroastrian Dualism." In *Light against Darkness: Dualism in Ancient Mediterranean Religion and the Contemporary World*, edited by Armin Lange, Eric M. Meyer, Bennie H. Reynolds, and Randall Styers, 55–91. Göttingen, Germany: Vandenhoeck & Ruprecht, 2011.

Slifkin, Natan. *Wrestling with Demons: A History of Rabbinic Attitudes to Demons*. Self-published online, 2011. www.zootorah.com/RationalistJudaism/Demons.pdf.

Smelik, Willem F. *Rabbis, Language and Translation in Late Antiquity*. Cambridge: Cambridge University Press, 2013.

Smith, Gregory A. "How Thin Is a Demon?" *Journal of Early Christian Studies* 16, no. 4 (2008): 479–512.

Sokoloff, Michael. *A Dictionary of Jewish Babylonian Aramaic of the Talmudic and Geonic Periods*. Ramat-Gan, Israel: Bar-Ilan University Press, 2003.

———. *A Dictionary of Jewish Palestinian Aramaic of the Byzantine Period*. Ramat-Gan, Israel: Bar-Ilan University Press, 1990, 1992.

Sophocles. *Antigone; The Women of Trachis; Philoctetes; Oedipus at Colonus.* Edited and translated by Hugh Lloyd-Jones. Loeb Classical Library. Cambridge, MA: Harvard University Press, 1994.

Sorensen, Eric. *Possession and Exorcism in the New Testament and Early Christianity.* Wissenschaftliche Untersuchungen Zum Neuen Testament 2. Reihe 157. Tübingen: Mohr Siebeck, 2002.

Steinfeld, Zvi Aryeh. "Adam Ḥashuv Shani." *Dine Israel* 13–14 (1987): 193–238.

Stern, David. "The Tale of the Jerusalemite." In *Rabbinic Fantasies: Imaginative Narratives from Classical Hebrew Literature,* edited by David H. Stern and Mark J. Mirsky, 121–42. New Haven, CT: Yale University Press, 1998.

Stern, Sacha. "The Rabbinic Concept of Time from Late Antiquity to the Middle Ages." In *Time and Eternity: The Medieval Discourse,* edited by Gerhard Jaritz and Gerson Moreno-Riaño, 129–45. Turnhout, Belgium: Brepols, 2003.

Stephens, Walter. *Demon Lovers: Witchcraft, Sex, and the Crisis of Belief.* Chicago: University of Chicago Press, 2002.

Stol, Marten. *Epilepsy in Babylonia.* Cuneiform Monographs. Groningen, Netherlands: STYX Publications, 1993.

Stratton, Kimberly B. *Naming the Witch: Magic, Ideology, and Stereotype in the Ancient World.* New York: Columbia University Press, 2007.

Strauch Schick, Shana. "Intention in the Babylonian Talmud: An Intellectual History." PhD diss., Yeshiva University, 2011.

———. "Reading Aristotle in Mahoza? Actions and Intentions in Rava's Jurisprudence." *Jewish Law Association Studies* 25 (2014): 262–91.

Stuckenbruck, Loren T. "The 'Angels' and 'Giants' of Genesis 6:1–4 in Second and Third Century BCE Jewish Interpretation: Reflections on the Posture of Early Apocalyptic Traditions." *Dead Sea Discoveries* 7, no. 3 (2000): 354–77.

———. "Satan and Demons." In *Jesus among Friends and Enemies: A Historical and Literary Introduction to Jesus in the Gospels,* edited by Chris Keith and Larry W. Hurtado, 173–97. Grand Rapids, MI: Baker Academic, 2011.

Styers, Randall. *Making Magic: Religion, Magic, and Science in the Modern World.* Oxford: Oxford University Press, 2004.

Swartz, Michael D. *Scholastic Magic: Ritual and Revelation in Early Jewish Mysticism.* Princeton, NJ: Princeton University Press, 1996.

Takahashi, Hidemi. "Syriac as the Intermediary in Scientific Graeco-Arabica: Some Historical and Philological Observations." *Intellectual History of the Islamicate World* 3 (2015): 66–97.

Tatian. *Oratio ad Graecos and Fragments.* Edited and translated by Molly Whittaker. Oxford Early Christian Texts. Oxford: Clarendon Press, 1982.

Tavadia, Jehangir C. *Šāyast-Nē-Šāyast: A Pahlavi Text on Religious Customs.* Hamburg: Friderichsen, de Gruyter, 1930.

Tavenner, Euguene. "Three as a Magic Number in Latin Literature." *Transactions and Proceedings of the American Philological Association* 47 (1916): 117–43.

Temkin, Sefton D. "Trachtenberg, Joshua." In *To–Wei*, edited by Michael Berenbaum and Fred Skolnik, 79. Vol. 20 of *Encyclopaedia Judaica*, 2nd ed. Detroit: Macmillan Reference USA, 2007.

Thompson, R. Campbell. *The Devils and Evil Spirits of Babylonia: Being Babylonian and Assyrian Incantations against the Demons, Ghouls, Vampires, Hobglobins, Ghosts, and Kindred Evil Spirits, Which Attack Mankind.* Vol. 1, *Evil Spirits.* London: Luzac, 1903.

Torijano, Pablo. *Solomon the Esoteric King: From King to Magus, Development of a Tradition.* Leiden: Brill, 2002.

Towner, W. Sibley. *The Rabbinic "Enumeration of Scriptural Examples": A Study of a Rabbinic Pattern of Discourse with Special Reference to Mekhilta D'R. Ishmael.* Studia Post-Biblica. Edited by J. C. H. Lebram. Leiden: Brill, 1973.

Trachtenberg, Joshua. *The Devil and the Jews.* New Haven, CT: Yale University Press, 1944.

———. *Jewish Magic and Superstition: A Study in Folk Religion.* New York: Behrman House, 1939.

Tuan, Yi-Fu. *Space and Place: The Perspective of Experience.* Minneapolis: University of Minnesota Press, 1977.

Ulmer, Rivka. *A Bilingual Edition of Pesiqta Rabbati.* Berlin: De Gruyter, 2017.

Urbach, E. E. "Concerning Historical Insight into the Account of Rabbah Bar Naḥmani's Death [in Heb.]." *Tarbiz* 34 (1965): 156–61.

Vanderkam, James C. *Enoch and the Growth of an Apocalyptic Tradition.* Washington, DC: Catholic Biblical Association of America, 1984.

———. *Enoch: A Man for All Generations.* Studies in Personalities of the Old Testament. Columbia: University of South Carolina Press, 2008.

———. "Jubilees, Book of." In *Encyclopedia of the Dead Sea Scrolls*, edited by Lawrence H. Schiffman and James C. Vanderkam. Oxford Biblical Studies Online.

———. "The Jubilees Fragments from Qumran Cave 4." In *The Madrid Qumran Congress*, edited by Julio Trebolle Barrera and Luis Vegas Montaner, 635–48. Leiden: Brill, 1992.

Veltri, Giuseppe. "The Rabbis and Pliny the Elder: Jewish and Greco-Roman Attitudes toward Magic and Empirical Knowledge." Special issue: Hellenism and Hebraism Reconsidered: The Poetics of Cultural Influence and Exchange, pt. 1. *Poetics Today* 19, no. 1 (1998): 63–89.

Verderame, Lorenzo. "Demons at Work in Ancient Mesopotamia." In *Demons and Illness from Antiquity to the Early-Modern Period*, edited by Siam Bhayro and Catherine Rider. Magical and Religious Literature of Late Antiquity, 61–78. Leiden: Brill, 2017.

Versnel, H. S. "Some Reflections on the Relationship Magic-Religion." *Numen* 38, no. 2 (1991): 177–97.

Wald, Stephen G. *B.T. Pesahim III: Critical Edition with Comprehensive Commentary.* New York: Jewish Theological Seminary of America, 2000.

Watkins, Calvert. *How to Kill a Dragon: Aspects of Indo-European Poetics.* Oxford: Oxford University Press, 1995.

Weiss, Abraham. *Le-Heker Ha-Talmud.* New York: Feldheim, 1954.

Widengren, G. "Manichaeaism and Its Iranian Background." In *The Seleucid, Parthian, and Sasanian Periods,* edited by E. Yarshater, 965–90. Vol. 3(2) of *The Cambridge History of Iran.* Cambridge: Cambridge University Press, 1983.

Wiesehofer, Josef. *Ancient Persia: From 550 B.C. to 650 A.D.* London: I. B. Tauris, 1996.

Williams, A. V. *The Pahlavi Rivayat Accompanying the Dādestān i Dēnīg.* Copenhagen: Royal Danish Academy of Sciences and Letters, 1990.

Wimpfheimer, Barry S. *Narrating the Law: A Poetics of Talmudic Legal Stories.* Philadelphia: University of Pennsylvania Press, 2011.

———. *The Talmud: A Biography.* Princeton, NJ: Princeton University Press, 2018.

Wintersmute, O. S. "Jubilees." In *The Old Testament Pseudepigrapha,* edited by James H. Charlesworth, 35–142. New York: Doubleday, 1985.

Wray, T. J., and Gregory Mobley. *The Birth of Satan: Tracing the Devil's Biblical Roots.* New York: Palgrave, 2005.

Wright, Archie T. *The Origin of Evil Spirits: The Reception of Genesis 6:1–4 in Early Jewish Literature.* 2nd edition. Tübingen: Mohr Siebeck, 2013.

Wright, Wilmer C. ed. *Julian.* Vol. 3, *Letters; Epigrams; Against the Galilaeans; Fragments.* Loeb Classical Library. Cambridge, MA: Harvard University Press, 1923.

Wyatt, N. "Qeteb." In *Dictionary of Deities and Demons in the Bible,* edited by Karel van der Toorn, Bob Becking, and Pieter W. Van der Horst, 673–74. Leiden: Brill, 1999.

Yamauchi, Edwin M. "Additional Notes on Tammuz." *Journal of Semitic Studies* 10, no. 5 (1966): 10–15.

Yassif, Eli. *The Hebrew Folktale: History, Genre, Meaning.* Bloomington: Indiana University Press, 2009.

———. *Sipur Ha-Am Ha-Ivri: Toldotav, Sugav U-Mashma'uto.* Jerusalem: Mossad Bialik, 1994.

Zenkovsky, Serge A. *Medieval Russia's Epics, Chronicles, and Tales.* New York: Dutton, 1974.

The Zohar: Pritzker Edition. Vol. 11. Translated by Joel Hecker. Stanford, CA: Stanford University Press, 2016.

Subject Index

Abaye, 93, 94, 101, 105, 107, 112–14, 121, 167–68, 170, 171, 174, 176, 178, 197, 198, 209
Abba Yose, 209–10
Abracadabra (incantation), 145
Abu 'Amir ibn Shuhayd, 190
Abu Zaid al-Qurashi, 190n68
Achaemenids, 181, 186
Acts of Mār Mārī the Apostle, 66n35, 173–74
Acts of Peter, 218
Acts of the Persian Martyrs, 201
Acts of Thomas, 174, 218
Adam (biblical figure), 43–47, 50, 52–54, 64n28
Adelman, Rachel, 53
Agag bat Baroq (demon), 171, 206
Agrat bat Maḥlat, 74, 99, 104n27, 107, 125, 169–71, 174–75
R. Agzar bar Dibšata, 207
R. Aḥa b. Jacob, 81, 196–201
Ahriman (Zoroastrian evil god), 78, 149, 180
Ahura Mazda (Zoroastrian good god), 6
Ahuvia, Mika, 15n42
Akkadian civilization. *See* ancient Mesopotamia
Alexander, Philip, 51, 71
Alfasi, R. Isaac (Rif), 7–8, 9
Amenar, 95
R. Ami, 114
The Amityville Horror (film), 195
Amoraim, demonic discourse of. *See* demons/demonic discourse; *specific Amoraim*
amulets, 100–101, 145, 201, 203–5
Anat (war goddess), 199
ancient Mesopotamia: Babylonian rabbinic community's interconnections with, 227, 228; chicken feet associated with Lamaštu in, 84n102; classification of demons in, 181–83; conceptualization of demons in, 22, 31; dragon/serpent slaying stories from, 198–200; extispicy and even numbers in, 138; legal discourse about demons and, 130; medical practices, Babylonian continuity of, 19, 23; moral neutrality of demons in, 22, 180–84; origin story of demon Pashittu in, 40; possession/exorcism and demonology of, 221–22; Sasanian Āsōristān, continuity with, 6, 109, 186–87; servants, demons depicted as, 180–88
"and if not" clauses, 142–44
angels: as both good and evil, 85n103; classification of demons and, 63–64, 68, 69, 72–73, 78–79; Dead Sea Scrolls, Community Rule, Angel of Darkness in, 34; demons as offspring of sinful sexual

angels *(continued)*
encounters between humans and, 35–41, 44, 50, 65; in early Christian writing, 51–52, 63–64, 65n30, 67, 68; fallen, 36, 50, 52, 65, 66, 72, 78, 128; incantation bowls invoking protection of, 207; privies, waiting outside, 113; rabbinic rejection of angelology, 50–54; Satan, rabbinic association with, 86n104
animals associated with demonic beings, 31, 47–49, 77
Anjra Mainyu (Zoroastrian evil god), 6
Anthony of Egypt, 200, 219
antisemitism, nonnormativization of Jewish demonology in face of, 10–11
anxieties about demonic superiority, rabbis dealing with, 158–65, 166–67
Aramaic incantation bowls. *See* incantation bowls/texts
Arginiton (bathhouse being), 211
Aristotle, 61n12, 86n105
Ascension of Isaiah, 218n64
R. Ashi, 94, 100, 117, 123
Ashmedai (demon king), 74, 95, 154–55, 158–65, 192, 193, 207
Ashurpanipal (Assyrian ruler), 181
Āsōristān, Sasanian province of, 5–6
R. Assi, 114, 132n5
Assyrian civilization, 181. *See also* ancient Mesopotamia
Athanasius of Alexandria, 54n72, 200, 219
attacks, demonic. *See* exorcisms and repelling demonic attacks
Aubin, Melissa Margaret, 11n30, 13
Austin, Jane, 166
R. Avira, 96
avoiding demonic danger, 21–22, 92–127; anxieties about demonic superiority, rabbis dealing with, 158–65, 166–67; the body, constructions of, 103, 119–24; classification as means of, 89–91; even numbers, 93–97, 111–13, 119, 120, 125; gender and, 124–25; morally neutral depiction of demons despite need for, 21–22, 28, 118, 196, 216; rabbinic knowledge and power regarding, 204–5; rabbinic self, constructions of, 126–27; space, constructions of, 103, 109–19; sugya b. *Pesaḥim* 109b–112a addressing, 93–103; time, constructions of, 103–9. *See also* exorcisms and repelling demonic attacks
Avot de-Rabbi Natan, classification of demons in, 75–81, 85–86
R. Ayvu b. Nagri, 176

Ba'al Cycle (Ugaritic), 199
The Babadook (film), 195
Babylonian Exile, 187n57
Babylonian incantation bowls. *See* incantation bowls/texts
Babylonian rabbinic community, 3–7, 224–29; constructions of rabbinic self in discussions of demonic danger, 126–27; demonic interest in Babylonian versus Palestinian rabbis, 168n5; R. Dimi traveling from Roman Palestine to, 95–96, 135; "filtered absorption" of existing cultural elements by, 194; late antiquity, concept of, 224–26; monotheism of, 12, 21, 23, 34, 149, 189n63, 194, 228–29; *naḥotei* (rabbinic travelers), 135n10; in Sasanian context, 226–29; space, demons and constructions of, 111. *See also* demons/demonic discourse
Babylonian Talmud, 4–5; amulets mentioned in, 205n27; classification of demons in, 75–80, 81, 82, 84, 85–86; R. Ḥanina b. Dosa in, 171; historiographic nonnormative view of demons in, 7–12, 15n43; incantation bowl, single mention of, 206; origin stories for demons, 29; study of demons/demonic discourse within context of, 12, 18–20; ubiquity of demons in, 3. *See also* **Index of Jewish Sources,** *for specific citations*
Balberg, Mira, 126n76, 150, 220n73
Bamberger, Avigail Manekin, 15n44, 187–88
Bar Ilan Responsa database, 154n47
Baris, Michael, 136–37
Bar Kappara, 79n85
Bar-Širiqa Panda (demon), 114, 187–88, 202
Bartholomew (apostle), as exorcist, 214, 218
Bar Tit, Bar Tama, and Bar Tina (generic demons), 202
Benayahu b. Yehoyada, 160–61
Ben Nefalim (demon), 124
Ben Talamion/Ben Tamalion (demon), 74, 212–15, 227
be rabbanan, demons in, 111–12, 197–201, 209
R. Berekhiah, 209
R. Bibi b. Abaye, 84
Bible. *See* Hebrew Bible; New Testament; Septuagint
the body: absence of bodily possession and exorcisms in rabbinic literature, 217–19; constructions of, and avoidance of

demonic danger, 103, 119–24; demons, corporeality of, 62, 65, 72, 78–80, 84n102; rabbinic anthropology and absence of bodily possession stories, 219–22
Book of the Watchers, origin story of demons in, 36–37
Boyarin, Daniel, 220
Boyce, Mary, 115
Brakke, David, 126, 218–19
Brand, Miryam, 39, 40
Brodsky, David, 66n35, 82n92
Brown, Peter, 224–25

Cameron, Averil, 224–25n1, 225
caper bushes, demons of, 100, 115
Carter, K. Codell, 123n66
categorization. *See* classification of demons
chiasm, 103
chicken feet, association of demons with, 84, 162
Chidester, David, 90
Christianity: afterlife of demons as servants in, 188, 190–92; angelology in, 51–52, 63–64; anthropology of soul/body in, 220; cataloging/classification and worldview of, 89; classification of demons/intermediary beings in, 57–59, 63–68, 85–88, 194, 207; conceptualization of demons in, 25; demonic possession and exorcism in Roman West, 22–23, 200–201, 213–15, 217–19; Enochic corpus, devaluation of, 53–54; holy men's power over demons in, 172–75, 180; importance of demons in early writings, 13n37; magic and religion distinguished in, 13, 14; Marcion and Marcionites, 172; monks and demons, 126; non-Christian gods, classified as demons, 25, 64–65, 66, 164; rabbinic differences from/interconnections with, 226; Second Temple Judaism, emerging out of, 63; servants, lack of demons as, 180; source materials for demonology in, 38n28; space, constructions of, 109–10; Syriac Christianity, 19, 22, 25–26, 172–75, 180, 186, 190–92; terms for demons in early writings, 26n65. *See also* New Testament
Chronicles of Jerahmeel, 53n71
Chrysippus, on classification of demons, 62
classification of demons, 21, 56–91; in ancient Mesopotamia, 181–83; angels and, 63–64, 68, 69, 72–73, 78; b. *Ḥagigah* and *Avot de-Rabbi Natan*, taxonomies of, 75–80, 81, 82, 83, 84, 85–86; by Christian writers, 57–59, 63–68, 70–73, 85–88; corporeality of demons, 62, 65, 72, 78–80, 84n102; by Greek philosophers, 57, 58–63, 69, 70, 85–88; Iamblichus's synthesis of Christian and Greek philosophical traditions, 58, 59, 68–70, 85, 86; in incantation bowls, 207–8; by late antique rabbis, 57–58; moral neutrality of rabbinic accounts, 73, 75, 78, 81, 82, 84, 85, 86, 88; mutability and invisibility of, 79–80, 90–91, 182; non-Christian gods, as demons, 25, 64–65, 66; rabbinic parallels to taxonomic accounts, 81–85; by scholastic elites, 56–58, 85; Second Temple Judaism and, 64, 66, 86, 88; significance of, 88–91; triangulation of Christian, Greek, and rabbinic accounts, 85–88; visual perception and, 79–84, 151
Clinton, Hillary, 2
Commodianus, 128, 130
Contra Celsum (Origen), 66n37, 67n40
corporeality. *See* body
corpse impurity and demons, 110–11n40, 147–48, 216
creation of demons by God, as origin story, 32–35, 42–44, 48–50
cress, demonic dangers of eating, 102, 121
Cruz, Ted, 1

daemōn (Latin term), 25
daimones (Greek term), 25, 26n65, 59–60, 73
Dalley, Stephanie, 187n56
Dan, Joseph, 157n54
danger, demonic. *See* avoiding demonic danger; exorcisms and repelling demonic attacks
Daniel the Stylite, 200
date-palm tree stumps, demons associated with, 100, 115–16, 123
David (biblical ruler), 35, 163n69
daxma, 148
Dead Sea Scrolls: origin story of demons in, 20, 32, 33–34, 44; possession and exorcism in, 217–18. *See also* **Index of Jewish Sources,** *for specific citations*
demons/demonic discourse, 1–28, 223–29; anxieties about demonic superiority, rabbis dealing with, 158–65, 166–67; avoiding demonic danger, 21–22, 92–127 (*see also* avoiding demonic danger); Babylonian Talmud, within study of, 12, 18–20 (*see also* Babylonian Talmud); classification of demons, 21, 56–91 (*see also* classification

demons/demonic discourse *(continued)* of demons); "demon," as translation term, 24–28; discourse, concept of, 23–24; exorcisms and attacks, 22–23, 195–222 (*see also* exorcisms and repelling demonic attacks); historiographic downplaying and nonnormativization of, 7–12; intermediary beings, rabbinic conceptualization of, 25–28; late antiquity, concept of, 224–26; in legal conversations, 22, 128–65 (*see also* legal discourse about demons); methodological approach, 20; in modern American politics and culture, 1–3, 195; origin stories, 20–21, 29–55 (*see also* origin stories); rabbinic culture of late antique Sasanian Babylonia, focus on, 3–7; religion and magic, within study of, 12, 13–16, 228; Sasanian context, Babylonian rabbis in, 226–29; servants of rabbis, demons as, 22, 166–94 (*see also* servants of rabbis, demons as); significance of, 3, 12; social-scientific study of, 12, 16–18; in Zoroastrianism, 6
De Mysteriis (Iamblichus), 68–70
De Principis (Origen), 67n39
Deuteronomy, intermediary/demonic beings in, 30, 31, 104–5n29
Devereux, George, 16
dēw (Pahlavi) or *devi,* 25–26, 78, 149
Dialogue with Trypho (Justin Martyr), 51–52
R. Dimi from Nehardea, 95–96, 135
Diocletian (Roman emperor), 210–11
discourse, concept of, 23–24
disease and demons, 122–24
The Divine Vengeance (Plutarch), 62n20
divorce, statements of, to repel demonic attacks, 206, 207n33
Doody, Aude, 89n119
dragon/serpent slaying stories, 196–201
drinking and eating. *See* food
dualism: of ancient Mesopotamian demons, 183; in Dead Sea Scrolls, Community Rule, 34; in early Christianity, 67; in Zoroastrianism, 6, 137–38
Dumuz/Dumuzi (Tammuz; god), 108n36, 185

eating and drinking. *See* food
R. Eleazar b. Yose, 81, 213
Eliav, Yaron, 194n79
Elijah (biblical figure), 156–57, 170n9
Elman, Yankov, 18, 120n57, 136n11, 146
El-Zein, Amira, 190n68
embodiment. *See* body
Enoch, books of: Jewish and Christian devaluation of, 51n61, 52–54; origin story of demons in Book of the Watchers, 20–21, 32, 36–37, 38, 39, 40, 44. *See also* **Index of Jewish Sources,** *for specific citations*
Enosh son of Seth (biblical figure), 48
Enuma Elish, 182n35, 182n37, 187, 200
epilepsy, 114, 124, 188
Ereškigal and Inana, Sumerian stories of, 184–87
Eshata (fever/fever-causing demon), 124
Eshel, Esther, 32, 35
ethnopsychiatry, 16–17
Evans-Pritchard, E. E., 13–14
Eve (biblical figure), 44–46, 50, 52–54, 64n28
even numbers: avoiding demonic dangers of, 93–97, 111–13, 119, 120, 125, 167–68; in legal discourse about demons, 130–40, 146, 147n35, 148, 149, 154–56; origins of problem of, 136–40; ritual gestures warding off evil of, 203
The Evil Dead (film), 195
evil eye, 111n41, 155n50, 177n25, 206, 217n59, 228
excretion/urination: avoidance of demonic danger during, 94, 100, 112–16, 120, 123–24, 125; outhouses/privies, demons in, 94, 112–14, 124, 125, 188; rabbinic prayer after, 220; Second Temple Judaism, possession and exorcism in, 217–18
exorcisms and repelling demonic attacks, 22–23, 195–222; absence of bodily possession and exorcisms in rabbinic literature, 217–19; amulets used to repel demons, 201, 203–5; *be rabbanan,* R. Aḥa b. Jacob's expulsion of seven-headed serpent from, 196–201; Christian/Roman West, possession and exorcism in, 22–23, 200–201, 213–15, 217–19; demonic attacks versus demonic possession, 22–23, 195–96; divorce, statements of, 206, 207n33; "good" demons allying with rabbis to expel evil forces, 209–16; incantation bowls/texts, 205–9, 217; intercultural influences, 198–201; moral neutrality and dangerousness of demons, interconnected discourse of, 196, 209, 216; prayer used in, 197, 200–201; rabbinic anthropology and absence of bodily possession stories, 219–22; rabbinic knowledge and power regarding, 204–5; red heifer ritual compared, 216; *Testament of Solomon,* on expelling demonic attacks, 72; verbal for-

mulas and ritual gestures, repelling demons with, 201–5
The Exorcist (film), 134, 195
extispicy, Babylonian, 138

fallen angels, 36, 50, 52, 65, 66, 72, 78, 128
First Apology (Justin Martyr), 65n29
food: ability of demons to eat, 77; avoidance of demonic danger and, 119–22; Leviticus, dietary rules in, 119, 122
Foucault, Michel, 24
Fowden, Garth, 225
Fraade, Steven, 80
Frankfurter, David, 90
Frēdōn/Θraētaona, slaying of Azdahāg/*Aži Dahāka* by, 198
Friedman, Shamma, 108n35

Gafni, Isaiah, 18
Gager, John, 14n41
Gaster, Moses, 192
Gayōmard (first man, in Zoroastrian tradition), 46–47
Geller, Mark J., 19, 138
gender: avoiding demonic danger and, 124–25; of demons, 74, 125, 182; important women, demonic attacks on, 96, 168; time, construction and experience of, 104n27; witchcraft and, 125
Genesis Apocryphon, 217
Genesis Rabbah: classification of demons in, 81–82; origin stories of demons in, 20–21, 43–48, 51, 53. *See also* **Index of Jewish Sources,** *for specific citations*
Gōgušnasp (Zoroastrian jurist), 147
Gordon, Cyrus H., 169n6
Goshen-Gottstein, Alon, 220
Graetz, Heinrich, 10, 223
Greek philosophy/mythology: apprenticeship of Sosipatra to daimones, 180n32; classification of demons in, 57, 58–63, 69, 70, 85–88; even numbers in, 138–40; Hercules and the Hydra, 198; legal discourse about demons and, 130
Gregory of Nazianzus, 64n28
Gribetz, Sarit Kattan, 104
Gudea of Lagaš, 183
Gunshow (webcomic), 27

halakhah le-moshe mi-sinai, significance of, 96, 135–36
Hamlet (Shakespeare), 80n91
R. Ḥanina b. Dosa, 107, 170–71, 174
R. Ḥanina b. Isaac, 51, 74nn70–71, 81, 151
Harari, Yuval, 14–15n42, 124, 213n52
Ḥasidei Ashkenaz, 9
Hayes, Christine, 135
Hebrew Bible: Deuteronomy, intermediary/demonic beings in, 30, 31, 104–5n29; Isaiah, intermediary/demonic beings in, 31; Jeremiah, intermediary/demonic beings in, 31; Leviathan in, 199; Leviticus, dietary rules in, 119, 122; origin stories for demons in, 30–32, 35; verbal formulae to drive off demons taken from, 202. *See also* Psalms
Herbert, George, "The Church-porch," 128
Hercules and the Hydra, 198
Hesiod, *Works and Days*, 59–60
Hillel (rabbinic figure), 175
R. Ḥinena b. Bibi, 94
R. Ḥisda, 94, 114, 156
History of the Jews (Graetz), 223
A History of the Monks of Cyrrhus (Theodoret of Cyrrhus), 218n65, 219
R. Hiyya b. Abba, 176
Homilies on Luke (Origen), 67n41
households, rabbinic. *See* rabbinic households
R. Huna b. R. Joshua, 97, 101, 105, 176, 178
Hydra, Hercules vanquishing, 198
hyena metamorphosis story, 48–50

Iamblichus, on classification of demons, 58, 59, 68–70, 85, 86
image and likeness of God, relationship of demons to, 81–82
Inana and Ereškigal, Sumerian stories of, 184–87
incantation bowls/texts: angels, invoking protection of, 207; for avoiding demonic danger, 110, 123; as discourse, 24; divorce, using statements of, 206, 207n33; exorcism and repelling demonic attacks, 205–9, 217; JBA 26 (MS 1928/43), 157n56, 207nn36–37, 217n59; JBA 42 (MS 2053/190), 207n34; JBA 55 (MS 1928/1), 208n38; JBA 58 (MS 2053/166), 207n36; legal discourse about demons and, 141, 143–45, 157, 163; Moussaieff 143, 163, 164; origin stories and, 26; servants of rabbis, demons as, 169n6, 170n9, 182
incense offered to demons, 177n26
Insidious (film), 195
interlaced fingers, 155n50
intermediary beings, rabbinic conceptualization of, 25–28

Interpreting Late Antiquity: Essays on the Post-Classical World (ed. Bowersock et al.), 225, 226
invisibility and mutability of demons, 79–80, 90–91
iron, as demonic protection, 140–41
R. Isaac Alfasi (Rif), 7–8, 9
R. Isaac b. Joseph, 106, 176, 177
Isaiah, intermediary/demonic beings in, 31
Islamic world, demons as servants in, 188–90

Jacobs, Andrew, 89–90, 91n119
James of Cyrrhestica, 172–73
Jeremiah, intermediary/demonic beings in, 31
R. Jeremiah b. Eleazar, 45–48, 51, 74n71
Jewish medieval afterlives of demons as servants, 188, 192–93
Jewish rabbinic communities and demonic discourse, 3–7, 224–29. *See also* Babylonian rabbinic community; demons/demonic discourse; Palestinian rabbinic community
jinn, 189–90
John Chrysostom, 205
John of Novgorod, 190n69
Jonathan/Yohanan (demon), 74, 157
Jones, Alex, 2
R. Joseph, 94, 95, 97
Joseph the demon, 74, 95, 153–58, 203, 207, 210
Josephus, 23, 39–40, 161n44, 175n33, 189n63, 195, 217. *See also* **Index of Jewish Sources,** *for specific citations*
R. Joshua b. Levi, 105n30, 108
R. Joshua b. Neḥemiah, 81
R. Joshua b. Peraḥia, 144, 207, 208
journeys, encountering demons on, 94, 112–13
Jubilees, book of, origin story of demons in, 32, 38–39, 44. *See also* **Index of Jewish Sources,** *for specific citations*
R. Judah the Patriarch, 53, 74n71, 80, 93, 106, 107, 150
Justin Martyr: on classification of demons, 58, 59, 63–65, 85, 86; origin stories and, 38n28, 51–52

R. Kahana, 100, 117
kallah, demons in, 111–12, 157–58
Kalmin, Richard, 15n44, 18–19, 87n107, 108n35, 162, 164, 165n75, 168n3, 171, 201, 212n48, 214
Kapfener, Bruce, 16
Kertir (Zoroastrian religious leader), 6n15
Kidd, Ian, 59, 64
Kiel, Yishai, 44–45n43, 46, 145
Kiperwasser, Reuven, 164
kishuf (forbidden witchcraft), 176
Kitz, Anne Marie, 183–84
Klingenschmitt, Gordon, 1–2
Kohut, Alexander, 9–20
kordiakos (demon), 159, 203
Kwasman, T., 123n67

Lamaštu (goddess/demon), 84n102, 222
language of demons, ability of rabbis to understand, 175–78
LASA beings, 183
late antiquity, concept of, 224–26
Laws (Plato), 138n18
legal discourse about demons, 22, 128–65; anxieties about demonic superiority, rabbis dealing with, 158–65; Ashmedai's usurpation of Solomon's throne and, 158–65; even numbers, problem of, 130–40, 146, 147n35, 148, 149, 154–56; on four cups at beginning of Passover meal, 130–36; *halakhah le-moshe mi-sinai,* significance of, 96, 135–36; liquids, dangers of drinking, 140–45; morally neutral, demons depicted as, 150, 154, 158; origins of even numbers problem, 136–40; personhood of demons, 150; rabbinic courts, demons as participants in, 149–53; scholastic elites, rabbis as, 130; tradents and teachers of rabbis, demons as, 153–58; Zoroastrian intersections, 22, 130, 137–38, 146–49, 165
leprosy, 123, 143
Levi, Israel, 214
Leviathan (in Hebrew Bible), 199
Levinson, Joshua, 91
Leviticus, dietary rules in, 119, 122
Liber Medicinalis (Quintus Serenus Sammonicus), 145
Life of Anthony (Athanasius), 200, 219
Life of Daniel the Stylite, 200
Life of James of Cyrrhestica (Theodoret of Cyrrhus), 172–73
Lilith (demon), 31, 38, 74, 170n9
Lincoln, Bruce, 11
Lotan (seven-headed serpent), 199
Lucarelli, Rita, 184n48

Ma'aseh Merkavah, 75
MacDonald, D. B., 190

magic and religion, demons/demonic discourse within study of, 12, 13–16, 228
Maimonides, 7–9
Malandra, William, 137
Mamzerim (demonic bastards), 38
Mandaeans, 6, 25–26, 109, 146
Manichaeans, 6, 109, 146, 180, 206n30
manuscripts: Arras 889, 80n89, 151n42, 151n44; Cambridge T-S F1 (1) 116, 97n10, 101n18, 102n23, 121n61; Columbia X893T14a, 97n10, 99n14, 102nn22–23, 121n61, 141n24; Enelow Manuscript Collection 271, 97n10, 99n14, 102n23, 121n61, 141n24; Florence II-I-9, 48n53, 105n32, 176n24; JTS Rab. 1608 (ENA 850), 99n14, 102n23, 121n61; Kaufmann, 42n40; London BL Harl. 5508, 141n24; Mingana Syriac Manuscript 205, 191; Moscow-Guenzburg 594, 74n70; Moscow-Guenzburg 1017, 74n70; Munich 6, 75, 97n10, 102n22, 121n61; Munich 95, 46n45, 74n70, 76n76, 96n8, 102nn22–23, 103n25, 114n49, 121n61, 141n24, 202n21; Munich 141, 74n70; NY JTS 1623/2, 97n10, 99n14, 102n23, 121n61, 141n24; Oxford Opp. 248 (367), 74n70; Oxford Opp. Add. fol. 23, 76n77, 96n8, 97n10, 99n14, 102n23, 103n25, 121n61, 141n24, 169n6; Paris 671, 141n24; Sassoon 594, 97n10; Vatican 109, 96–97nn8–10, 98n12, 99n14, 102n23, 121n61; Vatican 122a, 74n70; Vatican 123b, 179n29; Vatican 125, 93n1, 96n9, 107n34, 170n8; Vatican 130, 159n61; Vatican 134, 97n10, 99n14, 101n18, 102nn22–23, 103n25, 121n61
Mar b. R. Ashi, 151–52
Marcion and Marcionites, 172
Mār Mārī the Apostle (Syriac holy man), 173–74
Martin, Dale B., 57n2
Marx-Wolf, Heidi, 57, 58–59, 67–68
Mar Zutra, 123
Massekhet Soferim, 175n22
Massey, Doreen, 109, 118
Mastema/Satan, in Jubilees, 39
mazziqin (lit. harmers), 25–28
medieval Christian, Muslim and Jewish afterlives of demons as servants, 188–93
R. Mesharsheya, 97
Mesopotamia, ancient. *See* ancient Mesopotamia
Metatron (angel), 163
Michael (archangel), 36, 160n64
Milton, John, 1
Mishnah: origin story of demons in, 20. *See also* **Index of Jewish Sources,** *for specific citations*
Mohammed (prophet), 189
monks and demons, 126
monotheism and demonic discourse, 12, 21, 23, 34, 149, 189n63, 194, 228–29
Montgomery, James A., 170n9
morally neutral, demons depicted as: in ancient Mesopotamia, 22, 180–84; avoidance of demonic danger despite, 21–22, 28, 118, 196; classification of demons and, 73, 75, 78, 81, 82, 84, 85, 86, 88; exorcisms and repelling demonic attacks, 196, 209–16; legal discourse about demons and, 150, 154, 158; in origin stories, 47, 55; in rabbinic discourse generally, 27; servants of rabbis, demons as, 167, 180, 183–85, 188, 193–94
Moscovitz, Leib, 129–30n2
Moussaieff 164 (incantation bowl), 143, 163
Muehlberger, Ellen, 57, 90
Murphy, Trevor, 89
Muslim world, demons as servants in, 188–93
mutability and invisibility of demons, 79–80, 90–91

R. Naḥman b. Yitzḥak, 93, 97, 106, 131–32
naḥotei (rabbinic travelers), 135n10
names and naming of demons, 74, 157
Nasuš (Zoroastrian demon), 147–49
Nathan, Tobie, 17
Natural History (Pliny the Elder), 89
Nehardea, rabbinic center at, 95, 111
Neis, Rachel Rafael, 79
Neusner, Jacob, 41
neutrality, moral. *See* morally neutral, demons depicted as
New Testament: demons/intermediary beings in, 11n37, 58, 63; fallen angels in, 50n57; possession and exorcism in, 217; Satan as seven-headed dragon, in Revelation, 199; terms for demons in, 26n65
Ninurta (Sumerian war god), 199

Obama, Barack, 2
On Isis and Osiris (Plutarch), 62, 138–39nn19–21
On the Sign of Socrates (Plutarch), 61–62
Oratio ad Graecos (Tatian), 65n31
Origen, on classification of demons, 58, 59, 66–68, 85

origin stories, 20–21, 29–55; accidental emission, creation of demons by, 45–47; angels and humans, demons as offspring of sinful sexual encounters between, 35–41, 44, 50, 65; biblical, 30–32, 35; continuity of Second Temple traditions regarding, 41, 44, 46, 47, 49, 50, 52–54; creation of demons by God, 32–35, 42–44, 48–50; hyena metamorphosis story, 48–50; later rabbinic rejection of angel story, 50–54; in Roman rabbinic Palestine, 41–45; in Sasanian rabbinic Babylonia, 45–48; in Second Temple literature, 32–41; sin, association of demonic origins with, 35–41, 44–48, 65; spirits of wicked men, demons as, 39–40; Tower of Babel, transformation of humans into demons as punishment for, 47–48, 86n105
Ornias (demon), 72, 160n64
outhouses/privies, demons in, 94, 112–14, 124, 125, 188

Padel, Ruth, 118
Pahlavi Vīdēvdād, 22, 137, 146–48, 187n56
Palestinian rabbinic community: amulets mentioned in Palestinian Talmud and Mishnah, 205n27; classical rabbinic literature of, 4; demonic interest in Babylonian versus Palestinian rabbis, 168n5; R. Dimi traveling to Babylonia from, 95–96, 135; on evil eye and healing on Sabbath, 177n25; on four cups at beginning of Passover meal, 131; "good" demons allying with rabbis to expel evil forces in, 209–12; *nahotei* (rabbinic travelers), 135n10; origin stories for demons, 41–45; space, demons and constructions of, 111. *See also* **Index of Jewish Sources** *for citations to specific documents, e.g.*, Palestinian Talmud
Palga (demon), 100, 115, 123, 217n59
R. Papa, 94, 95, 97, 98, 101, 105, 112, 113, 154, 179, 187, 189n63
Paradise Lost (Milton), 1
Parthians, 137, 181, 186
Pashittu (ancient Mesopotamian demon), 40
Passover, 92, 106, 131–33
Patai, Raphael, 163n69
Payne, Richard E., 6n15
personal space, rabbinic legal expectation of, 116
personhood of demons, 150
Pesiqta Rabbati: on classification of demons, 70, 82–83; dating of, 82n95
Philo of Alexandria, 220
Pirqe de-Rabbi Eliezer, origin story in, 53
Plato: on classification of demons, 60–61, 62, 63, 69, 70, 86, 88; on even numbers, 138–40; Second Temple adaptation of Platonic binary of body and soul, 219–20
Pliny the Elder, 89, 155n50
Plutarch: on classification of demons, 58, 59, 61–63, 69, 85, 86; on even numbers, 138–40
Polymius (ruler), 214
possession. *See* exorcisms and repelling demonic attacks
prayer used in exorcisms/against demonic attacks, 197, 200–201
presidential elections (2016), demonic discourse in, 1–2
Pride and Prejudice (Austin), 166
Pritchard, J. B., 187n57
privies/outhouses, demons in, 94, 112–14, 124, 125, 188
procreation, by demons, 77–78
Psalms: intermediary/demonic beings in, 30, 31, 104–5n29, 199; verbal formulae to repel demons drawn from, 202, 203
Pseudo-Abdias, 214
pseudo-baraitas, 108
Pseudo-Clementine literature, 38n28, 52n64
Pseudo-Dionysius, *Celestial Hierarchy*, 70–73
Pseudo-Philo, origin story of demons in, 20, 32, 34–35, 43, 44
Pumbedita, rabbinic center of, 112, 156
Pythagoras, on classification of demons, 62

Qetev Meriri and *Qetev Yašud Ẓaharaim* (morning and afternoon demons), 101, 104–5, 108
Quintus Serenus Sammonicus, 145
Qumran texts. *See* Dead Sea Scrolls
Qur'an, *jinn* in, 189–90, 226
Qẓb (West Semitic god), 31

Rabbah b. Levai, 95
Rabbah b. Naḥmani, 97, 134, 211
Rabbah b. R. Huna, 94
rabbinic communities and demonic discourse, 3–7, 224–29. *See also* Babylonian rabbinic community; demons/demonic discourse; Palestinian rabbinic community
rabbinic households: avoidance of demonic danger by staying at home, 94–95, 112–13; demons as servants in, 178–80; privies/

outhouses, demons in, 94, 112–14, 124, 125, 188
rabbinic servants. *See* servants of rabbis, demons as
rābiṣu (lurkers), 183–84
Rami b. Ḥama, 114
Rashi (R. Shlomo Yitzchaki), 169n7, 176
Rav (Amora), 162
Rava, 86n105, 94, 95, 97, 113, 114, 132, 151, 167–68, 177n26
Ravina, 93, 97, 132–33
red heifer ritual, 216
Reed, Annette Yoshiko, 37, 38n28, 50n57, 51n61, 52
Reish Laqish, 51
religion and magic, demons/demonic discourse within study of, 12, 13–16, 228
religious toleration in Sasanian empire, 6
Rešeph (West Semitic god), 31
Rif (R. Isaac Alfasi), 7–8, 9
Rišpei, 100, 101
Roman empire, demonology in, 15n42
Roman Palestine. *See* Palestinian rabbinic community
Ronis, Margaret, 82n92
Rosenblum, Jordan, 119, 126
Rosen-Zvi, Ishay, 15–16n44, 220–21n77
Ross, Alec, 2
ruḥot (lit spirits), 25–28, 184n45

Sabians, 8
Safed, female pietists of, 9
Said, Edward, 91
Sanders, Bernie, 2
Sasanian Babylonia in late antiquity, 5–7, 224–29. *See also* Babylonian rabbinic community
Satan: angels, rabbinic association with, 86n104; in Hebrew Bible, 30; identification with demons in Christianity, 64n28; Jubilees, Satan/Mastema in, 39; lack of rabbinic association of demons with, 85–86; as seven-headed dragon, in Revelation, 199
satyrs *(śĕʿîrîm)*, 31, 114
Saul (biblical ruler), 35, 186
Sayings of the Desert Fathers, 191, 219
scholastic elites, concept of, 4, 12, 21, 56–57, 85, 130
Scholem, Gershom, 12
Schwartz, Sarah, 71–72n64
Second Apology (Justin Martyr), 38n28, 52, 65n30
Second Temple Judaism: Babylonian rabbinic community's interconnections with, 227; Christianity emerging out of, 63; classification of demons and, 64, 66, 86, 88; origin stories for demons in, 32–41; Platonic binary of body and soul, adaptation of, 219–20; possession and exorcism in, 217–18
šedim (Hebrew/Aramaic/Akkadian), 25–28, 78, 149
Sefer Ha-Halakhot (Rif), 7–8
Septuagint: "sons of God" as "angels of God" in Genesis, 51n58; use of δαίμωvon in, 26n65. *See also* Tobit, book of
serpent/dragon slaying stories, 196–201
servants of rabbis, demons as, 22, 166–94; ability of rabbis to summon/communicate with demons, 175–78; afterlife in Muslim, Christian, and Jewish contexts, 188–93; ancient Mesopotamian parallels, 180–88; anxieties about demonic superiority, rabbis dealing with, 166–67; holy men's ability to control demons, 107, 169–75; important people in community, demons more likely to attack, 94, 96, 113, 167–68; rabbinic households, demons as servants in, 178–80
shadows: avoiding demonic dangers of, 99–100, 101, 105, 111, 114, 115, 116–17; demonic casting of, 80, 143, 150–51; over corpses, 148; shadow of a shadow, 80, 151
Shakespeare, William, 80n91
shamir, 42, 159, 161
shavriri (demon/incantation), 144–45
Shema, 106
R. Shimon, 212–13
R. Shimon b. Laqish, 86n104, 97, 116
R. Shimon b. Yoḥai, 120
R. Shlomo Yitzchaki (Rashi), 169n7, 176
Shmuel, 97, 123n66, 162, 203
R. Shmuel b. Naḥman, 211
Shulḥan Arukh, 106n33
R. Simeon b. Yoḥai, 51
R. Simon, 209
sin, demonic origins associated with, 35–41, 44–48, 65. *See also* origin stories
six, rabbinic lists of, 79n85
sleep and avoidance of demonic danger, 94, 99, 102, 106, 108, 112, 117, 119
Smith, George, 187n57
social-scientific study of demons, 12, 16–18
Solomon (biblical ruler), 71, 159–65, 175n22, 189–90, 193, 217

Sophocles, *Antigone*, 60n9
Sorensen, Eric, 217–18n62, 222n79
Sōšāns (Zoroastrian jurist), 147, 148
Sosipatra (Greek philosopher), 180n32
space, constructions of, and avoidance of demonic danger, 103, 109–19
speaking to demons, 175–78
status, susceptibility to demonic attack as marker of, 168
Stol, Martin, 221
Stratton, Kimberly, 13
Strauch Schick, Shana, 146, 155
Stuckenbruck, Loren, 37
students of rabbis, demons as, 179n30, 190, 194
Styers, Randall, 13
Sukkot, 133
Šulak (Babylonian privy demon), 188
Sumerian civilization, 181. *See also* ancient Mesopotamia
Sura, rabbinic center of, 156
Syriac Christianity, 19, 22, 25–26, 172–75, 180, 186, 190–92
Syria-Palestine. *See* Palestinian rabbinic community

Tale of the Jerusalemite, 157n54, 192–93
R. Tanḥum b. Ḥanilai, 114
Tannaim, 49n54, 75, 79n85, 86, 106, 108n35, 110n40, 119, 135, 140–41, 146, 150, 170, 221n77, 227
Tatian, on classification of demons, 64, 65, 86
taxonomy. *See* classification of demons
teachers and tradents of rabbis, demons as, 153–58
Testament of Solomon, 70–73, 77n78, 160–61n64, 189n63
Theodoret of Cyrrhus, 172–73, 218n65, 219
Thomas (Apostle), 174
Θraētaona/Frēdōn, slaying of Azdahāg/*Aži Dahāka* by, 198
Tiamat (primordial goddess), 182n35, 199
R. Tifdai, 81, 82
Timaeus (Plato), 60–61
time, constructions of, and avoidance of demonic danger, 103–9
Tobit, book of: Ashmedai in, 162n66; exorcisms in book of, 23; use of *daimon* in, 26n65
totalizing discourse, 89, 90, 126n76, 167, 173
Tower of Babel, transformation of humans into demons as punishment for, 47–48, 86n105
Trachtenberg, Joshua, 10–11
tradents and teachers of rabbis, demons as, 153–58
travel and avoidance of demonic danger, 94, 112–13
Trump, Donald, 2

UDUG beings, 183
Udug-hul, 222n79
Ugaritic Ba'al Cycle, 199
Ulla, 94
Ulmer, Rivka, 82n95
urination. *See* excretion/urination

Veltri, Giuseppe, 155–56nn50–51
visual perception and demons, 79–84, 151
voces magicae, 141n24

Watchers, angelic. *See* angels; origin stories
Whitman, Walt, "The Sleepers," from *Leaves of Grass*, 92
Williams, A. V., 115n50
Wimpfheimer, Barry, 8
Wissenschaft des Judentums, 9–10, 13
Witchcraft, Oracles, and Magic among the Azande (Pritchard), 13–14
witches/witchcraft, 95–96, 98–99, 125, 141n24, 155–56nn50–51, 169, 176
women. *See* gender

Xenocrates, 62, 139
Xusrow I, 186–87, 200

Yalqut Shimoni, 53n71
Yassif, Eli, 213
Yazdgird, 123
R. Yehuda, 97
R. Yehuda Nesiah, 210–11
R. Yitzhak b. R. Yehuda, 94, 99, 113, 117, 168
R. Yoḥanan b. Zakkai, 175, 215–16
Yohanan/Jonathan (demon), 74, 157
R. Yose, 176–78

Zarathustra/Zoroaster, 6
zardata reeds, demons of, 100–101, 116, 123, 204
R. Zeira, 94, 112
Zlotnik, Jehuda, 192n74
Zoroastrianism, 5–6; accidental creation by emission in, 46–47; Ashmedai and, 163, 164; Babylonian narrative tropes in, 187; classification of demons, lack of interest in, 87; conceptualization of demons in,

47; even numbers, problem of, 137–38; Frēdōn/Θraētaona, slaying of Azdahāg/*Aži Dahāka* by, 198; human urine in, 115n50; legal discourse about demons and, 22, 130, 137–38, 146–49, 165; prayer used against demonic foes in, 201; primordial couple giving birth to demons and humans in, 44–45n43; rabbinic differences from/interconnections with, 226; servants, lack of demons as, 180
Ẓreida (demon), 100, 115, 123, 217n59
Ẓurva de-Rabbanan, 100, 101n18, 118, 127, 173

Index of Jewish Sources

SECOND TEMPLE JUDAISM

Damascus Document, CD XVI:2–4 • 38n27
Dead Sea Scrolls
1Q20 *(Genesis Apocryphon)* • 217
1QS (Community Rule, *Treatise on the Two Spirits*) 15–26 • 33–34, 44
4Q510 1.4–5 • 38
4Q560 1:3 • 218n63
Jubilees, book of
10:1–2 • 38n29
10:5 • 38
10:7–9 • 39
10:11 • 39
1 Enoch
1–36 • 36
7:2–6 • 36
7:5 • 37
10:12 • 37
10:15–16 • 36n20
15–16 • 36, 37
15:8–12 • 36n21
16:1 • 37
69:6 • 50n57
Josephus
Antiquities of the Jews
8.2.5 • 217n61
8.42 • 195
8.44–45 • 175n22
8.45 • 161n64
The Jewish War 7.185 • 40
Pseudo-Philo, *Book of Biblical Antiquities* • 34–35
Tobit 6–8 • 217n60

MISHNAH

m. *Avot*
4:4 • 155n48
5:6 • 42, 159n60
m. *Bekhorot* 5:2 • 159n59
m. *Gittin*
6:6 • 79–80, 150
7:1 • 159n59
m. *Keilim* 23:1 • 205n27
m. *Miqva'ot* 10:2 • 205n27
m. *Pesaḥim* 109b–112a • 92, 93
m. *Qiddushin* 2:8 • 155n48
m. *Shabbat*
6:2 • 205n27
8:3 • 205n27
16:5 • 159n59
m. *Sheqalim* 3:2 • 205n27

MISHNAH *(continued)*

m. *Terumot* 8:4–5 • 160n62
m. *Yevamot*
6:1 • 155n48
16:6 • 80n87, 150
m. *Yoma*
3:9 • 200n15
8:6 • 159n59
m. *Zevaḥim* 8:12 • 155n48

TOSEFTA

t. *Shabbat*
7:23 • 177, 178
10:19 • 155n48
t. *Terumot* 1:3 • 110n40

MIDRASH

Genesis Rabbah
7:5 • 43n42
8:11 • 81–82
20:11 • 45n44, 47
23:6 • 48n50
26:5 • 51
63:8 • 210–12
Leviticus Rabbah
4:8 • 83n97
24:3 • 209, 210, 211
Midrash Tanhuma on Exod. 23:20 • 78n81
Sifrei Numbers
Koraḥ 119 • 79n84
Naso 40 • 78n81

PALESTINIAN TALMUD

p. *Berakhot* 5:1 (38a) • 171n10
p. *Gittin* 7:1 (48c) • 159n59
p. *Nedarim* 2:2 (37b) • 155n49
p. *Pesaḥim* 10:1 (68b) • 131n3
p. *Sanhedrin* 101a • 177, 178
p. *Shabbat* 14:3 (14c) • 111n41, 217n59
p. *Ta'anit* 4:3 • 169n7

BABYLONIAN TALMUD

b. *Avodah Zarah*
12b • 144n31, 208n41
14b • 208n41
28a • 121n59
29a • 120n57
b. *Baba Batra*
16a • 86n104
92b • 121n62
134a • 175n22
b. *Baba Meẓia*
9b • 168n4
86a • 134
107b • 123n66
118a • 121n62
b. *Baba Qamma*
16a • 48–49
32b • 155n49
35a • 179n30
46b • 121n62
85a • 155n49
b. *Beiẓah*
11a • 142n25
20a • 142n25
30b • 133n6
32b • 79n85
b. *Bekhorot* 44b • 124
b. *Berakhot*
3a–b • 110–11, 127n78, 137n16, 175n21, 198
5a • 106
6a • 83–84, 112, 157–58, 210n44
31a • 200n15
34b • 200n15
35b–36a • 141n24
51a • 86n104, 132
51a–b • 79n85
51b • 142n25
55b • 155n50
57b • 120n57
60b • 113, 220n75
62a • 114, 127n78
b. *Eruvin*
18b • 45–47, 74n71
43a • 74n70, 74n72, 156
68b • 155n49
76a • 142n25
100b • 74n71
b. *Gittin*
53a • 155n49
66a • 80n89, 150–51, 158–59
67b • 159n59, 203
67b–68a • 189
68a–b • 74n71, 158, 193
68b • 84
69b • 208n41
70a • 108, 114, 124
b. *Ḥagigah*
13a • 142n25

16a • 75–80, 81, 82, 84, 85–86, 85n103
b. *Ḥullin*
9b–10a • 160n62
53b • 179n30
105b • 123, 151–52
105b–106a • 178–80, 188
106a • 122n64, 153
107b • 121, 124n70
b. *Keritot* 3b • 177n26
b. *Ketubot*
60b • 121n59
61a–b • 123
111a • 112n42
b. *Makkot* 6b • 151
b. *Megillah*
3a • 105n30, 105n32, 198n6
15b • 155n49
22b • 200n15
b. *Me'ilah* 17a–b • 23, 74n71, 212–15
b. *Mo'ed Qatan* 11a • 121n59
b. *Niddah*
17a • 110–11n40, 120
24b • 74n71
b. *Pesaḥim*
49b • 79n85
52a • 112n42
109 • 106
109b • 106n33, 167
109b–112a • 8n18, 93–103, 111, 115, 119, 123, 125, 131, 132, 135, 210n44
110a • 155n50, 203
110b • 135
111a • 147n35, 169n6, 202n20
111b • 114n47, 204, 217n59
112a • 140, 202, 208n41
112b • 169
112b–113a • 74n71, 107n34, 108, 170n8, 198n6
113b • 79n85
b. *Qiddushin* 29b • 23, 112, 127n78, 137n16, 196–201
b. *Sanhedrin*
8b • 155n49
44a • 105
67b • 125n73, 175–76
76b • 155n49
91a • 220n76
101a • 176
109a • 47–48, 86n105
b. *Shabbat*
12b • 76n74
38a • 155n49
59b • 168n4
66b–67a • 124
67a • 114, 202nn21–22
68b • 155n49
109 • 208n41
109b • 121n59, 141n24
110b • 122n63
112b • 79n84
113a • 121n59
119b • 85n103
151b • 74n71, 216–17n59
b. *Shevuot* 16b • 200n15
b. *Sotah*
33a • 76n74
38b • 132n5
b. *Sukkah*
28a • 175n22
38a • 142n25
45b • 133n6
47b • 142n25
b. *Ta'anit*
11a • 85n103
22b–23a • 107, 171n12
27b • 169n7
b. *Yevamot* 122a • 74n70, 80n88, 151n43, 157n55
b. *Yoma*
53b • 200n15
76a • 141n24
77b • 123–24
83b • 125n73

TARGUMIM

Targum Eccles. 2:5 • 175n22
Targum Sheni to Esther on 1 Kings 4:33 • 175n22

OTHER RABBINIC WORKS

Avot de-Rabbi Natan A 37 • 75–80, 81, 82, 83, 84, 85–86
Maimonides
Commentary to the Mishnah, Avodah Zarah 4:7 • 8n20
The Guide to the Perplexed 1.7 • 215–16
Massekhet Soferim 17:5 • 169n7
Pesiqta de-Rav Kahana 4:7 • 215–16
Pesiqta Rabbati 6 • 83n96
Pirqe de-Rabbi Eliezer 22:4 • 53n68
Rif, *Sefer Ha-Halakhot* on b. *Pesachim* 109b–112a • 8n18
Shulḥan Arukh Oraḥ Ḥayim 481 • 106n33
Zohar Song of Songs 69a • 169n6

Founded in 1893,
UNIVERSITY OF CALIFORNIA PRESS
publishes bold, progressive books and journals on topics in the arts, humanities, social sciences, and natural sciences—with a focus on social justice issues—that inspire thought and action among readers worldwide.

The UC PRESS FOUNDATION
raises funds to uphold the press's vital role as an independent, nonprofit publisher, and receives philanthropic support from a wide range of individuals and institutions—and from committed readers like you. To learn more, visit ucpress.edu/supportus.

www.ingramcontent.com/pod-product-compliance
Lightning Source LLC
Chambersburg PA
CBHW030530230426
43665CB00010B/829